Nature, Law, and the Sacred

MERCER UNIVERSITY PRESS

Endowed by

TOM WATSON BROWN
and
THE WATSON-BROWN FOUNDATION, INC.

Nature, Law, and the Sacred

Essays in Honor of Ronna Burger

Edited by Evanthia Speliotis

MERCER UNIVERSITY PRESS
Macon, Georgia

Copyright © 2019 by Mercer University Press

All rights reserved. No part of this book may be reproduced, stored in a retrieval system, or transmitted, in any form or by any means, electronic, mechanical, photocopying, recording, or otherwise, without the prior permission of Mercer University Press.

Printed in Canada

1 2 3 4 5 6   24 23 22 21 20 19

Library of Congress Cataloging-in-Publication Data
Names: Burger, Ronna, honoree. Speliotis, Evanthia, editor.
Title: Nature, law, and the sacred / edited by Evanthia Speliotis
Description: Macon, Georgia: Mercer University Press, 2019.
Includes bibliographical references.
Identifier: ISBN 978-088146-711-6 (hardback)
Additional Cataloging-in-Publication Data is available from the Library of Congress.

∞ The paper used in this publication meets the minimum requirements of the American National Standard for Information Sciences Permanence of Paper for Printed Materials, ANSI Z39.48–1984.

The typeface in this book is Monotype Ehrhardt.

Cover image: Temple of Solomon, fresco from the synagogue at Dura-Europos, third century CE, present-day Syria
Image credit: BP23FE; www.BibleLandPictures.com/Alamy Stock Photo

Cover design by Burt&Burt
Book design by S.P. Johnson

Published by
Mercer University Press
1501 Mercer University Drive
Macon, Georgia 31207
www.mupress.org

For each person, whatever is the essence or that for the sake of which they choose to live, this is what they wish to engage in with friends. That is why some drink together, some play dice together, while others exercise together and hunt together, or philosophize together (*sumphilosophein*)—each pass their days pursuing that which they most love in life.

— Aristotle, *Nicomachean Ethics* 1172a1–6

[Philosophic friendship (*sumphilosophein*) is] the way friends live together by sharing speeches and thoughts. . . . But sharing speeches and thoughts is supposed to define the distinctive mode of living together for human beings as such, which makes it the realization of our political nature at the same time that it expresses our rational nature. This joint fulfillment of our double nature, which is the essence of friendship . . . looks like the peak in the *Ethics* of the search for the human good and the good life for a human being.

— Ronna Burger, *Aristotle's Dialogue with Socrates*

Contents

Foreword

Ronna Burger's philosophic journey began with, and in many ways can be understood in light of, her first book, based on her dissertation, *Plato's "Phaedrus": A Defense of a Philosophic Art of Writing*. In her interpretation of that dialogue she explores and illuminates Plato's critique of writing as such, and at the same time, his defense of a philosophic art of writing implied by that critique. The charge against writing, which is raised most explicitly in the myth of Theuth and Thamuz near the end of the dialogue, is its tendency to cause forgetting and mindlessness, leaving the reader with the opinion of being wise merely by having read the author's work. The wholesale critique of writing that everyone associates with the *Phaedrus* proves to be no less a critique of the reader—whoever takes the written word to be authoritative, the embodiment of wisdom, as the recipients of ancestral tradition might do. The problem is that writings, like an inherited tradition, provide at best only "true opinion or the appearance of wisdom." Their meaning and truth "cannot be handed down" but "must be sought through an act of self-discovery." While the philosophic art of writing is one that leads the reader to replace "unmoving trust in the fixed authority of the tale [or tradition] with the motion of living thought" (Burger, *Plato's "Phaedrus,"* 1–2), the "motion of living thought" can only be accomplished by one who engages the writing with an artful, philosophic way of reading and thinking. This point becomes thematic in the *Phaedrus* at the true peak of the dialogue, which is not, as we might assume, "Socrates' 'mythic hymn' honoring the divine madness of *erōs*" (Burger, 5); for while that divine madness can inspire us, it will not of itself produce understanding (see *Phdr.* 265a6–b5, 265d1–266b1). Instead, Ronna proposes, the true peak comes after that grand, poetic speech, exactly at midday, when Socrates tells a story about the lovers of the Muses turned into cicadas, and warns against being lulled to sleep by their chirping; he and Phaedrus must avert that danger by engaging in dialogue (*dialogoumenos*, 259a7) and undertaking a critical examination of their preceding speeches.

Socrates elaborates the necessary way of proceeding for one who wishes to uncover the being of the beings with a twofold requirement: to "comprehend things dispersed in many places" and "lead them into one *idea*" as well as to "cut apart by forms according to where the joints have naturally grown" (265d3–e2). Ronna finds an application of this twofold analysis in the structure of a Platonic dialogue as a whole of parts, governed by the principle of "logographic necessity," and beyond that, in the relation among dialogues as parts of the Platonic corpus as a whole. In her book, *The "Phaedo": A Platonic Labyrinth*, Ronna's innovative interpretation of the *Phaedo*, she highlights the one moment in the dialogue—seemingly ignored by the interlocutors and the narrator—at which Socrates looks back to his trial and conviction. This allows her to discover, behind the arguments for immortality, that Socrates' motive for accepting the sentence of the city's court is not a hope for the release of his soul from the body, but his love of life and the worth of the life he lived.

The art of philosophic writing, which Plato describes in the *Phaedrus* and employs in all his works, calls for reading a text dialogically and dialectically, just as one would respond to a living interlocutor—in fact, just as Socrates is represented as doing in the texts Plato wrote. This approach provided Ronna with a key to her reading of Aristotle's *Nicomachean Ethics*, in her book aptly titled *Aristotle's Dialogue with Socrates*. One thread she traces through the course of Aristotle's argument is the meaning of "eros of the beautiful." The beautiful (*to kalon*) manifests itself first as the *telos* of ethical virtue, the excellence of the desiring part of the soul, which must be harnessed to *phronēsis*, seeking the means to achieve that end while directed toward what is beneficial. From the perspective of the virtuous person's self-understanding, Aristotle recognizes the nobility of this end, while standing back to uncover its internal conflicts and its limits. In the process he leads us to another conception of the beautiful, identified with wisdom (*sophia*), and a transformed understanding of *phronēsis* in its role looking to that *telos*.

Eros of the beautiful, as the desire for a self-standing perfection and completion, might seem to be satisfied only with the possession of wisdom and happiness, as Aristotle asserts at the end of the *Ethics*, fulfilled only in the purest life of contemplation. Ronna, however, highlights the qualifications with which Aristotle makes this claim, in particular, the charge he issues to evaluate the truth of these speeches in light of "deeds and life" (*NE* 1179a19). She locates the relevant deed, above all, in our own activity of thinking through the argument of the *Ethics*, following the dialogue Aristotle conducts with Socrates, in which he has "from the start invited the reader's participation" (Burger, *Aristotle's Dialogue with Socrates*, 215). This invitation is taken up by Ronna and offered to her readers by illustrating how we too may enter into this dialogue. Eros of the beautiful, on this reading, manifests itself as the desire for wisdom, *philosophia*, pursued by friends who "live together" in the distinctively human way, by "sharing speeches and thoughts" (Burger, 189).

In following this path, Ronna has explored bringing different thinkers into her conversation with a particular work. This is a special mark of her studies of the Hebrew Bible. In "Some Platonic Reflections on Genesis 1–3" (updated in a recent lecture, "The Fall from Our Ancient Nature: Plato's Aristophanic Speech on Eros and the Biblical Story of Adam and Eve"), she brings Platonic insights to bear on her reading of the opening chapters of Genesis, where she uncovers questions about the nature of human being and the human desire for wisdom. In another essay, "Woman and Nature: The Female Drama of the Book of Genesis," Ronna asks whether there might be a biblical recognition of nature vs. convention, which comes to light especially, as it does in *Republic 5*, through the issue of the status of woman. Ronna's lecture, "In the Wilderness: Moses as Lawgiver and Founder," includes Maimonides and Machiavelli along with Plato in the discussion, to help explore the problem of what a founding requires, why it might be important to identify the lawgiver with a divine source, and why the founder must withdraw from the people he shapes through the law. Through these studies and many others Ronna offers us her ever-deepening reflections on fundamental questions to which she was introduced by Plato.

This volume is presented as a tribute to Ronna Burger. The essays take up the themes that run throughout her work over the years: nature and law, the political and the sacred, the passions of the soul, especially eros and the desire for wisdom. Each of these themes has a history of its own, in the works of philosophers, poets, and the biblical authors, but they are all richly intertwined. With a view to the scope of Ronna's writings, these essays range broadly: from the Bible and Ancient Greek authors—including not only Plato and Aristotle, but also Sophocles, Euripides, Aristophanes, and Xenophon—as well as medieval thinkers, Maimonides, Dante, and Boccaccio, to modern philosophers, from Descartes and Montesquieu to Kant, Lessing, Hegel, and Kierkegaard. In gratitude for Ronna's thought, her teaching, and her extension of the gift of philosophic friendship, this collection is offered in the spirit of ongoing exploration, with encouragement to others to join in.

Evanthia Speliotis
Bellarmine University
Louisville, Kentucky
May 2019

Acknowledgments

I would like to thank Michael Davis for his help and encouragement in initiating this project, and Robert Berman and Stuart Warner for their advice and support as it progressed toward completion. I am deeply thankful for Marc Jolley's enthusiasm for the concept of this collection, and for offering a home for this volume at Mercer University Press. I also owe an incalculable debt of gratitude to Susan Johnson for her editorial assistance: it is thanks to her careful eye, attention to detail, and unflagging patience that this volume has the stylistic unity and consistency that it does. I thank all of the contributors to this volume for sharing their studies and reflections and allowing them to be part of a broader reflection on the themes of nature, law, and the sacred.

Finally, I would like to thank Ronna Burger for being such a wonderful teacher, mentor, and friend.

An "Introduction" by Seth Benardete

Ladies and gentlemen, I should like to welcome you to the seventh in a series of Forms and Works of Antiquity, which the Carl Friedrich von Siemens Foundation sponsors, and it gives me great pleasure to introduce Professor Ronna Burger, who will give a talk this evening on the argument and the action of Aristotle's *Ethics*.

As the title of Professor Burger's talk is rather unusual—one usually thinks of Aristotle as all argument and no action—it seems appropriate to sketch in Professor Burger's work on ancient philosophy in such a way as to indicate what may lie behind the title, which is not obvious at first glance.

Professor Burger was educated at the University of Rochester and the Graduate Faculty of the New School. She has been teaching at Tulane University in New Orleans for many years. She has written two important books on Plato. The first, a revision of her doctoral dissertation, was *Plato's "Phaedrus": A Defense of a Philosophic Art of Writing*. It dealt with the paradox at the heart of Plato, the writer who in defending the Socratic way of philosophy as living conversation, attacked writing and apparently contradicted himself. This self-contradiction seems to be a piece of the larger puzzle any interpretation of Plato must face, namely that which sets Plato the poet against Plato the philosopher, and again has him attack poetry on behalf of philosophy in forms that are entirely poetic. Through the publicity of writing and the apparitions of poetry, Plato tries to preserve the privacy of thinking and the truth and reality of what is. This

This is the text of a speech given by Seth Benardete as an introduction to a lecture by Ronna Burger, "The Argument and the Action of Aristotle's *Ethics*," at the Carl Friedrich von Siemens Foundation, Munich, in June 1994, by the invitation of Heinrich Meier.

twofold riddle, in which the means blatantly contradict the end, has always been a stumbling block in the interpretation of Plato and guaranteed that no one could ever say with any truth that he was a Platonist.

Now, what Professor Burger did was to show that these paradoxes are a necessary consequence of Plato's understanding of philosophy, and rather than being either logical self-contradictions or expressions of an unresolved conflict within Plato himself, they were the signs for unlocking the riddle. This meant that philosophy, in being a way of life, did not have and could never have a method that could dispense with the accidental. The erroneous was the necessary appearance that the truthful must take. The diversion from the truth belonged to the truth and was our only access to it. The world was not a book which could be read from start to finish if one knew its language. It therefore followed that only in a book where everything was intelligible and there was no chance could there be a representation of the life of the mind.

Professor Burger followed up this general conclusion of how to read Plato with an account of the *Phaedo*, the subtitle of which was "A Platonic Labyrinth." In this work, Professor Burger tried to topple the twin pillars of Platonism, the immortality of the soul and the existence of the so-called Platonic forms or ideas. If she did not succeed in blowing up the entire edifice of Platonism, she did manage to shake it. The kind of paradox that runs throughout Plato shows up in a particularly acute form in the *Phaedo*. Socrates, on his last day, argues for philosophy as the best way of life while seeming to defend the thesis that if and only if he is dead can he obtain what he wants, the contact of pure mind with pure being, and as long as he has a body, everything he perceives and everything he thinks on the basis of his perceptions are illusions. Professor Burger again tried to show that one could follow a thread or threads through the maze Plato had made that would not leave one as baffled as one was when one entered it. Her notion turned on the insight that the necessary way of analysis, in which a whole was articulated into its parts, points to a way of synthesis, in which the isolation of the parts gives way to a proof of their necessary togetherness. The division of body from soul therefore was only a preliminary, though indispensable, step on the way to its combination that both vindicated philosophy as the practice of dying and being dead and suggested how philosophy as *erōs* was not its contrary but its partner.

We now come to Aristotle, who seems as far away from paradox as a philosopher could possibly be. This sobriety of Aristotle makes him in a way less accessible to us than Plato. Before turning to Professor Burger, who promises to show the Platonic shadow in Aristotle, I would like to remind you of two things, which show how remote Aristotle's *Ethics* has become for us.

The story goes that Winston Churchill, who did not go to Oxford or Cambridge and was largely self-educated, got around to reading the *Nicomachean Ethics* in his fifties, and when he finished it remarked, "That was the way I was brought up." No one could say that now. The social system that bred the gentleman, who could understand himself as mirrored in Aristotle's *Ethics*, has long disappeared. When Hans-Georg Gadamer appealed to the *Ethics*, it was to the sixth book, on *phronēsis* or prudence, and not the five books preceding it, which largely concern moral character.

Martin Heidegger, in his letter "On Humanism," which was written in 1946 to Jean Beaufret, who asked whether an ethics was to follow from *Sein und Zeit*, had this to say: "Ethics came along with Logic and Physics for the first time in the school of Plato. These disciplines arose at the time at which thinking got transformed into philosophy, but philosophy was understood as *epistēmē*, science, and science in itself as a matter of school and school-industry. Science arises in the passage through philosophy so understood, and thinking disappears. The thinker prior to this time knows neither a Logic, nor an Ethics, nor a Physics. Still, his thinking is neither illogical nor immoral. *Phusis* or nature is thought in a depth and breadth that all later Physics could no longer achieve. The tragedies of Sophocles shelter and preserve in their speaking the *ēthos*—'character' in Aristotle, a place of dwelling or habitation in its original sense—in a more original way than Aristotle's lectures on *Ethics*."

Professor Burger, if I understand her summary, has set herself, correctly, the task this evening of bringing Aristotle's *Ethics* away from the discipline and science it seems to be, which Heidegger condemns, and back into the fold of philosophy and thinking.

Please welcome Professor Burger.

Nature, Law, and the Sacred

I.

Ancients:
Tragedy, Comedy, and Philosophy

1

Enlightened Piety in Sophocles' *Antigone*

Evanthia Speliotis

At the beginning of the *Antigone*, Kreon, the new ruler of Thebes, has just issued a proclamation prohibiting the burial of Polyneices, a native son who brought an army to march against his own city. The principle behind Kreon's proclamation is clear: traitors are to be punished, not rewarded, dishonored, not honored. In defiance of Kreon's proclamation, Antigone, who is Polyneices' sister, is determined to bury her brother. The principle guiding her action is also clear: the ritual of burial is commanded by the gods; burying her dead brother is therefore the pious thing to do. The conflict between Kreon and Antigone appears to be a conflict between justice and piety, between the authority and rule of man and the authority and rule of god(s).

Sophocles examines and addresses this conflict through a reflection on the nature and power of human being. Beginning with a ringing paean by the chorus to the power and capacity of human being (332–75), which culminates in the assertion that human beings are "all-resourceful" (*pantoporos*), Sophocles then proceeds to explore how far-ranging human power truly is. Offering Kreon as the champion of human beings' resourcefulness, and Antigone as the spokesperson for human beings' limitedness, and thus resourcelessness, Sophocles invites us to reflect on the nature and capacities of human being, on the extent and limit of human knowledge and power, and on where these situate us in the cosmos of time and being, justice and piety.

Polla ta deina

> There are many awesome wonders [*polla ta deina*]
> but none of them is more awesome than human being
> [*anthrōpos*]. (332–34)[1]

Thus begins the first choral stasimon, which proceeds to elaborate on and extol the amazing degree and kind of power that human beings have. Human beings, the chorus details, have an uncanny ability to control nature and harness it to their own ends. Confronted daily with seemingly impossible (*amēchanōn*) challenges, they can contrive solutions (*mēchanoen technas*, 365). They can create tools that allow them to yoke the forces of nature to their purposes and put them to use for their own will and benefit (335–51). Thus, they can build ships to sail the seas, yoke oxen to plow the fields, trap birds for food (335, 350, 345); they can protect themselves from the inclement and inhospitable conditions presented by nature (355–56); they can even "devise escape from impossible (*amēchanōn*) sickness" (361–63). To borrow a phrase from Francis Bacon, human beings have the capacity to be masters and possessors of nature.

What makes this mastery possible is that human beings are rational, artful beings, capable of thinking, speech, contriving, and learning:

> Speech [*phthegma*], wind-swift purposeful thinking
> [*anemoen phronēma*],
> and the passion for civic laws [*astunomois orgas*],
> these he has taught himself.
> (352–54)

Phrēn, phronein, and *phronēma,* the root of which means "sound thought, thinking, mind," abound in the play. *Phronēma* adds a layer of complexity,

---

1. The Greek text is *"Antigone,"* trans. Francis Storr, in *Sophocles,* vol. 1 (New York: Macmillan, 1912), http://www.perseus.tufts.edu. Translations are from Ruby Blondell, *"Antigone,"* in *Sophocles: The Theban Plays* (Newburyport, MA: Focus Publishing, 2002), 33–90, with an occasional emendation for greater literalness. For an excellent essay that also begins from this choral ode, see Charles Paul Segal, "Sophocles' Praise of Man and the Conflicts of the *Antigone,*" *Arion: A Journal of Humanities and the Classics* 3, no. 2 (Summer 1964): 46–66. All other translations are my own, except where indicated.

4

indicating not only thought but purpose or intention.[2] *Phthegma*—speech or utterance—is the vehicle for expressing and conveying one's thoughts to others.[3] Human beings—thinkers—are problem solvers: their thinking is prompted by the challenges they encounter and is aimed at addressing and resolving them.

One might be reminded here of Hesiod's account in the *Works and Days* of Pandora, who brings speech—which he expresses in three ways: *audēn* (61), *logous* (78), *phōnēn* (79)—for the first time to human beings. And, along with speech, she brings the arts (64).[4] Behind both speech and the arts is thinking. For it is because human beings have *logos*, the capacity for reason and speech, that human beings are able to learn and develop the arts. And it is because human beings have *logos* and artfulness that they are able to devise the greatest protection against nature—the city or political community (*astunomois orgas*).

Sophocles however speaks not only of *phronein* and *phronēma*, but *anemoen phronēma*: wind-swift purposes, thoughts like the wind (352).[5] *Anemoen* acknowledges that thinking allows human beings to soar above the immediate and actual, to imagine and envision possibilities that are not yet, and then to devise a way to put those possibilities in action. But these soaring, high-flying, free-wheeling thoughts, while they are the source of human beings' artfulness, power, self-rule, and preservation, are also the source of willful harm and evil. Whereas Sophocles' own deed of writing the *Antigone* is a manifestation of the greatest and highest possibilities of human beings' *anemoen phronēma*, the characters within his drama illustrate the dangers of letting our imagination soar too far and too high, of allowing will (*boulēsis*)

---

2. Throughout, Blondell translates *phronēma* as "purpose." But see also Seth Benardete, *Sacred Transgressions: A Reading of Sophocles' "Antigone"* (South Bend, IN: St. Augustine's Press, 1999), 25. Commenting on Kreon's introduction of *phronēma* at line 176, Benardete characterizes it as "the temper of one's devotion" (12.4). "Devotion" seems to include the idea of purpose, but adds also a sense of commitment and visceral attachment.

3. See Arist., *Pol.* 1253a9–15, on speech (*logos*) vs. voice (*phōnē*); cf. Plato, *Tht.* 189e6–190a6, on speech as the expression of thought.

4. Hesiod, *Works and Days*, ed. M. L. West (Oxford: Oxford University Press, 1978).

5. These are Ruby Blondell's and David Grene's translations, respectively. "*Antigone*," trans. David Grene, in *Sophocles I*, ed. David Grene and Richmond Lattimore, 2nd ed. (Chicago: University of Chicago Press, 1991), 159–212.

and passion (*orgē*) to overpower sound thinking (*euphronein*). Through his two protagonists, Kreon and Antigone, he illustrates how creativity can outrun evidence and logic; how it can make pronouncements that are impossible to enact in the world; how it can imagine fictions that have no bearing on reality. At the same time, however, through the dramatic action of the play, Sophocles also demonstrates how rationality gives human beings the ability to investigate proclamations and makings, to question judgments and purposes, to learn, and to correct our mistakes.

Astunomois orgas

Throughout the play, Kreon is the champion of the power of rationality. He embraces and extols it, and understands himself to embody it in his new position of rule. The culmination of this power, in his mind, is the *polis*—the state or political community—which is the greatest and highest human artifact (182–90). The *polis* is the vehicle and proof of human autonomy, the triumph of art over nature. Other artful activities work on natural materials, restructuring and reshaping them for human purposes, to be sure, but they are still in some sense constrained by the nature of those materials.[6] Political rule (the political art), by contrast, works entirely on *logos* and through *logos*. Employing speeches (proclamations, laws) to guide and direct human actions, it steers the metaphoric ship of state through the "seas" of nature, chance, and fortune. Just as a ship is self-contained and must carry within it all that it will need and use, the city is all-encompassing, comprehending the totality of activities necessary for human survival and progress. Unlike an actual ship, the "ship of state" has no timbers or sails to replace; its laws serve as vessel, delineating the whole, and its ruler as navigator, directing the parts. It is easy to see how one could conclude that, as it is only human beings that have such power over nature, human beings must be—must be destined to be—the highest of beings, the masters of nature. From this, it is but a short step to the claim that the ruler of the city—the one whose *phrēn*, *phronein*, and *phronēma* are steering the city (or ship) on its journey, the one who is ultimately responsible for the preservation and well-being of this ship of

---

6. For example, the earth allows for the plow, whereas the sea demands a ship; horses and oxen can be yoked, whereas fish require nets (335–41, 345–51).

state—bears both the greatest authority and power as well as the greatest responsibility of anyone in the city. For if the city is "tossed by perturbations" or, even worse, sinks, all other human purposes and endeavors will also be destroyed (see Plato, *Plt.* 302a2–5). The very being of the city—this acme of human artfulness and *phronēma*—appears to lie in the ruler's hands (191, 207–10).

The power of rationality, however, includes also the capacity to wonder about justice, and to question whether a given proclamation or rule is just or unjust and whether a given human ruler is ruling justly or unjustly. Mindful of this, an enlightened ruler, one who recognizes the power of his own reason but also understands that he rules over others with reason—as opposed to dumb beasts—will recognize that the best and most just ruler rules with persuasion and consent, not with brute force (see *Plt.* 276d2–e4 and passim). Kreon, who understands himself to be such an enlightened and just ruler, is at pains from the beginning not only to declare his *phronēma*—his good intentions and sound judgment—but also to explain and justify it. In his first address to the townspeople, therefore, he speaks both to the legitimacy of taking the throne and to the soundness and justice of his proclamation prohibiting Polyneices' burial (162–210).

As he explains, someone needed to assume the throne because the two brothers who supposedly had been sharing it—Polyneices and Eteocles—killed each other. Kreon stepped forward because he, being their closest male kinsman, is the natural person to assume the power and responsibility (170–74).[7] Immediately upon assuming this power, he issued a proclamation with the force of law (191–93) prohibiting the burial of Polyneices. The rationale for issuing this proclamation is that Polyneices, though a brother and native son, came as an enemy and, even worse, a traitor, bringing foreign armies to march against Thebes. But this means that he challenged and violated the highest principle of justice and, indeed, of all good, according to

---

7. There is a double irony here, revolving around "kinship," which implies a familial, and therefore, a natural bond. One irony, as Benardete notes, is that Kreon is related only by marriage and not by blood. This means that he does not in fact stand within the natural train of succession. *Sacred Transgressions* (12.2), 24. But there is an additional irony, which is that, in his *phronēma*, Kreon eschews any consideration of nature or familial relations; and yet he cannot justify taking the throne except by appealing to nature and family—that is, if he wants to insist he is not a tyrant, acting solely by force.

Kreon, which is that the city is the first and highest thing: fatherland and city are all in all (182–90). This means that what supports and protects and strengthens the city is good; what does not, is bad. Everything—every decision, every action, every association—must align with and contribute to the preservation and strength of the city. Anything that does not do this threatens the city and is therefore bad. Those whose actions support and promote the city are friends, those whose actions do not, are enemies. No person, not "friend" nor even relative—not niece, brother, or son—counts higher than the city. Everyone and everything, Kreon explains, is judged and ordered with a view to this principle and end. Polyneices, who, worse than enemy, was a traitor to his own city, deserves the harshest punishment (198–208).

Eusebeia sebasasa

Daring to stand up against and act in defiance of this all-encompassing declaration of power and authority is Antigone, sister of Polyneices as well as of Eteocles and Ismene, niece of Kreon and betrothed of his son Haemon. Unlike Kreon, whose stance is fixed and monolithic, becoming simply more entrenched as well as more extreme as he is challenged, Antigone's rationale is rather more fluid. When she is caught and brought before the king to answer for her defiant acts, she leads with a challenge to Kreon's comprehensive and totalizing view of the city and of political power.

> It was not Zeus who made this proclamation
> nor was it justice dwelling with the gods below
> who set in place such laws as these for humankind.
> Nor did I think your proclamation had such strength
> that, mortal as you are, you could outrun those laws
> that are the gods', unwritten and unshakable.
> (450–55)

Against Kreon, Antigone is arguing not only that there is more than just one kind of law and one authority, but also that the gods' laws stand higher than human laws and have a higher authority. Of particular concern to Antigone is "Hades," which signifies at once both the god and the realm of death and the dead. Matters pertaining to death belong to the gods, not to man; they are subject to gods' laws, not to human proclamation.

8

"Gods' laws" is however a rather ambiguous term. Initially, Antigone's appeal to "gods' laws" seems to be a reference to ancestral custom. If we look to the opening lines of the play, for example, where Antigone is trying to enlist Ismene to help move the corpse of Polyneices and give it the rites of burial, she seems to understand this act as according with and upholding ancestral custom (see 76–77). As we know from Homer, for example, burial is the ancestral custom and practice, the reverent and pious (*eusebes*) thing to do for the dead.[8] Furthermore, a part of this ancestral custom is that the responsibility of burial falls principally and primarily to the family.[9] It is no surprise, therefore, in the opening lines of the play, to see Antigone asking Ismene to help her bury their brother.

The traditional character of Antigone's desire to bury her brother and her request that Ismene help her highlights how iconoclastic and contrary to tradition Kreon's proclamation is. His iconoclasm suggests that the desire to bring everything within human control—i.e., the complete mastery of nature—implies and requires the demolition, or at least the appropriation, of the ancestral and traditional. For the ancestral and the traditional practices associated with "gods' laws," and therefore with piety, have as a principal focus matters concerning nature—namely, matters involving birth and death. For example, prohibitions against patricide and incest—both of which have to do with human origins and birth—are associated with the sacred, as we see in *Oedipus Tyrannus*.[10] And duties that have to do with death and the dead—that is to say, with the termination and end of human existence—are also understood as being prescribed by, hence owed to, the gods, as both Homer and the *Antigone* attest. Further, though the very nature of ancestral customs and traditions means that there is no one to whom one can turn to explain the rationale behind them (i.e., the gods' *phronēma*), one can nevertheless infer an explanation, namely, that as

---

8. For example, we know from Homer that, for the Greeks (as well as the Trojans) the dead must be buried if they are to be allowed to leave this world and enter Hades. See, for example, Homer, *Il.* 7.327–35, 23.65–71; *Od.* 11.51–78.

9. Consider, for example, *Il.* 24, where Priam, king of the entire Trojan empire, goes in person to retrieve the body of his slain son Hector, to bring it back home for burial.

10. Complement to *Oedipus Tyrannus* would seem to be Plato's *Republic*, which attempts to bring under the control and mastery of reason every aspect of the city, including birth (see *Rep.* 5, especially 459a7–461e9).

the family is the source of an individual's birth and beginning, it makes sense that to the family would fall the rituals attendant upon the individual's death or end. For the family is the placeholder and reminder of the natural, and the custom of burial recognizes this and serves as a reminder of it. Whether piety and justice are always and necessarily in tension remains a question; what is clear however is that piety and the belief that rationality enables human beings to be complete masters and possessors of nature are essentially at odds. Having the understanding he has, Kreon of necessity tramples on territory traditionally ascribed to the family and associated with nature and the gods.

Insofar as Sophocles presents Kreon as the one who has to learn a lesson—"Alas, you seem now to see justice, but too late" (1270)—we might expect that Sophocles will extol and defend the traditional and customary against the innovations of the new-fangled and iconoclastic; that he will uphold the old ways, which can be traced back to Homer, against the new ways being introduced by the emerging sophists.[11] What is striking about the *Antigone*, however, is that Sophocles only points in passing to the traditional rationale and understanding behind the ancestral custom of burial.[12] For while he has Antigone nod to tradition (*eusebeia sebasasa*) in the opening lines of the play, the line of argument she pursues in her quarrel with Kreon moves away from an insistence on adhering to and upholding ancestral custom and toward an almost metaphysical discourse on the being, power, and meaning of life and death. Thus, as Kreon insists ever more adamantly that human authority and power (especially his) comprehend everything, including what is traditionally understood to belong to the gods, Antigone ever more strongly emphasizes the ephemerality and impermanence of life over and against the eternality of death. And, whereas for Kreon everything is contained within the horizon of the city, for Antigone, what is substantive and lasting, absolute and enduring forever, is death, which lies far beyond the reach of the city. Beginning from what appears to be a disagreement about power, Sophocles drives the play toward a reflection on being.

---

11. See Segal, "Sophocles' Praise of Man," 53.

12. See, e.g., lines 74–77, 245–47, 278–79, 429–31, 692–99, 1114–15.

Pantoporos...

Kreon's initial response to Antigone's challenge and appeal to the law of Zeus appears to be to ignore it. Accusing her of being rigid and unyielding before the authority of his rule, he characterizes her defiance as an act of *hubris* (480). Initially, this might be understood to mean that, insofar as she is defying his proclamation, she is challenging and thus disrespecting his authority. Indeed, this is suggested when he says, "It is clear enough that I'm no man, but she's the man, if she can get away with holding power like this" (484–85). *Hubris*, however, also has undertones of challenging what is proper and right, as well as of challenging the gods. For example, when Agamemnon dishonors Achilles in the *Iliad* by threatening to take away Achilles' female war prize Briseis, Achilles calls this an act of *hubris* (*Il.* 1.203). Clearly Achilles cannot mean that Agamemnon is challenging his authority, for he knows well that Agamemnon is the commander-in-chief of the Achaeans. Rather, what he appears to have in mind is that Agamemnon failed to recognize and honor Achilles' natural right—his worth as a warrior. In the *Odyssey* as well, the suitors are several times described as hubristic.[13] While this might mean simply that they are being boorish guests, the emphasis on guest-friendship (*xenia*) and the connection, both explicit and implicit, between guest-friendship and the gods implies that to violate guest-friendship is to transgress against the gods.[14] That is to say, to invoke *hubris* is to suggest that it is something beyond the realm and power of human authority that is being violated or offended. As Kreon continues to argue, however, it becomes ever clearer that, in his mind, there is nothing higher than or beyond his rule. As he all but explicitly states, to defy and challenge his authority and proclamations is akin to defying and challenging the gods.

This is made clear through several passages. For example, when the guard first reports that someone has buried the body despite Kreon's proclamation, the chorus suggests that "maybe this deed was prompted by the gods [*theēlaton*]" (279). Kreon responds immediately and vehemently:

---

13. See, e.g., Homer, *Od.* 1.368, 15.328–29, 17.483–87.
14. See Homer, *Od.* 9.175, 268–79, 478–79.

11

The words you speak are unendurable—to think
divinities might be concerned about this corpse!
Did they conceal his body to bestow a special
honor on a benefactor—he who came
to burn their pillared temples and offerings,
to scatter into pieces their land and laws?
Do you see gods bestowing honor on the evil?
(282–87)

It is blasphemous, in Kreon's mind, to suggest that the gods might look kindly on one who has acted unjustly, especially one who has committed the greatest injustice by acting against the city's very being. Rather, the gods' pronouncements and judgments, and therefore what is pious (*eusebes*), must echo and support justice and the city, and thus also the pronouncements and actions of just and lawful human beings. Another example illustrating this understanding of the gods' judgments occurs in the first exchange between Kreon and Antigone. For Antigone, the dead lie beyond/outside the reach of the *polis* and politics, and belong rather to the gods and the realm of the gods. As reverence (*eusebeia*) is properly owed to the gods, reverence—in this case, burial—is owed to those who have passed over to the realm of the gods (i.e., the dead). Having just been challenged by Kreon—"Are you not ashamed" (510)—for wanting to bury Polyneices rather than obey his proclamation, she replies, "There is no shame in revering (*sebein*) one's own flesh and blood" (511). For Kreon, however, burial is an honor, and all honors belong to the city to confer or withhold. And, as the city's preservation and well-being is the highest good, persons and actions that support the city deserve to be honored, whereas those that hurt it deserve to be dishonored. Since, in his mind, piety echoes and upholds the principles of justice and the good of the city, what is worthy of reverence is identical to what is worthy of honor. For him, Polyneices' act of marching against the city was unjust and therefore "irreverent [*dussebes*]," and one should not honor (with burial) or show reverence to one who was unjust and irreverent, as if he were no different from one who was just (i.e., who died defending his city) and was therefore reverent. Anyone, Kreon believes, whether alive or dead, would agree: "Why give honor that is irreverent [*dussebes*] in his [Eteocles'] eyes?" (514).

12

This is echoed yet again later, when Kreon, conversing with Haemon, once more speaks out against "revering [*sebein*] the disorderly [*tous akosmountas*]" (730), namely those who would undercut or even threaten the stability, order, and well-being of the city.[15] The bad deserve to be called enemy, to be denied burial, not to be revered. Denying burial to someone who brought a foreign army to march against his own city is, for Kreon, in line both with justice and with piety.

As if bringing the gods entirely within the orbit and service of the city were not enough, Kreon takes his position one step further. Responding to Haemon's repeated questioning of his wisdom, and thus his justice, Kreon cries out, "So I'm at fault by revering (*sebōn*) my own rule?" (744). A far step from revering the gods, what he shows himself truly to revere is himself, his position, and his power.

...*Aporos*

Although Antigone's burial of Polyneices defies Kreon's proclamation while according with ancestral custom, her purpose or *phronēma* is actually much more radical, and stands at a far distance from both Kreon's understanding and the understanding embodied in ancestral custom. For Antigone does not merely accept her death as the penalty she must suffer for upholding piety over and against Kreon's wrongheaded proclamation. Rather, she positively embraces death—so much so that we are made to wonder if it is not the reverence of death that she truly understands as piety. Thus, whereas initially Antigone is focused on burying her brother because—despite Kreon's proclamation—it is the reverent thing to do, as she is forced to defend herself before Kreon, the focus of her argument turns increasingly to her own death and the meaning and being of death. She never ceases to defend the importance of burying Polyneices, but as she proceeds with her defense, her "reverence" (*eusebeia*) comes to refer not only—perhaps not even principally—to this act, but more to her willingness to accept—perhaps even to embrace—death (460–64; cf. 502–4, 555, 559–60).

---

15. Kreon thus upholds and remains consistent with his *phronēma*, as announced in lines 175–210.

Behind this embrace of death lies a much different understanding than Kreon's of the nature of this world and of life, and of where human beings stand in relation to the totality of the cosmos and of being. Whereas for Kreon this world—the visible, tangible, natural world that is found on the earth—is all that is, and human beings, because they are rational, have the capacity to be absolute masters and possessors of it, Antigone, by contrast, focuses on the ephemerality of human life, over and against the eternity of death. Human beings, human life, exist in time. They are born (come-to-be) and they die. The realm within which they dwell is constantly changing: rulers come and go; cities are sometimes at war, sometimes at peace. Human ingenuity and artfulness, which includes issuing proclamations and making laws, acts within and on this earthly, temporal, changing world. But while the power of human beings is vast, it is not limitless. Human artfulness works on "material" that it cannot create itself. Even political communities rely on human beings to come-to-be, which is a natural process and necessity. And, any given human being has power only as long as that human being is alive and walks on the earth. Once they have died, human beings are dead forever. The dead no longer live or act upon the earth; they therefore are no longer of or in the temporal realm, the realm of human power and artfulness. They now are in—belong to—"Hades," that aptly named "Unseen" realm, a realm that lies beyond the reach of human power, making, and law, a realm of the sacred, not the just. Whereas justice and obedience are what is owed to human rulers and human laws, reverence and piety (*eusebeia*) are what is owed to the gods and the gods' laws. By prohibiting the burial of Polyneices, Antigone charges, Kreon is intruding with his temporal human power into the realm of the atemporal and divine. He is therefore violating piety and the laws of the gods.

Although Antigone's embrace of death does not become entirely clear or central until her conversation with Kreon, there are already hints of it in the opening scene. When Ismene demurs, refusing to help bury their brother, Antigone says,

> You be as you think best, but I shall bury him.
> To me it is noble [*kalon*] to die performing such a deed.
> Dear, I will lie with him, with my dear friend, when I have

performed this crime of piety [*hosia panourgēsasa*]; for I
  must please
those down below a longer time than those up here,
since I shall lie there forever [*aiei*].
  (71–76)

We see here the association of the gods and the realm of the gods with eternity, a theme that Antigone repeats when she speaks of obeying the gods' laws instead of Kreon's proclamation (450–61), saying that "their laws are not for now or yesterday, but live forever [*aei*]" (456–57). But as Antigone proceeds, it is notable that her understanding of "eternal" does not extend back before birth, but only "forward," after death. She seems to have no thought or care for any god other than Hades, nor for any realm other than death: "Hades longs to see these laws fulfilled" (519), she says, speaking to Kreon. And, when Ismene wants to share the penalty with her, even though she did not help with the burial, Antigone replies, "Hades and those below know who can claim this deed" (542). Finally, and most tellingly: "You made the choice to live, and I, to die" (555); and "My soul has long since been dead" (559–60).

What, though, is the nature of this death that Antigone has embraced so wholly, even longingly? While her attention is set on burying Polyneices and defying Kreon, death seems to be for her an unarticulated ideal, connected, as we have discussed, with eternity and its standing outside of human power and human making. But as the moment of her death approaches and she is confronted with its imminence, she seems for the first time compelled to try to define or at least describe it. The only way that she is able to describe it, however, is through negation, which she expresses through a collection of alpha-privatives. She is going to Hades *agamos* ("unwedded," 867), *aklautos* ("unmourned"), *aphilos* ("without a friend" or anyone dear), *anhymenaios* ("unhymned," i.e., unaccompanied by wedding song, 876), and *adakruton* ("unwept," 882). And, a little later, *alektron* ("without a wedding bed"), and again, *anhymenaion* ("unhymned") (918). Her employment of alpha-privatives seems to imply that the cosmos, or the totality of all that is, is in her mind binary: there is the realm where there are tears, marriage, wedding song, and the realm that is devoid of these—the realm of life, and the realm of death. Contrary to Kreon, who seeks to comprehend everything within the power and control of human beings, and especially of the human ruler (himself), for Antigone, the realm of life and the realm of death are entirely disjunctive, other to each other. But what is more striking about Antigone's sudden proliferation of alpha-privatives is that, though she has privileged the realm of death and of the gods (or at least Hades) because they stand outside of time, eternal and forever, this eternal realm beyond the reach of temporal, earthly being and time appears to be a realm of perfect nonbeing.

In the face of this nothing or void that she finally seems to admit Hades is—this void which is, at the least, unknowable and unknown, but which might in fact be truly nothing, the absolute negation and other of being—all she can offer to comfort herself is a hope (or wish?). One part of this hope concerns what—or whom—she will find when she "arrives" in Hades: "I still nurse a hope (*en elpisin trephō*) that when I get there, I will arrive dear (*philē*) to my father, most dear (*prosphilēs*) to you, mother, and dear to you, my own dear brother (*philē de soi, kasignēton kara*)" (897–99). This hope expresses the longing of her heart, the longing she has expressed since the beginning of the play (73–74). Not knowing, however, the true nature and being of death, she entertains a second alternative, which she presents by likening her fate to the fate of Niobe. Quite possibly Antigone thinks of Niobe because her mind connects the stone-covering (i.e., the cave) that will be her death and her tomb with the stone that Niobe is transformed into, and which becomes her form and lot into eternity (823–28).[16] From this likeness, Antigone draws the following conclusion: "With me being most alike to her, a divinity [*daimōn*] puts me to sleep" (833). A stone covering (cave) will be her tomb, but under this possibility, the death she is about to enter is envisioned as akin to being asleep, a dreamless, never-ending sleep.[17]

Euphronein

The imminent approach of her own death forces Antigone to try to give articulation to the nature of this death, which in turn raises questions about what she understands death to be. Fittingly, having valued life and events

---

16. Indeed, the chorus suggests as much when they remark, "When you perish...you [will] have shared in the lot of the godlike in life and again in death" (837–38). See also Blondell's comment on that line, "*Antigone*," 69n139.

17. See line 811: "Hades who puts all to sleep." Cf. Plato, *Ap.* 40c5–e4.

in this world (the world of the living) as worth little to nothing over and against the eternity and, ostensibly, the full being that is death, it is the unfolding events of life and experience that challenge what she thinks she knows. In Kreon's case, it takes a concerted challenge to his logic and his thinking by someone whose wisdom he esteems perhaps equally to his own to open his mind to the possibility that there might be flaws in his thinking. But only when the unfolding of events forces him to see that human beings' actions have consequences—that his decisions set in motion a train of events that he could not control once started—does he truly begin to understand the limitations of both his knowledge and his power. For him to arrive at this self-knowledge and this insight is, however, no easy task.

Antigone presented the first challenge to Kreon's certainty but he was able to dismiss her rather easily, in part because she is "merely" a woman, in part because she simply asserted her view against his. In his mind, she could not touch either his wisdom or his power. When Haemon and Teiresias engage with Kreon, they automatically have some standing, in part because both are male, but also because one is his son and the other a trusted advisor. In addition, they do not simply declare a view contrary to Kreon's; rather, each directly questions and challenges the logic of Kreon's thinking. And, while Kreon in the end is as dismissive of Haemon as he was of Antigone,[18] when he is confronted yet again with many of the same questions and challenges by Teiresias, he eventually comes to realize that his judgment may not be as just and wise as he has believed.

From his first words, Haemon makes it clear that it is Kreon's judgment (*gnōmē*) that he is questioning: "Father...when, as it seems to me, you have good judgments [*gnōmas*], [then] you guide my path aright, and [then] I shall follow where they lead" (635–36).[19] Not hearing the implicit criticism, Kreon takes this statement as an invitation to praise himself and

---

18. This is because Haemon, by challenging Kreon, fails to live up to "the reason men pray to beget and keep obedient offspring in their house," which is so that "they may pay back evil to their father's enemies and give due honor to his friends, equally as their father does" (642–44).

19. Blondell translates this passage: "Your judgments, being good ones, guide my path aright, and I shall follow where they lead." But cf. her comment on this line at "*Antigone*," 60n112, where she says, "In Greek there is a subtle ambiguity in Haimon's words, which could mean 'When your judgment is good, I follow it.'"

display his great wisdom and judgment (639–40). As he responds, however, what emerges is not logic and rationality, but pride, even arrogance. He openly disparages Antigone, his son's betrothed (653–54); he appears certain that Zeus would not help save Antigone even if she were to pray to him (658–59); and, in the end, abandoning any pretense of upholding justice, he declares, "The one appointed by the city should be listened to, in small things and in just things and in their opposites" (666–67). Kreon's assertion of his authority, which originated in the twin foundations of knowledge and power, has devolved into power alone. Order, not justice, is now the only criterion for just rule, and order demands that the ruler be obeyed without question or challenge, regardless of whether his commands are just or unjust (see Plato, *Rep.* 1.339b7). His declaration to Haemon is the declaration of a tyrant.[20]

In the face of this tyrannical unrestraint, Haemon tries to tread carefully. Using language similar to that which Kreon had earlier employed against Antigone (see 473–76), Haemon warns Kreon of the dangers of remaining too rigid and unyielding (712–17). More directly, he tries to prompt Kreon to recognize that his thinking may not be as sound as he believes. Beginning with a statement that should accord perfectly with Kreon's own thinking, Haemon declares that "good sense" (*phrenas*) is the best possession human beings can have (683–84). But, he continues, "whoever believes that he alone has good sense [*phronein*], or that no one else has a tongue [*glōssan*] or spirit [*psychē*] such as theirs, when opened up, is seen to be empty" (707–9),[21] adding that even a wise man (*sophos*) can learn something (710–11). He then concludes, invoking the words and wisdom of Hesiod: while "it is best by far for men to be by nature full of knowledge in all things," since "things are not inclined to be that way, it is also fine to learn from others who speak well" (720–23).[22]

---

20. For a much fuller development and exploration of this point, see Socrates' discussion with Thrasymachus in Plato, *Rep.* 1.336b1–344c8.

21. On the triad of *phronein, glōssa,* and *psychē,* see Benardete, *Sacred Transgressions* (40.4), 88–89, who compares it with Kreon's initial triad of *psychē, phronēma,* and *gnōmē* (175–76).

22. See Hesiod, *WD* 293–95: "That man is best of all who is able to perceive everything by his own thinking, which things will subsequently and in the end be better; good also is he who is persuaded by [*pithētai,* obeys] one who speaks well."

Any argument that does not, however, accord with his own judgment (*gnōmē*) Kreon deems to be no argument at all. In the end, all he recognizes in Haemon's speech is that his son has failed to support his father's judgment. Such a son, he had declared at the beginning of their exchange, brings dishonor to his father by inviting "peals of laughter" from the father's enemies (647), and is therefore "evil" (*kakos*; see 652). He refuses to see himself in the mirror Sophocles has Haemon hold up or to heed the wisdom of Hesiod that Haemon conveys, instead interpreting Haemon's comments as a questioning of his authority, hence as a failure to obey. He thus categorically dismisses Haemon's advice and relegates Haemon to the same category as Antigone before him (see 740–56).

When it is Teiresias' turn to confront Kreon, he offers many of the same arguments as Haemon. But whereas Kreon shrugged off Haemon's words, in the end, Teiresias' arguments manage to break through Kreon's willful arrogance and make him turn to examine and question himself. In part, this might be because Kreon esteems wisdom and Teiresias is a trusted advisor who has always in the past advised truly (see 1092–94). In part also it might be because Teiresias does more than just exhort Kreon to pause and reconsider his views; he tackles the content of those views, in particular, Kreon's opinions about the scope of human knowledge and power and the relation between human beings and gods. Perhaps most decisively, however, Teiresias introduces a consideration that has been entirely absent from Kreon's thinking: that human decisions and actions have consequences, and that correct judgments must include the consideration and understanding of those consequences.

In order for someone to be open to listening to another's advice or counsel, the individual must first recognize that he might have less than perfect understanding. Haemon began with a reference to judgment; Teiresias begins with an allusion to ignorance. "O lords of Thebes, we have come by a shared road, two seeing through the eyes of one, for this is how a blind man makes his way, with someone else to lead" (988–90). The immediate explanation for this remark is prosaic enough: Teiresias is blind and therefore needs someone to guide him anytime he ventures out. But this line is also reminiscent of Diomedes' explanation in *Iliad* 10 for wanting Odysseus to accompany him as he goes to scout out the Trojan

army: for two going together see better than one.[23] Kreon, more like Dolon
than Diomedes up to this point, has been "going it alone," so certain has
he been of his own wisdom. Teiresias, however, bluntly challenges this
unquestioning self-confidence: "It is from your [bad] thinking [*phrenos*]
that the city is so sick" (1015–16). Then, echoing closely the message
Haemon tried to convey, Teiresias adds,

> To be at fault [*touxamartanein*] is common
> to all human beings. But when someone is at fault
>   [*hamartēi*]
> that man is no longer foolish [*aboulos*, lit.: without counsel]
>   or unfortunate
> if he attempts to heal the evil he has fallen
> into, and does not remain immovable.
> (1023–27)

The way to heal this evil, he concludes, pointing to Hesiod, is "to learn
from one who speaks well" (1031–32).

One "speaks well" if one has some expertise or knowledge. It is Teiresias, not Kreon, who supposedly has knowledge about piety and what is
owed or pleasing to the gods (see 998). Teiresias reminds Kreon of this
first by reporting what he experienced in his bird augury (999–1111). This
report invokes the traditional beliefs and ancestral customs regarding the
communication from gods to men through signs from birds and the success or failure of burnt offerings.[24] On the basis of these signs Teiresias
claims that the city is sick and polluted because of Kreon's proclamation
denying burial to the enemy (1015–22). Kreon, however, easily dismisses
this talk of bird augury (perhaps judging it to be mere superstition) and
categorically asserts against the seer that he knows well (*eu oida*) that "no
human being has the strength to taint the gods" (1043–44).[25]

---

23. "When two go together, one of them at least looks forward, to see what is best; a man
   by himself, though he be careful, still has less mind in him than two, and his wits have
   less weight" (*Il.* 10.224–26). The *"Iliad" of Homer*, trans. Richmond Lattimore (Chicago: University of Chicago Press, 1951).

24. See, for example, Poulydamas' advice to Hector (*Il.* 12.215–29).

25. See Blondell, *"Antigone,"* 76n173: "A human being could not literally taint the gods
   with pollution, but...this does not mean Zeus approves of Kreon's behavior."

Rather than try to convince Kreon to believe something that reason cannot prove, Teiresias turns instead to call into question Kreon's self-certainty that he is wise—"Does any mortal know or take into account... how far good counsel [*euboulia*] is the best thing to possess?" (1040, 1050). He then revisits Kreon's rationale for his actions in an attempt to prod Kreon to reconsider his thinking and judgment.[26]

In particular, Teiresias confronts Kreon's understanding of what is owed to the living and the dead and, by extension, his understanding of what is pious. He first speaks to Kreon's act of consigning Antigone to a cave to die. Kreon had claimed that since the cave lay outside the wall of the city, her death would not pollute the city—implying that his act was, at the least, not impious. Against this, Teiresias says, "You have cast down below one who belongs above, sending a living soul to dwell dishonorably in a tomb." Then, drawing a parallel between Kreon's treatment of Antigone and his treatment of Polyneices, he adds, "And you are keeping up here a corpse belonging to the gods below, without rites, without offerings, without holiness" (*amoiron, akteriston, anhosion,* 1067–71).[27] But this is to counter at once both Kreon's understanding of the nature of the cosmos and his corresponding understanding of what is pious. Drawing a sharp divide between the being of one who is "living" and the being of "a corpse," suggesting that each belongs to a separate realm, Teiresias challenges Kreon's belief that all of being is encompassed by and subject to human control. He goes further, however. Whereas for Kreon, "honor" aligns with justice and belongs solely to the city to confer or withhold, Teiresias here aligns honor more with holiness and piety, and suggests

---

26. This second part of Teiresias' exchange with Kreon is reminiscent (anticipatory) of Socrates' challenge to Euthyphro: "By Zeus, Euthyphro, do you believe that you have such precise knowledge concerning the divine things, how they are disposed, and the holy and the unholy, that, with these things having occurred as you say, you do not fear that, by bringing a lawsuit against your father, you might be doing an unholy thing?" (Plato, *Euth.* 4e3–6). For an excellent examination of the *Euthyphro* and the connection between self-knowledge and piety, see Ronna Burger, *On Plato's "Euthyphro"* (Munich: Carl Friedrich von Siemens Foundation, 2015).

27. Note how this is the reverse of Antigone. She, descending too soon to Hades, was going to miss out on several of the good things in life. In Teiresias' speech, the corpse of Polyneices is being deprived of what belongs to death.

that honor means to give to each being its proper due.[28] Because "the living" and "a corpse" have a distinct ontological status (i.e., being) and "belong" to two distinct realms, "due" or honor is not determined solely by whether someone has benefited the city or the ruler. Rather, what is owed to the living is one thing, what is owed to the dead is something else. Once Polyneices died, he no longer belonged to the realm over which Kreon rules, namely, the realm of the living and, more particularly, of the city. For, Teiresias continues, "Of these things [i.e., the dead], neither you nor the upper gods have a share [*metestin*]," and adds that to try to meddle in and control them is to "violate them by force [*biazontai*]" (1072–73). What is owed to a corpse is the recognition that the person that this was is now dead and is no longer within the realm of the living but rather now "belongs" to death (Hades). Recognizing this, one ought to "yield to the dead" (i.e., bury the corpse), rather than to "keep stabbing at a perished man" (1029–30).[29] Whether one buries the living while they are still living or denies burial to the dead once dead, one has failed to accord to them their due and this, Teiresias implies, is to violate holiness and piety.

To the counterargument, discussed above, Teiresias adds a dose of prophesy. Speaking to what Kreon values most highly, namely, himself, Teiresias prophesizes that, because Kreon has trespassed into the realm of the gods and violated it (*biazontai*, 1073), "the ruinous late-avenging Furies of the gods and Hades lie in wait for you, that you may be caught up in these same evils in your turn" (1074–76). Next, he speaks to the city, which Kreon has been claiming to champion and protect. Saying that the "unholy [*anhosion*] stench" of the rotting corpses of the slain enemy has

---

28. Cf. Plato's *Republic*, where to give to each what is owed, needful, or proper is offered as the definition of justice (*Rep.* 1.331e2–3; cf. 9.586e1–2). Similarly in the *Statesman*, the statesman's knowledgeable action, which would seem to align with justice, is described as doing what is needful, timely, and fitting (*Plt.* 284e5–8). If one looks however to the *Euthyphro*, Plato offers a model that harmonizes with Sophocles. This is the suggestion that "the pious" encompasses all that is, but that for the city, which is a subset of all that is, "pious" is (is called) "just" (*Euth.* 12b3–c8; cf. 15d6–8).

29. This passage might remind us of Achilles "dishonoring" Hektor by dragging his body around the citadel of Troy, especially since Sophocles concludes this speech with: "What prowess [*alkē*] is it to re-kill the dead?" Homer in the *Iliad*, however, underlines the savageness, hence the (im)morality of Achilles' action, whereas Teiresias' speech overall highlights instead the irrationality and illogicality of the act.

been carried back to their native cities and has stirred up enmity against Thebes (1080–83),[30] he implies that Thebes will suffer an attack in the future because of Kreon's wrongheaded proclamation and stubbornness. The bird augury with which Teiresias began purported to interpret the intentions of the gods, and thus stood independent of any proof. Teiresias' prophesying, by contrast, finds proof of piety and impiety within the earthly, temporal, human realm—in the unfolding of events through the passage of time. His prophesying therefore highlights that human actions have consequences and that correct judgment must include the consideration of consequences (see 1077–79).

Teiresias' status as a seer—as the chorus says, "We have never known him to utter anything false to the city" (1094)—causes Kreon, finally, to begin to question himself: "To yield is awful [*deinon*], but standing firm to strike with delusion [*atēi*] my proud heart, why, that is awful too" (1095–97). Human rationality and what it can achieve is admirable, awesome in its extent (*polla ta deina*; see 332–59). But to step beyond its limits is awful (*deinon*). It takes the unfolding of events, however, for Kreon to understand fully the extent of his ignorance. Thus, only when we see him returning to the palace with the body of his dead son in his arms, do we hear him acknowledge responsibility for what has transpired: "Oh! The rigid faults, death-dealing, of thoughtless wrongful thinking!" (1261–62); and, a few lines later, "You died, you departed, through my ill counsel, not your own!" (1268–69). And, when he learns of the death of his wife, Eurydice, he declares, "To me, to no other mortal, this responsibility will cling forever" (1318–19).

It is delusion to think that the world is infinitely pliable and malleable, for human beings to do with as they will. Right thinking recognizes that the world has an order and structure and being of its own, and that it is within this that any human doing or making is done: for "in no way must (can) one fight with necessity" (1106). As he begins to recognize and acknowledge these truths, Kreon also for the first time acknowledges that what has been driving his thinking and his judgment is not rationality or sound thinking (*phronein*) but his passions, his heart: "Reluctantly I let

---

30. Note that until this point it has been presented as if Kreon's proclamation was targeted specifically and only at Polyneices.

go of what my heart desires to do [*kardias...to dran*]" (1105). The implication is that in order to achieve correct thinking and judgment, the acme of rationality, we must not only direct our thinking toward making, producing, proclaiming, legislating. Rather, we must also turn it toward questioning ourselves, our logic and reasoning, our presuppositions and worldview, and our passions and motives.[31] Kreon's mistake was that he so firmly believed he was wise, he so completely believed in his own rationality, *phronēma*, and *gnōmē*, that he failed to realize the limited perspective and understanding that is the lot of every human being, as well as the strength and distorting effect of his passions. Consequently, he failed to allow for even the possibility that he might be wrong. Because of this, he trespassed where he had no authority to go.

To phronein... mēden aseptein

Sophocles concludes the play with the chorus underscoring the message that Haemon and Teiresias in particular have pressed about the importance of self-reflection and self-knowledge for anyone who wishes to assert and enact the true power of rationality. But the chorus also reminds us that the particular subject in question has been the subject of piety.

> By far sound thought [*to phronein*] is the foremost rule
> of happiness; and toward the things of the gods
> we should never act with irreverence [*mēden aseptein*].
> (1348–50)

The question remaining is, what is the correct understanding of piety?

The "good counsel" that Kreon understands and accepts in the end is that "it is best...to live until life's end preserving the established laws" (1113–14). His rationale for this conclusion, however, is not entirely clear. Most optimistically one might say that Kreon has been convinced by Teiresias' argument that there are two separate realms, the realm of the living and the realm of the dead (see esp. 1067–83). The truth seems to be

---

31. While the greatest part of the play seems to be addressing and tackling *phronēma* as purpose informed by judgment (*gnōmē*), which is how Kreon has understood it, at this crucial juncture in the play, he finally seems to admit that there may well be a large dose of *psychē* infecting one's purpose (*phronēma*) and skewing one's judgment.

more modest, namely, that Kreon recognizes at last that he cannot adequately defend or prove that his proclamation is what is best for the city.
Recognizing that he may not be as wise as he thought, he is ready to follow
the Hesiodic advice, which says that in the absence of complete knowledge,[32] one should "obey [*pithētai*] one who speaks well" (*WD* 295). That
this is indeed Kreon's understanding is suggested by his express willingness to follow the advice of the chorus (i.e., the townspeople) after Teiresias
has departed (1098–1102). For it is their understanding that Kreon articulates: that one should uphold ancestral custom—"the established
laws"[33]—presumably because they are ancestral.[34]

And yet, though obeying one who speaks well may lead one to do the
right action—in this case, to bury the dead—the one who (merely) obeys
does not himself understand the right reason for this action. Sophocles,
however, while displaying the path of Kreon's reform from iconoclastic
believer in his own wisdom to upholder of the ancestral laws and customs,
also offers to the reader (audience) a glimpse into the true explanation and
rationale for piety, the rationale available to the one who is able "to perceive for himself." For such a one, as for the townspeople, burial[35] is owed
to the dead. Unlike the townspeople, however, the one who is truly knowledgeable understands that the realm of the living and the realm of the
dead are two separate realms, that the realm of the dead lies "beyond" life
and is the "other" of life, and that the honor owed to the dead (i.e., burial)
is owed in recognition that they have passed beyond the reach and scope
of life and of the living. To act piously or reverently therefore, one must
first understand the limited sphere and scope of human knowledge, mastery, and power—that we neither create all that is nor can we control all
that is. Then one must acknowledge this recognition either in speech or
action. But this is to say that true "reverence" and "piety" derive from and

---

32. That is, the situation of "the man...who is able to perceive everything by his own
thinking" (Hesiod, *WD* 293–94).

33. 1114. See also 502–5; 688–700.

34. This seems analogous to Euthyphro, who, once he realizes that he cannot defend his
claim to have precise knowledge of what is holy and unholy, seems to fall back into
line with the conventional understanding (*Euth.* 14a11–b7; cf. 15e3–4). See Burger, *On
Plato's "Euthyphro,"* 103.

35. Or at least some funerary ritual.

are the expression of the knowledge of one's limits. If one knows the limitations of one's knowledge and one's being, then one will avoid trespassing on the things of the gods: "*mēden aseptein*."

2

Euripides' *Electra*:
The Marriage of Convention and Nature

Michael Davis

In the extant Greek tragedies, one story alone is treated by all three tragedians—the killing of Clytemnestra and Aegisthus by Electra and Orestes
is the plot of Aeschylus' *Choephoroe* and of the *Electra* plays of both
Sophocles and Euripides. The plots of the first two differ in a number of
ways (Sophocles, for example, gives Electra an additional sister), but they
are very much akin in making Orestes the primary agent of vengeance;
Electra drops out altogether halfway through the *Choephoroe*, and, while
her suffering is thematic throughout in the version of Sophocles, she is
curiously insulated from the action of the play, which would not change
at all were she not present. By comparison, the dominance of the agency
of Electra and the changes it effects in both plot and tone make Euripides'
version stand apart.

Moreover, Euripides' *Electra* begins with a prologue by an altogether
new character—the "husband" to whom Aegisthus has married Electra
off. He is an *autourgos*—a self-employed farmer. Now, while he is certainly
more complicated than he first seems, roughly speaking, this nameless
man is presented as good beyond anyone's expectation. He has not
consummated his marriage—perhaps because he does not recognize

---

The text of the play is from *Euripides, "Electra,"* ed. J. D. Denniston (Oxford: Clarendon
Press, 1998). The translations are my own.

Aegisthus' authority, perhaps because he is afraid of Orestes—but, in either case, the result is a marriage in name only. Neither he nor Electra accept the ritual they have undergone as indicating a real marriage. Electra is married to "no one." Euripides' *Electra* thus begins with characters who, in treating a *nomos* (law, custom, or convention) as a mere *nomos*, defy convention. In this way, Euripides begins with the tension that grounds all philosophic questioning. His *Electra* is about the wedding of nature (*phusis*) and convention (*nomos*), a marriage of the utmost importance for the thought of Ronna Burger.

The distinction between *nomos* and *phusis* is both underlined and made problematic by the status of the *autourgos*, who is throughout the play anonymous—he has literally made no name for himself. He was chosen to be Electra's husband because he is a nobody; he is weak (*asthenēs*—39), and so presumably could not generate sons sufficiently strong to be of danger to Aegisthus. This suggests a certain natural determinism— because he is lowborn, neither he nor those bred from him is a threat. And yet the *autourgos* is discovered by Orestes and Electra to be a *gennaios anēr*, a wellborn man (262). On the one hand, then, that *phusis* trumps *nomos* means that blood breeds true. On the other hand, it means that one can never trust a conventional hierarchy to reflect the natural order.[1]

Let us turn for a moment to the very end of the play. Castor, one of the Dioscouroi, the brothers (now stars in heaven, 990–92) of Clytemnestra and Helen, is addressing Orestes.

> But henceforth it is necessary to do
> What both Fate and Zeus ordained for you.
> On the one hand, give Electra to Pylades as wife in
> his house,
> and, on the other, you leave Argos.
> For it is not for you to set foot
> in this city, having killed your mother.
> (1247–51)

---

1. The one meaning would vindicate Agamemnon, the other Achilles.

Now, Electra announces early in the play that having been forced to leave home is a great trial for her (207–10). In addition, she has had no children because

> this [is] shameful, for a woman
> to rule over the household, and not the man.
>   And I hate also those
> children, whoever [of them] in the city has not been named
> from the father, but from the mother.
> For, of one marrying in a distinguished way and to a
>   greater marriage bed,
> there is no talk (*logos*) of the man, but of the females.
>   (932–37)

At the behest of Castor, Electra will be betrothed to Pylades, who neither says nor does anything in the play (he is only a name), and who is to remove her immediately from Argos, her home, for the marriage is to be "in his house." Is this really the happy ending it is meant to seem? Electra's marriage appears to be a punishment.

Euripides' *Electra* is a play about marriage. Its action is bookended by two versions of the marriage of Electra—one preceding the play with a husband who may be good and a real man, an *anēr*, but who has no name, and the other directly after the play with a husband who does nothing to show himself good, but who has a name. She moves from a marriage in name only to a marriage to a name only—from a denial of convention to the utterly conventional.

Both superficially and deeply, the whole of Aeschylus' *Oresteia* is about the power of the natural relation between mother and child as somehow greater and more permanent than the formed relation between wife and husband. Aeschylus sees that, while necessary to political life, this natural relation is always a threat to the *polis*. Accordingly, he concludes his story in the *Eumenides* by providing us with three possibilities. If the Furies are altogether victorious in their prosecution of Orestes for having killed his mother, the *polis*, the conventional, will be subordinated to the family, the natural, and so, in its way, be understood as altogether natural. This would be the complete victory of the female, the world in which family loyalty trumps all, the world in which revenge and vendetta prevail over justice.

If Apollo is altogether successful in his defense of Orestes, the family will be subordinated to the *polis*, utterly conventionalized, and ultimately destroyed. Apollo points out that the very existence of Athena is a sign that, should he wish, Zeus could altogether obliterate motherhood (*Eum.* 657–66). This would be the annihilation of the female—the complete victory of the male. And then there is the solution of Athena—the goddess whose only parent is a father. Her vote creates a tie. The issue is decided in favor of the defendant as the charge against him has not been proven (*Eum.* 734–53). True, the Furies lose, but by the thinnest and least insulting margin possible. Athena then convinces them (and so indirectly also Clytemnestra, who has lived on as a dream within them driving them furiously since the outset of the play) to dwell concealed beneath Athens and to become the patron deities of marriage. They are no longer to be *erinues*, furies, but rather *eumenides*, good spirits—their wild and natural anger tamed and civilized.[2] To honor marriage is to honor an institution, a *nomos*, as legally sanctioning or legitimizing what must happen in any case by nature.[3] To think through the significance of this reaffirmation of the natural by way of the conventional, Euripides' *Electra* asks what it means for marriage to be the most natural, and so in a way the deepest and most fundamental, of the conventions of the *polis*.

The action of the *Electra* seems at first to drive us to the conclusion that ritual or *nomos* is not important—it is at best something to be manipulated. So, on the one hand, Electra's first marriage is ignored and treated as though it were not real and its ritual insignificant; Aegisthus is killed while he is in the middle of performing a sacrifice—his piety is taken as an opportunity to catch him unawares (774–858); and Clytemnestra is killed (1165–67) after having been lured to Electra's home on the pretense that she was attending the "christening" of a newly born grandchild (651–60). And yet, on the other hand, the whole action of the play depends on accepting without question a certain *nomos*—the custom of naming or identifying a child through the male line. Aegisthus' mistake is to think his safety will be secured by refusing to allow Electra to marry someone

---

2. The chorus are never called the Eumenides in this play, although see line 868 for an indication of why they will be. See also Eur., *Or.* 321.

3. The Eumenides are also to be patron goddesses of the weather. Aesch., *Eum.* 903–9.

who is noble or "wellborn," as though, even if nature were all powerful and blood were to breed true, the relevant blood is, conveniently and conventionally, solely the male blood. By itself, female lineage is taken to be altogether insignificant. And yet, unlike Aeschylus and Sophocles, Euripides makes Electra the mastermind of his plot. She artfully manipulates a not very astute Orestes into avenging his father by killing both Aegisthus and Clytemnestra. Orestes behaves as though he were simply Agamemnon's child and not Clytemnestra's. Ironically, this formidable Electra assumes the primacy of the male as well.[4] She is much more like her mother than she is willing to admit.

These two issues are connected. The Greek custom (and, of course, it is not simply Greek) of tracing descent through the male line might be justified as providing the principle of a family's unity, but its consequence is that the woman of the family, the wife and mother, must always be perceived as a stranger, as coming from the outside.[5] What happens to Electra at the end of the play as a punishment is really simply the ordinary fate of women within conventional marriage—to be in exile. And this, in turn, requires the denial of the female line necessary if Orestes is to think he is perfectly justified in killing his mother. It is at the same time what is involved in Electra's preference for her father and brother over her mother. Both assume that "breeding true" has nothing to do with the woman. In calling our attention to this assumption, Euripides also calls our attention to the fact that Orestes' vengeance is conventionally determined. It requires an unequivocal continuity of the family across time, possible only when we ignore the necessarily dual origin of the family—as though there were no alternative to the convention of giving offspring of a marriage the surname of the father.

That these are the issues of the *Electra* is immediately brought to our attention in its prologue. The tension between nature and convention emerges in the ambiguity of its first line. Does the *autourgos* address the

---

4. "I came to be from Agamemnon, and Clytemnestra brought me forth" (115–16).

5. Accordingly, in Euripides' *Alcestis*, when Heracles arrives at the home of Admetus, finds the household in mourning, and asks who has died, Admetus first equivocates, telling him that Alcestis, who has given her life so that he might not die, both is and is not yet dead (521), and then says that the mourning is for a foreign woman (533) orphaned in his house (535). The mourning, of course, is for Alcestis.

ancient plain (*argos*) or the place, Argos—a natural land formation or a *polis*?[6] And how separable really are the two? The character of the female as by nature hidden also shows itself in the prologue, for the *autourgos* gives Clytemnestra no identity apart from the men to whom she is attached. She is first "the woman/wife [of Agamemnon]" (9), then "spouse/bedfellow of him" (i.e., of Aegisthus) and "daughter of Tyndareus" (13). The *autourgos* first mentions Orestes and then Electra as children of Agamemnon (15–16), but is silent about Iphigeneia. He makes not the female Electra, but an old *tropheus* (a male "nourisher") responsible for spiriting Orestes away as a baby. And, in a plot detail found only in Euripides, Electra is given multiple suitors, "the first men of the land of Greece" (21)—the whole story depends on her being primarily a potential wife.[7] Throughout, and this despite the deed of Clytemnestra and its echo here in the manipulative nature of Electra, the question of the nobility of women is treated as irrelevant.

The *autourgos*'s description of himself is also strange. He claims to come from an illustrious Mycenaean family (35–38), but then admits that being wellborn does not keep him from falling into poverty and weakness (38–39). And it is because he is weak that Aegisthus marries him to Electra. But then how is being wellborn not conventional, and so uninheritable? The *autourgos* goes on to say of himself, "This man (*anēr*) has not ever shamed her by her bed—Cypris is my witness—and she is yet in fact a virgin" (43–44). But, if we take his speech at face value, it shows that he is not in fact noble, and that he considers Electra's bloodline superior to his own. This, paradoxically, undermines his initial claims for himself.

The general point seems to be this. Orestes and Electra assume that their father is worth avenging because he is the famous Agamemnon—sacker of Troy. By beginning with the *autourgos*, the nameless, weak, and humble he-man, Euripides forces us to call this into question, for it is not so clear that the good descend from the good—after all Agamemnon and Aegisthus can claim the same ancestry. Nor is it clear that nobility cannot be lost, for example, through poverty. Nor is it clear that the *autourgos*,

---

6. That, shortly after, *argos* is used unambiguously to mean the city Argos (6) is Euripides' way of calling attention to this ambiguity.

7. "Electra" most obviously means "amber," deriving from *ēlektōr*, shining one, but it also suggests "without a marriage bed" (*alectron*).

though weak, will not be more noble than those who are strong. Nor is it even clear that the characters in the play believe that conventional nobility is real nobility, "for many, while being wellborn, are bad" (551; see also 367–90). But if all this were true, to justify the action they are contemplating, Orestes and Electra would need to make an argument for the worthiness of their father, and this they do not do.

Electra's first words are "Black night, nurse of golden stars" (54); whether wittingly or not, when applied to her own situation, her image suggests that the adversity she has faced has nurtured her nobility, that the bleakness of the one has made the other shine forth. Accordingly, it is important to examine this adversity. We first see Electra laboring—fetching water from the fountain. She laments having been thrown out of her house—discarded along with Orestes in favor of the children born to Clytemnestra and Aegisthus. And yet, by her own admission, she toils not from need, but in order to display to the gods the *hubris* of Aegisthus, which seems here to consist primarily in his having married her off. Indeed, her husband urges her to refrain from this labor and toil and to revert to the way of her previous life, a time when she was nurtured—one might say, pampered (64–66). To be sure, Electra is cast from the house, but, as this is the fate of all women who marry, it does not really single her out. It was, for example, true even of her mother, whom she identifies here by the name of her grandfather, Tyndareus. Of the "other offspring" of Clytemnestra, we will hear nothing more. They seem meant only to remind us that when Electra and Orestes succeed in killing Aegisthus, by their action they will reproduce in others the conditions for their own trials. The revenge will not stop here. In these and many other ways, Electra repeatedly exaggerates the adversity of her situation so that the golden stars of her nobility may shine.

For her own selfish reasons, Electra plays the role of selfless martyr. When she first speaks to Orestes, still thinking him to be a messenger from her brother, she enumerates the "heavy fortunes of me and of my father" (301). She laments the sorry state of her clothing, her general filth, her poor housing, and the necessity that she work. She complains that she must make her own clothing and carry water from the spring, that she is without a share in holy festivals and is deprived of dances (*chorōn*), and that, as a maid, she must turn her back on women and so is isolated. Now, shortly before this list of woes, the chorus of young maidens had entered. They are certainly not strangers to her. In their first speech, they invite her to a holy festival (170–74). When Electra declines, complaining that her hair is filthy and that she has nothing to wear (184–85), they offer to provide her with a cloak (191–92), and, of course, she might have used the abundant water she carries around (while having been urged not to do so) to bathe and to wash her dirty hair. The parodos (112–212) consists of an extended conversation in song and dance between Electra and a chorus of young maidens. Now, while the house of the unnamed farmer may not be up to the standards of the palatial home of her youth, we see that the rest of Electra's claims of woe—clothing, filth, toil, and the lack of festivals, dancing, and female companionship—prove false or hyperbolic even before they are uttered. The suffering they describe is metaphorical. Euripides' Electra is the poet of her own misery. In the parodos, she describes the murder of Agamemnon with an axe (160) and shortly thereafter with the two-edged sword of Aegisthus (164–65). It is not specified what weapon was used in the account given in Aeschylus' *Agamemnon*.[8] In Sophocles' *Electra* (97–99, 195–96, 484–87), it is an axe. Here, with apparent indifference, Electra says it is first one and then the other. It is both; accordingly, it cannot be said unequivocally to be either. Because Electra is so poetically fertile, we are never sure how exactly we are to take what she says. The chorus share our sense of her, for they chide her for preferring to make a show of her grief, for acting a part to make a point, rather than simply praying to the gods for help (193–97). Electra is a drama queen.

With one exception, Orestes is rather cautious when he first meets Electra. She, on the other hand, is strangely rash. While Orestes knows of her marriage (98), and knows to seek her outside of the city, he nevertheless feigns ignorance (248) and reveals himself initially only as an emissary from her brother. Caution fails him, however, in response to her fear that he might kill her. Orestes responds that he might rather kill others who are more hateful (222) even though there is none he might touch with

---

8. There is a longstanding and ongoing scholarly controversy about whether the weapon is an axe or a sword that goes back at least as far as Fraenkel's 1950 edition of *Agamemnon*. For a partial summary, see A. H. Sommerstein, "Again Clytemnestra's Weapon," *Classical Quarterly* 39, no. 2 (1989): 296–301.

more right (224). Electra does not question the propriety of these remarks, although they are surely odd coming from a stranger, even one who is an agent of Orestes; she substitutes poetry for reality, and so fails to recognize what is in front of her just moments before she begins to spin an elaborate fiction about the details of her daily life.[9] Altogether incurious, Electra accepts Orestes immediately as an emissary and abruptly elevates his status from a looming death threat to "most dear one"—*philtate* (229).[10] All of this fits the drama she has written and stars in. And so, within thirty lines, she will reveal to a total stranger who might well be a spy for Aegisthus, first, what otherwise she has been at some pains to conceal— that she remains a virgin—and then, most shockingly, that she would be willing to help her brother kill their mother. With the possible exception of the invention of the *autourgos*, this is Euripides' greatest departure from the other versions of the story. What was in Aeschylus and Sophocles delayed and carefully clothed in hesitation and double-talk here occurs early in the play and is absolutely up-front. Orestes does not hesitate to ask if Electra is willing to kill her mother. Electra does not hesitate to reply to a complete stranger, albeit one who is now "most dear," that she is. Then, she goes on to tell this stranger the details of her story, details that she never thought to relate to the chorus of maidens who have befriended her. When asked by Orestes whether her mother allowed this mistreatment, Electra replies, "Women, stranger, are friends of their men, not their children"; this is a most peculiar way to understand Clytemnestra,

---

9. It is remarkable how often in the play Electra fails to notice the obvious. For example, when Orestes' servant arrives to tell her of the death of Aegisthus, she doesn't recognize him even though she had seen him only a short time before (761–69).

10. Forms of the word *philtatos*, "most loved," occur eight times in the play, three times uttered by the old man, who uses it quite appropriately (to refer either to Orestes at 567 or to Orestes and Electra together at 576 and 679) and five times by Electra— referring to her father (153), Orestes in disguise (229), the *autourgos* (345), the messenger she has just failed to recognize (767), and Orestes when he is not in disguise (1322). For Electra, it seems to be a word unconnected to reality, an almost meaningless formula, like "like" or "awesome" or "Sincerely yours," that has infected her language. *Philtate*, which in Aeschylus would have been used to single out "the one I most love" here means "you to whom at the moment I am favorably disposed." This is the key to the play as a whole, which somehow altogether conventionalizes the story it borrows, and to Electra in particular, for whom words mean what she wishes them to mean.

the woman who killed her husband to avenge her daughter.[11] But no matter, it fits Electra's story line.

In the midst of this meeting, Electra's nameless husband arrives. Although he has admitted having no claims on her as a wife, the two quarrel like an old married couple. He asks her what she is doing hanging out in public with young men. She tells him not to be so suspicious, tells him they come from Orestes, and then asks them to forgive him his manners. He says he supposes that she's told them all about the ills that beset her. Since she has said nothing to the chorus, her only other companions, Electra must regularly nag her husband about her woes. He then chides her for her lack of hospitality in not having asked them in. These two may think they rise above their merely apparent, merely conventional, marriage, but their petty quarrelling not only reveals that both are concerned about appearances but also suggests how much more married they are than they imagine themselves to be.

How appropriate then that in introducing himself Orestes should give a long and unwittingly ambiguous speech about the relation of nature to convention (367–400). He begins by seeming to praise the *autourgos*. That "there is nothing precise in manly spirit" (368) seems intended as backhanded praise of the *autourgos* for his refusal to consummate his marriage to Electra. He is not as bad as he seems, for the truth of a man is not visible by signs. It is revealed neither by property nor family connection. A man is by nature more than the external conventional props for his identity. Of course, this is all true as well of the disguised Orestes, and so his speech about the hidden character of a man is for us a not so hidden defense of himself. He too is an example of the confused natures of men, for, like him, good children sometimes spring from bad parents (370), and there may be famine in the mind of a rich man and great judgment in the body of a poor man (371–72). And so, if one can judge at all, one must judge not by externals but by nature and goodness of soul (390). Yet the remainder of the speech (391–400) is strangely at odds with its beginning, for he now speaks of Orestes as the "child of Agamemnon" (392), who is presumably owed loyalty not because of his natural virtue but because of the very lineage just called into question. And then Orestes summons his slaves inside. Are they natural slaves?

---

11. Iphigenia is mentioned only once in the play, at 1023.

If Orestes really believes everything he says in the first part of the speech, why would there be any problem with Electra's marriage? Why would he praise the *autourgos* for refusing to shame him (365)? There is something deeply hypocritical about this seemingly generous speech, something self-serving in the extreme. A man who is "somebody," but knows that he does not seem to be, says that one can never tell if someone "is somebody." But his model for being somebody is still to be the son of Agamemnon. This is an altogether conventional rejection of conventionality. We know this because Orestes says, on the one hand, that the *autourgos* is a man who would manage the *polis* well as he manages his house well, comparing him favorably to "statues of flesh, empty of sense, in the marketplace" (386–88)—thus unwittingly suggesting that the *autourgos* is perhaps more competent than the dead Agamemnon, who did not manage his family very well and lost his city to Aegisthus. On the other hand, he still does not fancy a nameless peasant as a brother-in-law.

Orestes' self-praise in the name of nature reveals him to be conventional. Electra, more complicated, nevertheless suffers a similar fate, for she has made up her world—a poetic world in which metaphor replaces reality. In the *Choephoroe*, Electra disappears halfway through the play, before Orestes enters the home of Clytemnestra.[12] She plays no role in the unfolding of the action.[13] And, while Electra's suffering provides the motive for killing Clytemnestra in Sophocles' play, she is artfully presented as having no effect whatsoever on the action that unfolds. In both the previous versions of the story, then, Electra is affected but effects not at all. In Euripides, she becomes the active force of the drama, but at a cost, for she is transformed into a character who effects her own affects. As the poet of her own story, her artfully generated motives are no more natural than those of Orestes. In the *Eumenides*, Orestes' trial for matricide is represented in terms of the deep tension between the male and the female, which, in turn, is glossed as a tension first between political life and the family, and then between the artificial and the natural. Clytemnestra defends the natural by punishing Agamemnon for the sacrifice of Iphigeneia. And yet, to do so, she must become the "woman of manly

---

12. Probably at 584, certainly by 651.
13. The role she might have played (579) is performed by the nurse (734–82).

counsel" described by the guard at the very outset of the play (11). Apparently, one can only defend the principle of the natural conventionally.[14] To justify their deed, Orestes and Electra may appeal to the "natural" relation to the father; nevertheless, to kill the mother is to attack the natural. Electra unwittingly imitates not Euripides' humanly conflicted Clytemnestra (1102–10), but Aeschylus' more consistent "woman of manly counsel," the Clytemnestra Electra has invented. This conventional praise of the natural has something to do with Electra's elevation of marriage: "You speak just things, but justice holds shamefully, for a woman should defer to her spouse in all things, she who [is] of sound mind. To whom these things don't seem so, in saying [so], she does not even come to number among my things" (1051–54).[15] This good wife, however, cannot be a good mother. In making the principle of indeterminacy determinate, the fiction that marriage is natural conceals an attack on the natural that would compromise the relation between parent and child.

The prologue, the commos that serves as a parados, and the first episode are meant to establish the theme of the *Electra* as the tension between nature and convention, but the purpose of the stasimon that follows (432–86) is initially bewildering. Other than providing enough time for the *autourgos* to fetch an old man to serve Orestes a meal, it is not clear why this ode should be necessary. It seems merely decorative—fulfilling a dramatic convention. The stasimon consists of two strophic systems and an epode. In the first strophe, Agamemnon and Achilles sail to Troy accompanied by Nereids. In the first antistrophe, the Nereids bring Achilles his armor. The second strophe describes the rim of Achilles' shield and the second antistrophe the center of the shield, the helmet, and the breastplate. In the epode, the chorus describe Achilles' sword, and address Clytemnestra—reproaching her for having slain the ruler of "such spear-toiling men." With the exception of the end of the epode, what has any of this to do with the plot of the *Electra*?

If the first strophe presents Agamemnon together with Achilles on his way to Troy, it must occur directly after the killing of Iphigeneia. In

---

14. Consider Antigone's appeal to divine law in Soph., *Ant.* 450–70.

15. Denniston and others give these lines to the chorus, to avoid having Electra claim that justice is sometimes shameful, and so, in a way, unjust. However, perhaps the contradiction is the point here.

Euripides' full-length version of the sacrifice, Iphigeneia was lured to Aulis with a promise that she would be wed to Achilles. Since, at the end of the *Iphigeneia at Aulis* (1414–32), Achilles is angry enough that he is willing to fight the Greeks to free Iphigeneia, one would imagine him to be rather sullen on the way to Troy. However, here in the *Electra*, a light-footed, leaping son of Thetis is escorted, along with Agamemnon, by a dancing chorus of Nereids and a flute-loving dolphin (434–39). The mood is airy, not dour; Achilles is identified by his mother's name; and, given the plots of the *Iliad* in the future and of the *Iphigeneia at Aulis* in the past, he seems rather too easily coupled with Agamemnon.

We initially might think the first antistrophe is a retelling of *Iliad* 18, where Hephaestus forges new armor for Achilles, but we soon realize this cannot be. It is rather a reference to Achilles' first set of armor as a gift fulfilling a promise made at the wedding of Thetis and Peleus. (See *IA* 1062–79.) This is why, in the antistrophe, the Nereids are heading not toward Troy but toward Thessaly. The antistrophe, then, is earlier in time than the strophe. The second strophic system describes this armor. The description begs to be compared with the new armor forged in the *Iliad*. Perhaps the most significant difference is that the detailed contrast of the city at war with the city at peace (*Il.* 18.490–605) is altogether absent here, and so there is no highlighting of a marriage feast (*Il.* 18.492–96) and no substitution of courts for personal revenge (*Il.* 18.497–508). In addition to the Hyades and the Pleiades (*Il.* 18.486), two groups of daughters who have been transformed into clusters of stars, we are given a series of female monsters (the Gorgon, the Sphinx, the Chimaera). The imagery on the shield of Achilles' first set of armor thus either suppresses the female, reasserts the elevation of the female to stardom, or presents the female as monstrous. In the wake of the sacrifice of Iphigeneia, apparently women do not appear as women.

The reproach of Clytemnestra in the epode is strange. Can the chorus really mean to praise Agamemnon by making Achilles exemplary of those he ruled? Isn't the whole of the *Iliad* about how unnatural and utterly conventional that rule was? Accordingly, to establish the rule of Agamemnon over Achilles, the chorus must go back to the time before the war, and they must ignore the sacrifice of Iphigeneia. In addition, while they praise Agamemnon for having ruled such "spear-toiling men," they do not describe men but armor. And so, directly after a hypocritical speech about the priority of nature to convention, we are given a choral ode that praises Agamemnon in a way that proves entirely conventional. In the course of this praise, the ode either suppresses, idealizes, or demonizes the female. Moreover, the ode itself seems unnecessary and present only as a dramatic convention. As an obtrusive example of an excess of convention, in not fitting, it fits.

All Euripidean tragedy is about tragedy. The *Electra*, no exception, is nowhere more self-reflective than in its notorious recognition scene. An old man who took care of Orestes as a young boy arrives at the home of Electra. On his way, he has noticed that someone has sacrificed at the tomb of Agamemnon. Thinking it might have been Orestes, he urges Electra to compare the lock of hair that has been left to her own, to compare the footprint left behind to hers, and to look for any fabric that matches the material woven by Electra and worn by Orestes when he was taken away as a child. In other words, the old man urges that Electra reproduce the recognition scene from Aeschylus' *Choephoroe* (164–234). Her reasons for refusing to do so mock that scene. Even were the sacrifice to come from Orestes, she says, the hair will not match, for the one would belong to a man bred in the *palaestra*, while the other would be the combed hair of a woman. Nor would the footprints match, for that of a male is much larger. And, finally, not only was she far too young to weave when Orestes was taken away, but, even had she woven his clothing, he is now an adult and could no longer wear it. What is the point of Euripides' abrupt and seemingly churlish dismissal of Aeschylus? First, with respect to the lock of hair, Electra seems to claim that what it has undergone is far more important than what it is by nature. Apparently, for this Electra, the true Orestes cannot be made manifest by way of any natural connection to his natural origin, his family. Second, with respect to the footprint, after initially denying that the old man even saw it, Electra denies that it would prove anything even were it present, since generic sexual difference trumps particular family identity. And finally, with regard to the weaving, Electra does not acknowledge that Orestes' earliest clothing might be a keepsake— a conventional sign meant to remind him of his sister; she will not even allow herself to be the principle according to which Orestes is recognized. Orestes' identity will not be revealed by his nature nor by his connection to a female (whether natural or symbolic) but, of course, in the *Electra*, the two are really the same. Euripides' attack on Aeschylus is the counterpart of Orestes' speech on the relation of nature to convention. The principle of this parody is that nothing linked to Orestes' birth, his genetic make-up, is allowed to establish his identity. This, of course, is to minimize the importance of the mother. In the *Choephoroe*, Orestes is aided by his former nurse (*hē trophos*); in Euripides' *Electra* he is said to have had a male "nurse" (*tropheus*, or "nourisher," 16) who reared or nursed (*ektrephō*, 488) him—the same male nurse who once nurtured (*trephō*, 507, 555) Agamemnon. Ordinarily a boy is said to be nursed (*trephomenos*) only as long as he is in the care of women. Here, the female has been linked to nature and both have been suppressed in favor of history. The male has replaced the female.

The recognition scene that follows the parody turns on something else. Orestes says that the old man observes him as though he were inspecting the stamp, the *kharaktēr*, on a piece of silver (558–59). In fact, the old man says a god has revealed a dear treasure to him by way of a scar from a childhood wound on Orestes' brow (573–74). Not something natural but something stamped on by experience, not nature but character, reveals who Orestes is. But then why should it be so important that Orestes is the son of Agamemnon? If it is experience and not birth that makes us who we are, is the Orestes who was raised in Phocis even an Argive? That Electra understands this difficulty is clear from her relatively mild response. She does not give a speech of the sort that Sophocles' Electra gives (1282–1321) when she discovers her brother is not dead but stands before her. This Electra asks only, "Are you that one?" (581), and then leaves the rejoicing to the chorus (585–95). When Orestes launches into a discussion of their plan, she is more interested. Electra cares not so much who Orestes is but what he will do. She believes he is Orestes, but it is unclear what this means for her.

There is a difference between what one is and what one does. For the Clytemnestra of the *Oresteia* the former is what is important. Its sign is the relation to the mother. In his *Electra*, Euripides has made what one is problematic, and at the same time he has shifted the focus of what one is to the less certain descent through the father. Euripides thereby calls attention to the fact that the natural makes itself felt in political life in a very conventional manner. And so, Euripides' Orestes and his Electra are at odds with themselves; they vacillate—first affirming some natural ground for what they are about to do and then undermining this ground by way of the very reasoning they use to support it. They are engaged in a plot to kill their mother, eliminating the female principle and thereby altogether conventionalizing human life. Accordingly, neither will ever mention the fate of Iphigeneia, Electra can claim that women always prefer husbands to children, both Aegisthus and Clytemnestra will be killed using as a ruse rituals that have to do with childbirth and child-rearing, men replace women as nurturers of the young, and hereditary traits are discounted as part of identity. And yet all these things undercut as well the relation between father and children. Accordingly, Orestes and Electra really have nothing in common and are suspicious of one another; both seem primarily concerned with their conventional status. Insofar as they consider their father at all, they ground their elevated estimation of him on the status of a man whom he did rule, but nevertheless a man who is famous for having despised him. And it is not even the man they praise, but the splendor of his armor. Euripides' explicit debunking of Aeschylus, then, has to do with a disagreement over the extent to which the natural can be tamed so as to make it the ground of the political. What marriage gives with one hand, it withdraws with the other, for what stabilizes political life also inevitably disrupts it.

In response to Electra's "Are you that one?" (581), Orestes replies that he is only her ally.[16] Either the snare he sets will succeed, or the unjust things will be placed above justice, and one ought no longer to be led by gods. So, Orestes is nothing but what he will do. The old man says that, since Orestes has no *philoi*, friends or kin, from whom to expect help, his success will depend altogether on his own hand and on chance (610). Apparently, there is no room for the gods as causes. Having already conditioned his belief in the gods on the success of his own deeds, Orestes

---

16. The passage also, perhaps even more easily, might be translated "I alone am an ally." The sentence as I have translated it should be compared to the beginning of Aeschylus' *Choephoroe*, where Electra first prays that Orestes will come home (138) and, shortly after, that someone will come to avenge the death of Agamemnon by killing his killers justly in retribution (143–44). That she does not automatically equate the two means that Orestes is for her more than, and perhaps not even, an avenger, and so is more to her than what he does.

seems to agree. Now, while the success of the murder plan depends on the fact *that* Aegisthus is performing a ritual not on *what* it is, still, Orestes first assumes the ritual is for the sake either of the nurture of children or of a birth to come (626).[17] And Electra plans to draw her mother into a trap by announcing that she has recently borne a son.[18] Clytemnestra will be killed while on her way to perform a ritual of purification, perhaps for the new mother (654), who is, after all, her child (657), or perhaps for the child (1124–25, 1132–33). In each case, then, the plan involves the misuse of a ritual having to do with childbirth to facilitate a murder, and so the "killing of the mother" has been accomplished already by the means chosen to kill the mother. Aegisthus and Clytemnestra take children and the religious rituals that pertain to them seriously. Orestes and Electra use this piety impiously (which is to say, conventionally) to annihilate the principle that grounds the conventions according to which children are taken seriously. They demonstrate this by praying for success to gods in which they do not believe and to a father whose plight concerns them less than their own misfortunes.[19] Electra calls the planned killing of Aegisthus a contest, an *agōn*. This image of their deed dominates the remainder of the play.

The chorus deliver the second stasimon (699–746), the story of Atreus and Aegisthus, while Aegisthus is being killed. They sing of Pan, who lures a lamb from its mother with sweet music. The lamb has a golden fleece, and possessing it is taken to be a sign from Zeus that one will be the ruler of Argos.[20] This lamb is meant for Atreus, but his wife, Aerope, steals it for her lover Thyestes, the brother of Atreus. Angered, whether at the theft or at the adultery, Zeus reverses the natural motion of the heavens.[21] We remain in this state still, and so Atreus' recovery of rule is grounded in a

---

17. The old man tells Orestes he can count on the support of the slaves not because of who he is—none of them will recognize him; rather, that they are slaves will guarantee their support.

18. Electra, who no doubt thinks that her mother would not care about a granddaughter, is curiously obtuse in ignoring the significance of Iphigeneia.

19. Orestes names Zeus, god of fathers, and father Agamemnon, Electra names Hera with power over altars, and Mistress Earth.

20. The sign that one is a *turannos* (710), king or tyrant, is a marvel stolen from its mother.

21. Compare Plato, *Plt.* 267c5–277a2.

permanent reversal of nature.[22] The chorus conclude the stasimon with a strange remark.

> He is said (it has little trust, indeed with me) to turn hot sun to change his golden seat for an unhappy human for the sake of mortal justice, but fearful stories would be a gain for humans with regard to the tending of the gods, not remembering which, co-generator of famous siblings, you slew your spouse. (737–46)

The chorus give an account of a convention that would ground all convention, a belief in cosmic moral sanctions. On the one hand, they do not believe it; on the other hand, they think it salutary. Their ambivalence is borne out in the immediate sequel, where they first announce that they hear a shout that points to a death, then think it may have been something else—the rumbling of Zeus as a natural phenomenon, and end by announcing that the wind is not without moral meaning. Having first doubted the significance of nature, they now affirm it. This is typical of them. They are prepared to act on the basis of a poetic fiction (here, the story of the lamb) that they do not really credit. They take their cue from Electra, who, in what seems a thorough denial of nature, thinks she can hear an accent in a death cry (755). Apparently even death is conventional, an act in a drama.

According to the messenger's account, Aegisthus, behaving with perfect propriety, invites the Thessalian stranger, Orestes, to participate in the sacrifice he is conducting and even generously offers to let him display the skill in cutting up the bull for which the Thessalians are famous. Orestes, on the other hand, is not so authentic. He lies about having been previously cleansed for the sacrifice, replaces his sword with a cleaver suitable for butchering, not for facing a foe in battle, and kills Aegisthus as though he were a sacrificial animal. Orestes is saved from reprisal not owing to any manliness on his part, but because someone in the crowd recognizes who he is (making Electra's nonrecognition even more puz-

---

22. The chorus omit certain details (e.g., that Atreus punishes Thyestes by feeding him his children and Aerope by throwing her into the sea) for the sake of focusing on adultery as the cause of Zeus' anger.

zling). Orestes, crowned with garlands like a victor in games, brings the head of Aegisthus to his sister.

The commos that serves as the third stasimon (859–79) confirms this artificiality. The chorus tell Electra to "put her step in dance (*choron*)" and "sing a beautiful victory ode with their dance (*choröi*)." It is as though they say, "Look at us; we are a chorus." They compare Orestes' deed to the triumphs of athletes at the Olympic games. Electra replies first by invoking the cosmic gods—sun, earth (*gaia*), and night—and then says she will celebrate Aegisthus' death (not because it avenges Agamemnon but because it sets her free) by bringing out previously concealed ornaments for her hair (confirming the falsity of the previous description of her trials), and by crowning Orestes as victor (agreeing with the chorus's comparison to the games). After again calling attention to their choral dance (*choreuma*), the chorus rejoice that once more dear kings exercise rule over the land (*gaia*). So, eleven lines after Electra had invoked *gaia* as cosmic deity, it gets turned into dirt. In the immediate sequel, Electra makes two more parallels to games (883, 889), and Orestes all but collapses the gods into chance (890, 892). He claims that he killed Aegisthus not by speeches but by deeds, but by giving the head of their enemy to Electra, he makes it a symbol—all but a *logos*. From all of this, Orestes unwittingly draws the perfectly correct conclusion that "we have thrown together an enmity with this one without regard to laws of regular truce/drink offering" (906). This is what it means for there to be no distinction between gods and chance. Body, which is in its way the sign of the power of the particular and accidental, becomes altogether significant—as though life were an artificial event like the Olympic games or artfully contrived like a play. No quarter will be granted because one's enemy is pure enemy—a noun, not a person. The collapsing of nature and convention means obliterating the distinction between the ritual that distills reality and the reality it distills. When nature becomes completely civilized, it is rendered brutal and barbaric. And so, Aegisthus' corpse is punished as though it were he, and Electra addresses it as though it were he.

Oddly, Electra begins her long speech to Aegisthus' head (907–56) with an extended reflection about how best to structure her speech—what its proper beginning, middle, and end should be. So, on the one hand,

Electra seems curiously detached from her speech. On the other hand, she is curiously overwhelmed by her own speech. Aegisthus orphaned her and tainted her mother. Electra wants to punish him, and so she threatens him by warning that he can never be sure of Clytemnestra, for a woman who once betrayed her husband will do so again. Electra presents no evidence whatsoever that Clytemnestra did betray Aegisthus while he lived. She means her threat for now. But Aegisthus is dead. Electra then tries to shame him for being defined by a woman—he is Clytemnestra's man. But, again, there is no indication whatsoever in the play that this was Aegisthus' reputation while he lived. So, Electra seems to animate the dead Aegisthus by attributing to him her own anxieties. That it is shameful when the woman rules the household and not the man, when the children are given the name of the mother and not of the father, and when, with respect to making a great and distinguished marriage, there is no talk (*logos*) of the man but only of the females—this is what Electra fears from her own marriage to a nameless peasant. She seems also to attribute to Aegisthus an attachment to wealth for which there is no evidence in the play, although her own poverty causes her considerable anxiety. Nor is there evidence for any pride in his girlish, cute looks; the same cannot be said of her. The anger Electra displays at Aegisthus' head is thus only very tenuously connected to reality. The poetizing Electra once more gets consumed by the fire of her own images. Is this the point? To treat the body as though it were the person by threatening the head of the dead Aegisthus really means to treat it as something more than body—as though by itself it "embodies" significance. This is akin to a situation where the law perfectly describes and governs the way things are and so where there can be within the law no acknowledgment that there is a limit to law—no acknowledgment that the long arm of the law does not reach everywhere. This is what it means that Orestes does not acknowledge "laws of regular truce." When everything is determined by a *logos* unchecked by reality, what gets said is an indication solely of the will of the one who speaks. This is the rule of poetry. Reality, its sole obstacle, shows itself in the resistance to universality to which body points, and of which the mother is the poetic symbol. Accordingly, in the play that is about the totalizing of *nomos*, the mother stands as the final obstacle to be overcome. Clytemnestra must be killed.

Electra does not so much speak as give speeches—orations understood as artifacts meant to have effects.[23] What is curious about her speech to Aegisthus is that she uses his head to remember his actions against her, and this is sufficient for her to treat him as though he were still there—to reattach his limbs poetically. When she tells him that a wife who betrays once will do so again, she is trying to make him miserable *now* by altering what was true when he was alive. Electra makes no distinction between what a person is and what a person does. And she interprets what others do through what she undergoes or suffers—i.e., by what is done to her. She began her attack on Aegisthus by charging not that he killed Agamemnon unjustly, but that he orphaned her. Aegisthus is the actions of Aegisthus, and these actions are the effects Electra undergoes. Since these effects remain—she is still an orphan—Aegisthus remains. Electra is always play-acting, for in a play, characters are what they do—no more and no less. This is what it means that Electra leaves real body behind by making body totally meaningful. It becomes symbolic.

Electra had demanded her mother's death for herself (647), but here, when Orestes begins to have second thoughts about matricide, he assumes the task is his.[24] It is not clear why. Nor is it initially clear how Electra so quickly overcomes his new qualms. Yet perhaps both questions have the same answer. When Electra warns Orestes not to fall into unmanliness (982), she reveals the anomaly of her own position—she is a woman who speaks for manliness. She has lamented her marriage to an inappropriate man, disparaged Aegisthus as a woman's man, and claimed that the woman's attachment to her man is always more powerful than her attachment to her children. Electra and her brother are engaged in the destruction of the female. As a "she" cannot do it, he must.

---

23. See 907–12 and 1060, as well as 160–65, 247, and of course her exaggerations about her present condition at the beginning.

24. L, the superior of the two manuscripts of the *Electra*, reads *exaitisomai*, with a marginal correction (followed in the P manuscript) of *exaitēsomai* —"to demand for oneself"; so, Electra demands for herself the job of killing Clytemnestra. This is generally emended (although Denniston wonders whether the emendation is necessary) to *exartusomai*, "to ready" or "to prepare," in order to avoid the problem here—i.e., Orestes' assumption that he must kill his mother. But perhaps we are meant not to avoid but to be troubled by this problem.

This tension in Electra is clear at the end in her confrontation with her mother, for she is more the manly woman of the *Agamemnon* than is this Clytemnestra. When Clytemnestra arrives, the chorus praise her for her descent from Zeus, her relation to the Dioscouroi, and the wealth she has from Agamemnon's Trojan booty. In her first lines, alluding to what no one in the play has mentioned, Clytemnestra replies to this tacit insult by saying that it is all small recompense for the loss of her daughter. Electra counters that, as a part of this booty, despite being Clytemnestra's daughter, she is like a Trojan slave, and her mother is like Agamemnon. Clytemnestra is the sacker of Argos. To this Clytemnestra replies that Electra is no slave, and proceeds to speak in her own defense. First, marriage is not a right to kill, neither wife nor child, because family is not property. Second, Agamemnon used the ruse of a marriage to Achilles to trick her into sending Iphigeneia to Aulis. Third, to protect the city or the family this might have been defensible, but not to sustain someone else's marriage when the husband can't handle the wife. Still, in the end Clytemnestra might have stood for all of this if it had not been for Cassandra—i.e., for Agamemnon's expectation that he could have two wives in one house. Electra, of course, understands this as jealousy, but it isn't that clear, for all of Clytemnestra's objections can be summed up in one: Agamemnon did not understand marriage. He treated his wife as property. She demands some measure of equality (1035–48). Clytemnestra thus presents Aegisthus as her sole option—the enemy of her enemy, and so her friend. Her claim that Electra was no slave, not property, was meant very seriously even if, ironically, she felt forced to marry Aegisthus for his use-value.

Electra's reply, that a woman should yield to her husband in everything, confirms that the crucial issue is not so much Iphigeneia as marriage. Her long "free speech" involves a series of assumptions and exaggerations.[25] She assumes, with Agamemnon and Menelaus, that Helen was a willing victim, something she cannot possibly know and that Castor will deny (1278). She assumes that Agamemnon was the best of the Greeks. Her evidence for Clytemnestra's adultery before the killing of Iphigeneia is that Clytemnestra didn't stop trying to be attractive

---

25. "Free speech" is here *parrēsia*. It is the word the Athenians use to indicate the remarkable freedom of speech that prevails politically in Athens.

immediately upon Agamemnon's departure. Electra, then, draws conclusions on the basis of a view of marriage according to which a wife belongs entirely to her husband. For Electra, women play a part—they are wives or daughters; for Clytemnestra, they are more. This is what is at stake in the absolutizing of *nomos*. The chorus see that marriage is subject to chance (1097); Electra does not. Clytemnestra, who at once loves her daughter and knows her to be an enemy, gives a mother's response—"Yes, dear, but...." She says it is a matter of nature that some belong to the males and some love mothers (1102–3), and then owns up to being not altogether happy with herself and asks why Electra is such a mess. Clytemnestra admits to being internally at odds. Insufficiently manly to be an altogether consistent character, she may be a queen in a drama, but Clytemnestra is no drama queen.

When the chorus, Electra, and Orestes sing of Clytemnestra's death in the commos that follows (1147–1237), their high tragic tone is therefore strangely at odds with the scene we have just witnessed. The mother who fusses about Electra's unkempt appearance is hardly a "lioness" (1163).[26] Then suddenly everyone's tune changes. The chorus lament the matricide (1168) and wonder if there is any house more wretched than that of Tantalus (1175–76), Orestes invokes Earth and Zeus to proclaim both killings murderous and polluted (1177–79), and Electra claims to be responsible, having acted on account of fire against the one who bore her (1183–85). Killing the mother becomes killing "mom," but only for a moment. Orestes soon names himself a generic mother killer (1197), and Electra, lamenting her fate as unwedded (1198), becomes generically *alektros*. In the *Electra*, it is the character Clytemnestra who is a person, for the mother stands for whatever it is in us that is not exhausted by the role we play. The mother is who we are, not simply what we do—our natures. That Clytemnestra had divided loyalties and so could not be of one mind is to say that she had a soul. To have depth means to be at odds with oneself. Effortless conformity to principle, identifying oneself altogether with one's *onoma*, one's name or noun, is superficial and shallow—soulless.

---

26. The chorus's simile is particularly ironic, for in his *aristeia* in bk. 11 of the *Iliad*, Agamemnon is likened to a lion five times (113–21, 129–30, 172–78, 238–39, 292–95). The manly Clytemnestra who kills her husband is apparently still to be defined by her husband.

The Dioscouroi, who enter at the end of the play to dispense justice, provide a symbol for soul as by nature divided against itself. They are somehow divine but with an indeterminate status. According to the chorus, they are not mortals but either *daimones*, divine powers just short of being unambiguously gods, or they are *of* the gods of heaven (1234–35). Castor and Polydeuces are the twin brothers of Helen and Clytemnestra. The story goes that Polydeuces was immortal and his brother not. When his brother is killed, Polydeuces begs Zeus to grant him immortality. (See Pind., *Nem.* 10.62–90.) The request is granted, but at a steep price, for the two alternate in their immortality—one on one day, and the other on the next. They are the morning and evening stars—that is, they are the same star but appearing at different times and so fated never to be together. It is Castor who speaks here (1240), saying that, while the mother received justice, Orestes and Electra did not act justly, and that, while Apollo is wise, he did not prophesy wisely (1243–46). There is a difference between the actor and his actions. The Dioscouroi have responsibility for storms at sea; they deal with chance—with what exceeds *nomos*. Accordingly, Castor cites a double origin for what they are about to mete out—Zeus and fate. As we have seen, Electra is rewarded with a suitable marriage to Pylades but punished with exile from her home. Her husband in speech (1286) will go with her and be rewarded with wealth. Orestes is sentenced to play the role of Orestes in Aeschylus' *Eumenides*; he will be pursued by the Furies and must undergo a trial, but at the same time Castor assures him that there is no risk, for in the end he will be delivered and live happily (1291). Aegisthus and Clytemnestra will receive ritual burials. Finally, Castor announces that it was not the real Helen but her phantom image that went to Troy (1283); and so, apparently, the whole string of murders chronicled in the *Oresteia* was for nothing.

Orestes and Electra seemed for a moment to rise above the roles in which they are mere vessels for meaning, to break through the poetic world they inhabit. Then the Dioscouroi arrive on the scene; things are to be set to rights, but they seem instead to be set to rites. The *Electra* is, after all, a play. In the end, Clytemnestra only stands for the mother, and *autourgos* comes to be a name; determinate indeterminacy does not ensoul but rather creates a representation of soul. Much of Euripides' *Electra* is designed to show us that and why, "while you may throw nature out with a pitchfork, she keeps coming back" (Hor., *Epist.* I.10.24). Absent the limitations imposed by nature, the conventional is brutal. Still, at the end, the conventional reasserts itself, for we discover that even our awareness of these limitations must take a conventional form—the Dioscouroi, the two that are one and yet not one, are the visible poetic image of the gods in their necessary invisibility. Electra goes off to Phocis together with two husbands: the new one, Pylades, is "real" but is only a name; the old nameless one, while declining the name, is perhaps more really a husband. Both are present, but nevertheless, like the Dioscouroi, not at once.

The mastermind of the action of Euripides' *Electra* is a woman who defines herself solely in terms of men—father, brother, and suitors. She takes as ally a brother, but acknowledges him only by virtue of their common father. By manipulating Orestes into killing their mother, Electra conceals from herself her own manliness, her own attachment to convention. She pretends that she represents not the destruction, but the proper taming of the female. Her mother did not understand marriage. Any *Electra* will enact the murder of Clytemnestra to avenge Agamemnon. Euripides displays this vengeance as the destruction of the natural in the name of the conventional, albeit understood as the natural. Of course, it is all staged—a playful enactment in a drama. What the high drama of the play ultimately shows is a more mundane scene. Marriage can never be wholly successful; as an institution, it needs the threat of Clytemnestra to signal its necessary incompleteness. For marriage is at its most natural when, while seeking to wed nature and convention, it acknowledges that by nature, it can do so only conventionally. The most serious of conventions is playful.

3

Convention and Nature in Plato's *Protagoras*

Matthew Oberrieder

Plato's *Protagoras* depicts Socrates narrating to an unidentified auditor his encounter earlier that same day with the dialogue's famous sophist namesake.[1] The explicit, practical question of *Protagoras* is whether *aretē*, "excellence" or "virtue," is teachable (320b4–c2 with 318e4–319b3); yet, at the end of the dialogue, this issue remains unresolved (360e6–361c6; cf. *Meno* 70a1–2, 71a1–c4). This "aporetic" or inconclusive ending elicits the question of Plato's positive purpose in composing *Protagoras*. In depicting an

---

1. References to the *Protagoras* text, as well as to Plato's other dialogues, cite title and Stephanus pagination from *Platonis Opera*, ed. Johannes Burnet, 5 vols. (Oxford: Oxford University Press, 1900–1907). Translations from the Greek are my own. Early in *Protagoras*, Protagoras himself, whose name means something like "first-to-proclaim," calls himself "a 'Sophist'"—the first to do so openly, he claims—and asserts his venerability (316d3–317c3); later, he bluntly cites his Pan–Hellenic renown (335a4–8). Still later in the dialogue, Socrates references Protagoras' reputation, and self-promotion, to encourage him to continue their discussion: with whom else would Socrates discourse than with the one who, in calling himself "sophist," declares himself among all the Greeks to educate human beings (348e2–349a4)? The most notorious testimony in Plato of Protagoras' fame is in the *Meno*, when Socrates recounts for Anytus, Socrates' future accuser (cf. *Ap.*18b3, 36a5–b2), Protagoras' wealth and reputation for teaching "virtue" (91d2–e9). On the historical Protagoras and his reputation in antiquity, consult, e.g., *Plato: "Protagoras,"* J. Adam & A. M. Adam (1971; repr., Cambridge: Cambridge University Press, 1984), 219–22; *The "Protagoras" of Plato*, E. G. Sihler (New York, 1881), vii–ix; *Plato: "Protagoras,"* ed. Herman Sauppe, trans. Jas. A. Towle (Boston, 1892), 1–4; all aft. Diogenes Laertius, *Lives of Eminent Philosophers* 9.50–56.

extended interaction between Socrates and Protagoras, Plato presumably aims to illustrate the status of philosopher and of sophist in relation to one another (cf. *Soph.* 217a3–b2). The obviousness of this observation notwithstanding, this paper explores Plato's dramatizing of the encounter between philosopher and sophist as it engages the issue of the respective status of, and the relationship between, "convention" (*nomos*) and "nature" (*phusis*), for investigating the specific question of human nature.

Two signature features of *Protagoras* focus one's attention on the issue of human nature: Protagoras' Great Speech (320d1–328d2), and Socrates' debunking of the claim of the many that they choose (the) bad over (the) good due to being "worsted by pleasure" (352a6–358d5). Protagoras' Great Speech purports to prove that/how *aretē* is teachable (320b7–c2), prompted by the sophist's initial claims to "educate humans" (317b3) and to teach "good-deliberation" (*euboulia*, 318e4), which he affirms as "the political art" and the promise to "make men good citizens" (319a3–7). Protagoras' Great Speech begins with a creation myth that purports to chronicle the chthonic "*genesis*" and subsequent diversifying of all "mortal races," and specifically, "the human race," and it ends with the legendary rise of cities and establishing of civic life (320c8–322d5). Although Protagoras' myth invokes "the human race" (*to anthrōpōn genos*, 321c2), this sole instance of this designation in the dialogue actually denotes a negative determination, one from which human nature emerges as completely indeterminate originally. In the sophist's presentation of human origins and civic life, the human as human depends on the force of *nomos*, the various customs, conventions, and laws (*nomoi*) of the city, conveyed and instilled through traditional education and civic punishment, for its distinct determination. Protagoras' Great Speech thus expresses the conceit of the city that it completely determines the human as such, which identity it conflates with and reduces to mere citizen. Only in Socrates' conclusion to his debunking of the claim of the many to being "worsted by pleasure" (358a1–d4) does the dialogue offer a positive proposition regarding human nature (*anthrōpou phusei*, 358d1), namely, that no one willingly prefers (the) bad (things), as "human nature" wishes to pursue (the) good (things) (358c4–d3). By interpreting these two signature features of *Protagoras* and clarifying their internal connection, one discovers that Plato's fundamental purpose in depicting Socrates' ostensibly aporetic encounter with Protagoras is to dramatize the problematic relationship between human nature and civic life.

Preliminary Action Propaideutic to Protagoras' Great Speech

Before Socrates reenacts his encounter with Protagoras, he reenacts his encounter with a young Athenian aristocrat named Hippocrates (310a7–314c2). In the darkness of "deep-early dawn," Hippocrates hurries to Socrates' house (310a7–b3) to enlist him for an introduction to the sophist (310b8–311a2). Socrates concedes to Hippocrates' request, but not before questioning him concerning Protagoras specifically and sophistry generally: "What is Protagoras?"; "What is a Sophist?"; and "What will Hippocrates become (or what will become of Hippocrates) in patronizing Protagoras as a Sophist?" (311a3–314c2). A small Socratic dialogue unto itself, this preliminary encounter between Socrates and Hippocrates anticipates Socrates' encounter with Protagoras—who will affirm that he is "a Sophist" and claim to "educate humans" (317b4–5)—and functions to establish preemptively the positive pedagogical purpose of Socrates' philosophizing. When Socrates finally does introduce Hippocrates to Protagoras (316b1–c4), he invokes his "nature" (*autos de tēn phusin*, 316b9) in presenting him as a promising and ambitious Athenian youth (316b8–c2); moreover, he questions the sophist, like he did Hippocrates, about what will ensue for the youth from his tutelage (318a1–4, b1–d4). Socrates, then, is a protector, not a corruptor, of the youth (cf. *Ap.* 24b4–26a7).

Protagoras' responses to Socrates' questions initially are evasive (316c5–317c1, 318a6–9), but ultimately the sophist asserts that what his students learn (*to mathēma*) is "good-deliberation" (*euboulia*, 318e4); upon a further question from Socrates, he then affirms that he teaches "the political art" (*tēn politikēn technēn*) and promises to "make men good citizens" (319a3–7). Socrates initially questions Protagoras' claim and requests that the sophist demonstrate that, or how, "*aretē*" is teachable (319a8–320c1).[2]

---

2. Socrates argues that *aretē* is not teachable from two examples, one public, and one private. First, he references the reputed wisdom of the Athenians, evident in the operation of the city's Assembly (319b3–d7). On issues involving technical expertise, only recognized, specialized artisans may advise the city; the Assembly rejects counsel from non-experts, and even from experts in a different field (cf. *Euth.* 3b9–c2). In political

Protagoras responds by delivering a lengthy exhibition (320c8–328d2), traditionally dubbed his Great Speech. The precise organization of Protagoras' Great Speech emerges as highly complex, but Protagoras himself divides its overall structure into roughly two halves, which he designates as his *"muthos"* ("likely-story") and his *"logos"* ("rational-account"), respectively.[3]

Protagoras' Great Speech "Muthos": The Origin of "The Human Race" and Civic Life

"Once there was a time," Protagoras blithely begins his myth, "when gods were, but mortal races were not" (320c8–d1). Without identifying these posited pre-existent gods, the sophist immediately reports the advent of the "allotted *genesis*" of the not-yet-existent, and so prematurely referenced, "mortal races" (*thnēta genē*): "gods molded them within the earth from earth and fire" (320d1–2). Protagoras' vagueness in reporting this *genesis* invites one to wonder when, and how, exactly, various distinct mortal races came to be, and especially, what originally and specifically distinguishes "the human race" (*to anthrōpōn genos*, 321c2), as such. At stake is the question of the status of human nature.

---

affairs, however, anyone may advise the city. Second, Socrates references the "wisest and best of our citizens," who, he argues, fail to transmit to others, even to their own sons, the *aretē* that they themselves possess (319d7–320b3; cf. *Meno* 93a5–94e2). Socrates concludes that these phenomena prove that *aretē* is not a political "art" involving transmissible expertise.

3. Cf. 320c2–7, 324d6–7, 328c3. One may divide Protagoras' *"muthos"* (320c8–324d1) into a myth (320c8–322d5) and a non-myth (322d6–324d1), reflecting the content of these respective sections. The myth is, in brief, mythical. The non-myth addresses the first example from which Socrates doubts Protagoras' affirmation that *aretē* is teachable. In comparison to the content of the myth, the non-myth seems to belong to Protagoras' *"logos"* rather than to his *"muthos."* Protagoras seems to have designated the whole *"muthos"* by the characterization appropriate to only the first of its two halves. Protagoras' *"logos"* (324d7–328c2) addresses the second example from which Socrates doubts the sophist's affirmation that *aretē* is teachable, but one can still divide it too into two halves. In the first (324d7–326e5), Protagoras insists that there is one thing of which it is necessary for all "citizens" to partake "if ever a city is about to be," and then expounds the operation of education in the city. In the second (326e6–328a8), Protagoras explains why many "paltry" (*phauloi*) sons still "become" to good fathers despite both the fathers' own possession of *aretē* and the operation of education in the city.

That the gods' molding did not produce an original diversity of distinct mortal races emerges from Protagoras' report next that the unidentified gods appointed "Prometheus" and "Epimetheus" to "order" (*kosmēsai*) and to "distribute" (*neimai*) initially-unspecified "powers" (*dunameis*) among the moldings (320d4–5). Once undertaken, the purpose and meaning of this delegated task clearly are to introduce the essential characteristic features that finally do individualize and differentiate the emergent mortal races. As Protagoras presents it, Epimetheus alone (320d6–7) deliberately distributes distinguishing powers among the originally undifferentiated group (320d8–322c2); but, in the process, he also inadvertently exhausts all of them on "the irrational-creatures" (*ta aloga*, 321b7–c1). The result of this distributing, during which, apparently, no ordering occurs, is that "the human race" remains "still without-order" (*akosmēton eti*, 321c2). In its first and only explicit reference in *Protagoras*, "the human race" is an empty designation: it suggests that humans are completely indeterminate by nature.

This dire situation of so-called humans seems, initially, to find some "salvation" (*sōtērian tōi anthrōpōi heuroi*) in Prometheus' subsequent intervention: his stealing of fire and gifting of fire and the arts to humans (321c3–e3). Apparently, Prometheus' gift of the arts affords so-called humans a high degree of self-sufficiency, allowing them to exist, albeit in apolitical, scattered isolation (*kat' archas ... ōikoun sporadēn poleis de ouk ēsan*). In this situation, however, they suffer destructive attacks from otherwise unidentified "wild-beasts" (*thēriōn*) (322a8–b3). With each human seeking his own preservation (*sōizesthai*), they eventually crowd-together (*hathroizesthai*), and cities arise (322b6). These first cities soon fail, however, due to some unspecified mutual injustice (*ēdikoun allēlous*) among their inhabitants (322b7–c1); this situation prompts one to wonder whether at least some of the destructive wild-beasts were actually other so-called humans.

After the failure of the first cities, these so-called humans teeter on the brink of extinction (322b8–c1). Lest they then perish completely from the earth, "Zeus" instructs "Hermes," Protagoras explains, to distribute (*nemein*) among them universally "reverent-shame" (*aidōs*) and "just-penalty" (*dikē*) (322c1–d2). Zeus' explicit purpose in commanding Hermes to perform this specific distribution is to establish "order [*kosmoi*] and uniting bonds of friendship" in cities (322c3). Without universal participation in "reverent-shame" and "just-penalty," Protagoras quotes (!) Zeus, explaining, "Cities would not come-to-be" (322d1–4). Yet, cities did already arise (322b6), they just did not last (322b7–c1). Protagoras' report of the intervention of Zeus and Hermes, then, indicates that first cities were merely mutual defense pacts, whereas these second cities are to be civic communities, complete with common values enforced by a common authority. As such, Protagoras' myth abruptly ends with Zeus' stipulation of the first "law" (*nomon*)—its first occurrence in *Protagoras*— a death-penalty edict for those "not capable" (*ton mē dunamenon*) of participating in Zeus' commanded universal reverent-shame and just-penalty (322d4–5).

On the surface, Protagoras' myth presents the natural, even if mythological, origin of humans, complete with the recognizably civic character of recognizable human life. Nevertheless, specific details of his myth imply the underlying assertion that humans are indeterminate by nature and that the human as such is determined by convention. Consider Protagoras' sole invocation of "the human race" (321c2) as the first and indeed the only explicitly named mortal race. Upon scrutiny, this otherwise affirmative reference emerges as simply the empty appellation that designates as much of the original, indeterminate mortal race as remains "still without-order" after Epimetheus' incomplete distribution of distinguishing powers (320d6–321c2). When Hermes subsequently distributes among humans "reverent-shame" and "just-penalty," Zeus ensures their complete distribution with his imposition of *nomos*. Thus, not by nature, allegorized in the unidentified-gods-delegated distribution of Epimetheus, but only by convention, allegorized in the specified-Zeus-ensured distribution of Hermes, does the so-called human race finally experience "order" (320d5, 322c3), i.e., emerge with a determinate and distinguishing human identity. Finally, one must notice that Zeus, in this exercise of his own, exclusive political art (cf. 321d4–5), enacts Protagoras' promise to teach "the political art" and to "make men good citizens" (319a3–7). Protagoras' implied identification in his myth of the human with citizen, there being no natural human as such, emerges more explicitly in the second half of his Great Speech, its purported "*logos*." As the sophist therein repeatedly avers, Zeus-like (cf. 322d1–3), everyone in the city must partake of "political (citizen) virtue" (*politikē aretē*), or there would be no city (cf. 323a1–3, a5–7, 324d7–e1, 327a1–4).

Protagoras' Great Speech "Logos": Civic Education

The main feature of the second half (324d6–328c2) of Protagoras' Great Speech is his description of education within the (now-established) city. In brief, beginning at birth and continuing until death, one either learns "virtue" and the city's laws (*nomoi*), or one suffers "straightenings" (beatings) until one does (325c5–326e1 with 325a5–b1). This operation of education in the city corresponds to the civilizing-as-humanizing actions of Hermes and Zeus in Protagoras' myth: as "virtues," "moderation" (*sōphrosunē*) and "justice" (*dikaiosunē*) are civic equivalents to Hermes' distribution of "reverent-shame" and "just-penalty," and the city's conventions affirm Zeus' original *nomos* (324d7–325b1). As Protagoras later plainly explains, without the city, the would-be human is simply a "savage" (*agrios*), who would prompt even the greatest misanthrope to cherish the company of the greatest villains within the city (327c5–e1). Yet, those "reared among laws and humans" have "education, law-courts, laws and ... [the] necessity through which [they] are compelled always to care about virtue" (327c6, d1–3).

Protagoras' enumeration of the amenities of those reared among "laws and humans" (*nomois kai anthrōpois*, 327c6)—whose pairing implies their identity—is not simply an inventory of the features of civilization; rather, it concisely reiterates in descending order the ascending stages of the process of humanization. Consider how the cardinal virtues of "moderation" and "justice" within the city correspond to "reverent-shame" and "just-penalty" from Hermes' distribution in Protagoras' myth. Although the virtues seem elevated, their mythic sources and origin indicate that they really reduce to the shame of reproach and fear of punishment. Civic education in virtue, then, reduces to coercing these passions into conforming to the prevailing conventions of the city. Protagoras' myth allegorizes the city's ideological conceit that it completely determines humans as such, through a fundamentally coercive and, finally, punitive pedagogical practice, now expounded more explicitly in Protagoras' "*logos*" (cf. 325c5–326e1).

Regarding this education by the city, its principal initial mode of instilling conformity to convention is "admonition" (*nouthetein*; cf. 323d1, e3, 324a2, 325c6, 326a1), literally, "to put mind" in someone. When one resists, or fails to heed, this oral imparting of intelligence, the city then literally tries to knock sense into him by beatings (325c6–d7, 326d8–e1 with 324a4–c5). The good citizen (cf. 319a5) eventually learns to avoid these blows by conforming to the customs that are the subjects of admonition; thus, he exhibits justice, as well as moderation, or "sound-mindedness" (*sōphrosunē*). This supposedly mindful learning of virtue, however, reduces to (a) calculation about pain and pleasure. This calculation constitutes, at least within Protagoras' Great Speech, fundamental human rationality.

Protagoras' Great Speech:
"Rational Punishment" and Unwitting Hedonism

To prove that "political (citizen) virtue" (*politikē aretē*, 323a1, a7, b2, 324a1) is teachable (323c6, d7) and comes from learning (*mathēseōs*, 324a3), Protagoras invites Socrates to consider "punishment" (*to kolazein*) in its "power," or what it is "capable to do" (*dunatai*) (324a3–5). In Protagoras' subsequent exposition, he asserts the pedagogical character of punishment by developing a distinction between retribution and deterrence. From the start, the sophist insists that no one punishes the unjust for the sake of penalizing their injustice, unless he "irrationally revenges" (*alogistōs timōreitai*, 324b1), just as a "wild-beast" (324a6–b1). As the alternative to irrational revenge, Protagoras explains the operation of "punishment with reason" (*meta logou kolazein*, 324b2) or "rational punishment," which, he asserts, punishes in the present solely to prevent injustice in the future (324b1–5). The "intention" (*dianoia*) of rational punishment is explicitly "deterrence" (*apotropēs*, 324b6), Protagoras avers; as such, he insists, it is not punitive, but pedagogical: it teaches "virtue" (*dianoeitai paideutēn einai aretēn*) (324b5–7).

As Protagoras expounds irrational revenge, the revenger irrationally supposes that his would-be punishment can and will undo something already done (324b3). Thus, to punish the unjust for the sake of their (past) injustice is as "thoughtless" or "mindless" (*anoētos*, 323d4), Protagoras claims, as punishing those born ugly, small, or weak (323c8–d5). Insofar as any punishment has such action in mind (*pros toutōi ton noun echōn*, 324a7), it has no mind. This explains why Protagoras emphasizes the "intention" or "intelligence" (*dianoia*, 324b5), more literally, the "mind" (*nous*) "throughout" (*dia*), of rational punishment. While "admonition" (*nouthetein*) seeks to instill "mind" (*nous*) in citizens, when it fails, so-called rational punishment tries to knock sense into them. The intelligence or mind that the city seeks to instill is calculation about future pain(s) and action(s), in light of the experience of present pain and its connection with past actions.

Protagoras' exposition of the power of punishment extends and elaborates the issue of the original indeterminacy of the human from his myth, to underscore the civic determination of the human. When Protagoras scorns one who "irrationally revenges," just as a "wild-beast" (*thērion*) (324b1), he implicitly confirms that the "wild-beasts" (*thēriōn*) of his myth (322b2, b4) were, in fact, the indeterminate, original humans, who were destroying one another insofar as they sought retribution or revenge for past wrongs. This identification likewise explains the vague mutual injustice that ruined the first, pre-Zeus cities (322b7–c1), and it clarifies the significance of Protagoras' remark that original humans lacked the "political art" (322b5, b8; cf. 319a4) then exclusive to Zeus (321d4–5). Protagoras' report of the founding and the failure of the first cities, and their refounding by Zeus, is his allegorical assertion of the role of convention in determining the human and making it rational. Before Zeus' intervention and inaugural *nomos* to ground the second cities, the original, so-called humans were not yet determined as (rational) human. Prefiguring Protagoras' rational punishment, Zeus' death-penalty *nomos* teaches one to mind the future, rather than try to undo the past, or else lose one's life in the present. Zeus' stipulation of this first "law" (*nomon ge thes*, 322d4) also anticipates admonition in the city: "legislation" (*nomothetein*) parallels "admonition" (*nouthetein*) in both its grammatical formation and its citizen formation.

Recall that Zeus' *nomos* is for those "not capable" (*ton mē dunamenon*, 322d4)—those without any "power" (*dunamis*)—to partake of reverent-shame and just-penalty. In contrast with "wild-beast" "irrational revenge," then, what Protagoras' rational punishment is capable of doing (*ti pote dunatai*, 324a4) is to humanize the so-called human by making him rational.

Rational punishment as the enforced conformity to the city's conventions thus achieves what Epimetheus failed to do: it gives a distinctive order (*kosmos*) to human beings and distinguishes them from other mortal creatures. Now endowed with rationality through the coercion of the city, humans, as citizens, will (must) conform to convention and act according to "good-deliberation," which "learning" Protagoras himself promises to teach (318e5–319a7); such is the pedagogical conceit of Protagoras' rational punishment.

The education in "political (citizen) virtue" of Protagoras' rational punishment is that it previews the painful consequences of unjust actions, which seem to reduce to failing to conform to the city's customs and laws (*nomoi*). The rationality of this rational punishment, then, reduces to the calculation that to avoid future punishment and pain, one must avoid transgressing *nomos*. Yet, precisely because the instilling of this reductive rationality occurs through suffering the actual pain of coercive education and punishment in the city, so-called rational punishment reduces to a hedonistic calculus to avoid pain. Due to this negative determination, however, it actually promotes hedonism, as it implies that pleasure, as the opposite of pain, is the good. Ultimately, then, the promised rationality of Protagoras' rational punishment proves to be self-contradictory, insofar as it prompts the many unwittingly to pursue pleasure, which impulse inevitably leads them to transgress *nomos*, which results in the very punishment and pain that their education sought to teach them to avoid. In brief, though the content of education in the city explicitly teaches that pleasure is *not* the good, the manner of this education implicitly instructs that pleasure *is* the good; thus, the many claim to *know* the good, even as they act contrary to it, not understanding that they unwittingly pursue pleasure *as* the good. This confusion about pleasure points to the popular paradox, familiar in the experience of most humans, of how anyone can act contrary to his knowledge of the good.

Being-Worsted by Pleasure

In the operation of education in the city, failure to heed admonition to virtue in childhood or to observe the city's customs and laws (*nomoi*) into adulthood results in physical pain. Yet, according to Protagoras' Great Speech, this infliction of pain is not punitive, but pedagogical. Nevertheless, despite its promise to promote virtue, this pedagogy actually promotes among the many an unwitting and self-contradictory hedonism. This paradoxical hedonism manifests itself in the seemingly common, yet morally urgent, phenomenon of "being-worsted by pleasure" (*hēdonēs hēttasthai*) (352d4–353a5), as the many express it. Socrates illuminates this issue late in the *Protagoras* (352a1–358a5). Prompted by Protagoras' evasiveness about the status of the "virtues" and his claims about "courage" (349b1–351b2), Socrates questions him about the good life for humans regarding their experience of pain and pleasure (351b3–c1). As Protagoras avoids answering Socrates directly about whether "pleasure itself" (*hēdonēn autēn*) is (the) good (351c1–e11), Socrates himself must investigate the relationship between pleasure and the good (352a1–8).

Socrates begins his investigation by raising the question of the status of "knowledge" (*epistēmē*, 352b1), asking Protagoras whether he agrees with the "opinion" (*dokei*, 352b3) of "the many humans" (352b1–3). They say, he says, that while knowledge is "often present-in a human" (*enousēs pollakis anthrōpōi*) (352b5–6), it is "not vigorous, neither hegemonic nor fit-for-rule" (*ouk ischuron oud' hēgemonikon oud' archikon einai*) (352b3–4). By this popular claim, what "rules" (*archein*) the human is not knowledge, but something else, such as pleasure, which drags around knowledge like a slave (352b6–c3). When the many assert, then, that they "know the best-things" (*gignōskontas ta beltista*), but are "not willing" to do them, even though they are able, Socrates asks them the "cause" (*hoti pote aition*) of their acting otherwise (*alla prattein*) (352d6–8). They answer that they are "worsted" (*hēttōmenos*) by pleasure or pain, which "compulsorily-rules" (*kratoumenous*) them (352d8–e2).[4] The many further describe their experi-

---

4. Commentators on *Protagoras* routinely identify the experience described by the many with the phenomenon that Aristotle later (*NE* 7.1–4) famously calls *akrasia*. Yet, nowhere in *Protagoras*, or even anywhere in Plato's dialogues, does "*akrasia*" ever actually occur. This scholarly convention seems due, in no small part, to Aristotle's remark in the *Nicomachean Ethics* that Socrates believed that "*akrasia* is not," wherein he also cites *Prot.* 352b6–c3 about knowledge being dragged around like a slave (7.2, 1145b24–26 passim). Plato does elsewhere sparingly use the term "*akrateia*," and with even less frequency, "*akratēs*." Plato's twelve total uses of "*akrateia*" are: *Gorg.* 525a4; *Laws* 1.636c6, 5.734b5, 10.886a9, 908c2, 11.934a4; *Rep.* 5.461b2; *Tim.* 86d6. Plato's four total uses of "*akratēs*" are: *Laws* 4.710a7, 9.869a2; *Soph.* 252c4; *Phil.* 53a6. Leonard Brandwood, *A Word Index to Plato* (Leeds, UK: W. S. Maney and Son, 1976), 29.

ence as being a conflict between the individual and external, "villainous" (*ponēros*) "pleasant things" (*hēdeōn ontōn*)—"food, drink, and the things-of-Aphrodite"—which "compulsorily-rule" (*kratoumenoi*) the individual (353c6–7).

Socrates' subsequent examination exposes the incoherence of the many in blaming pleasure, which they implicitly consider to be (the) good, as though it were an external agent compelling them to do bad, contrary to their professed knowledge of the good (354e5–355e4).[5] When the many claim, initially, that knowledge is often "present-in [*enousēs*] a human" (352b5–6), but does not rule him, they imply a pun on the purported instilling of intelligence or mind (*en* + *nous*) by the city. From childhood through adulthood, the city seeks to knock sense into humans to be good citizens; yet, this purported intelligence or mind (*nous*) reduces to convention (*nomos*). As the city considers this indoctrination in *nomos* to be education, when duly educated citizens transgress (the) *nomos*, they cannot plead ignorance of it. Thus, when the many claim, finally, that they are "worsted by pleasure," they affirm their indoctrinated conceit of knowledge of the good and blame "pleasure," as though *it* acts as an external agent that has compelled them to violate (the) *nomos*. While the many assert that their (conceit of) knowledge of the good is too weak to withstand pleasure, in fact, they lack any positive knowledge of the good, having only civic indoctrination. In their unwitting hedonism, they are ignorant of their own ignorance; specifically, they lack self-knowledge.

"Unlearnedness" and the City as the Greatest Sophist

Socrates eventually demonstrates that what the many experience as being-worsted by pleasure—contrary to their professed knowledge of the good—actually is their unwitting affirmation of pleasure as the good in conflict with their conventional conceit of knowledge of the good (357c1–358c5). Socrates calls this phenomenon *amathia*, "unlearnedness" (357e1); in fact,

---

5. Moreover, Socrates illuminates the incoherent self-conception of the many that under-lies their description of their experience, which emerges as an *internal* battle between a better and a worse "self." Thus, in "being-worsted by pleasure," what begins as a contest between "you . . . [and] these-things-here" (*humin . . . en toisde*) (353c5; cf. 353c2)—food, drink, the things-of-Aphrodite—that overcome "you," culminates in a psychological struggle "to win-victory within yourself" (*nikan en humin*) (355d3–4; cf. 356a1).

he calls it the "greatest unlearnedness" (*amathia hē megistē*, 357e2), for it is having a "false opinion and being-false concerning affairs of much worth" (358c4–5).[6] As ignorance of one's own ignorance, *amathia* is a counterpart to *aporia*. In various Platonic dialogues, Socrates' interlocutors experience the phenomenon of *aporia*, "perplexity," when they fail to answer Socrates' questions about subjects about which they are (were) certain they know (cf. *Meno* 79e5–80b4 with 71b9–e1). Their *aporia* reflects their conceit of knowledge. In their perplexity, they experience their ignorance, even as they still cling to their conceit. "Being-worsted by pleasure," as *amathia*, differs from *aporia*, however, in that those who experience it fail to experience their ignorance of their ignorance as ignorance.

To try to clarify "unlearnedness" further as the lack of self-knowledge, consider Plato's *Republic*, where Socrates invokes the issue of the "philosophic nature" and discusses its corruption in so many of the few who are potentially philosophical (6.490c8, d6, e2–3 with 491a8–b2). The sources of its ruin are great and many (6.491b4–5), but Socrates focuses on "learning" (*mathēseōs*, 6.492a2)—upon which the soul is nourished or reared—just as he did early in *Protagoras* (cf. *mathēmasin*, 313c6–7 with 313e4, 314a2, b1, b2), when he forewarned Hippocrates of the danger of patronizing Protagoras, whom Hippocrates identified as a sophist (313a1–314b4). In the *Republic*, discussing good and bad instruction, Socrates introduces "certain private sophists," whom the many assert individually corrupt the city's youth (6.492a5–8). Nevertheless, Socrates questions this allegation and proposes instead that the many themselves are the "greatest sophists" (*megistous sophistas*, 6.492a8–b1), in their far more pervasive reach and influence (cf. *Plt.* 303b8–c5), as they "educate most-completely and produce young and old, men and women, to be such-a-sort as they wish them to be" (6.492b1–3).

This popular, sophistic education occurs, Socrates explains, whenever (the) many "crowd-together" (*hathrooi*) in "assemblies, law-courts, theaters

---

6. Socrates in Plato's *Apology* scorns the conceit of one's own wisdom (*doxosophia*) as the "reproachable unlearnedness" (*eponeidistos amathia*) of "supposing that one knows what one doesn't know" (29b1–2 with 22e3). In Plato's *Sophist*, the Eleatic Stranger characterizes *amathia* as "some big and difficult *eidos* of ignorance," of someone "not knowing something that he opines [*dokein*] that he knows" (229c1–9). Cf. *Alc.* I 117e9–118a5.

...or any other common meeting of a multitude" (6.492b5–7), and, with "much clamor" (*pollōi thorubōi*, 6.492b7) of exclamation and applause, they excessively praise some of the things said or done and blame others (6.492b7–9). Socrates' *Republic* description parallels Protagoras' Great Speech myth claim about original humans, how they "crowd-together" (*hathroizesthai*) to form first cities (322b6), as well as his assertion about the humanizing function of "education, law-courts, laws and...[the] necessity through which [those reared among 'laws and humans'] are compelled always to care about virtue" (327d1–3, c6). Furthermore, Socrates in the *Republic* references the "greatest necessity" of the operation of popular education: these "educators and sophists impose [*prostitheasi*] in deed when they don't persuade in speech," and "they punish [*kolazousi*] the one not persuaded with dishonor, fines, and death" (6.492d2, d5–6; cf. *Ap.* 36b3–38b9).

In his relating the "great clamor" (*pollōi thorubōi*) of the crowds in assemblies, law-courts, theaters, and the like (6.492b5–7), Socrates in the *Republic* adds that this "clamor [*thorubon*] of blame and praise" echoes and resonates off the "rocks" around and the surrounding "place" (6.492c1–2). While its civic institutions indicate that this "place" (*topos*) is the city, Socrates' details implicitly identify it with the both odd and placeless (*atopos*) domain of the Cave (7.515a4). The perniciousness of the *amathia* of those "worsted-by pleasure" finds a profound parallel in describing the plight of the prisoners of the Cave (7.518a7), who mistake "shadows of artificial-things" cast on the wall before them for "the things-that-are" (*ta onta*) (7.514a1–515c2). Socrates later describes their deformity of soul that, in "being-unlearned" (*amathainousa*), "wallows in *amathia*, just-as a swinish wild-beast [*thērion hueion*]" (7.535e3–5).[7] In the clamorous competition among its prisoners to name the shadows they see within it (7.515b4–c2 with 516c8–d2, 516e3–517a6, d4–e2), the Cave is the city, the city is the Cave, and it is the many who actually are the source of sophistic corruption (*amathia*), not the private, individual, wage-earning sophists (cf. *Ap.* 24c10–25c1 with 18a7–b6, 18c4–7). Protagoras himself implies as much near the end of his Great Speech, when he asserts about

---

7. Compare Socrates' description at *Rep.* 3.411d7–e2 of the misologist, the "hater-of-*logos*," in his *amathia*: "he not-a-whit still uses persuasion through *logos*, but does everything through force and savageness [*biai de kai agrioteti*], just-as a wild-beast [*thērion*]."

education in the city, "All are teachers of *aretē*, according to as much as each is capable [*dunantai*]...just as if you should seek some teacher of speaking Greek" (327e1–328a1; cf. *Alc.* I 110d5–111a4).

What is the status, then, of the individual, private sophist, like Protagoras? Rather than rival the city in its teaching, Socrates explains in the *Republic*, this sophist learns the very "dogmas of the many [*ta tōn pollōn dogmata*]—which they opine [*doxazousin*] whenever they are crowded-together [*hathroisthōsin*]" (6.493a8–9)—calls it "wisdom" (*sophian*, 6.493a9, b6), organizes it "as (if) an art" (*hōs technēn*), and teaches it (6.493b6–7). Protagoras enacts this very description when he introduces himself to Socrates and Hippocrates (316c5–317c5). Invoking "the sophistic art" (*tēn sophistikēn technēn*, 316d3–4), he venerates it (and himself) as being "ancient," and he names certain foundational figures of Greek culture, e.g., the poets Homer and Hesiod and the religious figures Orpheus and Musaeus (316d6–9), as his previously unrecognized predecessors.

Though Protagoras affirms the title "Sophist" and claims to "educate humans" with his "art" (317b4–5, c1 with 349a1–4), Socrates has already warned Hippocrates, before they meet Protagoras, that the sophist indiscriminately praises his teachings, not knowing which and/or whether they actually help or harm (313c8–e1). As Socrates explains in *Republic*, the individual sophist knows "nothing in truth about which [popular] dogmas [*dogmatōn*] and appetites are beautiful or ugly, or good or bad, or just or unjust" (6.493b7–c1), nor does he care. Instead, following popular "opinions" (*doxais*), he simply calls "good" whatever pleases and "bad" whatever pains, "neither having seen nor being-capable [*dunatos*] to show someone else how much the nature [*phusin*] of the necessary and [the] good differ in their being [*tōi onti*]" (6.493c2–3, c5–6). Insofar as the individual sophist fundamentally affirms the shadows of the Cave, which represent the various, often conflicting, or simply incoherent, conventions of the city, Protagoras, as the epitome of the professional sophist (*Prot.* 335a4–8, 348e2–349a4; cf. *Meno* 91d2–e9) illustrates how the city is the greatest sophist.[8] It should be no surprise, then, that the many are "unlearned,"

---

8. Insofar as the city magnifies the individual, writ large enough to examine its less observable status (cf. *Rep.* 2.368c7–369a3), Protagoras, the individual sophist, embodies and enacts, writ small, how the whole city is the greatest sophist (cf. *Rep.* 6.492a5–493d9).

lacking in self-knowledge, and unwitting, self-contradictory hedonists, confused about the true status of the good.

"The Measuring Art" and Hedonistic Calculus

Insofar as Protagoras' Great Speech exhibits how the city is the greatest sophist, and "being-worsted by pleasure" is the experience of the many of their "unlearnedness" in their unwitting hedonism, a third signature feature of *Protagoras*, and traditionally one of its more puzzling, becomes clearer upon examination. As Socrates culminates his exposing of "being-worsted by pleasure" and identifies it as "the greatest unlearnedness," he appears to endorse Protagoras and his fellow sophists (357e1–8) as teachers of "the measuring art," as the basis of a hedonistic calculus and the "salvation of life" (356d1–e4, e6, 356e8–357a1, a6–7). In fact, the "measuring art" illuminates what Protagoras' promised "good-deliberation" (318e4) might provide, were it not reduced to the unwitting-hedonism-inducing, incoherent calculation of the city's "rational punishment."

As a practical problem, "being-worsted by pleasure" indicates the past failure to foresee the future pleasure or pain that will result from one's present actions. As present pleasure and pain are proximate, they appear to be greater than future pleasure and pain, which, being remote, appear to be lesser (356a2–c8). Yet, which pleasure or pain actually is greater, and which less, and so, which actually is better, and which worse, is unclear, precisely due to the distortion of "the power [*dunamis*] of appearance" (356d4), which, Socrates explains, induces one to err about "acting well" (*eu prattein*), i.e., happiness or the good life (356d1–7, 357d3–7 with 351b3–c1). Were one able to see future pleasures and pains clearly—as if they were present—one could compare them to present, proximate pleasure and pain, and calculate accurately which is greater and which is less, and which to choose. "The measuring art," then, promises to dispel the "apparitions" (*phantasmata*; cf. 356d8) surrounding pleasure and pain and to clarify "the truth" (*to alēthes*), which would "save [our] life" (356d8–e2).

This clarity of "the measuring art" is exactly what civic admonition and rational punishment are supposed to provide, insofar as they induce intelligence or mind and instill rationality. The problem with Protagoras' rational punishment in particular, however, is its negative determination about the status of pleasure. Just as retributive punishment focuses on the past, rather than the future, Protagoras' rational punishment teaches only to avoid the pain(s) resulting from transgressing (the) *nomos*. Even as it implies that pleasure is the good, insofar as pleasure is the opposite of the pain one should avoid, so-called rational punishment fails to provide positive guidance for choosing (among) pleasure(s). Thus, the "power" of Protagoras' "rational punishment" proves to involve the same distorting effect as the misleading "power of appearance." In its conceit that it is pedagogy, not punishment, Protagoras' rational punishment produces "apparitions" (*phantasmata*) regarding the status of pleasure and pain. Socrates' apparent advocacy that Protagoras and his fellow sophists teach the measuring art—as the basis of a hedonistic calculus—aims to elucidate this implication while it illuminates that Protagoras' Great Speech is an expression of the city as sophist in its pedagogical conceit that it humanizes so-called humans. Insofar as the city is the greatest sophist and indoctrinates citizens into an unwitting hedonism, only if private, individual sophists taught a measuring art that involved a true hedonistic calculus might they develop their own actual art and be true teachers of a life-saving learning.

The Human as Socratic Philosophizing

Protagoras' Great Speech conveys the city's conceit that it instills in humans the rationality that finally determines and thus distinguishes as human the otherwise naturally indeterminate "human race." Socrates' clarification of the issue of "being-worsted by pleasure" elucidates the implication of this conceit of instilling rationality as actually reducing to an unreliable calculation about the good regarding experiences of pleasure and pain. In brief, the city's pedagogical program does not teach good-deliberation about affairs, either domestic or civic—as Protagoras promises about his own instruction (318e5–319a7)—but rather, it instills an unwitting and self-contradictory hedonism. This hedonism, developing from the city's coercive conventions, which claim to civilize and make humans human, actually dehumanizes the human. For Plato, the human as such emerges in concert with the activity of Socratic philosophizing, as the realization and the fulfillment of natural human rationality, and the truth of the good-deliberation promised by Protagoras as sophist. What this would look like emerges early in the dialogue, prior to Socrates' encounter with Protagoras, in the preliminary discussion between Socrates and Hippocrates (311b2–314c2), before they even venture to Callias' house to meet Protagoras.

When Hippocrates arrives at Socrates' bedside (310c1) to enlist him to meet Protagoras (310e2–5), the time is "still deep-early dawn" (310a8; cf. *Crito* 43a4). Hippocrates hurries Socrates to depart immediately (310e7–311a2), but Socrates resists the youth's haste and proposes that they instead stroll in the courtyard until it "becomes light" (*phōs genētai*) (311a3–5). The significance of this "light" emerges once one recalls from Protagoras' myth that the unidentified gods appoint Prometheus and Epimetheus to their task just as the gods "were-about to lead [mortal races] toward light [*pros phōs*]" (320d4). Nevertheless, Protagoras' subsequent report of Prometheus' inspection of Epimetheus' incomplete distribution of powers—wherein he observes the remaining orderlessness of "the human race" (321c5–6 with c2)—specifies: "Already the allotted day was present on which also [the] human needed to go-out from earth into light [*eis phōs*]" (321c6–7).[9] Protagoras reports that "mortal races" originated "inside the earth" (320d), and apparently, "the human" remains so, in the dark, all along; nowhere in his myth does Protagoras report that "the human" ever actually emerged into the light. Though Protagoras' myth does relate the rise of cities and civic life, insofar as humans remain(ed) indefinitely in some subterranean realm, Protagoras' myth, and actually his entire Great Speech, enacts the puppet show and shadow play of the Cave (*Rep.* 7.514a2–515c2).

In contrast, the "deep-early dawn" dialogue between Socrates and Hippocrates, set within Socrates' own house, culminates in genuine illumination from the natural light of the sun, an image for the good (*Rep.* 6.505a2–4, 506d8–e5, 508a4–509b10 with 7.515e1–516b7, 517a8–c5). First, Socrates leads Hippocrates out of his dark house into the open courtyard (311a3–8). Second, when Hippocrates realizes the implication of Socrates' questions concerning what he himself will become in patronizing Protagoras, Socrates observes the youth's embarrassment because "already some day [*hēmeras*] was evident, so that he himself [*auton*] became manifest" (312a2–3). Thus,

---

9. This third occurrence of "light" (*phōs*) in *Protagoras* is the last of only three instances in the dialogue. Brandwood, *Word Index to Plato*, 953. Plato's deliberate use seems intended to pun on *phōs* as "light" and *phōs* as "man" or "mortal."

the only certain emergence into the light of anyone in the entire *Protagoras* occurs from Socrates' questioning of Hippocrates about his conceit of knowledge and his ignorance of the implications for his very "self" of patronizing Protagoras as a sophist. Note that Socrates' questions to Hippocrates ask him, "were you of-mind" (*ei epenoeis*, 311b5, c4), and, what he "has in mind" (*en nōi echein*, 311c6, d7), with respect to Protagoras' "being" and his own "becoming." Socrates' questions clearly illuminate Hippocrates' deficiency of mind (*nous*), yet rather than trying to knock sense into him, Socrates philosophizes with him.

Socrates' preliminary dialogue with Hippocrates, then, enacts Socrates' allegory from the *Republic* about the philosophy-aided ascent out of the Cave (7.515c4–516b7), i.e., the *periagōgē*, or the turning (leading) around of the soul to the natural light of the good (7.515c6–8, 518b7–d7 with 521c1–8).[10] This enactment also clarifies why Socrates ultimately assents (314b4–c2) to Hippocrates' request to introduce him to Protagoras, despite Socrates' warning about the danger of engaging any sophist (313a1–314b4): the philosopher must perennially descend back into the Cave and examine the shadows of convention (*Rep.* 7.516c4–517a6 with 520c1–6). For Plato, then, the city and its conventions do serve a crucial role in human flourishing, but only as the ground for Socratic philosophizing, that is, the ground for the discovery of one's own ignorance, which constitutes the self-knowledge of "human wisdom" (cf. *Ap.* 20d6–23b4).

---

10. When Socrates in *Republic* first introduces the periagogic ascent out of the Cave (7.515c6–8), he proposes that this happens "by nature" (7.515c5). Moreover, in introducing the Cave allegory, Socrates says that it is an image of "our [human] nature in its education and lack of education" (7.514a2). In *Protagoras*, Socrates explicitly contrasts the "unlearnedness" of "being-worsted by pleasure," and "having a false opinion and lying about affairs of much worth" (358c1–5), with the positive proposition about "human nature" (*anthrōpou phusei*, 358d1)—its sole expression in the dialogue—that no one willingly prefers (the) bad (things), as "human nature" wishes to pursue (the) good (things) (358c4–d3).

4

Bad Seeds, Chance, and
the Soothsaying *Daimonion*:
A Note on Plato's *Theages*

Jason Tipton

There has been a revival of interest in some of the lesser-known Platonic dialogues, including the *Theages*, in recent years.[1] The previous lack of interest in the *Theages* and other dialogues was due, in large part, to questions of authenticity. But as Cobb notes, "Objections to the authenticity of the *Theages* are based entirely on interpretations of its style and content. There are no philological or historical grounds for rejecting it as a forgery."[2]

Translations are excerpted from *"Theages,"* trans. Thomas L. Pangle, in *The Roots of Political Philosophy: Ten Forgotten Socratic Dialogues*, ed. Thomas L. Pangle (Ithaca, NY: Cornell University Press, 1987), 132–46.

1. Mark Joyal, *The Platonic "Theages": An Introduction, Commentary and Critical Edition* (Stuttgart: Franz Steiner, 2000); Christopher Bruell, *Socratic Education* (Lanham, MD: Rowman & Littlefield, 1999), 103–13; William S. Cobb, "Plato's *Theages*," *Ancient Philosophy* 12, no. 2 (1992): 267–84; Thomas L. Pangle, "On the *Theages*," in Pangle, *Roots of Political Philosophy*, 147–74; Michael Davis and Gwenda-lin Kaur Grewal, "The Daimonic Soul: On Plato's *Theages*," in *Socratic Philosophy and Its Others*, ed. Christopher A. Dustin and Denise Schaeffer (Lanham, MD: Lexington Books, 2013), 35–52. To these works, I would add Seth Benardete, "The *Daimonion* of Socrates: An Interpretive Study of Plato's *Theages*" (master's thesis, University of Chicago, 1953).

2. Cobb, "Plato's *Theages*," 268. An even stronger formulation of the problem is given by Benardete: "The one dialogue in which the *daimonion* is dealt with at some length,

While I am convinced of the arguments made by Cobb and others, and assume the dialogue is authentic, I do not wish to argue one way or the other for the authenticity of the dialogue. I believe one can fruitfully offer an interpretation of the substance and structure of the dialogue without determining, once and for all, its status in the Platonic corpus. In other words, I believe it is possible to offer an interpretation of some aspects of the content and structure while bracketing the question of authenticity. Those who argue that the dialogue is authentic or are interested in the topics broached in it might find such interpretive suggestions worthwhile; those who argue that it is spurious will surely view the effort as somewhat superfluous, if they do not take the suggestions offered here as proof for their own thesis.[3]

The *Theages* is a peculiar dialogue, in part because the second half contains one of the most extended accounts of Socrates' *daimonion*. In this account, Socrates paints himself as a prophet or soothsayer, making pronouncements about athletics, political intrigues, and military expeditions. This is strange in light of what is said of the *daimonion* in the *Apology*; there it seems to qualify Socrates' claim to serve the city, or explain why Socrates did not lead a political life (31c4–32a3). The discussion of the *daimonion* in the *Theages*, by contrast, follows an accusation of playfulness:

---

the *Theages*, has been rejected as spurious by most modern scholars (as contrasted with those of antiquity who accepted it) on the curious ground that it clashes with the account of the *daimonion* to be found in the canonical dialogues. This judgment presupposes that one understands what we may call the canonical account of the *daimonion* and that that account is unambiguous. Yet few of the scholars who reject the *Theages* lay claim to understanding the *daimonion*, though their rejection presumes such understanding." Benardete, "*Daimonion* of Socrates," ii–iii. While much work has been done on the question of the *daimonion* since Benardete's assessment, especially as treated in the canonical works, a consensus has yet to emerge on its function or status. For an illustration of some of the issues of the debate surrounding the *daimonion* and Socratic piety, see Gregory Vlastos, "Socratic Piety," in *Socrates: Critical Assessments*, vol. 2, *Issues Arising from the Trial of Socrates*, ed. William J. Prior (New York: Routledge, 1996), 145–66, and Mark L. McPherran, "Socratic Reason and Socratic Revelation," *Journal of the History of Philosophy* 29, no. 3 (1991): 345–73.

3. As Joyal has most recently suggested: "Scholars have made the question of the dialogue's authenticity almost the exclusive focus of their endeavours and have thereby been led to ignore what should be of primary importance, namely the detailed interpretation of the work from beginning to end." *Platonic "Theages,"* 9.

Theages believes that Socrates mocks him when he claims to know only a small matter, erotics, and Socrates responds by appealing to his soothsaying *daimonion*.[4]

Socrates' reference to his *daimonion* might easily be dismissed if the issue of soothsaying had not come up unexpectedly in the first half of the dialogue. This connection will in turn direct our attention to questions about when to consult an oracle or the divine, what role chance plays in the affairs of humans, and the sacredness of counsel. An examination of the connection between Socrates' description of his *daimonion* and the issue of soothsaying as it unexpectedly arises early in the dialogue therefore might provide a clue to the structure and content of the work. This will be a way to draw the two halves of the dialogue together through an analysis of the introduction of soothsayers (124d9), the manner in which the *daimonion* is discussed, and the emergence of chance (130a9), which will be discussed below. My hope is to try to provide a framework in which to make sense of these odd moments in the dialogue and certain elements in the movement of the argument.

Ostensibly, Demodocus, the father of Theages, has run into Socrates by chance, or as Demodocus himself exclaims, "You have therefore showed up at a beautiful (*kalos*) moment" (122a7). But from their conversation, it appears that Socrates is approached by Demodocus right at the start, one might say, as a soothsayer. One seeks a soothsayer when things are uncertain, when one wants divine wisdom to direct one's affairs. Telling Socrates that Theages desires to be wise, Demodocus asks Socrates for a measure of help in satisfying the desire. Demodocus wants to somehow satisfy Theages' wish to become wise and apparently believes Socrates can play a part.

Socrates attempts to examine Theages' desire for wisdom more closely, proceeding through a number of seemingly unrelated analogies. The conversation is directed in this way along a number of awkward steps. First, Socrates mentions the wisdom that a charioteer has, which is used to rule (*archein*) a team of horses, then the wisdom of a pilot, which is employed

---

4. Pangle suggests that the *daimonion* is meant to account for Socrates' powers as an educator, while at the same time absolving him of responsibility for the effects of his influence. "On the *Theages*," 168.

in ruling (*archein*) ships (123d1–e2).[5] At first glance, these are simply two examples of kinds of wisdom, each with a different object. But they are also both examples of a kind of rule. This leads us to wonder whether Theages' desire for wisdom is really just a wish to rule and whether Socrates, by offering these examples, helps illuminate this fact about Theages. Or is Socrates imposing something on him?[6]

While Theages admits that he is seeking the wisdom regarding rule, he has difficulty naming the kind of rule he means in a straightforward, un-hesitant manner. Socrates manages finally to elicit from Theages an expression of desire for the ultimate kind of political rule: in Theages' acknowledgment of his wish to "govern men," Socrates uncovers the desire for tyranny, and pressures Theages to name his desire for what it is.[7] As he leads Theages in this direction, Socrates calls to mind the discussion in book 9 of the *Republic* about the erotic and melancholic temperament of the tyrant. Here he moves from the desire for wisdom to the desire for tyranny, in part with the aid of a pun: tyrants wish for rule (*archē*) and wisdom seeks a first principle (*archē*). Wisdom and tyranny both seem to desire an *archē*, to master the city or to understand nature. This connection might be more than a linguistic accident: The order imposed on the city may be a metaphor for the order imposed by first principles. The connection between tyranny and wisdom might lie in a certain kinship between those desiring political mastery and those desiring understanding for the sake of some mastery of nature.

Once Theages is led to specify the object of his desire as rule over human beings, Socrates presents him with a list of particular tyrants—

---

5. For the way in which *kubernan* becomes *archein*, see Joyal, *Platonic "Theages,"* 22.

6. In making a comparison between *Alcibiades* I and the *Theages*, Joyal notes that "whereas Alcibiades assumed that his background was enough to prepare him for political life and he refused to acknowledge the need for any further skill, Theages at least admits that a certain *epistēmē* or *sophia* is lacking in him and realizes that what he has thus far accomplished simply will not suffice." *Platonic "Theages,"* 19–20; cf. also 31–33. On the larger question, see David K. O'Connor, "Socrates and Political Ambition: The Dangerous Game," in *Proceedings of the Boston Area Colloquium in Ancient Philosophy* 14, no. 1 (1998), 31–52.

7. Davis and Grewal note that "Socrates scolds the boy for this desire [to become a tyrant] and at the same time, strangely, scolds his father for not satisfying it." "Daimonic Soul," 35.

without ever using that word—beginning with Aegisthus and Peleus, and going on to Periander, Archelaus, and Hippias. He then adds two "soothsayers," Bacis and Sibyl (124d9). The model provided by Socrates' addition of the two "soothsayers" is meant to push past some trepidation and allow Theages to identify the first set as "tyrants." Socrates presents him with a list of particular tyrants without using the words "tyrant" or "tyranny." Whatever Socrates' motivation for pushing to "uncover" Theages' desire for tyranny, we are shocked when that effort is interrupted by his sudden introduction of the soothsayers. The issue of soothsayers appears to come from out of nowhere. It does not appear to play any role in the argument at hand; in fact, it disrupts the pattern of the argument up to that point.[8]

Soothsayers are consulted when the wisdom of the gods is required. Such divine counsel is thought to be needed when things are uncertain or ruled by chance, such as in agriculture or matters of war.[9] The need for oracular consultation would be something familiar to Demodocus. As a farmer, Demodocus knows the planting of seed and preparation for planting are relatively easy; it is when what has been planted takes on life (*bios*) that things become difficult (121b7–c7). In the case of crops, we could imagine difficulties arising in two ways: (1) the crop could become unmanageable or fail to grow in the desired way due to some internal mechanism; and (2) the crop could be affected by some external source like climate or infestation by some pathogen. Because crops are susceptible to nature or chance, humans have prayers and religious ceremonies surrounding the art of agriculture. Agriculture is an imperfect art insofar as it cannot control things like the weather; the felt need to appeal to the gods amounts to an admission of its shortcomings as an art. The apparently random way

---

8. Joyal offers an interpretation of the emergence of soothsayers by drawing a comparison between the *politikoi* and *chrēsmōdoi*, especially in that neither are *technai*. See, for example, *Platonic "Theages,"* 25–26. This is consistent with his attempt to analyze the structure of the dialogue as a whole (9–63). I take a significantly different approach, attempting to determine how the first half of the dialogue relates to the latter half, which will become clear below as I argue for the relationship between the appeal to soothsayers, Socrates' characterization of his *daimonion,* and the emergence of chance.

9. Ronna Burger, *On Plato's "Euthyphro"* (Munich: Carl Friedrich von Siemens Foundation, 2015), 93.

the topic of soothsaying comes up points to chance, and chance is the condition under which the human arts reveal their limits, and we experience the need to appeal to the gods. Of course we should note that the topic of the gods is explicitly introduced when Theages says he would pray (*euxaimēn*) to become a god (125e10–126a5) and returns in the end when Theages will suggest that he might pray or make sacrifices to the divine if things do not go in the way he anticipates (131a5).[10]

Demodocus extends his knowledge of agriculture to all living things, thus explicitly providing an explanation for how Theages has become corrupted—how he has taken on a life of his own, as indicated by the challenge he presents to his father's control.[11] Theages is like a crop which, once sown, has gotten out of hand—out of the control of the farmer. Even if Demodocus is unaware of the mechanics of his son's corruption, we can hypothesize that an internal mechanism (some as yet unarticulated

---

10. As has been pointed out to me, the connection implicitly raises the question whether "the divine" is the same as the gods. Even before this, Theages' name, as Socrates notes, points to the sacred or divine (122e1). Cf. Joyal's suggestion that the significance of this passage lies in establishing the individuality of Theages. *Platonic "Theages,"* 17–18. On the question of Theages' revelation, Pangle says, "To be sure, Theages admits that he (like everyone, in his view) would pray to become the tyrannical ruler over as many people as possible or, taking this thought a step further, to become a god. If he could become a tyrant through prayer, that is, through divine assistance, Theages would circumvent the necessity of having to subordinate himself to a tyrannic human teacher. But would he know how to maintain his rule without political science? And would his rule be manly and independent? It seems that only by becoming a god, a being who transfigures human science and manliness, could he be certain that he could resolve the tension between tyranny, based on science, and manly independence. The concentration of oaths by Zeus in this immediate section (125d7, 126a10, b3) reminds us that Theages discloses his remarkable prayer for tyranny while standing in a place consecrated to Zeus, the patron god of political liberty." "On the *Theages,*" 161. Among other things, Pangle reminds us that the setting of the dialogue also compels the reader to think how the divine might figure into the discussion at hand.

11. Pangle notes (151) that "the old democrat's outlook is determined by the fact that his life is rooted in the soil and concerned with tending the things that grow (*phuta*) from the earth. He is, as we would say, close to nature (*phusis*). As a result he is oblivious to nature, and, partly as a consequence, the term 'nature' is conspicuously absent from this dialogue. For to conceive of *phusis* is to distinguish man from the other beings, while Demodocus' experience has produced in him the conviction that there is no fundamental distinction between the 'way' of the human being and the 'way' of all the other 'things that grow.'"

desire) works in concert with some external pathogen. Demodocus' understanding of agriculture provides the reader with a model by which to understand what is happening to Theages, but also explains why Demodocus approaches Socrates for help and why Socrates takes such an appeal for help as some kind of appeal for sacred counsel (122b2–6). What is ironic in Demodocus' coming to Socrates for counsel on this issue is that Socrates appears to be responsible for some of the behavior that is troubling the old farmer.[12] Socrates might, in fact, be the pathogen that has unintentionally spoiled the crop.

Socrates' infection or impregnation[13] of Theages appears to be unintentional. Socrates has never had any direct contact with Theages. Theages has heard certain Socratic speeches (126d1–2) that are circulating among the young men in the city of Athens. Additionally, he has seen the effect Socrates has produced in his friends (128c2–5). In rejecting the path that would lead to a life of farming, Theages has taken on a life of his own and is out of the control of his father; likewise, it is as if some of Socrates' speeches have also taken on a life of their own, getting out of his control. These speeches have found fertile soil in Theages and have contributed to his assumption of independence, which is a source of concern for his father.[14] The desire for tyranny or wisdom that Theages exhibits seems to be intensified by the climate in Athens, due to the influence of Socrates. The effect of Socrates' speeches on Theages is beyond the control of both Socrates and Demodocus. Socrates compares the perfect writing to a living being (cf. *Phdr.* 264b2–9, 275d4–276e7); here we have speeches that

---

12. Cf. Joyal, *Platonic "Theages,"* 58.

13. I use this word in thinking about the ambiguous discussion of Socratic *maieutics* in the *Theaetetus*. There it is not clear whether Socrates has in fact "impregnated" some of those he tries to help give birth. Burger was the first to point this out to me.

14. I believe that Benardete was the first to clearly articulate the relationship between the *Theages* and the *Clouds*, especially as a reply to the charges of the *Clouds* and in drawing attention to the similarity of the characters of both dramas. See also Pangle, "On the *Theages*," 149–50, and Bruell, *Socratic Education*, 103–4. But if we can say that the clouds are somehow a creation of Socrates that get out of his control, there is a certain sense in which the *Theages* confirms this Socratic "defect": the speeches of Socrates, like the clouds, have gotten out of his control and have helped to corrupt Theages. In this sense, Demodocus and Socrates both have something that has "taken on a life" and is out of their control.

are not written, but have in a sense taken on an independent life. They float around the city haphazardly until they find fertile soil. If Socrates lacks control of his speeches, and is in this way without an art, perhaps Plato's writing is meant to be a more technical art of planting (cf. *Phdr.* 276e7–277c7). The desire Theages has for something beyond what his father can offer has certainly not been passed on in the act of reproduction. Theages does not share his father's farmer "genes": he is a bad seed.

If Demodocus' crops had failed or gotten out of his control, he would have sought answers from the gods. Like an oracle, Socrates has been consulted by Demodocus regarding the education of his son, who, he feels, has gotten out of his control. Socrates suggests however that counsel is sacred (*hieros*), especially regarding matters of education (122b2–6). If true, this would make Demodocus' appeal to Socrates intelligible.

One might say that by chance Theages desires wisdom or rule and is not, by nature, a farmer. The notion that chance can produce a condition that may result in a felt need of the gods—hence the appeal to soothsayers—is bolstered by Socrates' discussion of his soothsaying *daimonion* in the dialogue. That discussion is meant to provide a reason why Theages might not progress as an associate of Socrates. Theages had rejected the suggestion that he associate with one of those skilled in politics because of their apparent inability to transmit their knowledge or capacity, even to their own sons. He has learned this from one of Socrates' speeches that is floating around Athens (126d1–2) because some of Socrates' associates are circulating in the city (128c2–6). Socrates does seem to be the hidden source of Demodocus' fears about his son (121d1–4).[15]

A politician can generate a child, but apparently he cannot reproduce his knowledge in that offspring. He transmits something in the begetting, but not his ability in politics. Demodocus had no problem "planting" or begetting Theages; yet Theages has a thirst for more than his father can offer, for something that was not transmitted, not inherited from the

---

15. See Pangle, "On the *Theages*," 163, and Bruell, *Socratic Education*, 108–9. Burger describes Socrates' aim in his conversation with Euthyphro as an attempt "to bring this young man back into the fold of generally accepted opinion." But the dialogue, she adds, "also reveals how much Socratic philosophy is in the air, and hence perhaps a contributing factor, albeit unintentional, in the partial, and therefore dangerous, liberation that has led Euthyphro to his supposedly free-thinking plan." *On Plato's "Euthyphro,"* 35.

sometime politician (127e2–3), sometime farmer. Instead, Theages has gotten hold of a Socratic teaching. What he does not understand about the problem of transmission with regard to political skill is that this Socratic "teaching" equally applies to Socrates' own "teaching." Socrates' speeches can be transmitted, while philosophy cannot. His speeches can circulate easily enough throughout the city, but not everyone who hears them will understand their meaning, and this is beyond Socrates' control. Socrates is not in charge (*enkrateis*) of who will advance in understanding. To make this clear, he turns to speak of his *daimonion*.[16]

Socrates offers as evidence for the power of his daimonic voice certain prophetic warnings he was able to give in instances such as Charmides' training for a race in the Nemean games (128e), some fellow Timarchus, involved in a plot to kill Nicias, the son of Heroskamandrus,[17] and the Athenian campaigns against Sicily (129a2–d2), as well as against Ephesus and Ionia (129d6–9). In the *Apology*, the digression on the *daimonion* follows the digression on the Delphic oracle. The conversation in the *Theages* moves from Socrates' admission of a certain knowledge of erotics to his description of an oracular *daimonion*. All of the instances Socrates addresses of his daimonic voice could be said to be political or to involve political figures; this seems to be in contrast to the two occasions Socrates

---

16. A remarkable exchange between Socrates and Theages occurs when the latter asks whether Socrates is not a gentleman (127a9) and thus capable of teaching and keeping company for free (127a1–7). This exchange prompts Bruell to rightly say: "Putting to Socrates a question—whether he is not himself one of the gentlemen—that needs no answer since it admits of only one (cf. *Gorg.* 521d6–8), the boy declared that he would be perfectly satisfied, if Socrates for his part is willing, to be placed with him. And Theages' declaration accomplished something all but unheard of: it rendered Socrates, in effect, speechless (127b1)." *Socratic Education*, 110.

17. It is worth noting that Timarchus escapes the attention of the daimonic voice when Socrates fails to notice his third attempt at getting up to execute the deed (129c4). With regard to the prophetic power of Socrates, Benardete makes the very interesting point that Socrates demonstrates his prophetic power right at the beginning when he asks what the fitting name of the beautiful youth is: "Demodocus then would surely have been offended if Socrates, his son possessing some unpretentious name, had asked him the youth's noble name. But as it is, he accepts the compliment as perfectly just: yet we cannot. The coincidence seems uncanny and preternatural; it suggests something of divination, as if Socrates somehow knew beforehand what kind of name Theages would bear." "*Daimonion* of Socrates," 9.

alludes to at his trial, where the *daimonion* is said to have failed him—the trial of the ten generals after the battle of Arginusae and the execution of Leon of Salamis (*Ap.* 32b1–e1).[18] These seem to illustrate the dangers of overt political activity, justifying Socrates' decision to avoid it as far as possible. I say that the *daimonion* "failed" Socrates in these instances because it was not able to keep him from the political activity that he viewed as dangerous, which is supposed to be its function (*Ap.* 31c4–32a3). Perhaps this goes too far, and we can simply note that there seems to be a limit to the power of the *daimonion*; it seems that it cannot keep Socrates from all political activity. There is no doubt that Socrates acted nobly in these two cases, but these actions seem necessitated by the failure of the *daimonion* to keep him from trouble in the first place.

Socrates is, in a sense, forced to paint the picture of the *daimonion* as he does because Theages believes that Socrates' claim to know only the small subject of knowledge limited to matters of erotic love is a joke and further that Socrates is only toying with him and his father (128b9–c2).[19] For the second time (the first being at 126d1–8), Theages brings up the issue of the Socratic speeches he has heard from the associates of Socrates (128c2–6). It appears as if Theages is interested not in erotics, but only in the effect Socrates has had on his peers. As Socrates explains it, there are several things that can happen in his association with the young men:[20] the *daimonion* can oppose the potential student so he would not be able to

---

18. See Davis and Grewal, "Daimonic Soul," 36.

19. Or as Strauss says, "Socrates has recourse to his *daimonion* after the recourse to his being *erotikos* was of no avail; his *daimonion* replaces his being *erotikos* because it fulfills the same function—because it *is* the same. Socrates cannot profitably be together with people who are not promising, who are not attractive to him." Leo Strauss, "Plato's *Apology of Socrates* and *Crito*," in *Studies in Platonic Political Philosophy*, ed. Thomas L. Pangle (Chicago: University of Chicago Press, 1983), 47. Cf. Joyal, *Platonic "Theages,"* 96–97, 101–2.

20. Bruell remarks that "the question of Socrates himself as a teacher is the theme of a dialogue called, after its young hero, the *Theages*. Yet that work culminates in the depiction of a strenuous if not altogether successful effort on Socrates' part to avoid having to comply with the boy's own request, urgently seconded by his father, that he undertake to teach him. It thus compels us to approach the question of Socrates as a teacher from the direction of a consideration of a reluctance of some sort on his part to teach." *Socratic Education*, 103.

keep company with Socrates; the *daimonion* might not oppose him and yet he would still not benefit; the daimonic thing could contribute (129e3–5) and the student could benefit in a lasting way or, alternatively, he could gain something at first, only to lose it later. The *daimonion* is usually said to act only negatively and to hold Socrates back (e.g., 128d4–7). Here, however, in his description of the effects of his associations with the young men, it seems as if the *daimonion* can have a positive effect, actually contributing to the benefit of some. Socrates abandoned the tack with Theages that stressed his knowledge of erotics in favor of an appeal to his *daimonion*. Very unexpectedly, the appeal to the *daimonion* seems to be abandoned in the end in favor of an appeal to chance: "If it should be dear to the god, you will make very great and rapid progress, but if not, not so. Consider then, whether it would not be safer for you to be educated by one of those who are themselves in charge (*enkrateis*) of the benefit by which they benefit human beings rather than, with me, to act according to what turns out by chance (*tuchē*)" (130e5–8). Just as the issue of soothsaying unexpectedly arose like a chance event in the first half of the dialogue, the replacement of what is "dear to the god" by chance or luck here is also quite unexpected.

The *daimonion* was presented as an alternative way in which to speak about the Socratic knowledge of erotics: chance seems to be an alternative way to understand the *daimonion*. But this is not quite accurate. Socrates had made himself, or his *daimonion*, responsible for the problem of transmission. With the suggestion that chance will dictate whether Theages progresses with Socrates, we might hypothesize that chance will be a factor when Theages' character is considered: if Theages has the capacity to progress, he will; but this is a matter of chance; philosophers cannot be bred. All men may by nature desire to understand (Arist., *Met.* 980a20), yet the desire to learn or philosophize may not be natural to all. It seems as if chance plays the major explanatory role in the attraction between two people, including, perhaps, Socrates' attraction to certain young people.

Theages does not recognize that the outcome he desires is not subject to his control. He believes that Socrates' *daimonion* can be appeased with prayers or sacrifices; he does not see that Socrates has put the emphasis on chance, which might amount in part to putting the emphasis on Theages' character and Socrates' own attraction or lack of attraction to that character. It is not at all clear whether Socrates is attracted to Theages or whether Socrates is an attraction for Theages. It does seem clear that Theages desires for himself what Socrates has done to and for his comrades. That Socrates senses failure is suggested by his putting on the cloak of fate in the last line of the dialogue: "If it seems that that's the way it has to be done (*chrēnai poein*), then that's what we'll do (*poiōmen*)." It is not an accident that Socrates' emphasis on *poiēsis* reminds us of poetry:[21] poetry is the process of making chance seem like fate or necessity.[22] Poetry has a certain relation to soothsaying in the way each points to the divine. Once it appears to Socrates that he has failed in what he wants to accomplish with Theages by bringing forward the soothsaying *daimonion*, it should not be a surprise that he resorts to a kind of poetry in the last line of the dialogue.

---

21. Poetry is also used more explicitly as an issue in Socrates' examination of Theages' desire. Socrates appeals to a line he attributes to Euripides, "Tyrants are wise through keeping company with the wise" (125b6). In a comment that will bolster my own interpretation, Pangle observes that Socrates "treats Euripides as a kind of oracle whose gnomic utterance requires a dialectical interpretation, and the interpretation he develops here is rather different from the one suggested for the same line in the *Republic* (568a–b)." "On the *Theages*," 160.

22. In discussing the plot structure of tragedy, Aristotle remarks that the events that are most amazing are those that happen through chance or luck but appear as if they are providential. *Poet.* 1452a1–11.

5

Erotic Revolutions
in *Ecclesiazusae* and *Republic 5*

Derek Duplessie

Introduction

In Plato's *Apology of Socrates*, Socrates signals that the charges brought against him by the city of Athens originated out of the comic poet Aristophanes' caricature of Socrates in his play, the *Clouds*. Plato's dialogues assign a central role to Aristophanes despite, or because of Aristophanes' critical posture towards Socrates. Precisely because Aristophanes' critique is at least partially, if not preeminently, political, this essay will undertake an interpretation of Socrates' purported vision of the best regime in *Republic 5* so as to get a handle on Plato's own presentation of the disagreement—to the extent that there is one—between Aristophanes and Plato with respect to politics. While book 5 certainly provides one of the most central points of entry into Socratic political thought, it has special relevance to the question concerning Plato's relation to Aristophanes. For book 5 shares common features with, and was perhaps even modeled after, Aristophanes' *Ecclesiazusae*.

By considering the texts both on their own and in relation to each other, we will pay special attention to the ways in which Aristophanes and

Translations are from Jeffrey Henderson, *Aristophanes*, *"Frogs," "Assemblywomen," "Wealth,"* Loeb Classical Library (Cambridge, MA: Harvard University Press, 2002); and Allan Bloom, *The "Republic" of Plato* (New York: Basic Books, 1968).

Plato's Socrates handle the distinction between public and private life—especially how they understand the prospects of attempts to collapse that distinction. Finally, while indicating important points of agreement between the Aristophanic and Platonic analyses of political life, this essay will attempt an outline of a remaining difference—of a Platonic critique of Aristophanic poetry. For in spite of the comic poet's efforts to move beyond the domain of the merely conventional so as to generate a *mimēsis* of it, there are nevertheless important respects in which Aristophanic poetry remains ineluctably bound to the conventional, or to "the many beliefs of the many."

I. Praxagora's Scheme:
Political Innovation in Aristophanes' "Ecclesiazusae"

Ecclesiazusae begins in the early hours of the morning, just before sunrise. Praxagora has called upon the women of Athens to join her in her efforts to persuade the Assembly that, due to the chronic incompetence and corruption of Athens' political class—constituted entirely of men—it is time to enact a measure that would put power into the hands of the city's women. Praxagora justifies her radical proposal in her rehearsal speech, paradoxically, by appealing to the greater moderation of women.[1] In particular, she claims women are arch defenders of the "old ways" and as such would regard with apprehension the sorts of half-baked political innovations that are responsible for Athens' decline. As Praxagora argues in her rehearsal speech,

> [Female] character is superior to [male], as I will demon-
> strate. First, [women] dye their wool in hot water according

---

1. Praxagora's *actual* speech before the Assembly is, for one reason or another, concealed from the audience. We are forced to reconstruct her remarks on the basis of the rehearsal speech made before the women and the testimony of Chremes (who was in attendance at the actual speech). Aristophanes' concealment of Praxagora's speech recalls his concealment of Socrates' "indoor" instruction in the *Clouds*. Whatever the purpose of these omissions, one might at least surmise that, in Aristophanes' view, neither the Socratic education nor Praxagora's political proposals are in themselves as laughable as their consequences. That an argument or a teaching should be less ridiculous than its ramifications perhaps points towards Aristophanes' awareness of the fundamental cleavage of *praxis* and *theōria*.

to their ancient custom, each and every one of them; you'll
never see them try anything new. But the Athenian state
wouldn't hold on to that custom if it worked just fine; no,
they'd be fiddling around with some innovation. (214–20)

Women would be superior custodians of the city because of their adherence
to ancient custom; this is emphasized by the repetition of "as they always
have" (*kai pro tou*) throughout Praxagora's speech. Furthermore, women
have long demonstrated their competence as "stewards and treasurers" of
the household (221–29; cf. 232). Praxagora's appeal to the success of
women in household management as evidence for their qualification to
lead the city suggests early on the conceit that is operating underneath the
entire proposal: That there is no essential difference between the city and
the family—or, more precisely, that the city can be refashioned using the
family as a model. It therefore looks as if the policies enacted by the women
once they are installed follow organically from the logic used to justify their
installment to begin with. The truth of this conceit can be confirmed or
disconfirmed by the success or failure of Praxagora's revolution.

Before moving on to examine the content of that revolution, one might
ask the following: What is the inner connection between the two prongs
of Praxagora's argument for this changing of the guard? Or, what is the
relation between women as defenders of ancient custom and women as
devoted to the family? As a provisional response, I would like to suggest
that family—also understood as the attachment to one's own—is needed
in order to make a case for the intrinsic goodness of the old ways. Because
the ancient customs originate with distant kin, we can be sure of the beneficence of those customs. To deviate from the old ways is to disrespect
progenitors to whom we must always acknowledge a debt of gratitude.
This debt of gratitude, if properly acknowledged, would compel us to
defend the laws instituted by those progenitors; at bottom, adherence to
ancient custom is adherence to the law. The connection between the devotion to family and the adherence to the old ways points towards a category
that subsumes both, namely, the ancestral.

The speech Praxagora intends to give before the Assembly will involve
a double deception. Not only will she make her appeal while disguised as
a man, but her case for the desirability of female rule runs counter to the

specific policies that end up being enacted by the women. This "bait-and-switch" is all but announced when Praxagora exhorts the Assemblymen in her rehearsal speech to "hand over governance of the city to the women, and let's not beat around the bush or ask what they plan to accomplish. Let's simply let them govern" (229). The Assemblymen are urged to pass the measure so that they can find out what the measure involves![2]

The details of Praxagora's revolution are revealed to the audience at the same time as they are revealed to Praxagora's husband, Blepyrus, who is informed while in the most disgraceful of situations. He first becomes aware of Praxagora's absence in the early hours of the morning when he awakes with an urgent need to defecate. Unable to locate his cloak and boots, he is forced to steal away into the night in his wife's nightgown and slippers. While Blepyrus is relieving himself and bemoaning what he takes to be his wife's infidelity, Praxagora is in fact making her case before Athens' ruling class. Blepyrus wears Praxagora's slip, while Praxagora wears Blepyrus' cloak. Praxagora's ascent coincides perfectly with Blepyrus' descent. Praxagora, then, appears to be initiating a revolution that mirrors the revolution that has already unfolded in her own home.

It is worth noting the discrepancy between Praxagora's rehearsal speech and the speech as it is reported by Chremes to Blepyrus: In Chremes' account, Praxagora's pitch omits all of the central arguments presented above, namely, that women are qualified to rule because they are faithful guardians of ancient custom and are devoted to the welfare of the family (and, relatedly, competent in overseeing the interests of the household). Instead, according to Chremes, Praxagora argues that "a woman is a creature bursting with brains, a moneymaker, and that women never divulge the secrets of the Thesmophoria" (441), and that the women "lend each other dresses, jewelry, money, drinking cups, privately and

---

2. But here it is necessary to address an apparent inconsistency in the foregoing analysis. In a rather complicated sense, Praxagora's policies both do and do not follow from her justification for rule by women. In the sense that the city—as we will soon see—is to represent a certain triumph of the private over the public, and insofar as Praxagora touts the competence of women as custodians of private households, the policies follow from the justification for female rule. But in the sense that the policies are novel, while Praxagora had argued that women should rule due to their adherence to the old ways, the policies seem to be at odds with the justification for female rule.

without witnesses, and always return everything and don't cheat" (446). Finally, according to him, Praxagora argues that women deserve to rule because "they don't inform on people, don't sue them, don't try to overthrow the democracy" (454). There is no mention of the female comportment towards hearth and home, nor is there any suggestion that women are uniquely faithful to the old ways.

Perhaps most significantly, Chremes suggests that the Assembly voted to turn the city over to the women because "that seemed to be the only thing that hasn't been tried" (455). In stark contrast to the argument that Praxagora had made in her rehearsal speech, according to which women were suited to rule because of their prudent contempt for foolish political innovations, the men of Athens are apparently captivated by the utter novelty of the proposal. The fact that Chremes' account of the Assembly's logic for endorsing Praxagora's proposal runs counter to the arguments that she herself had rehearsed suggests either that Praxagora abandoned those arguments or that the Assemblymen were simply indifferent to them.

Before unveiling her specific policy proposals, Praxagora expresses the following concern as regards their reception: "I'm sure my proposals are worthwhile, but I'm awfully worried about the spectators: are they ready to quarry a new vein and not stick with what's hoary and conventional?" (583). Praxagora is in fundamental agreement with the men of the Assembly regarding the defectiveness of the conventional.[3] This agreement confronts us with a puzzle: If neither Praxagora nor the men whom she hopes to persuade are moved by an appeal to ancient custom, what purpose is the argument presented in the rehearsal speech meant to serve? Why does she take such pains to contrive an argument designed to persuade nobody? If the argument *is* intended to persuade, it looks as if it is perhaps meant to persuade the women rather than the men. That the women were impressed by Praxagora's initial arguments while the men perhaps were not suggests that there may be some truth to those arguments: women *do* in fact exhibit greater fidelity to custom and family than men do. It

---

3. "Convention" is distinguishable both from the novel and the natural. But since nature is older than convention, even the oldest customs appear to be novel from the standpoint of the natural. Does Praxagora's subversion of custom suggest an allegiance to the novel or to the natural?

appears, then, to be the women and not the men who fall victim to Praxagora's bait-and-switch. Praxagora reveals herself to be, in a certain respect, more akin to the men of the Assembly than to her female allies; her immoderation belies her femaleness.

Indeed, Praxagora's proposals—specifically, her endorsement of communism and free love—betray her own utter disregard for ancient custom. Praxagora's first proposal is stated as follows:

> I propose that everyone should own everything in common, and draw an equal living. No more rich man here, poor man there, or a man with a big farm and a man without land enough for his own grave, or a man with many slaves and a man without even an attendant. No, I will establish one and the same standard of life for everyone.... My first act will be to communize all the land, money, and other property that's now individually owned. We women will manage this common fund with thrift and good judgment, and take good care of you. (588–97)

Praxagora attempts to assuage Blepyrus' concerns about this first proposal, insisting that all men alike will willingly contribute to the common fund, since the common fund will provide for every need and desire. There will be nothing that can be purchased with private funds that will have not already been provided for with public funds.

Blepyrus next asks whether public funds will be available for the solicitation of prostitutes. His question, though playful, anticipates a sensible objection to Praxagora's initial proposal. It suggests his awareness that there remains a distinction between public goods and private goods—a distinction that communism seems unprepared to handle, as communism endeavors to make the common good so primary that private life and its attendant private goods are utterly suspended. Blepyrus' objection acknowledges that there are certain private appetites that compromise our concern for the good of the city. Why, indeed, should public funds be provided to make possible an activity that is at best indifferent to and at worst inimical to the common good?

Praxagora responds to Blepyrus, offering a second proposal: "I'm making these girls common property too, for the men to sleep with and make babies with as they please" (614). Praxagora's second proposal stands in a somewhat complicated relationship with the first. On the one hand, as already noted, the liberation of eros that the second proposal prepares for would seem to function so as to create a private sphere of erotic entanglements that would loosen the attachment to the public good, which was the chief aim of the first proposal. On the other hand, the second proposal certainly seems to be the logical fulfillment of the first proposal. Equality with respect to public goods alone is not enough. The only way to stomp out private quarrels once and for all is to ensure that no person has a greater share of private pleasure than any other. In order to bring about this effect, it is stipulated that men and women are free to sleep with whomever they like, but each must sleep with a less desirable suitor before moving on to the true object of his or her desire. It's only fair, after all.

Eros must therefore be brought into the public sphere via legal mandates. The city's effort to provide for equal shares of sexual gratification carries along with it a necessary corollary: the abolition of family—or more precisely, the abolition of *families*. Praxagora's endorsement of "free love" leads to the consequence, as Blepyrus notes, that no man will be able to recognize his own children. (Cf. *Rep.* 460–65.) He asks, "Then from now on won't sons methodically strangle each and every older man? Because even now they strangle their acknowledged father; what will happen when he's unacknowledged?" (638). Praxagora responds, "No, the bystanders won't allow it. They didn't use to care who was beating other people's fathers, but now if they hear a man getting beaten they'll worry that the victim is their own dad, and fight the attackers" (641). According to her analysis, far from creating a situation in which there are no familial obligations or attachments, the new arrangement will create the impression that the city is simply one big family. Strikingly, no mention is made of the flip side to Praxagora's argument. That is, if every older man is to be regarded as at least potentially one's father, every older woman must also be regarded as at least potentially one's mother. This fact suggests that, even if Praxagora's proposal succeeds in preventing parricide, it does so in such a way as to make incest all but inevitable. Praxagora intends to make customary what has in all times hitherto been understood to be a crime of the first order.

Praxagora's plan to fashion a single family out of a city of many families is finally announced a few lines later. She intends to "convert the city into one household by breaking down all partitions to make one dwelling, so that everyone can walk into everyone else's space" (675). Additionally, the courthouses and porticoes will be transformed into dining rooms, and speakers' platforms into cabinets for the storage of mixing bowls and water jugs. Praxagora intends not to refashion the family so as to make public affairs primary, but rather to refashion the city so as to make private affairs primary.

The play's final episodes take pains to examine whether or to what extent this repurposing of public life is successful. In spite of Praxagora's efforts, does there remain some cleavage of the public and the private? First, the play probes the prospects of the first proposal by presenting a dispute between a "selfish man" and a neighbor regarding the wisdom of obeying the law that commands all citizens to hand over their private belongings to the state. The selfish man cannot believe that anyone would leap to obey such a law. Unlike the law-abiding neighbor, the selfish man intends to remain cautious until he is able to "see what most people do" (770). He very much doubts that others will comply with the mandate because of its incompatibility with the "national character" (779). Indeed, as he notes, even the gods of the city are wont to receive without giving anything in return.

The dispute involves, at bottom, a disagreement concerning the *wisdom* of forfeiting one's possessions to the common store. Is it the man of sense (*sōphrōn*) or the imbecile who does what he's told? The question here is not whether it would be wise from the perspective of the city, but rather, whether it would be wise from the standpoint of an individual in the city to voluntarily comply with such mandates. This doubt seems to be the crudely materialistic version of Blepyrus' earlier *erotic* concern about the possibility of collapsing private and public life. The question now is not whether political innovations will succeed in satisfying private desires, but whether what is good for the city as a whole will be materially beneficial for the individuals who compose that city. To act in a way that is contrary to one's own benefit is to make oneself "brainless." The disagreement between the selfish man and the neighbor therefore hinges on the follow-ing question: Is it possible to entirely erase the distinction between the good of the citizen and the good of the city? If not, is it ever wise to subjugate one's private good to the public good? The answer for the selfish man is, of course, a resounding "no." The selfish man, in spite of his "total skepticism" with regards to whether or not citizens will comply with the new law, has no reservation about attending the public banquet—he will seek self-benefit by sapping the common store without contributing to it himself.

While this first episode is intended to explore the prospects of the first proposal, a second episode is offered up as a comic reflection on the implications of Praxagora's second proposal. Here we are introduced to a girl waiting for her lover to arrive. Upon his arrival the young couple is assailed by a parade of old hags, each more hideous than the last, and each attempting to make a claim on the object of the young girl's affection. After a long struggle between the first old woman and the young couple, the old woman finally stands down after the young girl makes explicit a possibility previously only alluded to. She proclaims, "He's the wrong age to be sleeping with you—you're more his mother than his wife. If you people start enforcing a law like this, you'll fill the whole country with Oedipuses" (1038).[4] That this proclamation is enough to discourage the old woman in her efforts suggests a profound limitation to Praxagora's decree.

Following the first old woman's retreat, two additional old hags come on the scene, each claiming a right to sleep with the young man, who is finally forced to capitulate to the demands of the law. Before doing so, he exclaims, "I'm damned three ways from Sunday if I have to fuck an old bag all night and all day, and after I get free of her, start in again on an old toad with a funeral urn already standing by her chops!" (1098). Indeed, if the young man's interpretation of the law is correct, it is not clear how or whether the most attractive among the Athenians would ever be entitled to satisfy their erotic longings. The new arrangement favors only the indigent and the unsightly.

---

4. Saxonhouse notes Praxagora's insistence that the difference between a household and a *polis* is one of magnitude only. The consequence of this failure of identification— the city of Oedipuses—seems to confirm Aristotle's argument at the beginning of his *Politics*. Arlene W. Saxonhouse, "Boundaries: The Comic Poet Confronts the 'Who' of Political Action," in *The Political Theory of Aristophanes*, ed. Jeremy J. Mhire and Ryan-Paul Frost (Albany: State University of New York Press, 2014), 104.

Both episodes presented above display unexpected or problematic features of Praxagora's regime, but because Aristophanes so often expresses his final estimation of the schemes presented in his comedies by presenting the fates of his "heroes," a further question remains: How does Praxagora herself fare in the wake of her own revolution? There are, in fact, few concrete indications as to Praxagora's situation following the institution of her new laws. Is it possible that Praxagora's absence in the second half of the play is intended to suggest that the outcome of her proposals for the city as a whole is of little concern to her? If her disappearance suggests her indifference to or insulation from the effects of her own revolution, perhaps we are meant to surmise that there remains an ineradicable distinction between private and public interests, thereby giving the lie to Praxagora's conceit that such a distinction can be subverted. To the extent that we are provided with no sense of how Praxagora fares—not to mention whether or not she herself is surprised by the outcome of her laws—the comedy leaves open the possibility that Praxagora is not ridiculous, even if her proposals result in certain ridiculous consequences.

II. An Approach to "Republic" 5

The radical proposals set forth in book 5 of the *Republic* are introduced as a way of addressing a question haunting Polemarchus: How will the community of women and children described in the preceding stage of the dialogue operate? In particular, how will the children be begotten and reared? These questions provide the occasion for Socrates to introduce proposals that otherwise may never have been made explicit.[5] It is revealing that the question is made apparent through a whisper uttered by Polemarchus to Adeimantus. This whisper, a private communication, becomes publicized through the drama of the dialogue in such a way as to make

---

5. If a private whisper is the cause of the digression that will occupy bks. 5–7, the effect of that whisper is also Socrates' "arrest" at the hands of his young interlocutors (450a1). A public action, however metaphorical, is the consequence of a private communication, and the playful capture of the philosopher sets the stage for a philosophical proposal according to which philosophy both rules and is protected against the *polis*. The discussion to follow is thus framed by two fundamental questions raised by dramatic elements in the first few moments of bk. 5: (1) what is the proper relation between the private and the public? and (2) to what extent can philosophical or rational rule ever prevail in political life?

the subsequent discussion possible. At the same time, this attempt at a private communication, as we shall soon see, seems to be precisely the sort of thing that the city soon to be proposed must eliminate in order for that city to become possible.[6]

Before considering Socrates' response to Polemarchus as to how, specifically, the community of women and children is to be arranged, we must first consider the *problem* for which this community is intended to be a solution. In book 4, Socrates alludes to the need to reorganize the family in the context of a discussion of the conditions that would have to be in place in order to secure the perfect *unity* of the best city. This unity is prepared for by the principle of justice, according to which each man devotes himself singularly to that job for which he is most suited. A harmonious political order must discourage "jacks of all trade" and "busybodies" from encroaching on the work designated for others. Consequently, we are told, "the whole city will naturally grow to be one and not many" (423d7). This principle of justice announced in book 4 requires that citizens be properly assigned to the class for which they are suited according to their natural abilities. "Education and rearing" are to play a crucial role in this determination, and for the first time we are provided with a passing allusion to the radical reforms that such an education will necessarily entail: "The possession of women, marriage, and the procreation of children must as far as possible be arranged according to the proverb that friends have all things in common" (423e5–424a3). The central proposal of book 5 will spell out precisely how this desideratum is to be brought about.

As a final step, before finally turning to the proposal specifying that women and children be shared in common, it will be necessary to provide a brief sketch of the first proposal, which argues for the equality of male and female guardians, and which also seems to serve both as a consequence of and a necessary condition for the realization of the community of women and children soon to be proposed. This first proposal appears to serve as a fitting beginning point in the following ways: First, if the

---

6. As Benardete aptly puts it, "The whisper represents the gravest threat to Socrates' proposal on communism...for any private communication between bride and bridegroom would suffice to cancel the publicity which communism is meant to institutionalize." Seth Benardete, *Socrates' Second Sailing: On Plato's "Republic"* (Chicago: University of Chicago Press, 1989), 110.

integrity of the guardian class is to be guaranteed, women must be granted entry as a matter of biological necessity. Only once—or only if—it is established that women, too, can be guardians will it be possible for the best to mate with the best, for the generation of the best citizens. If women are not naturally equal to men, the guardian class will necessarily undergo a slow and steady diminution as the souls of the best citizens are "watered down" by female contributions. Aside from the practical necessity of female guardians for replenishing the guardian class, the argument that justifies their inclusion provides a first indication as to the larger sweep of the argument: the best city depends upon an effort to rationalize politics, and the success of this project depends, as we shall soon see, upon abstracting from the subrational elements of human psychology supplied by body.

The discussion of female equality begins with a question posed by Socrates to Glaucon as to whether the women should share in the work of the male guardians, or rather, serve a different function entirely, tending to household management and the rearing of the children. Since Glaucon insists that everything must be in common, the women will have to perform the same tasks as the men and therefore must also receive the same education. Before continuing on to examine "whether female human nature can share in common with the nature of the male class" in all deeds, in none, or in some, Socrates asks Glaucon, "Do you want us to carry on the dispute and represent those on the other side ourselves so that the opposing argument won't be besieged without defense?" (453a8–10). With Glaucon's assent, Socrates gives voice to his imagined opponents, raising the possibility that the argument has contradicted itself.[7] Justice was earlier understood to be minding one's own business according to *nature*, but because Glaucon insists there is a natural difference between women and men, the

---

7. Berg raises the possibility that, if Aristophanes is included among the disputants now being acknowledged, Socrates is giving voice to some version of the question Aristophanes may have intended to raise at the end of Socrates' speech in the *Symposium* prior to Alcibiades' drunken interruption: what is the precise relation between the good and one's own? This general question shows up here as: how does the universalism entailed by Socrates' vision of the good relate to his earlier identification of justice as "minding one's *own* business?" Steven Berg, "The Woman Drama of *Republic* Book V," in *Nature, Woman, and the Art of Politics*, ed. Eduardo A. Velásquez (Latham, MD: Rowman & Littlefield, 2000), 58.

opposing argument brings to the fore the absurdity of claiming simulta-neously that women differ from men by nature and that women neverthe-less should tend to the same business as men. Glaucon is stumped and enjoins Socrates to once again switch sides and respond to this objection.

Although the conversation has postulated that one's job will be deter-mined by one's nature, the discussion has not yet given sufficient consid-eration to "what type of difference and sameness of nature we had in mind and what was our aim in reaching a definition when we assigned different tasks to different natures, but the same tasks to the same nature" (454b7–10). The ensuing argument attempts to parse out the specific aspects of "nature" that are relevant to the determination of one's job in the city. Just as baldness has no bearing on one's capacity to become a cobbler (454c6), perhaps men and women can differ in nature with respect to gen-der without also differing in every other respect, or as Socrates concludes,

> If [the two sexes] appear different with regard to some trade or other job we shall agree that we must assign them separ-ately, but if they appear to be different only in that the female conceives, while the male fathers the child, then we shall say that nothing has yet been discovered to say that a woman is different from a man in relation to what we are talking about, so we shall still think that our guardians and the women should do the same job. (454d9–e5)

So the question that Socrates now submits to his opponents is, quite sim-ply, do women differ from men by nature such that women would be inca-pable of practicing the political art? Is the bodily capacity to conceive as irrelevant to guardianship as baldness is to shoe repair?

Although it certainly seems quite plausible that a capacity for child-bearing *would* affect one's psychology in a more profound way than, say, baldness, Socrates diminishes the significance of all bodily differences to the point where they can play no crucial role in determining one's natural capacity for political rule, at least. In the final analysis, the person with a better nature differs from the person with a worse in the following way: "the one learns something connected with that thing easily, the other with difficulty" (455b5). The primary way in which natures differ—indeed, the *only* way mentioned here—is that some humans have a greater natural aptitude for learning.[8] Even though it is agreed upon, without any supporting argument, that women are inferior to men in this one crucial respect, it turns out that, though women are inferior to men in terms of their capacity for learning *in every area*, there is no practice for which women are uniquely suited; women can do everything that men can do, only worse.[9] Like men, some women are suited to be guardians and others are not.

Following this, the second proposal is finally introduced: "All these women are to belong to all these men in common, and no woman is to live privately with any man. And the children, in their turn, will be in common, and neither will a parent know his own offspring, nor a child his parent" (457d1–5). The equality of the sexes means that women will no longer be distinguished from men by their role as child-bearers and homemakers. But if they are no longer expected to preside over the private household, the family must take on a radically different shape or disappear altogether. The community of women and children, however, is not merely a practical implication of the first law; it also brings to completion what the first law began. To overcome the attachment to one's own private good is first to overcome the attachment to one's own bodily existence and then to one's own family.

This ultimate goal will require that private erotic desires be publicized and rationalized—that they be transformed so that they can serve an instrumental function. Specifically, women and men will all live and eat together in common houses, "with no one privately possessing anything of the kind" (458c10). Furthermore, sexual relations will have to be carefully managed. "Irregular intercourse" is the term of disapprobation

---

8. A necessary corollary to this argument is that, if the *bad* or the harmful is the true standard of the ridiculous, and if the *good* man is he who learns with ease, such a man cannot be the object of any comedy, as long as that comedy takes its cues from nature and not merely from convention. This conclusion is confirmed in the subsequent analysis.

9. Socrates adds a wrinkle to the argument, asking Glaucon, "Do you know of anything that is practiced by human beings in which the class of men doesn't excel that of women in all these respects? Or shall we draw it out at length by speaking of weaving and the care of baked and boiled dishes—just those activities on which the reputation of the female sex is based and where its defeat is most ridiculous of all?" (455c6–d3). Socrates thereby suggests that the greatest comedy would be something like the mirror image of Aristophanes' *Ecclesiazusae*—that men taking over the household would be a more comic sight than women taking over the city.

applied to any act of intercourse that occurs without the intention of generating the best possible citizens or—what amounts to the same—is beyond the scope of the law. The law can only make use of eros for its own purposes if it is able to eliminate the beautiful as the object of eros. Socrates' discussion of intercourse indicates the full extent to which the beautiful has been eclipsed by the good in the argument's effort to identify the two (457b4). Accordingly, "there is a need for the best men to have intercourse with the best women, and the reverse for the most ordinary men with the most ordinary women; and the offspring of the former must be reared but not that of the others" (459d9–e1). Finally, the offspring of the best are to be sent to a pen where they will be raised by nurses, and the offspring of the worse and those with other deformities will be deposited in an "unspeakable and unseen" place.

That all of this micromanaging must happen out of view reminds us that these reforms are ultimately intended to make what is wholly artificial appear as if it were entirely natural—as if it could not be otherwise. The necessity that the best city's operations remain unknown to its citizens is already signaled in book 3, in which it was agreed upon that the flourishing of the city will depend upon the promulgation of falsehoods designed to disguise the origins of the city and its tripartite class structure (414d1–e6). Specifically, citizens will be conditioned to believe that they are born of the earth and that their class status is determined by the specific metals of which their individual souls are constituted. Socrates' city depends upon a hierarchy of classes but, in order to forestall class resentment, those at the lower rungs must believe that their lot is determined by natural necessity. Precisely because these myths—and indeed the practical reforms introduced in their service—must appeal to a fictitious natural order, we are incidentally made aware of the artificiality that seems to lie at the base of every city. Class structures, even or especially when rationalized, are not strictly speaking natural. The best city, one in which every aspect of life is placed in the service of the public, depends upon keeping its own origins entirely private. This, in a way, would therefore seem to be a practical reflection of a literary observation already made. Namely, just as the whisper provides the occasion for the founding of a city that would seek to eliminate the whisper, complete opacity is needed in order to bring the whole of private life out into the open.

After setting forth this preliminary sketch, Socrates continues on to examine whether such an arrangement would, in fact, be for the best. Socrates asks, "Have we any greater evil for a city than what splits it and makes it many instead of one? Or a greater good than what binds it together and makes it one?" (462b1–3). The greatest good for a city is for the citizens of a city to rejoice and feel pain together about the same "comings into being and perishings." As already acknowledged, this great good cannot be achieved as long as there are private interests in the city, and private interests cannot be squelched without eliminating private possessions, including, of course, private families. The best city is that in which "most say 'my own' and 'not my own' about the same thing" (462c6–8). Or, to put it differently, the best city is that which functions most like a single body, where the good of every part is inseparable from—or even identical to—the good of the whole.

In spite of his insistence that the body should serve as the model for the city, Socrates nevertheless indicates the body is also the true obstacle to the best city when he asks, "Won't lawsuits and complaints against one another virtually vanish from among [the community of guardians] thanks to their possessing nothing private but the body, while the rest is in common?" (464d6–e1). In a city in which all "money, children, and relatives" are held in common, there will be fewer opportunities to legitimately take legal action on account of some perceived inequality. Still, Socrates' remark amounts to a grim reminder that the body *will* continue to persist as private and individuated, and therefore as a problem that politics cannot altogether manage. All of his best efforts to abstract from or overcome the body notwithstanding, Socrates here grants that the body remains a source of private pains and pleasures, that is to say, of private interests, and therefore prevents the city from becoming a perfect whole; the body prevents the city from becoming a body.

Following this reminder of the persistence of the body and of its attendant private pains and pleasures, Socrates addresses the possibility of "assault and insult" in the community of guardians: "There would justly be no suits for assault or insult among them. For we'll surely say that it is fine and just for men to take care of their own defense against others of the same age, thus imposing on them the necessity of taking care of their bodies" (464e5–8). To propose a penal code would perhaps not be "just," since to do so would be to anticipate in advance the failure of Socrates' reforms. Though there is no proposed legal remedy to assault and insult, it is not denied that there may well be strife even after all belongings have been designated common property. In the absence of any legal recourse, citizens must be permitted to tend to their own self-defense. They must train their bodies so as to prepare for external assaults from peers. Even in this city, where peers are to be regarded as brothers, there will be violence between men of the same exact class. Regarding one's peers as brothers is not enough to eliminate the possibility of injury and insult. Fratricide, it seems, always remains a possibility.

III. Socrates and Aristophanes on the Public and Private

Socrates and Aristophanes, each in his way, seems to be aware of the deep difficulty in severing private interests from the common good, and vice versa. In *Ecclesiazusae* private family life is suspended in favor of free love. The final good is the satisfaction of each citizen's sexual desire, even if the law ultimately fails to make good on its promise. There is absolutely no consideration of childbearing in Praxagora's city; no distinction is made between the good and the pleasant, and consequently, the good is sacrificed to the pleasant. Whereas Socrates demands that bodily desires be subverted so that the city as a whole can become as close to a single body as possible, Praxagora endorses communism because such a political arrangement should be most capable of providing for the desires of our bodies—specifically, the desire for sex, food, and drink. Aristophanes' comedy, at bottom, seems to expose the private—and often base—desires that underlie the pretense to political idealism.

Still, although both Aristophanes and Plato employ communism and the abolition of the traditional family to reveal something about the difficulty involved in collapsing private and public spheres, Socrates' reimagining of the family—or, more precisely, his dissolution of the family —turns Praxagora's proposals on their head. The Socratic analysis begins with the individual body before turning to the private family, and aims to show what would have to be modified in human nature, or in nature as such, in order that the distinction between the private (or individual) and the public (or whole) could be resolved in favor of the public. Although Socrates' proposals are designed to attenuate the attachment to one's private good, the physical body, according to the Socratic analysis, ultimately emerges as the chief obstacle to the city becoming like a single body. Even if everything else is shared in common, the irremediably private character of our embodied existence with its concomitant private pleasures and pains ensures that there will remain the likelihood of "assault and insult" among citizens. This reality compels Socrates to advise that citizens tend to their bodies so as to train for self-defense. The body furnishes a problem for which it itself turns out to be the best solution (464e5–8).

What, though, is the purpose of Plato's inversion of Aristophanes' presentation of political idealism? If Aristophanes' comedy draws our attention to and elicits our laughter at the insuperable character of sub-rational appetites for earthy pleasures, Plato seems to draw our attention to the silliness of reason's pretending to transcend the bodily, and especially the erotic attachments. This pretense culminates in a final proposal, which Socrates grants will drown him in "laughter and ill repute" (473c8): rule by philosophers. Whatever the merits of Socrates' vision of the best regime, his analysis exposes the extent to which the body and its demands serve to frustrate every effort to manage political life according to reason. Plato's comic representation of reason's hubristic attempt to transcend bodily and erotic needs implies his own knowledge of the perils associated with attempting to "rationalize" politics. Because Plato's comedy is in fundamental *agreement* with Aristophanes' own critique of philosophy in the *Clouds* as, at best, politically oblivious and, at worst, politically dangerous, Plato refutes the comic poet in deed. Plato's ostensible absorption of Aristophanes' insights provides evidence that Aristophanes was wrong in his supposition that philosophy is necessarily self-ignorant with respect to its relation to politics. *Political* philosophy is possible after all.

*   *   *

Although the chief goal of this essay has been to bring out a fundamental point of agreement between Plato and Aristophanes with respect to politics, Plato nevertheless makes available a criticism of comedy as excessively dependent upon and supportive of the merely conventional or doxic. Through his allusion to the "wits" who in the past laughed at the sight of naked gymnasts (452c4–e1)—or, more generally, by pointing out that people in the past laughed at what is now totally commonplace, Socrates indicates that makers of comedy ridicule what is unconventional, not what is ridiculous by nature.[10] They literally do not *know* what they're laughing at. Socrates insists:

> He is empty who believes anything is ridiculous other than the bad, and who tries to produce laughter looking to any sight as ridiculous other than the sight of the foolish and bad; or, again, he who looks seriously to any standard of beauty he sets up other than the good. (452d8–13)

To make a laughingstock of a person or phenomenon in the absence of a reasoned account of the badness of that person or phenomenon is to appeal to mere appearances or conventional "seemings."

Book 5 concludes with an attempt to identify the philosopher, and in doing so also negatively determines the philosopher's other. Those who are *not* philosophers are determined to be, at bottom, "lovers of opinion" (480a6). We are therefore left with the unmistakable impression that Aristophanes himself is lumped into this second category. Indeed Aristophanes' comedies certainly depend upon opinion insofar as they must, to some extent, accommodate themselves to it. They must appeal to the popular applause of the many. As for Aristophanes the man, to the extent that he does not seem to care to turn towards the unchangeable ideas and to reason about them, he must be understood to be bound to the horizon of opinion or convention (479e3). Still, it would seem to be precisely the laughter provoked by Aristophanes' comedy that served to inspire Plato's own *philosophical* treatment of the same issue. Although conventional laughter is presented as an obstacle to the acceptance of Socrates' radical proposals, Aristophanes' laughter appears to serve as prelude to Plato's own philosophical analysis of those proposals.

---

10. See Benardete's rich analysis of laughter's relation to convention in *Socrates' Second Sailing*, 115. Noting the ambiguous character of laughter, he remarks, "The laugh might be the noise of shame and due to the sudden recognition that everything beautiful is by law; but it might be no less the triumphant vindication of convention and due to the realization that the old ways are best."

6

Self-Reliance and Roguishness: On the Surprising Modernity of Xenophon's Socrates

Clifford Orwin

It's easy to want to contribute to a *Festschrift* for Ronna Burger. Who of us, whether students or colleagues, has not basked in her great warmth and kindness, on the one hand, and her invigorating readings, on the other? Ronna and I were strangers in our youth, and first met only in middle age. Yet from when I first began to read her I never doubted that she was remarkable. So she is easy to love and admire, but difficult to emulate.

Why Xenophon as my choice of topic for this volume? Well, if there ever was a guy who matched Ronna in combining down-to-earthness with analytic rigor (and that little touch of devilish wit), it was him. As it happens, my own acquaintance with him is even more recent than my acquaintance with her. It was just eighteen months ago that I fell under the spell of his Socratic writings in particular. It was in the context of teaching, and I found him wonderful for teaching graduate and under-graduate students alike. The present contribution grew from that engagement. So I must stress that I am not a specialist in Xenophon, but really just one of his rawest recruits.

My thanks to Christian Wendt and his colleagues at the Free University of Berlin for their comments on an earlier version of this essay.

At this stage of his own career, however, Xenophon might find even my attention flattering. Since the eighteenth century he has languished as the most neglected of major classical writers. (Does he even still qualify as a major classical writer?) Some leading scholars have bucked this trend, notably the late Leo Strauss, and his readers in America and Vivienne Gray in New Zealand. On the whole, though, Xenophon remains a misplaced name craving rediscovery.

Yet it is not just the occasional active scholar who has battled this modern indifference to Xenophon, but at least one retired philologist who had gone on to better things. There is no more striking modern statement on Xenophon and his Socrates than that of Nietzsche in Aphorism no. 86 of the final section of *Human, All Too Human*, "The Wanderer and His Shadow."

> If all goes well, the time will come when one will take up the *Memorabilia* of Socrates rather than the Bible. In him converge the roads of the most different philosophic modes of life, which are in truth the modes of the different temperaments, crystallised by reason and habit and all ultimately directed towards the delight in life and in self. Socrates excels the founder of Christianity in being able to be serious cheerfully and in possessing the wisdom full of roguishness that constitutes the finest state of the human soul. And he also possessed the finer intellect.[1]

Given the neglect into which Xenophon had already fallen by 1875, Nietzsche's readers must have been as surprised by this verdict as we are. That the *imitatio Socratis* might entirely dislodge the *imitatio Christi*, with the Socrates so privileged explicitly identified as the Xenophontic one: that's pretty strong beer. So too is the related claim that the pathways of all philosophical modes of life lead back to him. (I never caught any philosophy professor of my acquaintance tracing his or her theoretical genealogy back to Xenophon.) Yet perhaps the most striking assertion of all is that the Xenophontic Socrates, unlike Christ, possessed that *wisdom full of roguishness* (*Weisheit voller Schelmenstreiche*, emphasized in the original),

---

1. Friedrich Nietzsche, *Human, All Too Human*, trans. R. J. Hollingdale (Cambridge: Cambridge University Press, 1986), 332.

which *den besten Seelenzustand des Menschen ausmacht.* Obviously this is a far cry from the obtuseness that so many scholars have ascribed to Xenophon and his Socrates alike. And then the final twist of the lance in Christ's wounds, that Socrates also possessed the finer intellect.

Nietzsche, then, here offers Xenophon's Socrates (not that other fellow's) as *the model* for modern man, the indicated alternative to Christ as the spirit of the dawning age. Consider that had he persisted in this position Xenophon's Socrates would have preempted the role of the *Übermensch* in Nietzsche's fantastic cast of characters. (That would have been all to the good: no fascist has ever drawn inspiration from Xenophon's Socrates.)

Unfortunately neither here nor in his later writings does Nietzsche offer further illumination of the "cheerful roguishness" of Xenophon's Socrates. He leaves it to us to figure out why his doubts about the Platonic Socrates did not preclude so resounding an affirmation of the Xenophontic one.

I'll mention one other reader of Xenophon whose enthusiasm for him has piqued my own. That was Benjamin Franklin. Franklin and Nietzsche had surprisingly much in common. To begin with, both were emphatically modern. While more cautious than Nietzsche, Franklin too belonged to the theoretical avant-garde of his time.[2] He too combined deep reserva-

---

2. For recent treatments emphasizing the conscious modernity of Franklin's thought, see Jerry Weinberger, *Benjamin Franklin Unmasked: On the Unity of His Moral, Religious, and Political Thought* (Lawrence: University Press of Kansas, 2005); and Lorraine Smith Pangle, *The Political Philosophy of Benjamin Franklin* (Baltimore: Johns Hopkins University Press, 2007). See also Steven Forde, "Benjamin Franklin's *Autobiography* and the Education of America," *American Political Science Review* 86, no. 2 (1992): 357–68; and Christopher S. McClure, "Learning from Franklin's Mistakes: Self-Interest Rightly Understood in the *Autobiography*," *Review of Politics* 76, no. 1 (2014): 69–92.

Noting Franklin's early engagement with Xenophon and Socrates, Lorraine Pangle remarks that "he shows a remarkable affinity for the earthly practicality of Xenophon's Socrates and resembles him in his constant readiness to make his companions more sober, moderate, and useful members of their community." *Political Philosophy of Benjamin Franklin*, 12. While proceeding to elaborate the similarities between the two, she concludes that Franklin departed decisively from the Socratic model (whether Xenophontic or Platonic) by throwing in his lot with theoretical modernity. She does not consider the possibility that his affinity for the Xenophontic Socrates in particular might have reflected his perception of certain intimations of modernity in him. It is

tions about Plato, Aristotle, and much of the Western legacy with a lively admiration of Xenophon. Indeed, in his youth he had read and admired the *Memorabilia*. Under its spell he had not only set about composing Socratic dialogues of his own but had modeled his own speech on that of [Xenophon's] Socrates. And the *Autobiography*, like his other writings, abounds in wisdom full of roguishness.

I will offer a possible explanation of the appeal of Xenophon's Socrates to Franklin and Nietzsche, even while both moderns shrank from the Platonic version. The question is what they saw as present in him that was lacking in Plato's Socrates and perhaps what they saw as lacking in him that was present in the latter. (It also mattered that it was not so much the Xenophontic as the Platonic Socrates who had inspired the subsequent "Socratic" tradition in philosophy, including Aristotle and his school and vast posthumous following.) For simplicity's sake I will reduce the modern dissatisfaction with this Socratic mainstream to just two points. Plato through his Socrates had preached two related doctrines (both also promoted by Aristotle) with which the moderns had decisively broken. The first of these was a life according to nature. Rather than impose their will on nature, human beings were to recognize its beneficence to them and to respond with appropriate gratitude. The second (and again related) doctrine was the primacy of the theoretical life over the practical one. This supported what we might call acquiescence in the natural status quo, for however generous or stingy she may be to human beings in other respects, nature supported the permanent possibility of theoretical contemplation of herself.

Let us briefly sketch the modern break with these teachings. Machiavelli, another great admirer of Xenophon who never so much as mentions Plato or Aristotle, had defined the modern imperative as the conquest of fortune. Conquest is of course a practical matter rather than a theoretical or contemplative one. Bacon, following Machiavelli, had restated (and

---

worth noting that at the time he read the *Memorabilia* Franklin was also reading Shaftesbury's *Characteristicks*, in which that great outlier of modernity emphatically praises Xenophon's Socrates at the expense of Plato's (noted and quoted by Weinberger, *Franklin Unmasked*, 18, 299n28). Lorraine Pangle's excellent later article, "Franklin and Socrates," in *Benjamin Franklin's Intellectual World*, ed. Paul E. Kerry and Matthew S. Holland (Lanham, MD: Rowman & Littlefield, 2012), 137–52, alludes to Xenophon but seems to rest primarily on the comparison of Franklin with the Platonic Socrates.

expanded) this project as the mastery of nature for the relief of man's estate. So too Descartes, Hobbes, Spinoza, Locke, Adam Smith, and the British Utilitarians—and in their different ways, Hegel, Marx, and Nietzsche—are all urging us ever forward on this project from which there has proved no retreat. Today even those most critical of modern progress (deep environmentalists, for example) have no choice but to look to technology to mitigate the effects of technology. Even in the defense of nature her conquest must proceed apace.

For the modern thinkers, then, not a life according to nature but rather one of self-reliance through emancipation from her, whether as individuals or as a species, has loomed as the goal of the human endeavor. Modern science, whether natural, political, or economic, has served under the banner of Bacon. Its practitioners have rejected Plato and Aristotle as obsolete stick-in-the-muds if not something worse.

But might there have been an alternative antiquity, one more friendly to, which is to say anticipatory of, the modern outlook on the world? Might this have been what Franklin and Nietzsche saw in Xenophon's Socrates? Begin with two surprising facts about Xenophon's presentation of Socrates. He never calls him a philosopher—the term appears in the *Memorabilia*, but only in the mouth of Socrates' adversary Antiphon (1.6.2). Accordingly Xenophon, unlike Plato and Aristotle, never openly promotes Socrates' way of life as philosophic or for that matter philosophy as a way of life. Rather, the *Memorabilia* praises the utility of Socrates' advice to mostly ordinary people facing practical dilemmas. This is not to say that Socrates' way of life is not a theme or even the theme of the *Memorabilia*. It is to say, however, that Xenophon presents that life very practically, an aspect of which is his focus on Socrates' practical advice to others.[3]

Here we will look at some of that advice, hoping to see in it what might have delighted Franklin and Nietzsche. Space being limited, we will consider just three passages of the *Memorabilia:* one chapter (2.7), and some sections drawn from two other chapters (1.1 and 3.9). These passages are of a piece with each other and with Xenophon's overall presentation of Socrates.

---

3. Including Xenophon himself (1.3.10–13).

Socratic Piety: Standing on One's Own Two Feet

The first chapter of the work offers Xenophon's defense of Socrates' piety.[4] It begins with an unconvincing attempt to assimilate Socrates' notorious *daimonion* or "divine voice" to the city's approved view of divination. As if to make matters worse (a recurrent feature of Xenophon's highly ironic defense of Socrates) he next launches into an exposition of Socrates' views on divination in general (1.1.6–9).

In these passages Socrates makes the following argument concerning the proper role of divination in human life and, by inference, of recourse to the divine in general. For so far as art or science or more generally human reason extends, divination is superfluous and even the gods disapprove when we resort to it. Socrates states this point as strongly as possible by declaring that it is not only *daimonān*, or "crazy," in a sense suggesting divine possession, with an obvious play on *daimonion*, but *athemis* or "contrary to divine law," to invoke the divine when human self-help is available.

Socrates thus casts maximal human self-reliance as not only the most effective course but the most pious one. The gods not only permit us to study the maximum enhancement of human power that as such would permit us to achieve maximum independence from theirs: they actually command us to do so. The gods are exacting: they accept no excuses for our failure to set our human house in order. For them to shield us from the consequences of human unpreparedness would therefore amount to rewarding us for our impiety. At most they help those who have done all they can to help themselves.

Socrates further insists that there are certain questions that it would be *daimonān* to put to the gods by seeking answers to them through divination. The only specific examples he offers are all versions of the same

---

4. On this chapter see now Thomas L. Pangle, "Humanity and Divinity in Xenophon's Defense of Socrates," in *In Search of Humanity: Essays in Honor of Clifford Orwin*, ed. Andrea Radasanu (Lanham, MD: Lexington Books, 2015), 115–28. My own readings of Xenophon are much indebted to Pangle's readings here, as they are to Leo Strauss, *Xenophon's Socrates* (Ithaca, NY: Cornell University Press, 1971). Pangle's magisterial *The Socratic Way of Life: Xenophon's "Memorabilia"* (Chicago: University of Chicago Press, 2018) appeared too late for me to consult it, but I have noted one of his readings in n. 6, below. These debts notwithstanding, all errors are my own.

question: whether to put the most artful human being in charge of each particular situation. This question is *daimonān* because the answer is so obvious, and it is so obvious because it follows from the general principle forbidding superfluous reliance on the gods. Piety dictates reliance on the most competent human beings to minimize your reliance on the gods. You don't ask the gods to confirm you in this policy—that would just call their attention to your impiety as newly redefined. You just go ahead and act on it. This is Rule One alike in human affairs and in managing our relations with the divine. It's why Ronna Burger gets to head Tulane's program in Judeo-Christian Studies.

Why the particular examples of the experienced teamster and helmsman as subjects of questions to pose, which to the gods would be *daimonān*? Can it be because both suggest confronting the unpredictable through reliance on experience? Both the best teamster and the best helmsman might encounter contingencies that would strain or exceed the capacities of their respective arts. They are no less exposed to such vagaries than a lesser artisan would be. Yet their superior experience offers them and their clients their best hope for success in the face of the unexpected. While all human power conferred by art is by definition limited, we would still be derelict in the eyes of the gods if we did not rely on those human beings who, because most artful, may be presumed most efficacious.

Art, while more reliably useful than the gods, can never entirely abolish the realm of chance or the gods. Yet the gods themselves do not just tolerate but demand of us that we leave no stone unturned in extending the frontiers of the power of art, thus progressively (and aggressively) reducing our dependence on the gods. Under these circumstances, to rest content with the present degree of one's tutelage to the gods would itself count as impiety. The genuinely pious man, while recognizing that he can never entirely free himself from dependency on the gods and fortune, and while never deluding himself that he has succeeded at doing so, will pride himself on ever striving to liberate himself as much as possible. Every one of us should emulate the expert helmsman, who through mastery of his art has subdued fortune as completely as is given to humankind.

True, Socrates looks primarily to greater experience in an art, rather than to superior inventiveness in it, to advance such improvement. In this respect he remains situated in the old world of artisanship rather than in our shiny new one of science and technology. Still, he thus looks to progress in the arts, not to any version of placation of the gods, to improve human life on earth.

So much for the limits of the gods' approval of divination or any other mode of recourse to them. The question remains whether divination, when tried, proves effective. Is faith in its effectiveness itself a demand of piety (as the city in its confrontation with Socrates clearly held)? Precisely in the context of his defense of Socrates' piety, it might have been advantageous for Xenophon to impute to Socrates the teaching that, as it is *daimonān* to seek for divine guidance in matters that remain within the province of man, so it is to deny that the gods offer guidance in matters beyond it. His Socrates says no such thing. This omission cannot be accidental: Xenophon's Socrates is no more accident-prone than Plato's. And if not accidental, it is not incidental. It implies that we may without impiety reject the notion of providential deities whose will is accessible through divination.

Yet is there not evidence that Socrates himself both subscribed to divination and practiced it? That evidence is most uncertain. Yes, he recommended to certain of his interlocutors who wished to know what was humanly unknowable that they seek guidance from an oracle or some other form of divination. Xenophon offers, however, no report of their success at so doing, nor does he present Socrates as recommending this course to those closest to him, his associates. Not surprisingly, then, neither does he suggest that Socrates himself ever pursued it. He goes no further than to quote him as saying that "the gods give signs to those toward whom they are gracious" (1.1.9). Evidently the gods are gracious to some but not to all human beings. How then to know whether a given instance of divination is a genuine communication from a god rather than a merely human imposition on human credulity? How to know whether the god supposedly responsible for an alleged sign is in fact gracious to the party seeking the sign, whether it be an individual or (as more commonly) a *polis*? In Shakespeare's *Henry IV, Part Two*, 3.1, the Welsh chieftain Owen Glendower, who prides himself on his occult powers, makes a claim parallel to that of Hellenic diviners: "I can call spirits from the vasty deep." To which Hotspur replies (insolently and, given that Glendower is a crucial ally, imprudently): "So can I; so can any man. But will they come when

112

you do call for them?" Socrates stops well short of affirming that the gods are at the beck and call of the diviners. Do these last lure us down the wrong path, encouraging us to rely on an illusion of divine aid rather than developing our natural powers? It would be no dishonor to the gods to maintain that they require us to get by without them.

At this point someone will likely raise the question of Socrates' afore-mentioned *daimonion*. Even or precisely if it resists assimilation to the city's notion of divination, are we not to grant it as a case of genuine communication from the divine? We won't have time in this short essay to explore the riddle of the *daimonion*. The question is whether it is anything more than an aspect of Socrates' popular presentation of that greater riddle which is his way of life. Precisely if divination is, as suggested in our passage, a crutch for human beings unable or unwilling to stand on their own two feet—which is to say, for the vast majority of human beings, including most of his own associates—Socrates might not wish to leave the public diviners a monopoly of it. The necessities of his situation would compel him to beat them at their own game.

From Aristocracy to the Money Economy:
Socrates' Enlightenment of Aristarchus

We turn now to Socrates' encounter with one Aristarchus in *Memorabilia* 2.7. Xenophon begins this chapter by announcing the transition to a new subject that will prove to occupy the remaining four chapters of book 2: Socrates' advice to his friends. He suggests two distinct problems that Socrates sought to address among his friends: ignorance, which he sought to cure by advice; and want, which he sought to relieve by explaining how they could help one another. The two categories are not exclusive, because the failure of the friends to see their way to cooperation in matters of want could itself be seen as a case of ignorance.

Chapter 7 forms a pair with chapter 8: both concern friends in need, indeed dire need. As emerges from the text, these were hard times for Athens. Having lost the war, she lost her empire as well, including her citizens' private holdings in the former subject cities. She endured regime change and restoration, both accompanied by violence and expulsions.

None of this will have affected Socrates' manner of living. (We recall that according to Xenophon's *Apology* Socrates had remained unruffled even by the Lacedaemonian siege that drove other Athenians to desperation.) Aristarchus, however, has been pushed to the brink, and unlike Socrates, is very worried about his future. Once prosperous, he is so no longer. Numerous female relatives have sought refuge with him—his household now numbers fourteen in all—and he has neither the resources to sustain them nor even (money being so tight) much hope of borrowing in order to do so. It deeply distresses him that he may fail in his fundamental aristocratic/patriarchal obligations. While he, like many characters in the work, is otherwise known to us, it is worth noting that his name is deeply, even perfectly aristocratic: "rule of the best" or "best ruler."

It has evidently not occurred to Aristarchus that he could put the women crowding his house to work. (He must not have not read Plato's *Republic,* where the supposedly progressive introduction of the same way of life for men and women follows from the observation that women no more than female dogs should be permitted to dodge their fair share of work.) Can it be that on the present occasion Socrates is mindful of the former one? In any case, just as putting all her women to work would benefit the city in speech, so Aristarchus' harnessing of the efforts of his would benefit them as well as himself. Yet this won't happen unless he casts off certain class prejudices.

As so often, Socrates' argument is amusing. He begins by noting that even in these difficult times and with a large family to feed, the baseborn Ceramon has succeeded just swimmingly. Why does Aristarchus suppose that is? Because, he replies, Ceramon's house is full of slaves, mine of gentlefolk. And which are better, asks Socrates, slaves or gentlefolk? The latter, Aristarchus predictably answers. Then why should he, surrounded by gentlefolk, fare so much worse than Ceramon amidst his slaves? Because, replies Aristarchus, those slaves were educated as artisans, while his own dependents were educated as free.

Except that even as free women they had been educated in the arts, those arts practiced by free women. As Socrates proceeds to observe, the practice of these arts, when commercialized as it has been by certain men, can be quite lucrative. Great fortunes have been made from the humble groat, as they have from baked loaves, to say nothing of cloth and the garments made from it. Why should not Aristarchus and his dependent females set out to profit from the practice of these arts just as these baseborn males have done? Not surprisingly, not one of the artisan entrepreneurs whom Socrates names is known to us from any other source. It is as if he seeks to create a whole new role model: the self-made man risen from need to prosperity through the commercial exploitation of an art so far beneath the notice of gentlemen as to be consigned by their class entirely to its women.

Aristarchus still doesn't get it. Of course, he replies, if he had slaves to employ, like all these merchants and manufacturers, he would emulate them. But his household is made up of "free people" who are his relations to boot.

To which Socrates responds with a blast that anticipates Locke, Montesquieu, and Adam Smith, those great modern enemies of aristocratic idleness. He uncannily foreshadows them by updating the notion of a free man to include useful activity and therefore productive labor. This requires some adjustment of the notion of virtue, and Socrates proceeds to effect it. Through a long series of rhetorical questions, he relegates idleness, aristocratic and otherwise, to the dustbin of history (or at least of Aristarchus' history).

Socrates next offers a penetrating critique of Aristarchus' family situation, encumbered as he is by all these idle women. He contends that compelling them to labor will greatly improve matters. Aristocracy perpetuates dependency, and dependency necessarily breeds mutual mistrust and resentment. In vain will the patron look for gratitude; in vain the client for respect. To depend and to be depended upon are equally recipes for unhappiness. Here Socrates anticipates Rousseau's critique of personal dependency: "for those who call themselves masters are no less slaves for that."

Socrates concedes the aristocratic point that death would be preferable to the women's submitting to disgrace. He can point out, however, and even without recourse to his earlier argument for the dignity of labor as such, that traditional female pursuits had never incurred dishonor, not even among aristocratic women. (Consider that exemplary lady Penelope.) The unspoken difficulty is that, had ladies been compelled to practice these arts commercially (as here), it would have been deemed disgraceful.[5]

---

5. Abram Shulsky has noted that Aristarchus swears three times by Zeus (the only character in the work to do so) to express his incredulity at Socrates' suggestions. Abram N.

Finally, at section 11, Aristarchus has gotten the message, and he immediately sets out to implement his Socratic business plan. The new enterprise proves a roaring success. The only complication is that the women protest that Aristarchus himself is not at work as they are. They disclose themselves, however good-naturedly, as proto-Marxists. They presume that it is only their labor that has created the value of the enterprise, which the idle Aristarchus unjustly confiscates.

In response, the always helpful Socrates provides Aristarchus with an entrepreneurial/managerial rationale for his taking his share of the profits. He does so with typically Socratic ingenuousness, offering a fable about sheep who complain about the superior rewards and honors lavished on their sheepdog. This fable justifies Aristarchus in receiving not merely a share of the common proceeds but the largest share. Also typically for Socrates, this ingenuousness is suspect, for Aristarchus is parallel not to the sheepdog but to the shepherd, whose benevolence toward the sheep is ambiguous.[6]

Consider also that in the first sentence of this chapter, Xenophon suggests that Socrates addressed the problem of need among his friends by encouraging them to cooperate with each other. We might have supposed from this that Socrates was a founding saint of socialism, who promoted cooperation rather than competition. But how has Socrates in fact addressed this very first concrete situation that Xenophon presents to us, without reference to other friends of his or to friendly cooperation of any kind, unless we are to suppose this among the women? He enjoins on Aristarchus entrepreneurship, pure and simple, guided only by considerations of the market. The struggling aristocratic household, the prisoner of its fixed assets, must become a business, exploiting its hitherto untapped reserves of labor. Its women, formerly its burden, emerge as its ongoing resource. Rather than Aristarchus supporting them, their labor will now support him. The patriarchal family is dead; long live the family firm.

Shulsky, "An Introduction to the *Ways and Means*," in *Xenophon*, "*The Shorter Writings*," ed. Gregory A. McBrayer (Ithaca, NY: Cornell University Press, 2018), 189–210.

6. For the possible "theological" implications of Socrates' rendering of this originally Aesopian fable, see Thomas L. Pangle, *Socratic Way of Life*, 106–7.

Similarly the virtues demanded of Aristarchus are no longer aristocratic virtues. Rather they are those of the market: those required for efficient production so as to sell at competitive prices. He must exploit the freedom the market offers by respecting the discipline it imposes.[7] Nor is this market in any sense a cooperative of friends, unless we redefine friendship as mutuality of need, and cooperation as the nexus of supply and demand.

Aristarchus' former stodgily aristocratic notion of *eleutheria* or the virtue worthy of a free man ("liberality" in its original sense) gives way to a new, more relaxed one that can only be described as protoliberal. Where the old understanding deprecated participation in the market, the newer one endorses it. And if such participation is in principle good, then so is economic expansion. Let a thousand Aristarchuses bloom, and let 13,000 kinswomen be freed to profit from their handicrafts. If, again, this reminds you (as it does me) less of Plato or Aristotle than of Locke or Smith, you will understand why I might suppose that it would have appealed to Franklin.

It's true, of course, that Xenophon no more than Plato presents a Socrates who lives according to these suggestions of his to Aristarchus. His Socrates too is notoriously impecunious and notoriously unashamed of it (cf. especially Xenophon, *Apology of Socrates to the Jury* 18). In the *Memorabilia* itself he has earlier delivered a critique of devoting one's life to accumulating wealth. In so doing he appears predictably "Socratic," thus justifying Lorraine Pangle's assimilation of his position to that of the Platonic Socrates.[8]

Yet precisely insofar as this was a matter in which the aristocratic prejudice against commerce supported the philosophic critique of it, we might have expected Socrates to defer to it here. Instead he subjects that prejudice to a withering critique, and with the intention of leading Aristarchus not to a life of philosophy but precisely to one of commerce. However indifferent to gain himself, he is only too willing to encourage its pursuit as tending to the good of all.

---

7. Compare the discussion of the market in Pierre Manent, *"Préface: Situation du libéralisme,"* in *Les libéraux*, ed. Manent, 2 vols. (Paris: Hachette Pluriel, 1986), 1:7–40.

8. Lorraine Pangle, *Political Philosophy of Franklin*, 26; cf. 15.

Eupraxia and Eutychia

We'll draw our final examples from *Memorabilia* 3.9. This might be the work's most challenging chapter. It reads as if someone had set out to compress Aristotle's *Ethics* into three pages.

What is the theme of this chapter? Apparently one by this point familiar to readers of the *Memorabilia*: the relation of knowledge to virtue. Yet we here encounter a variation on the theme: now the question is rather the relation between knowledge or virtue, on the one hand, and power or success, on the other.

We'll consider just two sections of the chapter, 14 and 15. Section 14 raises the question of the relation between *eupraxia* and *eutychia*. Both terms signify success, but the etymological contrast between the two is striking. *Tychē* ("chance") is by definition that which befalls you, independently of any action on your part. *Praxis,* by contrast, signifies action. In ordinary usage *eupraxia* was ambiguous, sometimes meaning "faring well" (a sense that Socrates has himself employed in section 8 of this chapter) and sometimes "acting well." Socrates' argument in this section responds to this ambiguity. If someone has fared well, and if his faring well has resulted from his acting well, i.e., from the practice of an art (i.e., of an activity informed by knowledge) then his is a case of *eupraxia*. If he has fared well for some other reason, his case is one of [mere] *eutychia*.

Just what is going on here? Socrates exploits the availability of two terms for success, of which one implies no more than a favorable outcome and the other may imply something more. He uses them to distinguish between two kinds of success. One kind is praiseworthy, the other not. He cannot plausibly claim that only those who merit success achieve it. Nor does he go so far as to claim that the proper practice of an art qualifies as *eupraxia* even where the outcome is disadvantageous. He does not attempt to purge *eupraxia* of its sense of "faring well" in favor of that of "acting well." He does insist, however, that no success qualifies as *eupraxia* unless it follows from the practice of an art. Only that success is to be esteemed which is earned. While Socrates can't deny that some people succeed only due to chance, he wants to deprive such success of its lustre. Something like self-madeness in the modern sense of that term emerges as the new core of virtue. While Socrates speaks here not of *eudaimonia* but only of *eupraxia*, the tendency of his argument is to replace the former with the latter. As in his conversation with Aristarchus, he emphatically endorses honest labor.

Dearness to the Gods

The final section I'll discuss is that immediately following: 3.9.15. It raises the question of whom to deem dear to the gods. Usually those who enjoy worldly prosperity—wealth, health, offspring, honor—are so regarded. And perhaps those who succeed by fortune are so regarded rather more than those who succeed by virtue. If the gods are presumed to intervene in the world on behalf of their favorites to avail them when their own means are insufficient, might we not pronounce the winner of the Mega-lottery dearest to the gods? After all, his victory is arbitrary, inexplicable, and incomprehensible: why him rather than another of the 130,000,000 entrants? Of the man of *eupraxia*, however, who owes his success to his own efforts and whose success is proportionally modest, why single him out as dear to the gods? There is, after all, no evidence that they have intervened on his behalf or otherwise signified their approval.

Socrates turns this popular view on its head. It is in fact all (and only) those who practice *eupraxia* within their walks of life, how much or little they have to show for it, who must be deemed dear to the gods. Here the sense of *eupraxia* evoked is clearly that of right practice rather than successful practice.

Nor however is there any suggestion here that the gods intervene on behalf of those dear to them. Here too Socrates inverts the popular view. Dearness to the gods is what universities call a status-only appointment: it confers no emolument. It resembles the Queen's Award to Industry. A British firm that succeeds at exporting its products basks in the Queen's approval, but her approval does not relieve it of maintaining its competitiveness. Rather that approval remains contingent on its continued success at so doing. So it is with dearness to the gods. The gods smile on a world in which we are all artisans striving to our utmost, and for that very reason they offer us nothing tangible beyond what we are capable of obtaining on our own. We must learn to be satisfied with our dearness to them.

As must be clear by now, my suggestion is that Xenophon's Socrates surprisingly anticipates the moderns in the emphasis he places on self-reliance understood much as the moderns do. I wouldn't claim this as the whole story about his Socrates,[9] but I do see it as an important part of it—which may well explain at least in part his attractiveness to Franklin and Nietzsche.

A Concluding Question

To conclude I'd like to return briefly from Franklin's sly appreciation of Xenophon's Socrates to Nietzsche's more poetic one. "In him converge the roads of the most different philosophic modes of life, which are in truth the modes of the different temperaments, crystallized by reason and habit and all ultimately directed towards the delight in life and in self." "The delight in life and self" (*die Freude am Leben und am eignen Selbst*): this formulation suggests something still more modern than the promotion of self-reliance: the turn to subjectivity. Conceptually, the two are related: consider the role of subjectivity in so early a modern thinker as Montaigne. Yet it is only with Rousseau that subjectivity, having dethroned the Cartesian ego, shines forth as itself the core of self-reliance. Only he stands alone who mans a fortress of sentiment sprung from his unique blend of sensibility and history and accessible only to himself. Music to the ears of Nietzsche, perhaps, but are we really to ascribe it to Socrates, whether in Xenophon's or any other ancient version? A question for Ronna.

---

9. Compare Christopher Nadon, "Xenophon and the Conquest of Nature," in *Mastery of Nature: Promises and Prospects*, ed. Svetozar Y. Minkov and Bernhardt L. Trout (Philadelphia: University of Pennsylvania Press, 2017), 120: "The city must both exploit and respect nature. It must both encourage and restrain industry, the human capacity to take matters into our own hands and care for ourselves." Nadon's essay is an exploration of this ambiguity and its implications. In that sense it begins where my discussion leaves off.

7

A Shrine to the Graces: Justice and Tragedy in Book 5 of Aristotle's *Nicomachean Ethics*

Mary P. Nichols

Aeschylus' *Oresteia* is set in a world of violence, in which the house of Atreus suffers a cycle of horrible crime and brutal retribution. Only when Athena sets up a court of justice to hear the case of Orestes' matricide does the cycle seem to end. Political justice replaces family vengeance (*Eum.* 681–95). Aeschylus' tragedy, however, does not announce the end of tragedy in the city (*polis*), even if it shows the potential for political life to moderate tragic suffering. When the court delivers a tie vote, Athena breaks the tie in favor of Orestes. Political institutions seem to require divine interventions for their institution and success. Aristotle's treatment of justice in book 5 of the *Nicomachean Ethics* offers other ways in which politics can hold back tragic conflict. Without relying on divine interventions in political life, Aristotle shows that political life can be guided by a reciprocity that holds the city together, by a natural justice that supports shared governance, and by equity, which corrects the universality of law in particular cases.

For many years Ronna's work has enlightened and challenged my understanding of Plato and Aristotle and of the fundamental questions of philosophy. Her friendship has enriched my life as much as her thoughts have stimulated my own. I shall always be grateful.

Aristotle's argument also addresses Plato, whose Athenian Stranger in the *Laws* founds a regime that he insists is "the truest tragedy" and understands the tragic poets as his rivals (*Laws* 817b1–d8). So too in Plato's *Republic*, Socrates suggests that the best regime he founds is a tragedy when he calls upon the Muses to assist his story of its decline in "high tragic talk" (*Rep.* 545e1). When its citizens are no longer willing to do what is best for the city, but choose instead to compete for honors and wealth, the "noble city" (*kallipolis*) falls to faction and conflict (547b2–c4; 527c2). The conflict between one's own good and the common good that spurs Socrates' description of this city, or between the advantageous and the noble, cannot be held in check over time. Complementing his tragic presentation of political life, Socrates locates justice in the proper ordering of the soul rather than in the relations and interactions of human beings within political communities.[1] Aristotle, in contrast, insists on the latter (cf. *Rep.* 443c9–444a2 with *NE* 1129b32 and 1138b4–13). Indeed, Aristotle indicates that his treatment of justice is a response to Plato's when he observes that "justice alone of the virtues is held to be another's good," converting Thrasymachus' criticism of justice in the *Republic* into praise (1129b26–34 and 1138b4–13; cf. *Rep.* 343c1–5).[2]

In the first section of this essay, I explore the ways in which justice is manifest in the laws of political communities, both as the lawful, and in the distribution of goods such as honors and property and in the correction of violations. While acknowledging the necessity of law, Aristotle also indicates that the law is not sufficient for avoiding conflict. A range of difficulties appear, including controversy over the ways in which goods are

1. Kraut argues that Aristotle's analysis of justice in bk. 5 is an implicit criticism of Plato's approach in the *Republic*, especially its definition of justice as the proper order in the soul, and the "idealistic aloofness" from political life that this understanding of justice permits. Richard Kraut, *Aristotle: Political Philosophy* (Oxford: Oxford University Press, 2002), 100, 121–22, 135, 169–74.

2. Citations in parentheses, unless otherwise noted, are from *Aristotelis "Ethica Nicomachea,"* ed. I. Bywater (1890; repr., Oxford: Clarendon Press, 1962). For references to Plato, see *Platonis Opera*, ed. Johannes Burnet, 5 vols. (Oxford: Oxford University Press, 1900–1907). Translations are my own, but I have consulted throughout the excellent *Aristotle's "Nicomachean Ethics,"* trans. and ed. Robert C. Bartlett and Susan D. Collins (Chicago: University of Chicago Press, 2012). For other classical texts, I have relied primarily on the Loeb Classical Library editions (Harvard University Press).

distributed, the inadequate compensation awarded to the injured, and more generally, the dependence of law on particular human beings to formulate and apply it.

By expanding his discussion to other forms of justice that supplement or even complete the law, Aristotle takes a step beyond Aeschylus toward minimizing tragic conflict. I treat these in the remaining sections of this essay. I first address justice as reciprocity, which Aristotle supports by divine models of both justice and grace that discourage vice and support virtue, appealing to the judgments of Rhadamanthus and the encouragement of the Graces. I then examine Aristotle's treatment of the natural justice manifest in shared ruling, which good law supports. In the third place, I turn to equity, which is a kind of justice that modifies and even corrects the law as circumstances demand. In order to make a case for equity, Aristotle returns to the question of when actions are voluntary and when not, and argues for the justice, and even the grace, of forgiveness. Thus, by making room for equity, looking to divine models for reciprocity, and embodying natural justice in political forms, political communities can moderate tragedy. Finally, I conclude with brief reflections on suicide—the last topic Aristotle brings up in book 5—and how the law against suicide that he implies belongs to all cities affirms the goodness of life that his politics supports.

Justice and the Law

Aristotle begins book 5 by reminding the reader of the method and the goal of the inquiry—to examine justice and injustice, what sort of actions they happen to involve, what sort of mean this virtue is, and between what extremes it is a mean. Although Aristotle claims that he will use the "same method of inquiry" that he has been following (1129a5–6), his treatment of justice does not follow this pattern. Unlike the extremes of the other virtues, those of justice share the same name, injustice. The virtue is not easily located as a mean between extremes when its extremes are both described by its negation. Anomalies abound.[3] By reminding us of the

---

3. Burger points out the difficulties with the various ways in which Aristotle appears—and fails—to present justice as a mean between extremes. Ronna Burger, *Aristotle's Dialogue with Socrates: On Aristotle's "Nicomachean Ethics"* (Chicago: University of Chicago Press, 2008), 92, 253n46. Kraut acknowledges justice in Aristotle's account

general rule he has been following in defining each of the virtues, from which he then proceeds to deviate, Aristotle prepares us for his discussion of justice understood as lawfulness, and the limits of that understanding. His treatment of justice thus can serve as a model for the justice he later calls equity, which deviates from the law when required by particular cases (1138a24). In both Aristotle's treatment of justice and in equity as he describes it, justice requires looking beyond the rule that virtue is a mean, even if there is ample precedent in Aristotle's "rule" concerning ethical virtue itself—that it is a mean between excess and deficiency not in a mathematical sense but in relation to us (1106a26–b4).[4]

Moreover, unlike the other virtues, justice has two senses. In the first sense, justice is the lawful, for law commands the deeds of every virtue and forbids those of every vice (1129a32–b1, 1130b20–24). Aristotle of course does not infer that the just person is obedient to the law neither more nor less than he should be, as prudence or right reason dictates (see 1106b21–24, 1107a1). He never explicitly applies the mean to a citizen's obeying the law. Nevertheless, he observes, almost in passing, that a good man and a good citizen may not always be the same (1130b29). At the end of the first book of the *Ethics*, Aristotle claims that the statesman must contemplate the soul, for he wishes to make the citizens good and obedient to the laws (1102a9–10). But making citizens obedient to the laws—and hence good citizens—is not the same as making citizens good, no more than obeying a law, however reasonable the law may be, is the same as obeying the rational part of one's soul (1102b26). In the latter case, obeying and commanding belong to the same soul.[5] The statesman who contemplates the soul and its parts as Aristotle presents them at the end of

---

does not conform, like other virtues, with his teaching about the mean. He claims that Aristotle is not "troubled by this." *Aristotle: Political Philosophy*, 98–99.

4. Aristotle even says that ethical virtue "is not one and the same for all" (1106a32–33).

5. In explaining that there is something in the soul that resists reason, Aristotle gives the example of paralyzed limbs of the body that move in their own way. He says "perhaps it must be held (*nomisteon*) that there is something in the soul that no less [than a paralyzed limb] resists reason" (1102b23–25). That is, we must "hold it as a law" (*nomos*). As is often the case, Aristotle's precise use of words captures a range of meanings, or the imprecision of words. *Nomizein*, "to suppose" or "to hold," means literally to hold or to enact as law or convention for ourselves. Statesmen, in other words, must understand the citizen's capacity for self-legislation.

book 1 would see this. His wish to make the citizens both good and obedient to the laws is a wish that his work involved both. Perhaps it is even a wish that the distinction could be overcome, and hence that his own work would be unnecessary. If citizens were good men, they could act as laws for themselves. In book 3, Aristotle distinguishes wish from deliberation and choice: we deliberate about and make choices about what is in our power, while we might wish for the impossible (1111b20–26).

In the second sense, justice is part of virtue, a part of what the law commands, when it aims at the "equal" or the "fair," the distribution of what is due. In this sense of justice as well, the mean does not easily apply. The unjust person "grasps for more" (*pleonektēs*) (1129a33), and the just one seeks what is his due, but Aristotle does not present grasping for less as a vice on the side of the deficiency. To be sure, the unjust person, who takes more of the good things for himself, would also take less of the bad, but doing the latter means grasping more of the good (1129b6–10). So too when Aristotle describes doing justice as a mean between doing injustice and suffering it (1133b30–32), he does not consider the latter a vice for which one is responsible. He does not blame the victim. Considering "the good of another," as justice requires us to do, apparently, takes precedence over finding the mean in one's own passions and actions.

Aristotle brings up another question about justice at the outset, one that also arises in the *Republic*: if a just person is good at guarding or keeping safe, as Polemarchus says, does it not follow that he is also good at stealing, just as a doctor who is good at guarding against a disease is also good at producing it (333e3–334b6)? Aristotle immediately insists that the just person is not like a doctor, but rather like a healthy person. "What holds for skills and capacities does not hold for dispositions": the former involve opposites, while the latter do not. As a consequence of health, one does only healthy things (1129a12–16). The just person does just deeds; in other words, he is not a "clever thief" (*Rep.* 334a5).

Aristotle's clear answer to the discussion in the *Republic*, however, leaves open several questions applicable to his own discussion of justice. The just person is "lawful," while the unjust is a lawbreaker (1129b11). But who lays down the law (see *Ap.* 24e1–2)? Aristotle insists that justice is a disposition and not a skill or capacity, but he immediately refers to "the legislative art" (*nomothetikē*), which "defines the lawful" (1129b13).

Even if justice is a disposition for the good citizen rather than an art or skill, does the lawgiver have a skill that is analogous to the doctor's? Can he be a good lawgiver without such skill? But if he does have such a skill, can we trust him? Aristotle underlines these difficulties when he proceeds to point out that laws aim at the common advantage "either for all persons, or for the best or for those who have authority, whether on the basis of their virtue or on the basis of some other such thing" (1129b14–17). Laws command virtuous actions and forbid vicious ones, "correctly when correctly laid down, but worse when laid down haphazardly" (1129b24–25). Laws are necessary and good, but they are only more or less good, depending on the lawgiver. That the laws coincide with justice, and the just with those who obey them, is only Aristotle's first word in his discussion.[6] Justice and injustice, however, "are spoken of in many ways" (1128b8, 1129a33).

Turning to the particular virtue of justice that the law commands, Aristotle observes that the law pursues the equal (*ison*) or the fair through a distribution of goods such as honors and wealth or any of those things divisible among those who share in the regime—in proportion to the worth of the individuals to whom they are distributed (1130b30–35). This is a formula for equality, in which what one receives is equal to what one deserves. As Aristotle explains, the proportion in distributive justice is one that mathematicians called "geometric," in that it involves a ratio between the persons and things involved (1131a30–b15). Corrective justice, in turn, restores the balance when the proportion established by the law is violated. In such a case, corrective justice takes from the one who has taken from another and returns it to the one from whom he took it (1132a9–19).

Distributive and corrective justice, like justice understood as the lawful, depend on the regime and its laws. Because the equality involved in distributive justice is proportionate to worth, "fights and denunciations

---

6. Burger argues that "the movement of the argument in the course of Book V can be understood precisely as an effort to put into question" the claim "that obedience to the laws of one's community, whatever they are, is sufficient to make one just." *Aristotle's Dialogue with Socrates*, 96. See also Delba Winthrop, "Aristotle and Theories of Justice," *American Political Science Review* 72, no. 4 (1978): 1201–16; and Aristide Tessitore, *Reading Aristotle's "Ethics": Virtue, Rhetoric, and Political Philosophy* (Albany: State University of New York Press, 1996), 38.

arise," as when those who are equal are distributed unequal things, or those who are unequal have been distributed equal ones. Disagreements arise because all do not mean the same thing by "worth." Indeed, such disagreements, Aristotle warns, account for the differences in regimes: democrats say that all who are free and not slaves are equally worthy; oligarchs would measure worth by wealth; others by good birth; and aristocrats by virtue (1131a23–29). Mathematics does not address these fundamental political problems, and anyone who has such an expectation would expect more precision than the subject warrants, failing to distinguish, for example, between mathematics and questions of the just, noble, and good (see 1094b23–27). This is the very observation with which Aristotle introduced his own inquiry in the *Ethics* in book 1. When Aristotle proceeds to offer mathematical formulations as determinations of justice, he is therefore aware of their inadequacy, or rather of their utility for understanding justice only "up to a point"—specifically, up to the point that one accepts the underlying presuppositions of worth in one's regime.[7]

Just as we can ask whether justice as the "lawful" means that the just person is the one who makes or the one who obeys the laws, we can ask whether the just person is the one who makes the distribution or the one who receives his just portion.[8] Or is he both? Aristotle's observation that

---

7. As Winthrop observes, "No significant political controversy would be resolved by the application of the principle of distributive justice as stated. It is too general, and it abstracts from the hardest political problem." "Aristotle and Theories of Justice," 1204. Similarly, Mathie points out that the distributive justice that Aristotle describes is "neutral" toward "the criteria of merit belonging to the various regimes" and that its operation presupposes that the question of who should rule has already been settled. William Mathie, "Political and Distributive Justice in the Political Science of Aristotle," *Review of Politics* 49, no. 1 (Winter 1987): 64–66. Winthrop argues that the difficulties with justice that Aristotle presents point to the need to move beyond theories of justice to friendship, as he explores it later in the *Ethics* (1201–2, 1212–15). While I agree with her analysis that "the problems that arise in politics can be solved only in the spirit of friendship, trust and goodwill, not in the spirit of punitive justice or even impartiality" (1212), my analysis (i.e., of reciprocity, political justice, and equity) attempts to show that these characteristics, which are more fully developed in friendship, can arise in political life itself.

8. In his discussion of distributive justice, Aristotle more or less avoids the question of who distributes by referring to the distribution in the passive voice (1131a24; see also 1131b5).

the just accords with the proportion, whereas the unjust is more or less than the proportion (1131b16–17) does not answer the question. If the just person practices distributive justice, distributing the goods of the community in accordance with worth, the question of his possessing a skill or knowledge—and if so, why he should be trusted—applies here as well. If the just person is accorded honors or wealth according to his deserts, he is the recipient of justice rather than the doer of just deeds. Inasmuch as justice is the last of the ethical virtues Aristotle lists in his outline in book 2, Aristotle's treatment of the ethical virtues would conclude with a virtue that resides in receiving (or being acted upon) rather than in acting, and therefore would not fit Aristotle's definition of happiness as an activity of virtue (1098a16–17; see also 1095b32–1096a1). Or if the just person distributes both to others and to himself, he acts as judge in his own case. When Aristotle later suggests that the just person includes himself in his distributions (1134a3–6), he almost immediately indicates the danger of tyranny that arises from someone's distributing to himself (1134a30–b1; see also *Pol.* 1280a15–16).

Leaving these issues unresolved, Aristotle turns to a second form of justice as the equal or fair, which comes into play when laws are violated. Then the judge, Aristotle says, takes from the perpetrator what he gains from his crime and returns it to the victim from whom he has taken it (1132a9–19). Aristotle suggests the inadequacy of corrective justice by his deceptively simple mathematical language, as if subtracting and adding could restore what existed before the "exchange." His examples of gains and losses, however, include not only cheating in business deals, but also theft, adultery, poisoning, pandering, stealing slaves, abduction or rape, assault, maiming, and murder (1113a1–9). His inclusion of rape or abduction reminds us of the Trojan War and Paris' abduction of Helen (see Hdt. 1.3.1). Would the Greeks have been satisfied merely by the return of Helen? And could she have been restored in the same condition as before the abduction? Moreover, Aristotle includes murder among the examples of unjust actions. Would even the execution of the murderer restore the balance? A life for a life, to be sure, might be just, but it could hardly be said (as Aristotle does) that corrective justice deprives the unjust of gain and restores the loss so that one who has suffered injustice "has [no] less than he had at the beginning" (1132b13–16; see also 1132b19–20).

In all these ways, Aristotle leads us to the inadequacy of law for securing an end of violent conflict, to say nothing of cultivating good human beings. The distributions of the community's goods can be—and are—contested, and Aristotle's list of crimes, some of them violent, indicate the limits of the law in controlling crime and in providing satisfactory corrections when it occurs. If Aristotle's account of justice stopped here, he would have an insufficient answer to tragic conflict, and would echo Plato's suggestion that political life is tragic. But Aristotle does not stop here. In the remaining parts of book 5, Aristotle proposes three things that, I argue, minimize the tragic character of human and political life: reciprocity, natural justice, and equity. I discuss each in turn.

Reciprocity

"Reciprocity" (*antipeponthos*) means literally "suffering in turn." It occurs when one suffers what he has inflicted on another. As Aristotle says, "People seek to reciprocate harm for harm—if they do not, that is held to be slavish" (1132b34–1133a1). Unlike the case with corrective justice, there is no judge to "correct" the injustice; the one wronged takes it upon himself to do so. If leaving a crime against oneself unpunished is slavish, however, would it not also be slavish to leave its punishment up to the law, or up to the judge, even one whom Aristotle described as "wishing to be justice ensouled" (1132a21–22)? Aristotle soon mentions rulers in his discussion of reciprocity: if a ruler strikes another, he ought not be struck in turn, or if someone strikes a ruler, he should not only be struck but punished (1132b28–30). Aristotle's example is strange, if only because striking and being struck are not the most obvious interactions we would wish to attribute to ruler and ruled. On the other hand, this example may be the most appropriate for indicating the problem to which he is calling attention, for those who inflict harm in return because not doing so is slavish are likely also to resist being ruled by another. Homer's Achilles serves as a famous example.

Moreover, it is not only the one wronged who seeks reciprocity, for Aristotle observes that people "wish" justice as reciprocity to mean "the justice of Rhadamanthus" (1132b25–27). Rhadamanthus was a mythical judge in the Underworld, one of the judges that Socrates claims to look forward to meeting after his death, one who is "truly a judge" rather than those who merely claim to be judges in this life (*Ap.* 41a1–2). In Plato's

Gorgias, Socrates' myth about the afterlife indicates what people might wish from the justice of Rhadamanthus. Before the reign of Zeus, as Socrates tells the tale, human judges judged the living on the day they were to die. Their judging was done badly. They were hindered from seeing clearly since their bodies obstructed their souls' visions, while the souls of those whom they judged were hidden by beautiful bodies, ancestry, and wealth. For the sake of justice, Socrates recounts, Zeus changed the practice, appointing three of his sons, one of whom was Rhadamanthus, to judge souls when they arrive in Hades, visible because stripped of their bodies (*Gorg.* 523a3–524a8). Needless to say, their insight into souls is shared neither by the judge who restores losses in Aristotle's account of corrective justice nor by the one who inflicts suffering on the one who harmed him. It is only the god who can claim to be "justice ensouled," although human beings "wish" their justice were that of Rhadamanthus.[9]

Instead of dwelling on the ways in which harm for harm falls short of the justice we might wish, and its correction after death, Aristotle turns to the workings of reciprocity in an exchange of goods (1132a1–2). He gives the example of the exchange of goods and services between those who possess different arts or skills like doctors and farmers, housebuilders and shoemakers. Exchange makes it possible to acquire the diversity of goods necessary to life, and even an abundance that one can share with others, as Aristotle's example of the exchange of a house for quite a few shoes suggests (1133a7–25). His example also makes clear the need for a medium of exchange, or "money," that makes the exchange of products of different worth possible. Aristotle emphasizes that money (*nomisma*) exists by convention or law (*nomos*) rather than by nature and is therefore "up to us" (1133a28–31), using the same expression that he uses for voluntary actions. Whatever we use for the medium of exchange, that there is some such medium established by law or convention makes possible the exchange within cities essential to the variety and bounty conducive to

---

9. Socrates' tale casts doubt even on the justice of Rhadamanthus, when he explains that when two of the judges, Rhadamanthus and Aeacus, disagree, they can be overruled by the third judge, Minos (*Gorg.* 524a5–7). Thus when he mentions Rhadamanthus in the Apology, he imagines meeting him along with others, and "examining and investigating those there, as [he] did here, to find out who among them is wise, and who believes he is when he is not" (*Ap.* 41b5–7).

both living and living well. The need for a variety of goods that different human beings share and to which they contribute in different ways, Aristotle says, leads to the mutual giving (*metadosis*) that "holds the city together" (1132b33–34).

Aristotle speaks more broadly, although more briefly, of the mutual exchange of goods that holds the city together when he mentions the Graces, the daughters of Zeus, as Hesiod recounts in the *Theogony*, who dwell with the Muses in "delight" or "good cheer" (*thalia*) (*Theog.* 64). Because communities remain together through mutual exchange, Aristotle observes, "[People] place a shrine to the Graces (*Charites*) in the roadway, to foster reciprocal giving, for this belongs to gratitude" (*charis*) (1133a3–5). Scholars have no knowledge of where and when there was such a shrine to the Graces, or even whether one ever existed. We have only Aristotle to trust for the existence of such shrines. The phrase of Aristotle's that I have translated as "in the roadway" (*empodōn*) is literally "in [the way] of one's feet." It is "in the way," and thus serves as a "stumbling block." Perhaps it is Aristotle himself who is setting up the shrine, metaphorically speaking, to serve as a reminder of the Graces as a stumbling block to those who desire simply to return harm for harm, rather than good for good.[10]

Rhadamanthus, the punitive judge whom souls encounter on their way to the Underworld, must be supplemented by these feminine deities, whose shrine encourages us not only to render service in turn (*anthupéretē-sai*) to those who have been gracious to us, but also to "initiate (*arxai*) acts of graciousness" (1133a5). Like the great-souled individual whom Aris-

---

10. According to Winthrop, the exchange of harm for harm as well as the need that gives rise to the exchange of goods indicates for Aristotle "nature's imperfection." Aristotle "characteristically obscures the harshness of nature and human nature," she argues, "by emphasizing economics, speaking *as if* the exchange necessary for survival were an exchange not of harms but of goods like beds and shoes" (emphasis mine). Winthrop mentions Aristotle's reference to the Graces in this context, but she understands it in the same light—as a way of obscuring the harshness of nature implied in justice's requiring "reciprocal harms." "Aristotle and Theories of Justice," 1205, 1205n8. Frank, in contrast, understands this passage as crucial to Aristotelian reciprocity, including the importance of the initiation of benefits that the Graces encourage. As she points out, "most commentators treat [Aristotle's references to the Graces] as not germane to his account." Jill Frank, *A Democracy of Distinction: Aristotle and the Work of Politics* (Chicago: University of Chicago Press, 2005), 100.

totle described earlier, those encouraged by the Graces confer benefits on others. But unlike the great-souled, who thinks he is worthy of the greatest things, they do not insist on giving rather than receiving; nor do they forget the benefits they receive (1124b11–15). Aristotle's Graces are a stumbling block not only to those who insist on returning harm for harm, but also to great-souled individuals, in that they remind them that good deeds, theirs included, are fostered by the Graces, and therefore that they must share responsibility for them. They render service not merely by conferring benefits on others, but also by prompting others to serve *in turn*. They are not the sole givers. Their benefiting others is not an act of self-sufficiency (see 1125a11–12), but of grace, and makes them part of a community of reciprocal giving.[11]

In his own way, Aristotle takes his turn at rendering service by furthering Aeschylus' attempt to convert the avenging Furies, who torment Orestes for his matricide, into "Eumenides," "kindly" goddesses who support the city, on which they confer their grace or favor (*charis*) (*Eum.* 865–69, 881–926, 937). Aristotle's Graces, also "kindly" goddesses, as is the meaning of the new name Athena gives the Furies, remind human beings to initiate and return acts of graciousness. They hold out the prospect that human life involves an exchange of goods that goes beyond that exchange measured by money, even if the latter exchange teaches us both our common needs and our ability to meet them, and thereby prepares us to worship at the shrine of the Graces.

As he moves away from his discussion of reciprocity, Aristotle reminds us that human beings cannot attain the insight of Rhadamanthus into souls, when he again points out the discrepancy between a person's actions and the disposition of his soul. Judgment will always be imperfect, but it is possible for natural justice to inform the laws, conventions, and political structures of a community, as he discusses next, especially in cases of reciprocal ruling and being ruled. And there is a kind of justice Aristotle calls equity, which gives beyond what is due, at least in the sense of the lawful. The Graces, metaphorically speaking, remain at work when Aristotle takes his turn serving with his discussions of natural justice and equity.

---

11. Whereas Aristotle associates "serving" with the virtue of women in the *Politics* (1260a21–25), it cannot be only that of women, for in "serving" and "serving in turn" lies the reciprocity that holds the city together.

Natural Justice

Aristotle discusses natural justice as a form of political justice. Although the forms of justice that Aristotle has been discussing thus far might be called "political," Aristotle now brings his discussion of political justice further—to the fundamental character of just human association: "The just in the political sense ... exists among those who share a life in common," "who are free and equal," and exists for those for whom law is natural, namely, those for whom there is equality in ruling and being ruled (1134a26–31, b14–15). "Equality in ruling and being ruled" does not imply a simple democracy. As in the distribution of goods such as property and honors, so in the distribution of ruling offices, the "equal" means the portion equal to one's merits in relation to others.

The ruler about whom Aristotle is speaking here is one who is ruled by the law that structures his sharing rule with others, insofar as "there is equality in ruling and being ruled." Whatever proportionate equality exists for those "for whom the law is natural," no one is so different from others as to be "a law unto himself" (*Pol.* 1283a3–14). The law (*nomos*) that establishes and maintains institutions that structure shared governance, as Aristotle said of money (*nomisma*), facilitates the mutual exchange of goods that holds the city together (1132b34).[12] Where there is "equality in ruling and being ruled," structured by law, lawgivers are also ruled by the laws, and those who obey the laws also have a part in ruling. There is a reciprocity between rulers and ruled, and it does not consist in striking and being struck, but in shared governance, in which ruler and ruled fulfill their potential as political and rational animals. To be sure, where there is such "equality of ruling and being ruled," we cannot rely on the knowledge or skill of a legislative art that militates against error. But there is greater opportunity for citizens to develop a capacity for deliberation and to make more considered choices. Nature may ordain

---

12. In the *Politics*, Aristotle says that "reciprocal equality preserves cities" in the context of discussing ruling among the free and equal, and he refers his addressee to his discussion of reciprocal equality in the *Ethics* (*Pol.* 1261a30–35; see also 1277b8–13). See also Bernard Yack, *The Problems of a Political Animal: Community, Justice, and Conflict in Aristotelian Political Thought* (Berkeley: University of California Press, 1993), 136; Frank, *Democracy of Distinction*, 101; and Mary P. Nichols, *Citizens and Statesmen: A Study of Aristotle's "Politics"* (Lanham, MD: Rowman & Littlefield, 1992), 88.

this, but it takes human beings to accomplish it (see 1103a23–26 and *Pol.* 1253a31–32). After elaborating this understanding of political justice, Aristotle turns to the naturally just as a meaning of political justice.

The naturally just, Aristotle says, "has the same potential everywhere" (1134b19). As suggested by Aristotle's previous discussion, this potential would include that of human beings to share in ruling and being ruled, who are neither slaves nor masters by nature, and who are no longer children. There are many ways in which this potential might become realized, just as there are many regimes that are not tyrannical, all based on some degree of equality among their members.[13] Thus whereas fire burns the same here and in Persia, for us what is just by nature is "altogether changeable," since the regimes differ from one another. And yet, "there is only one regime everywhere that is in accord with nature, the best regime" (1134b24–1135a5). Aristotle notoriously says very little here about this best regime, which alone exists according to nature, but he has laid out its foundations and limits, namely, in the human potential to rule and to be ruled, and that finds expression in various ways, although Aristotle might not have seen it yet among the Persians (see 1160b27–32).[14] The particular structure and organization of the best regime by nature, such as the one he describes in the *Politics*, depend on human choices and actions.

After discussing the naturally just, Aristotle turns to the conventionally or legally just. Here, Aristotle explains, things that make no difference in the beginning do make a difference once they have been set down—such decrees as determine the sum of money to offer for ransom, whether to offer a sacrifice of a goat or two sheep, whether or not to sacrifice to Brasidas, or other such things (1134b20–24). Aristotle's examples show that the naturally just—and the human potential on which it is based—is relevant to the legal or conventional form of political justice. Conventions are just when they favor the freedom of human beings. While Aristotle says it is conventional or "up to us" to determine how much we should offer

---

13. For a discussion of Aristotle's account in the *Politics* of the many forms of democracy and oligarchy, and how the more moderate of each tend toward greater inclusiveness or shared rule, see Nichols, 85–100.

14. In commenting on Aristotle's description of the naturally just, Winthrop points out that the Persians worshipped fire as a god (Hdt. 1.131). "Aristotle and Theories of Justice," 1208n13.

for a ransom, he does not say the same about whether or not we should offer a ransom if circumstances permit. So too while it is a matter of indifference whether a goat or two sheep are originally designated for sacrifice, it is not a matter of indifference whether there is to be a sacrifice, or more generally, some way in which humans worship the divine. And human sacrifice is never a matter of indifference (see also *Pol.* 1324b40–41).

Aristotle's third example of a law or convention that may be a matter of indifference until it is decided is that of sacrificing to Brasidas, a custom adopted by the Greek city of Amphipolis after the Spartan general sacrificed his life for the city's freedom (Thuc. 5.11.1, 5.9.9). This last example, however, is problematic. When the people of Amphipolis celebrate Brasidas' act by worshipping him as a god, their honors suggest that achievements such as his are beyond what human beings can ask of themselves. But they must ask such deeds of themselves in order to preserve their freedom. By sacrificing to Brasidas, and thereby treating him as divine, the Amphipolitans give more to Brasidas than his due and less to themselves. If honoring a human being as a god implies or presages their own loss of freedom, Brasidas' noble sacrifice for their freedom fails to achieve its purpose. The loss of freedom is not a matter of indifference.

Although conventions or laws set down "at the beginning" might be decided one way or another, once they are set down they become binding. But what cannot be binding are those things that undermine the equality and freedom that make possible the shared governance appropriate to human beings. Laws or conventions such as human sacrifice treat human beings like beasts. Those such as worshipping Brasidas treat them as gods. Because they undermine human equality and freedom they are not a matter of indifference, and therefore cannot be decided one way or another at the outset. Justice cannot simply consist in abiding by law or convention; rather, it requires preserving the equality and freedom that serve as the indispensable support for the laws' justice.

Tragedy and Equity

Aristotle's last way of speaking about justice in book 5, the justice of equity, is embedded in references to tragedy and allusions to problems that appear in tragedy. Aristotle makes a host of distinctions that tragedy ignores, and that equity, as he will soon describe it, will be able to address. He begins

by pointing out that while law legislates just actions and forbids and punishes unjust ones, "someone acts unjustly or performs a just act [only]
when he does so voluntarily." Voluntary acts are those that are up to the
one acting, and they are performed "with the knowledge of" (*eidōs*) the
person affected by his action, of the means he uses, and his purposes in
acting (1135a17–25). Aristotle illustrates his point: if someone strikes his
father not knowing that it is his father whom he is striking, his act is involuntary (1135a28–30). His example applies directly to Oedipus.[15] Here he
expresses his reservations about tragedy, or at least about those who in ignorance commit horrific acts such as patricide or incest, and are held responsible, or who hold themselves responsible. They are pitiable, to be sure, but
forgiveness, not blame, is appropriate (see 1111a1–2).

Even when one harms another while knowing what one is doing, Aristotle also observes, one's act is not necessarily unjust. One might have
acted from spiritedness or other natural passions. In such a case, it is
"noble" (*kalon*) to judge his act as "unintended" (*ouk ek pronoias*) (1135b25
–26), that is, to render a judgment that supports pardon or forgiveness.
This is one of the few times that Aristotle uses "the noble" in book 5. He
applies it not to the act of a spirited or angry person (one might think of
the wrath of Achilles), but to the one who forgives him. Aristotle's usage
is in accord with his calling the mean with respect to anger "gentleness"
in book 4, and in explaining that "the gentle person inclines to forgiveness
rather to revenge" (1126a2–3). It is also anticipated by his quick move in
his discussion of reciprocity from returning harm for harm to initiating
and returning good, from the justice of Rhadamanthus, to the beneficence
of the Graces, even though those who do not exact the former are held to
be slavish (1132b25–1133a5). While Aristotle does not deny this, he
responds in effect that the greater freedom lies in an act of grace.

Aristotle gives further examples that point us in this direction. He asks
whether it is possible to do an injustice to oneself, and denies it, inasmuch
as no one wishes to harm himself (1134b12). He gives an example from
Homer: Glaucus, who gave more to Diomedes than he received from him,

---

15. Aristotle calls the harm or injury (*blabē*) that occurs when a person acts in ignorance
"error" (*harmartēma*) (1135b12), using a noun related to the word he uses in his *Poetics*
to describe the tragic protagonist (*hamartia*). *Poet.* 1453a10, 17.

"gold for bronze, the worth of a hundred cattle for nine," Aristotle quotes from Homer (*Il.* 6.236). Glaucus is someone who takes less for himself in an exchange but neither suffers injustice voluntarily nor does injustice to himself, Aristotle claims, for his "giving is up to him" (1136b1–14). Homer's story, however, is not about liberality or voluntary giving. Rather, Glaucus gives away his own resources, because "Zeus stole his wits" (*Il.* 6.234). He does not suffer injustice voluntarily, but it is not because his act is "up to him," for it is Zeus who is responsible. Aristotle transforms Homer's account, for he does not mention Zeus, and makes Glaucus responsible for his act. Aristotle's Glaucus is a liberal man. Aristotle's revision of Glaucus' story delivers another strike against the poets and their presentation of the divine. Just as Homer's Glaucus expends his resources when deprived of his wits, protagonists in tragedies seem deprived of their wits, metaphorically if not literally (as in the case of Ajax), as they move toward self-destruction.

Aristotle reflects back on his revision of Homer at the end of this section of book 5. "The just things exist among those who share in the things simply good," he remarks, "and who can have an excess or a deficiency of them." Only for the gods, perhaps, "is there no excess of goods, whereas for those incurably bad, there is no beneficial portion" (1137a27–31). Whatever Aristotle may mean by the gods, to whom the goods belong without limit, they occupy a pole opposite to the "incurably wicked." They would not deprive us of our wits; nor would they contribute to the horrific human suffering from oracles and commands, as they do in countless Greek tragedies.

Aristotle quotes another line from a tragedy, from one of Euripides' plays, when the play's title character Alcmaeon admits that he killed his mother. Alcmaeon supposes that his admission of the deed is sufficient, for he can reduce his tale to "a brief speech," as he says in the line that Aristotle quotes. But Aristotle also quotes the question of his interlocutor in the play, "Did you [kill her] voluntarily, and [was she killed] voluntarily, or was she killed involuntarily and did you do so involuntarily?" (1136a10–14). Even within tragedy, at least in this play, someone asks about the circumstances of the actions and the state of the doer and sufferer of the deed. Because Euripides' play has been lost, we do not know how or if Alcmaeon responded, nor do we know who asked the question. But like the questioner, Aristotle thinks that more should be asked about Alcmaeon's deed in order to judge it properly.

One might ask, for example, whether Alcmaeon killed his mother voluntarily, if he was asked to do so by his father as he lay dying due to his wife's treachery (cf. 1110a28–29). As Aristotle has just said, claims of justice can often be made by both sides in a conflict (1135b27–1136a1). The tragedian Aeschylus dramatized this point in the *Oresteia*, when the votes of the court trying Orestes' case produce a tie. There were certainly extenuating circumstances, in that his mother had murdered his father and Orestes had been commanded by Apollo to kill her in turn (*Ch.* 269–77, 1026–32; *Eum.* 458–67). Athena resolves the deadlock in favor of pardon, proclaiming that she gives her vote to Orestes, inasmuch as she is born solely of Zeus and "favors the male in all things," even if she wouldn't marry one (*Eum.* 734–35). Aristotle finds a less arbitrary reason for pardon when he discusses a more human expedient, equity, which modifies the law as circumstances demand.

Because law necessarily speaks in universal terms, it holds only "for the most part," while "not being ignorant of its error (*hamartanomenon*) in its doing so" (1137b15–16). Like a tragic protagonist, the law errs, but unlike the tragic protagonist it knows that it is doing so—that it must speak in universal terms although it cannot know the particular cases that will occur over time. The lawgiver who understands this also understands that he can rule only in part, even if it is for the most part, and that there will be limits to the extent that he can legislate about everything in the city.[16] He has learned what Aristotle has been trying to teach from the beginning of the *Ethics*, namely, in political matters, where the just, the noble, and the good are involved, matters hold only "for the most part" (1094b11–23).

When extenuating circumstances occur, then equity comes into play. Although Aristotle points out that common usage refers almost inter-

---

16. In the *Rhetoric*, Aristotle admits that the defects in the law are sometimes involuntary, and sometimes voluntary on the part of lawgivers, in the former case when it escapes their notice, in the latter case when they must speak in universal terms about what holds only for the most part (1374a27–32). In the *Ethics*, Aristotle speaks of law, which is not ignorant of its error, whereas in the *Rhetoric* he speaks of lawgivers, who may or may not be so. He does not speak universally of all lawgivers.

changeably to the equitable and the good, he gives it a specific meaning (1137a34–b2).[17] Equity is a kind of justice that corrects the defect of the law stemming from its universality (1137b11–14).[18] Whereas the just person first appeared in book 5 as "the lawful," and the unjust as "the lawbreaker" (*paranomos*, 1129a32), equity looks at and gives justice to what falls "outside" (*para*) the law (1137b20) due to the circumstances that arise. Equity applies the universal rule, as it were, neither more nor less than it ought, when it ought, toward whom it ought, and for the sake of what it ought, presumably according to correct reason, as Aristotle's formula for acting according to the mean requires (1106b21–24, 1115b11–20).

Because the universal terms of the law capture only what holds "for the most part," law is partial. So too is the justice of equity, which applies only in the case at hand and does not become a new law for others. Equity

---

17. Although Aristotle has used "equitable" on many occasions throughout the *Ethics*, in most cases he does not distinguish what he means by it other than the good (e.g., 1113b14, 1132a2). Translators use a variety of terms to translate *epieikēs*, for example, "decent," "virtuous," and "good." Whether Aristotle's usages of the term are relevant to the specific definition he gives it, as he elaborates it in the book on justice, depends on the context. See Burger's discussion of his use of it in the context of shame at 1128b27. *Aristotle's Dialogue with Socrates*, 90. So too one might consider Aristotle's use of "the equitable person" in his discussion of wittiness in book 4 (1128a18).

18. Hamburger points out that "the concept of *epieikeia* [equity] as defined by Aristotle has no antecedent in the whole of pre-Aristotelian literature." Max Hamburger, *Morals and Law: The Growth of Aristotle's Legal Theory* (New Haven, CT: Yale University Press, 1951), 90. The usages prior to Aristotle that Hamburger cites (91) confirm Aristotle's observation that the word was used interchangeably with the good, with a range of meanings, including clemency, leniency, indulgence, forgiveness, and moderation. In Plato's *Statesman*, the Eleatic Stranger recognizes the deficiency of a law that is promulgated "about all things and for all time," when "human things are never at rest." Therefore the lawmaker who makes law for all collectively will fail to provide what is proper for each individual (*Plt.* 294b2–6 and 294e8–295a2). But there is no mention of equity here, either the word or the meaning that Aristotle gives it as a response to this problem. The Stranger criticizes the law in order to establish that the best rule is that "without laws" by "the wise (*ton meta phronēseōs*) king" (294a8). In his absence, the rule of laws that allow no deviation or questioning can be a "second" best (297e1–4). The wise ruler does not err (297a5–b3), and the erring laws allow no correction. Once again, Aristotle's treatment of justice is an implicit response to Plato. For a rich treatment of Aristotle's differences with Plato's Eleatic Stranger, see Kevin M. Cherry, *Plato, Aristotle, and the Purposes of Politics* (New York: Cambridge University Press, 2012), especially 99.

does not replace the law; nor does the person who corrects the law in the particular case replace the lawgiver, for he decides cases "as if" the lawgiver were present (1137b11–24). His judgment must nevertheless supplement that of the lawgiver, for he looks not merely to the law that has been violated, as Aristotle elaborates in the *Rhetoric*, but to the sort of person the wrongdoer is or has been "always or for the most part" rather than "in the moment" he acts. Equity looks not to the "action" of the wrongdoer, but to the "choice" (*proairesis*) behind it. In the *Rhetoric*, moreover, Aristotle connects equity to pardon or forgiveness. "Equity pardons what is human" (*Rhet.* 1374b3–16; see also *NE* 1143a19–24).[19]

The questions that equity considers address the conflicts that might lead to tragedy. Matricide is against the law, but should Orestes be pardoned for his matricide? Or, to use another example familiar to us from tragedy, burying the city's enemy may be forbidden by the ruler, but should one bury the city's enemy if he is one's brother? Is Antigone's intention to violate Creon's decree or to obey a divine one? And what sort of person has Antigone been always or for the most part rather than in the moment of her act? Equity, as Aristotle describes it, would consider all these things.

Aristotle concludes his discussion of equity by describing the equitable person himself: he is inclined to take less for himself, "even though he has the law on his side" (1137b34–1138a3). The one who tends to forgiveness in his judgment of others, and thereby grants them more leniency than the law requires, also takes less than the law grants in cases when he himself is involved. He is not "exacting about justice," Aristotle says (1137a1–2). In taking less for himself, Aristotle makes clear, he does not do injustice to himself or wish his own harm, for he "grasps more of another good, such as reputation or what is simply noble" (1136b20–23). He exchanges good for good, although a lesser good for a greater. He is therefore a more apt illustration of someone who does not do injustice to himself than is Homer's Glaucus, who gives more than he receives only because Zeus has

---

19. Max Hamburger compares and contrasts Aristotle's treatment of equity in the *Magna Moralia*, the *Nicomachean Ethics*, and the *Rhetoric* and finds the most developed form of Aristotle's theory of equity in the *Rhetoric*. *Morals and Law*, 99. Aristotle does add helpful remarks in the *Rhetoric* about the character of the equitable person. In his discussion of justice in the *Ethics*, Aristotle's emphasis is on equity's relation to the law.

deprived him of his wits. The equitable person has his wits about him, for he understands the nobility that he derives from taking less.

Aristotle's description of the equitable person here offers a model for the noble that contrasts with the characteristic tragic figure, who chooses the noble over his own good. Aristotle gives the example of Achilles in the *Rhetoric* as someone we praise for doing what is noble, disregarding his own benefit, for whom death was nobler than living, although living was advantageous (1359a5–8). Death for Achilles was noble but not simply good (see also *NE* 1094b17–19). He grasped the noble, like the equitable person, but only at the cost of his life. When Aristotle describes the equitable person as taking more of the simply noble by taking less for himself, he severs the connection between nobility and death, just as he earlier connected nobility with forgiveness rather than with spiritedness or anger. The equitable person achieves the noble, with no disservice to himself. Resembling the one encouraged by the Graces, and unlike the great-souled individual Aristotle describes in book 4, the equitable person "remembers the benefits he received rather than the ones he conferred" (*Rhet.* 1374b18–19; cf. *NE* 1124b12–13). To lovers of the noble, who are eager to sacrifice themselves, Aristotle will offer a different way to take both less and more in friendship, in the later books of the *Ethics*. Here, in his discussion of equity, he offers them the "superior" justice he calls equity and assigns to them the noble work in the political community that someone who takes less for himself might accomplish with less ostentation than Achilles' sacrifice.

Conclusion: The Question of Suicide

After his discussion of equity, Aristotle returns to the question of whether it is possible to do injustice to oneself, and this time he mentions suicide explicitly. Suicide seems to call into question Aristotle's view that one cannot do injustice to oneself, along with its underlying assumption that no one wishes to harm himself (1134b11–12 and 1136a34–b9). Is Aristotle ending his discussion of book 5 with an exception to his general rule? Doesn't one who commits suicide wish to harm himself? Or does Aristotle's general rule have the character more of a command than a description, or rather a description of what might come to be, if not only law but human life itself were informed by Aristotle's understanding? Oedipus laments that he is evil, and born from evil, soon after he blinds himself, for example, while Jocasta's silence when she leaves the stage is still more ominous (*OT* 1397, 1073–75). These characters doubt their own goodness. They suppose that it is better for them not to live, or at least that it is better for others not to have to live with them. Oedipus, for example, asks that he be sent away from Thebes, for he is hated by the gods (1518–19). Such characters are harsher on themselves than Aristotle teaches they should be, and they have a harsher view of the gods than any Aristotle countenances.

Aristotle attributes to the city a law that forbids suicide and that imposes penalties and dishonor on those who kill themselves (1138a9–14). One might understand Aristotle here to confirm the all-embracing character of the city and its laws that order everything in it, inasmuch as they treat even the life of the individual as not his own to take. But a law against suicide indicates not the city's power, but its weakness, its failure to protect life, and its weakness in the face of death. In imposing dishonor and penalties on those who take their lives, it punishes those whom it is too late to save from death, almost like a tragic protagonist whose actions come "too late" to prevent death (see Soph., *Ant.* 1270). By dishonoring suicide, however, the law honors life, and the good for which it is the condition. It thereby asserts the goodness of life, even of the one who disavows it by committing suicide. It may be too late for punishing, but it is not too late for teaching. This is the work of a good city. Aristotle does not accept the tragic lament, "too late."

The law that Aristotle presents, indeed, transforms, in the course of his discussion of justice is not one that asserts its all-embracing authority over human beings, but one that supports human choice and action, as we have seen in so many ways. There are laws or conventions (*nomismata*) that facilitate the exchange of goods; there is ruling and being ruled that is just for those for whom "law is natural"; there is a law that knows it errs and therefore that it must be supplemented by equity; and finally, in response to the poets whose tragedies are replete with suicides, there is law that dishonors suicide and thereby insists on the goodness of life.

So too do laws that command the deeds of virtue and forbid those of vice, regardless of their success, affirm which deeds are worthy and which are not. If the law succeeded in guaranteeing that the deeds of citizens were always virtuous, citizens could not satisfy their desire to trust their own goodness, for their goodness would come not from themselves but from the law. Trusting one's own goodness nevertheless does not belong to a self-contained soul, whose virtue lies in the proper relation between its parts, as Aristotle suggests in his concluding allusion to the *Republic* (1138b5–14). Trusting our goodness requires confirmation from our deeds, deeds that involve others, such as those that Aristotle's treatment of justice in book 5 brings to light: pardoning when appropriate, for example, or sharing in ruling and being ruled, or erecting shrines to divinities who encourage our initiating acts of goodness and benefiting others in turn. Aristotle's elaborations of such experiences offer us models for directing or perhaps reforming the political communities in which we live.

Aristotle in effect offers Glaucon and Adeimantus a better political life than they could imagine from watching the unjust prosper, or even from watching Socrates found a city that will remain only in speech while advising them to cultivate justice within themselves (see *Rep.* 472d9–473a3; 592a7–b5). Aristotle can therefore turn the young toward political life, not away from it. So too he does not exclude the poets, not even the tragedians, from the city, as Socrates does in the *Republic* (607b1–3). Citizens can learn from the poets the tragic dilemmas they face without despairing that they have no recourse. For Aristotle, the poets—and Plato—serve not only as his foil, but as an incentive to a reformed politics.

II.

Art, Beauty, and Truth

8

Matelda, Dante, and Beatrice in the Earthly Paradise: Poetry and Philosophy on Trial in the Court of Biblical Theology

Steven Berg

Dante's *Purgatorio* begins with a resurrection. It is, however, one of a distinctly non-Christian character. Dante prays to the Muses, to whom, he declares, he belongs, to "let dead poetry rise again" (I.7–9).[1] Dante's *Comedy* and in particular his *Purgatorio* represent precisely this revival of a poetry consigned to the sepulcher for over a thousand years. To accomplish this renewal, Dante insists, requires the aid not only of all the newly reborn goddesses of song, but in particular of Calliope. Dante solicits the Muse of epic to accompany his poem with the same strain she employed to defeat the nine daughters of Pierus, those fatuous and pretentious girls who believed themselves the Muses' superiors and so challenged them to a contest in song (I.9–11). This contest, of course, ended in the Pies' defeat and their transformation into a flock of magpies, whose voices imitate the sound of the human voice, while lacking all reason and sense.[2] Dante and Calliope, it would seem, are engaged in a new contest of song

---

1. All translations of Dante's *Purgatorio* are taken from *The Divine Comedy of Dante Alghieri*, trans. and ed. Robert M. Durling and Ronald L. Martinez, vol. 2, *Purgatorio* (Oxford: Oxford University Press, 2003). I have occasionally altered their translations in order to reflect more literally Dante's text.

2. Ovid is the source for Dante's knowledge of this ancient tale. See *Met.* 5.294–678.

against a new usurper of poetry's prerogatives. Who is this opponent and what is the song this opponent sings?[3]

The contest between the Muses and the Pies, taken by Dante as a model for his own work in its competition with an as yet unspecified foe, is restaged in the second canto of the *Purgatorio* as the competition between the psalm sung by the pilgrims newly arrived at the shores of Mount Purgatory and the song performed by Dante's friend Casella at Dante's request (II.43–48, 106–17). The pilgrims arrive in a boat piloted by an angel or "divine bird," as Dante calls him, who, the poet observes, "shuns all human argument" (II.31, 38). The psalm the pilgrims sing— *In Exitu Israel de Aegypto* (Ps. 114)—explains precisely why their pilot eschews all human reason and sense (II.46–48). It celebrates the power of God as the Redeemer of Israel from her slavery under the Egyptians. It portrays the miraculous effects of that power as the inevitable accompaniments of God's redemptive action: "The sea looked back and fled; Jordan turned back. The mountains skipped like rams, the hills like lambs" (Ps. 114.3–4). The whole of the earth "trembled" in the presence of the Lord and nature's courses were entirely diverted (114.7–8). The psalm sings of a God of miracle and mystery whose will surpasses and overturns any putatively necessary natural order. This is the song of the new Pies.

In response Casella, at Dante's urging, puts to music one of Dante's own poetical compositions, the second canzone from the *Convivio*—*Amor that reasons with me in my mind*. As Dante explains in his comment upon this poem in the third book of that work, the beauty whose charms and virtues are celebrated in the canzone is not a mortal woman, but Lady Philosophy (*Convivio* III.11). Dante and Casella's song celebrates the attractions of the study of philosophy, a study devoted to uncovering through the agency of human reason alone the necessary character of the nature of things. What Casella's song or Dante's canzone reveals, therefore, is that Dante's poetry, the poetry he has awakened from its millennial slumbers, is not an independent or autonomous poetry. It is poetry in the service of philosophy.

---

3. Since, at the very moment of poetry's rebirth, she must do battle with a challenger who would confine her to the grave once more, this same challenger must have been responsible for her previous entombment.

If Casella's song points to and defines the character of the *Comedy* as a whole and particularly that of the *Purgatorio*, the psalm sung by the pilgrims under the tutelage of the divine bird who shuns all human argument points to and defines the character of biblical revelation. In the *Letter to Can Grande* (7), Dante declares that though the literal meaning of *In Exitu Israel de Aegypto* concerns God's redemption of Israel from her bondage under the Egyptians, its allegorical and moral meanings concern Christ's redemption of man from his bondage under sin. In its literal and allegorical meanings, the psalm expresses the central themes of biblical revelation, the Old and New Testaments. The contest that Dante establishes at the opening of the *Purgatorio*, then, is a contest between Dante's *Comedy* and the Bible.

Since the greatest claim of the Christian revelation concerns the issue of the salvation of the human soul, and the soul is said to be saved or redeemed by being purged, on the one hand, of the sin or vice that has accrued to its nature and, on the other, invested with all the virtues, natural and supernatural, the contest between the Bible and Dante's philosophic poetry must be played out first upon the terrain of the issue of the true character of virtue and vice of soul. Dante employs the Sermon on the Mount, the beatitudes of which punctuate the transitions from one terrace of Purgatory to the next, to serve as representative of the biblical teaching regarding virtue and vice of soul.

What Dante shows throughout the course of the *Purgatorio*, up to and including especially the terraces of pride, envy, wrath, sloth, and avarice, is that the Christian teaching regarding virtue and vice is misconceived in three respects. First, the biblical teaching confuses extreme states— excessive or defective—in regard to the passions, and actions in accordance with these extreme states, for virtuous conditions and virtuous actions: humility, love of one's enemies, meekness, zeal, and poverty stand at the opposite extremes from pride, envy, wrath, sloth, and avarice (XII.109–11, 118–20, XIII.34–42, XV.49–57, XVI.16–24, XVII.67–69, 85–87, XIX.112–23). The Christian teaching lacks knowledge of the measure of the mean. As Dante argues, however, first in the *Convivio* and then in the *Purgatorio* through the mouth of his Statius, the mean, as discovered by Socrates and articulated by Aristotle, is the true measure of all practical and moral virtue (*Purgatorio* XII.49–54; *Convivio* III.6). Second, the Christian teaching mistakes a condition that is predominantly bodily—an affective disposition—for a condition of soul. It therefore mistakes not a sound bodily condition, but an unsound or vicious condition of body for virtue of soul.[4] Finally, it unwittingly identifies certain affective dispositions as simultaneously virtues and vices, e.g., Oderisi's humility proves to be indistinguishable from Sapia's envy, and St. Stephen's love from Amata's self-destructive wrath.

Thus, in Cantos IX–XXII of *Purgatorio* and particularly in the central cantos of the work, wherein Virgil offers his "demonstration of love" (XIV–XX), Dante simultaneously refutes the mistaken biblical understanding and articulates his alternative philosophical understanding of the true nature of the virtue and vice and the purgation and salvation of the soul. As Virgil's speech and its context shows, the true virtue of soul is intellectual, not moral virtue, and the truth of purgation and salvation entails the purification of love from wrath and the salvation of the soul from the false images and opinions lodged within the imagination that are built upon the foundation of this fusion of desire and anger.

This demonstration of the truth regarding virtue, purgation, and salvation, on the one hand, and the consequent victory of poetry in the service of philosophy over the parables and images of the Bible in the service

---

4. That all of the affective conditions (the states of the various passions) identified by the Christian teaching as virtues and vices of soul are in fact closer to dispositions of body is indicated by Dante through his alteration of the beatitude that stands as the penultimate member of the series of beatitudes that he has borrowed from the Sermon on the Mount and used to punctuate the transition from one level of Purgatory to the next. Dante transforms Christ's central beatitude, in which hunger and thirst are clearly to be taken in a strictly metaphorical sense, into a dietitian's prescription: "Blessed are those who hunger and thirst for righteousness, for they shall be filled" becomes "Blessed are those whom so much grace illuminates that love of taste (*gusto*) does not smoke with too much desire in their breasts hungering always for the right amount" (XXIV.151–54). Dante thereby insists on the corporeal character of the core of the Christian moral teaching. Moreover he insists on the fact, recognized by both Plato and Aristotle—the discoverers or inventors of the doctrine of the mean—that the virtues that are the concern of all moral teachings are not virtues of the soul primarily, but of those aspects of the soul that are so close to body as to be indistinguishable from it: the blanch of fear, the blush of modesty, and the flush of righteous indignation all indicate the bodily character of the passions with which morality is chiefly concerned.

of its moral teaching, on the other hand, are both presupposed when, at the verge of the entrance to the earthly paradise, Virgil declares Dante's will or judgment to be "free, standing upright (*dritto*), and sound (*sano*)" (XXVII.130–40). When Virgil crowns and miters Dante "himself over himself," he does so in the name of a philosophy and poetry newly liberated from the dominance of the Christian revelation (XXVII.142).[5] Thus at the moment Dante enters the earthly paradise, encounters the wondrous Matelda there (XXVIII.37–39), and, with any thought of Beatrice banished from his mind, is ready to take her as his own, he is encountering and attempting to appropriate a figure that, like Dante's beloved Casella, represents the beauties of poetry as made suitable to the pursuit of philosophical understanding. Matelda is a new, tenth muse; she is the most beautiful of the Muses. (See Plato, *Laws* 667a10–b3.)

Thus Matelda appears to Dante within the "ancient wood" of the earthly paradise, "singing and separating flower from flower"; later, when Dante compares the light of her gaze to that of Venus in love, and describes her as "laughing while standing upright" before him, he speaks of her weaving together these same flowers (XXVIII.23, 41, 64–69). Singing her song, she both separates and combines. She is the work of poetry and dialectic mixed in equal measure, or rather, of the former as adjunct to the latter.

As has often been observed, Matelda is a figure who has leapt from the pages of Guido Cavalcanti's ballata, *In un boschetto trova' pasturella*. She therefore recalls the relationship of Dante to the man he once called his "first friend" (*Vita Nuova*, 30.2). Dante's understanding of friendship in the proper sense is articulated in his *Convivio*—it is friendship in philosophy (*Convivio* III.11). The pleasure Matelda inspires and the attractions she displays, then, are connected to the pleasures and attractions of friendship inspired by a mutual passion for the pursuit of truth or the love of wisdom. Matelda, however, is also an image of human life in its perfection. With the exception of Dante himself, she is the only living human being found within the pages of the *Comedy*. This distinguishes her sharply from Beatrice, who will, in the following cantos, insist upon her own dead flesh.

---

5. See Ernst H. Kantorowicz, *The King's Two Bodies: A Study in Medieval Political Theology* (Princeton: Princeton University Press, 1957), 491–92.

Dante's amorous inclinations toward Matelda, then, reflect the fact that the pursuit of truth or love of wisdom, precisely as undertaken in the company of the friend, entails a love not only of knowledge, but of human life in the proper sense and so entails a love of self and a knowledge of self. As Aristotle suggests in book 9 of his *Nicomachean Ethics*, the friend is another self whose activity provides, as it were, a reflective medium within which to perceive one's own activity and so one's own life mirrored (*NE* 1169b28–1170a4). Indeed, the friend in dialogue with the friend may be said to be constitutive of the reality of what we call "the self."[6]

Human life, however, is above all the life of the mind (*NE* 1170a27–b8), and as Dante observes in his *Convivio*, "the use of our mind is most of all delightful to us. And whatever is most of all delightful to us constitutes our happiness and our blessedness, beyond which there is no greater delight" (*Convivio* IV.22).[7] Matelda, therefore, also embodies the good of man that lies beyond and is superior to the moral understanding of good and evil, according to which not the use of the mind, and the pleasures of such use, but the possession of morally virtuous character traits and the performance of morally virtuous actions are what is required for the achievement of happiness. Such a trans-moral understanding of the good entails an understanding of human life as innocent, an understanding according to which error is no longer defined in terms of vice or "sin," but transfigured and redeemed as the precondition for doubt and so for the pursuit of truth. As Dante insists in his *Paradiso*, "doubt springs up like a shoot at the foot of truth; and this is nature which urges us to the summit from height to height" (*Paradiso* IV.130–32). Matelda represents human life insofar as it has left behind the moral imagination and the passions that animate it, namely, hope, fear, and the desire for revenge—what

---

6. See Ronna Burger, *Aristotle's Dialogue with Socrates: On Aristotle's "Nicomachean Ethics"* (Chicago: University of Chicago Press, 2008), 182. The reader will find here a very powerful and insightful discussion of these issues, central to an understanding of the question, What is philosophy? The question What is philosophy?, however, is inseparable from the question What is God? and Professor Burger takes up this question with an equally penetrating thoughtfulness (156, 180–82, 193–94). See also Ronna Burger, *On Plato's "Euthyphro"* (Munich: Carl Friedrich von Siemens Foundation, 2015), 55–57.

7. *Dante's "Il Convivio" ("The Banquet")*, trans. Richard H. Lansing (New York: Garland Publishing, 1990), 212.

Virgil called "spirited love" (XVII.91–96, 112–23). She is human life as having completed the ascent to the good appropriate to man, the good of the intellect, an ascent and appropriation that can be undertaken only on the basis of what Virgil calls "natural love" (XXVII.91–96). She is a non-biblical Eve who offers Dante the "sweet apple" that Virgil promises him he will taste upon his entrance into the earthly paradise (XXVII.115). She is herself the most delicious fruit of the Golden Age of which, as Matelda herself suggests, the ancient poets sang when they dreamed the earthly paradise on Mount Parnassus, the Muses' home (XXVIII.139–44).

Matelda is fruitful in this way. She is fruitful in a second sense as well that makes it wholly appropriate that she has been anticipated in the figure of Leah as she appeared to Dante in the dream he had on the night before his entrance into the ancient wood. In this dream Dante had seen Leah weaving garlands of flowers with which she adorned herself while gazing upon her own image in her mirror. She had contrasted her activity with that of her sister, Rachel, who never left off gazing at herself within her mirror and therefore lacked such works and self-adornment (XXVII.94–108). The Leah of Dante's dream was, like the biblical Leah, fecund and productive of works. Her sister, again following the biblical precedent, was barren of works. Matelda, then, represents not simply the friendship in philosophy of Guido and Dante, but this friendship as productive of works, a friendship in poetry. She embodies the love of wisdom or mind as employing the images of the imagination to its own purposes. Matelda stands to Leah as Beatrice to Rachel, and Dante to Jacob. Dante is Jacob with a difference, however. He prefers the fecundity of his new Leah to the barrenness of the new Rachel. Dante's love for Matelda has driven any affection for Beatrice from his soul.[8]

---

8. Dante's preference for the perfectly human Matelda over the divine or "trans-human" Beatrice is an echo of Aristotle's argument in the *Ethics* that we would not wish what is often thought to be "the greatest good" for our friend, namely, to be a god. "For the friend will wish for the greatest goods for the other as a human being" (*NE* 1159a7–12). "Also no one chooses to possess every good by becoming another" (*NE* 1166a21). *Aristotle's "Nicomachean Ethics,"* trans. and ed. Robert C. Bartlett and Susan D. Collins (Chicago: University of Chicago Press, 2011), 175. Aristotle's argument in its turn echoes Homer's Odysseus' rejection of Calypso's offer to make him a god: he prefers to live the life of a human being (*Od.* 5.206–20). To embrace the human, however, is not, in Dante's view, simply to put aside the divine. See Lansing, "*Convivio*," 92–93, 153.

It is the fruitfulness of Matelda that permits Dante to compare her not only to Eve and Leah, but, leaving biblical allusions behind, to Proserpina, the incarnation of vernal renewal whose mother is Ceres, the goddess of the life-bearing earth (XXVIII.49–51). Dante, however, compares Matelda to Proserpina at the moment immediately prior to her abduction and rape by Pluto, the god of death, and then amplifies this hint of looming danger by further comparing her to Venus in love with Adonis and Hero with Leander (XXVIII.64–75). Something threatens to thwart the well-prepared consummation of the union of Dante and Matelda.

The Hellespont that separates Matelda's Hero from Dante's Leander is the "little stream" that runs between them (XXVIII.26–27). The stream is one of two running through the earthly paradise; and though these two streams have a single source, they are divided as they flow forth from it. The one stream is called Eunoe or "good mind," and the other Lethe. The first restores all thought of the good, the other erases all memory of sin (XXVIII.121–32). Between them and their effects the streams separate knowledge of the good from innocence. One can retrieve innocence while lacking knowledge of the good, and possess knowledge of the good while suffering from the shame of recollected sin. The biblical teaching concerning these matters, according to which, for man as man, the knowledge of good and evil is necessarily accompanied by shame and innocence by ignorance, is still haunting the earthly paradise despite Dante's completed ascent beyond the moral or lawful teaching regarding good and evil and the confirmation of Dante's self-sovereignty by Virgil. What is the source of this lingering apparition?

This question is answered immediately when we discover that the terrain that Dante was to have occupied and ruled over as his own realm, with Matelda as his consort, has already been invaded by alien and hostile forces: the books of the Old and New Testaments personified and ranked as in a military cohort or triumphal procession (XXIX.82–150). Dante identifies these forces in his first encounter with them as a "false appearance" (XXIX.43). The hallucinations of the imagination, animated by anger or spirited love, have regrouped and staged a counter-attack that challenges the victory of the reborn Muses over the new Pies. The divine law has reclaimed as its engines of war the images of the imagination that philosophic poetry declared to be its proper instruments of thought.

Somehow, despite their best efforts, Virgil and Dante have failed to vanquish this hostile power. The new weapon this power holds in its arsenal that allows for the overturning of the victory of the Muses is Beatrice and all that she represents.

If Matelda is the perfection of the imagination, insofar as she represents the imagination as perfected by being employed towards the aims of philosophy, Beatrice is the perfection of the imagination, insofar as she represents the notion of perfection as seen from the viewpoint of the imagination. She is the false appearance of a trans-human perfection of humanity. She is divine wisdom incarnate. As such she takes the place of Jesus in Dante's "eschatology." Beatrice can take the place of Jesus as the figure of divine wisdom because she is the incarnate *logos* armed with a new *logos*. She is equipped with the concatenation of biblical revelation and Greek philosophy: theology. Accordingly, she purports to fulfill the promise that Christianity has always made, that its teaching is the truth of philosophy or the resolution of philosophy into wisdom.[9]

Thus Beatrice appears not only dressed in the colors of the theological virtues, but crowned with Minerva's olive leaves, not only as the focal point of the biblical procession, but ensconced within an antique triumphal chariot drawn by a bestialized Christ (XXIX.106–20, XXX.1–33). The books and authors of the Bible and the teachings of Jesus have been inspired with a new and militant life by the divine science that Dante portrays here as their culmination and truth. Only in the train of this putative science can the Bible claim to bring the Muses to heel and consign them to the tomb once more. Only if philosophy is properly subordinate to a divine wisdom that completes it can poetry as ancilla to philosophy be disenfranchised. Thus the very appearance of Beatrice is enough to chase Virgil—"our greatest Muse" (*Paradiso* XV.26)—from the field and back to his fortified position in the noble castle of limbo.

Dante's "ship that singing makes her way" (*Paradiso* II.3; *Purgatorio* XVII.78, XXIV.1–4) is deprived of its Palinurus just as it runs straight into the armada over which Beatrice presides as admiral (XXX.58–66).

---

9. See, for example, Gregory of Nyssa, *The Life of Moses*, trans. and ed. Abraham J. Malherbe and Everett Ferguson (San Francisco: HarperCollins Books, 2006), 34–42; see also Origen, *On First Principles*, trans. and ed. G. W. Butterworth (Gloucester, MA: Peter Smith, 1973), 224–25, 257–58.

He is supported only by an alliance with Statius, who has already declared himself a turncoat,[10] and an attachment to Matelda, who is immediately forced to acknowledge her servile relation to the queenly Beatrice. It would appear that in this renewed battle of the books Dante suffers a crushing defeat in his first engagement with the enemy. This defeat was prepared by Dante's abstraction throughout the *Purgatorio* from the core claim of the Christian revelation. In treating that revelation as primarily a moral or lawful teaching, Dante failed to acknowledge the most vaunting of Christianity's claims, namely, that the teaching it offers is not a moral teaching at all, but a speculative one, that the salvation it offers is not completed primarily in the purification of the soul of vice and the installation within it of moral virtue, but in the enlightenment of the mind through the aid of the theological virtues and their support for a cognition of and union with the first principle of all things. Theology in its culmination (scholasticism) represents the complete articulation of this claim. To confront Christianity's claims to dominance, then, requires, it would seem, not simply a confrontation with Christianity's political pretensions and its moral teachings, but above all its claims to embody a trans-legal and trans-moral experience of the truth of love that has at its core the contemplation of first principles.[11]

It will take Dante the better part of the *Paradiso* to lend full articulation to and provide a complete refutation of these claims, but in the final cantos of the *Purgatorio* he gives the reader a taste of the strategy he will pursue

---

10. Statius has explained that he has been converted to the Christian faith by, of all things, his reading of Virgil (XXII.31–93).

11. This is a convenient place to give a general outline of the subject matters of Dante's *Comedy* as they are presented in its three-part structure. The *Inferno* is an articulation and refutation of Christianity's teaching regarding the political community and its perfection in the best regime, along with an exposition of the truth regarding the status of the political community and its perfection in the best regime. The *Purgatorio* is an articulation and refutation of Christianity's teaching regarding the soul and its perfection in moral virtue, along with an exposition of the truth regarding the soul and its perfection in practical wisdom or prudence. And the *Paradiso* is an articulation and refutation of Christianity's account of mind and its perfection in the ascent to and union with the first principle of all things, along with an exposition of the truth of the nature of the mind and its paradoxical perfection in doubt and a never to be completed inquiry into the first principles of all things.

there. Dante snatches victory from the jaws of defeat by illustrating, precisely in the depiction of his humiliation at the hands of the victorious Beatrice, the falsehood of Christianity's claims to have ascended beyond the legal and moral realm in a flight of the mind on the wings of love.

Dante portrays Beatrice's triumphal advent as a second coming.[12] The second coming of Beatrice takes the place of the second coming of Christ. She comes in power and glory—not as a savior, but as a judge. Yet she comes to judge not the world, but only her former lover, Dante. Her first coming, after all, was an advent for the young poet-protagonist of the *Vita Nuova* alone. He alone, on the basis of the experience of his love, took her to be more than a mortal woman, a new divinity of love, a Christianized Venus.[13] It is, then, this experience of "first love"—as represented in Dante's first book—that the author of the *Comedy* here resurrects. As soon as he catches sight of "the high virtue that had already transfixed [him] before [he] was out of [his] boyhood," he knows the signs of the "ancient flame" (XXX.40–48).

The phrase "ancient flame" is taken, of course, from book 4 of Virgil's *Aeneid* (4.23). It is used by Dido to describe her experience of falling in love once more after having vowed to renounce all further entanglements following the murder of her husband Sychaeus (*Aen.* 4.15–30). The flame that burns her is ignited by Aeneas and, as everyone knows, ultimately becomes a conflagration that drives her first to madness and finally to suicide. Dante thus uses his Virgil to suggest that the sort of love experienced by the protagonist of the *Vita Nuova* is, like the ancient flame that kindles the passions and ignites the imagination of Virgil's Dido, a form of insanity. Virgil, how-

---

12. Beatrice stages the second of two resurrections that Dante presents to the reader in *Purgatorio*. In contrast to the first, the second is of a distinctively Christian character, though a Christianity far from orthodox. *Purgatorio*, therefore, begins and ends with portrayals of resurrections—competing and colliding resurrections. Beatrice's resurrection is the Muses' re-entombment.

13. Dante's "Christian Venus," however, is not the mother of the god of love, Amor, whom Dante declares inspires his poeticizing (XXIV.52–54). She is, rather, barren, virginal, and ultimately an opponent of Amor and all the gods who make up the ancient pantheon. In this regard Beatrice is a "creature" who has broken free of and turned upon the guidance and power of her master (*Vita Nuova*, 3.1–12). One might say, then, that Amor and the rebellious Beatrice contend for the possession of Dante's poetic art (XXIV.52–54, XXXIII.52–81).

ever, in book 4 of the *Aeneid* follows Lucretius' analysis of love from book 4 of *On the Nature of Things*.[14] According to that analysis, there is scarcely a greater source of madness in human life than that species of love rooted in sexual attraction. This is so, above all, because it leads one, "blinded by desire . . . to ascribe to others qualities which in reality they do not possess" (Lucr. 4.1153–54).[15] At its maximum this tendency results in the attribution of qualities to the beloved that are more than "it is right to grant a mortal" human being. This tendency, explains Lucretius, is exploited by these beloved "Venuses" who "all the more strive to conceal everything behind the scenes of life from those they wish to ensnare and hold fast in love," for example, certain "foul odors" (Lucr. 4.1183–87).[16]

On taking sight of Beatrice, again and again experiencing the symptoms of his former love, Dante turns to Virgil to express his condition. As Singleton and other commentators have remarked,[17] in recounting Virgil's disappearance, Dante refers to Virgil's work a second time, now to the fourth of his *Georgics* (4.525–27) in which he portrays Orpheus, even in death still expressing his despair at losing Eurydice to the hostile power of the infernal gods.[18] Dante thereby suggests that, whatever may have been Beatrice's intention in summoning Virgil to his aid, Dante's dominant aspiration was to lead Virgil up from out of the realm of the dead, beyond the reach of the infernal powers, and into the precincts of the earthly paradise.

---

14. That Virgil is a great reader of Lucretius is a fact not often noted by students of Dante's *Comedy*. All the same, more than one commentator has suggested that Dante had first-hand knowledge of Lucretius' *De Rerum Natura*.

15. Translations of *De Rerum Natura* are from *Lucretius, "On the Nature of Things,"* trans. Walter Englert (Newburyport, MA: Focus Philosophical Library, 2003).

16. The desacralizing effect of even the suggestion of bad smells perhaps explains the ubiquitous employment of incense in religious rites (Hdt. I.183) and is remarked upon sagaciously by Lessing in his *Laocoön*—see G. E. Lessing, *Selected Prose Works*, trans. E. C. Beasley and Helen Zimmern (London, 1879), 148–49.

17. *Dante Alighieri: "The Divine Comedy,"* trans. and ed. Charles S. Singleton, vol. 2, *Purgatorio*, pt. 2, *Commentary* (1973; repr., Princeton: Princeton University Press, 1982), 741.

18. As Virgil's verses thrice call upon Eurydice's name, so Dante does Virgil's (XXV.49–51).

When Dante weeps for Virgil's loss Beatrice speaks for the first time. Her speech is animated by anger and her anger by jealousy. Dante's tears demonstrate that he is more grieved to lose Virgil than delighted to regain Beatrice. Given the choice, he would retain Virgil and let Beatrice return to the dust from which she has risen. The reason for this becomes clear if we take the first three words of Beatrice's utterance in isolation, words that bind Dante and Virgil together at the very moment of their apparent separation: "Dante, perche Virgilio..." (XXX.55). Dante exists as Dante only because Virgil exists—no Virgil, no Dante. That is to say, Dante's poetic accomplishments would have been impossible without Virgil's precedent. Dante does not stand in a similar relation of indebtedness and intimate community of mind vis-à-vis Beatrice. Indeed, one must rather say that because Dante exists, Beatrice exists. She is entirely the product of his poetic art.

Beatrice finds Dante's tears at Virgil's departure intolerable. "How did you deign to ascend this mountain? Did you not know that here man is happy?" she exclaims (XXX.74–75). If Virgil represents most obviously the guidance of the soul by reason, Beatrice insists that man "here" ought to be happy even or especially in the absence of the guidance of reason. Yet Beatrice has no intention of drying Dante's tears or demanding that he assume a joyful demeanor. On the contrary, she herself will give him something to cry about: "Do not weep yet, you must weep for another sword," she insists (XXX.56–57). He must weep for the offense of not loving Beatrice and Beatrice alone. His love of and friendship with Virgil is a crime for which he must be made to pay the penalty.[19]

In order to try Dante for this putative love-crime, she establishes a court in which she will act as both prosecutor and judge. She will read the charges and Dante will be compelled to confess his guilt. Prior to charging the defendant, however, she provides a preamble to the indictment that is meant to remove any thought of extenuating circumstances in this case. She declares that Dante was endowed by both nature and grace with such a disposition that every "right habit would have made marvelous proof in him" (XXX.115–17). That he was virtually such in his youth was made

---

19. This passage cannot help but put us in mind of those several biblical passages in which God upbraids the Children of Israel for their "whoring after foreign gods."

manifest, she declares, in his "new life," his *vita nova*. This *vita nova* was conducted under the gaze of her countenance and as long as this sustained him he followed "the right goal" (XXX.121–23). Having completed her preamble, and shown to her satisfaction that neither incapacity nor lack of proper guidance can serve as excuses for Dante's delinquency, she proceeds with her indictment. The charge amounts to one of infidelity to her own person: when she left this life for the next, he turned away from Beatrice and gave himself to others. Dante's *Convivio* documents his turn away from Beatrice and all that she represents and towards the beautiful lady Philosophy. From that day forward all of his poetic activity and each of his writings were devoted not to the celebration of Beatrice but to the pursuit of philosophy (*Convivio* III.12). It is this pursuit that Beatrice condemns as a turning of his "steps along a way not true, following false imaginings of good which pay no promise in full" (XXX.130–32). Taken together, this preamble and indictment also prove to be a somewhat extreme form of literary criticism: everything that Dante has produced after his completion of the *Vita Nuova*, up to and including Canto XXIX of the *Purgatorio,* is, according to Beatrice, misguided, false, and bad, because it takes philosophy and not Beatrice, the wrathful queen of the religion of love, as its central theme.

As we have seen, Dante's poetic endeavors in the service of philosophy are embodied in the figure of Matelda. Beatrice's initial jealous anger may have been provoked by Dante's attachment to Virgil; her formal accusation, however, involves his passionate attraction to Matelda. Though Beatrice rejects Dante's love of philosophy as the love of a false good, she does not insist that he should have remained devoted to her alone on the basis of her goodness. In fact, she never once mentions her own goodness. Rather she insists on her bodily beauty or her splendid appearance, which, she declares, surpassed in its splendor all other products of art or nature.[20]

---

20. Beatrice remarks upon the attractiveness of her "countenance" or "aspect" (*volto*), of her "youthful eyes" (XXXI.121–22), of her increased "spiritual" "beauty and virtue," her nobility, in taking on her "second age" or new "life" (XXXI.124–28), of the pleasure presented by her "beautiful members" (XXXI.50), and of the supreme attractiveness of her "buried flesh" (XXXI.48). She does suggest that this supreme attractiveness and the "highest pleasure" offered by her inordinately lovely body, both living and, above all, dead, should have led Dante to "love that good beyond which there is nothing

Beatrice's vanity knows no bounds. Having lost to death this supreme beauty and "highest pleasure" (XXXI.52), she argues, no mortal thing ought to have detained him. Rather he ought immediately to have "risen up," turned in the opposite direction from all things mortal, and followed after her "buried flesh" (*carne sepolta*). In his love for the beauty of her buried flesh he should himself have become buried flesh so that they might be together, buried flesh with buried flesh.[21] Beatrice's corporeal beauty should have led Dante to love this, namely, death, as "that good beyond which there is nothing to which man may aspire" (XXXI.23–24).[22]

Dante is made to offer a confession of his "sins" under the compulsion exercised by the "confusion of his virtue" that his fear of Beatrice and the "bitter taste" of her "harsh piety" engender: he did indeed turn his steps towards "present things" and away from Beatrice. Beatrice specifies the character of these "present things": a "young girl" or "new thing" (XXXI.34–36, 52–75). At the conclusion of her tirade Beatrice bids Dante to "lift up [his] beard" so that he "will have more pain in gazing" at the source of this prolonged invective. Dante complies, but with resistance, and suggests that

---

one can aspire to" (XXXI.22–24). In the context, however, it is clear that the "good" to which she invites him to aspire is death.

21. The word that Martinez and Durling translate as "flesh," namely, *carne*, can also be translated as "meat." In which case Beatrice might be construed as suggesting that Dante follow her into the grave to dine upon her supremely delicious bodily organs (*membra*). This would invert the relationship of food and feeding upon it that we see presented in the first poem, a sonnet, of the *Vita Nuova*, wherein the naked Beatrice, held like a child within the arms of the god Amor, is compelled to feed upon Dante's burning "heart" (3.1–12). Obviously the sacrament of the Eucharist cannot be far from Dante's mind when offering up these most remarkable images for the reader's delectation.

22. We see here that Beatrice refers to, approves of, and insists upon, the inclinations that Dante portrays in the central canzone of the *Vita Nuova*. He himself describes these inclinations in the comment to that canzone in the following terms: upon seeing his lady dead, "It seemed that women covered her—that is, her head—with a white veil; and it appeared that her face had so much the aspect of humility that she seemed to say: 'I am beholding the font of peace.' In this imagining I felt such humility at seeing her that I summoned Death, and said: 'Sweet Death, come to me, and be not unkind, for you must be noble: in such a place have you been! Now come to me, I greatly desire you.'" Dante calls this entire feverish episode an "erroneous fantasy," "a false imagining," and "an empty or vain imagining" (23.1–24.1).

"when she referred to my beard I knew well the venom of the argument"
(XXXI.67–75). Gazing on the veiled face of Beatrice, Dante is to conclude
that the uncovered loveliness of Matelda, representing all that is eternally
present and new, and with all of her consequent attractions, ought to have
been rejected in favor of keeping faith with the "past things" that the religion
of love declares to be the ultimate reality of all future things: the dead body
of Beatrice. The present and the new—human life devoted to discovery—
are declared by Beatrice to be "Sirens" leading Dante astray (XXXI.43–46).

Beatrice has made two chief claims in her indictment: First, that Dante
had a duty, a duty he neglected, to keep faith with her not only unto death,
but also beyond it and through it. Second, that she herself in her unpar-
alleled beauty is the highest object of love. The first claim seems to be
dependent upon the second. Through the first claim, Dante points to the
foundational character of the concept of faith for theology. According to
the arguments of theology, faith is the root or ultimate first principle of
all human knowledge. Such faith, however, is not ultimately a faith in certain teachings or doctrines, since the latter presupposes a faith in the person who is the source of those teachings or doctrines.[23] Dante ought to
have remained perpetually faithful to the person, even to the body, of Beatrice. Such faith appears, at first glance, then, to be one in kind with the
faith a lover must offer his beloved if he is to qualify as a lover at all. On
closer inspection, however, it proves to stand in combination with the faith
or trust that one is duty bound to offer to the law and its authority. Those
who break faith with the authority of the law are compelled to acknowledge that authority again through the juridical apparatus and punitive
force that the law employs. Dante portrays Beatrice's jealous accusations
in the trappings of a legal prosecution. The spontaneity of erotic attraction
and devotion, however, and the compulsions of the law make for strange
bedfellows.[24] The discordance between the two is highlighted in Dante's

---

23. Aquinas, *Summa Theologica*, Prima Pars, A.1, Q.8, second reply.

24. This fusion of love and law is pervasive in the Bible, in the Old and New Testaments:
for the latter, Jesus as the ultimate beloved and the final judge of mankind; for the former, the God of the Law as He who must be loved with "all one's heart, all one's might,
and all one's soul." Such a fusion is "possible" only on the basis of a complete ignorance regarding the true character of love and the true character of the Law and the
passion that animates it: anger. It is possible, that is, only on the basis of a complete

presentation of Beatrice's second claim, namely, that she is, on account of her beauty, the highest object of love. In this connection Dante invites his reader to observe that his Beatrice does not behave in any way like the transcendently beautiful beloved might be expected to behave. Such beauty, that is, such perfection and self-sufficiency, ought to render its possessor sublimely indifferent to whatever love she might inspire, or whether, indeed, her beauty be the cause of any love at all.[25] On the contrary, Beatrice's anger and jealousy reveal her need and her neediness, her defectiveness. Beatrice is ugly. She is the ugly and defective, inspired with a furious ambition to be taken for the beautiful or non-defective. Beatrice is not simply the beautiful as a false appearance of the good, she is the ugly attempting to take on the false appearance of the beautiful as the false appearance of the good. Beatrice is at best twice removed from any genuine object of love. She is neither lovable nor a lover, unless one is to take

---

absence of any analysis of the nature of the human soul. Homer, who is the first author known to have provided such an analysis, turns his capacious mind to a complete unfolding of the passion of anger and its effects, which he perceptively describes as both "sweeter than honey" and "devastating" or "ruinous" (*Il.* 1.1–2, 18.110). Compare this with Heraclitus' observation that "anger (*thumos*)...buys what it wants at the price of the soul" (Heraclitus, frag. 85, ed. Robinson). There are no similar observations to be found in Holy Scripture. On the contrary, see 2 Kings 1:1–2:25.

25. Arist., *Met.* bk. 12, ch. 7. Miguel de Cervantes, in his portrayal of the star-gazing shepherdess Marcella, seems to have devised an anti-Beatrice. Cervantes sums up the splendid and sovereign indifference of Marcella to the legions of young men who have fallen under her spell in these words: "And over one and the other, over these and over all, the free, the unconcerned, the beautiful Marcella triumphs." Cervantes also allows Marcella to offer her own defense against the charge of cruelty leveled at her by a young man named Ambrosius, whose friend Chrysostom has done away with himself in despair of any hope that his mad love for Marcella might find requital. At the opening of her apology Marcella offers the following argument: "By the help of the small capacity which nature has bestowed upon me, I know that which is beautiful is lovely, but I can by no means conceive why the object which is beloved for being beautiful, is bound to be enamored of its admirer." Cervantes, *Don Quixote de la Mancha*, trans. Tobias Smollett, ed. Carlos Fuentes (1755; repr., New York: Farrar, Straus, and Giroux, 1986), vol. 1, bk. 2, chs. 4–5. Marcella's argument regarding herself as an object of love seems to anticipate Spinoza's reflections regarding God considered from a similar point of view: "He who loves God cannot strive that God should love him in return." Benedictus de Spinoza, *Ethics*, bk. 5, prop. 19, in *The Collected Works of Spinoza*, trans. and ed. Edwin Curley, 2 vols. (Princeton: Princeton University Press, 1985), 1:604.

as a species of love the root of her punitive anger that Virgil has called "spirited love." Virgil's "spirited love," however, is what the medieval Aristotelian tradition called the irascible faculty. Beatrice conjures up once more the false identification of anger and love that Virgil had analyzed and refuted in his "demonstration of love" at the center of the *Purgatorio* and of the *Comedy* as a whole. Her claim to represent the fulfillment and embodiment, through faith and love, of a good beyond the moral good or a life of the mind beyond the horizon of the law is therefore spurious. She embodies all of the ugliest aspects of the law and its punitive justice.

Thus rather than, like Virgil or Matelda, cultivating the reflections of mind or the affect of love in Dante's soul, Beatrice instills there the passions of fear and shame (XXX.76–78, 97–99, XXXI.1–3, 13–15, 64–69, XXXIII.31–34). The fear and shame she induces debase Dante from the state of a man sovereign over himself and taking his own pleasure as his leader, to the state of a tearful, repentant, and speechless child (XXX.79–81), and finally to a state of unconsciousness or a condition resembling that of a stone (XXXI.85–90). Beatrice is non-mind or anti-mind disguising itself as the ultimate object of mind. She is everything inimical to love parading as the ultimate object of love. When Beatrice calls Matelda and all that she represents a false good or Siren, this is the crow calling the swan black. Beatrice is the true Siren.

It is now made clear that Dante's dream of the Siren and the *donna presta* or "swift lady" (XIX.25–27) who discovers her deception is, like his later dream of Leah and Rachel, a dream prefiguring his encounter with Beatrice and Matelda (XVII.94–108). Indeed, and as has been observed more than once, Beatrice announces her advent in words that resemble those with which the Siren makes her identity known (XIX.19, XXX.73). Both echo the words of the biblical God, employed in response to Moses' demand that he reveal to him his name: "I am that I am" (Exod. 3:14). Both therefore represent the rock upon which Christian theology is founded. Dante has shown that this insistence upon self-identity and seamless unity conceals a complex incoherence. The ultimate *theologoumenon* of Christian theology is a self-contradictory aggregate of incompatible traits: the punitive wrath and jealousy of the god of the Law in combination with the self-sufficient beauty and separate mind of the god of Aristotelian philosophy. The "swift lady" (*donna presta*) of Dante's dream encourages Virgil to strip the Siren's womb and uncover there the effluvium of retributive justice in all of its mindlessness beneath the fraudulent promise of the complete satisfaction of the desires of the mind—she uncovers the foul odor of spirited love beneath the empty appearance of the highest desideratum of natural love. So Matelda, who declares to Dante and Virgil that she "has come swift (*presta*) to all your questions" (XXVIII.83–84), proves to be the touchstone against which Beatrice's specious claims to embody the most perfect beauty and the highest object of love may be gauged. The lovely Matelda, with all of her sweetness, reveals Beatrice in her unlovely and bitter squalor. Beatrice, she shows, is, precisely as Virgil suggests, the "ancient witch," who alone is the cause of tears in the earthly paradise (XIX.59–60). She is Circe, whose charms once diverted Ulysses from his proper course (XIX.22–24) and whose enchantments effect the bestialization of the human under the false aspect of its apotheosis or, as Dante has it, "trans-humanization" (*Paradiso* I.70–72).

9

Reflections on the First Three *Novelle* of Boccaccio's *Decameron*

Nathan Tarcov

The *Decameron* is deservedly famous for containing many funny or sexy stories, and I would recommend it on that basis alone. I wish, however, to suggest that it also explores serious questions about the divine, the law, and nature through the *novella*, a form marked by brevity, competing narrators, and a complicating frame. Thomas Pavel notes that *novelle* tend to feature an element of surprise: "a single uncommon situation or turn of events triggers an unexpected response from the characters, inviting readers to infer a specific truth about human nature."[1] I suggest that this element of surprise in the first three *novelle* of the *Decameron* serves to make them funny while also provoking serious thought about religion.

First, a few remarks about Boccaccio's preliminaries.[2] We read in his proemium that he writes the book moved by compassion (*compassione*) for

---

An earlier version of this essay was presented at "The Novel as a Form of Thought," a conference of the John U. Nef Committee on Social Thought at the University of Chicago, May 16–17, 2014.

1. Thomas Pavel, *The Lives of the Novel* (Princeton: Princeton University Press, 2013), 77.

2. My summaries, paraphrases, and quotations are based on the text of Vittore Branca's edition of the *Decameron* (Turin: Einaudi, 1980). I consulted the translations of Mark Musa and Peter Bondanella (New York: Signet, 1982), G. H. McWilliam, 2nd ed. (London: Penguin, 1995), and Wayne Rebhorn (New York: W. W. Norton, 2013). I refer to stories by day and number, e.g., "1.2" for the second story of the first day.

those suffering from love as he did, especially for ladies in love, who are forced to follow the dictates of their parents, brothers, and husbands and to conceal their love without being able to enjoy the diversions men can enjoy, such as hunting, fishing, riding, gambling, and business. It is to amend this sin of fortune (*peccato della fortuna*) against ladies that he offers succor and refuge by presenting a hundred *novelle*, whether fables or parables or histories (*o favole o parabole o istorie*), told in ten days by seven ladies and three young men in a time of pestilence, as well as the songs they sang. The pleasing and bitter incidents of love and other accidents of fortune they recount, which happened in modern as in ancient times, will offer ladies both delight and useful counsel (*utile consiglio*). Having been freed from the bonds of love himself, Boccaccio is able to minister to the ladies' pleasures. He does not say whether he means to help them to be freed from the bonds of love or to obtain pleasures or both.

The seven ladies and three young men sought refuge in the countryside from the plague that killed more than 100,000 people in Florence in 1348. Boccaccio's introduction initially leaves open whether the plague was sent by the just wrath of God (*giusta ira di Dio*) to punish the people's iniquitous deeds. He leaves open whether medicine was of no avail because of the nature of the illness (*natura del malore*) that did not admit of any cure or because of the ignorance of those treating it, often without any medical learning; in either case, the plague's general fatality is explained as a result of nature or human ignorance rather than divine intervention. Although Boccaccio says the plague began to show its painful effects in a miraculous manner (*miracolosa maniera*), he reports that humble supplications to God by the devout were of no avail against it. And far from correcting human iniquity, the plague almost overthrew and dissolved the revered authority of the laws, divine and human (*la reverenda auttorità delle leggi, così divine come umane*). Accordingly, Boccaccio drops his initial equivocation as to whether the plague was sent by a just God and attributes it instead to "the cruelty of heaven."

Given the emphasis on love in the prologue, the reader may be surprised that the first three *novelle* deal more with religion than with love.[3]

---

3. Franco Fido interprets these three stories as parts of a series that articulate "a discourse of moral theology." "The Tale of Ser Ciappelletto (I.1)," in *The "Decameron" First Day in Perspective: Volume I of the Lectura Boccaccii*, ed. Elissa B. Weaver (Toronto: Univer-

Could religion be a form of love, an impediment to love, or both? The proemium's mention that the *novelle* are modern as well as ancient (there are only five ancient *novelle*, counting the Hebrew and the Chinese as well as the Greek and Roman *novelle*)[4] may suggest the religious and resulting erotic differences between ancient and modern times or indicate that the work achieves a perspective that transcends a specifically modern or Christian view.

*   *   *

The first *novella* is told by Panfilo, one of the young men, who introduces it by saying he will tell of one of our Maker's marvelous things so that our hope in Him may be firm and His name always praised by us. For we could not endure the trouble, anguish, toil, and infinite dangers of transitory and mortal, temporal things if the special grace of God (*spezial grazia di Dio*) did not lend us force and discernment. Divine grace does not descend upon us by any merit of ours, Panfilo continues, but by His kindness, which is moved by those who followed His pleasures when they were alive and have now become eternal and blessed, and through whom as our advocates we make our prayers. Grace thus appears at first to depend on saintly intermediaries. Panfilo contends, however, that we discern God's merciful liberality toward us more when opinion mistakes one of the damned for a saint, since the human eye is unable in any way to penetrate into the secret of the divine mind (*segreto della divina mente*). Despite the asserted impossibility of penetrating the secret of the divine mind, Panfilo confidently concludes that God regards the purity of the one who prays more than the damnation of the one prayed to. The problem in this case, however, is the difficulty or impossibility of penetrating the secrets of the human mind, distinguishing saints from sinners.

Panfilo illustrates this unorthodox theological claim by telling the story of a man known as Ser Ciappelletto, a notary who delighted in committing forgery, giving false testimony, and stirring up enmities and scandals

---

sity of Toronto Press, 2004), 59–76; see 69–70. Similarly, Marga Cottino-Jones reads the first three *novelle* as conveying a central message "concerning the mutual relations of man, God, and the Church." "The Tale of Abraham the Jew (I.2)," in Weaver, 77–88; see 78. Pamela D. Stewart calls them "a triptych on the paramount value of our faith in God." "The Tale of the Three Rings (I.3)," in Weaver, 89–112; see 98.

4. 5.1, 7.9, 9.9, 10.3, 10.8.

among friends and relatives, who willingly participated in homicides and other evil deeds—a very great blasphemer against God and the saints, who never went to church and scorned the sacraments with abominable words, instead visiting taverns and places of ill repute. Moreover, he did not at all desire women but delighted in their opposite. He stole and robbed as conscientiously as a saintly man makes offerings. He was very gluttonous, a great drinker, and a solemn gambler with rigged dice. Panfilo sums up by saying he was the worst man perhaps ever born (*il piggiore uomo forse che mai nascesse*).[5]

That such a man came to be worshipped as a saint is surprising and incongruous and therefore funny, but also thought-provoking. Who would expect the worst man in the world to be finally worshipped as a saint? And who would expect that to be a demonstration of God's kindness (*benignità*) and pious or merciful liberality (*pietosa liberalità*) toward us?

Ciappelletto contracted a fatal illness while lodging in the house of two Florentine brothers who were moneylenders in Burgundy. He overheard his hosts worrying that, as he had led such a wicked life, he would not make confession or receive the sacraments and a Christian burial—and if he did make confession, his sins were so great and horrible that no friar or priest would be willing to absolve him. They feared that the townspeople, who every day spoke ill of them for their profession, which they considered very iniquitous, would rob and kill them. Ciappelletto told them not to worry and to fetch the most saintly and able friar they could find— "if there is such a one"—to take his confession, for since he had committed so many injuries against God while living, committing one more at his death (by making a false confession of his sins, just as he had previously delighted in giving false testimony against others) would make no difference, and he would make both their affairs and his turn out well, and they would be content.

The brothers fetched an old friar who had led a saintly and good life. He was, moreover, a great master of Scripture. The confession whereby Ciappelletto convinced the holy friar not only that he deserved a Christian burial but even that he was a veritable saint is a hilarious mixture of out-

---

5. This extensive but not comprehensive list of vices does not assert Ciappelletto was a fool or a coward. The story shows rather that he was clever and brave.

right lies, misleading truths, double entendres, and trivial trespasses—confessed as if they were the greatest sins,[6] because only a most saintly man would consider them his greatest sins. Ciappelletto, who had never made confession in his life, started by claiming to have done so at least once a week. He nonetheless begged the friar to ask him everything as if he had never confessed before, so he might confess all the sins of his whole life rather than risk the perdition of his soul, which his Savior had redeemed with His precious blood (*perdizione dell'anima mia, la quale il mio Salvatore ricomperò col suo prezioso sangue*), which pleased the saintly man. (Although Ciappelletto never went to church he is fluent in Christological language.)[7]

The friar first asked if Ciappelletto had ever committed the sin of lust with a woman, to which Ciappelletto, who delighted in men rather than women, presumably truthfully replied that he had not done so once since he was born, while professing to be worried that he might thereby be committing the sin of vainglory. When asked if he had ever committed the sin of gluttony, he confessed to enjoying water and craving herb salads during his alleged weekly fasts, to which the friar responded that such sins were natural. (The naturalness of human desires becomes a great theme in many of the erotic *novelle* later in the book, including the one incomplete *novella* Boccaccio tells in his own name in the introduction to Day 4.) Ciappelletto's rejection of such consolation made the friar pleased by his pure and good conscience (*tua pura e buona conscienza*). When the friar asked if he had ever sinned from avarice, he replied that he should not be thought guilty by association with his usurer hosts, for he had come to admonish and castigate them and draw them away from this abomination. (His eavesdropping hosts must have been uneasily amused by this.) When asked how often he had gotten angry, he confessed he had done so very

---

6. On Ciappelletto's false confession, cf. Nora Martin Peterson, "Sins, Sex, and Secrets: The Legacy of Confession from the *Decameron* to the *Heptaméron*," in *Reconsidering Boccaccio: Medieval Contexts and Global Intertexts*, ed. Olivia Holmes and Dana E. Stewart (Toronto: University of Toronto Press, 2018), 403–24. Fido presents a review of the wide range of critical interpretations of Ciappelletto and his confession. "Tale of Ser Ciappelletto (I.1)," 59–65.

7. Peterson points out that Ciappelletto "shows an understanding of which sins would have been condemnable and why." "Sins, Sex, and Secrets," 408.

often, seeing men every day do obscene things, not following the commandments of God, and not fearing His judgments, seeing youths go after vanities and hearing them swear and perjure themselves, go to taverns rather than church, and sooner follow the ways of the world rather than that of God (*seguir più tosto le vie del mondo che quella di Dio*). The friar assured him this was good anger (*buona ira*) and required no penance. The possibility of divine mercy toward the wicked of the world contrasts with human indignation at wickedness provoked by the divine commandments. Similarly, Ciappelletto confessed that it was out of pity for his neighbor's poor wife that he spoke ill of the man, who beat her every time he drank too much. When the friar dismissed as trivial his violation of the Sabbath by having his servant sweep the house, Ciappelletto lectured the friar about the importance of the Sabbath, the day when "our Lord was resuscitated from death to life" (*risuscitò da morte a vita il nostro Signore*). When his confession that he once spat in church elicited from the friar a smile and an admission that priests do so every day, Ciappelletto admonished the priests for committing a great villainy by defiling the sacred temple where sacrifice is offered to God.

Finally Ciappelletto tearfully said that from shame he had never confessed one sin for which God would never show mercy (*misericordia*). The friar assured him that if all the sins that had been and would be committed by all men while the world endures were all committed by one man who repented of them like Ciappelletto and confessed them, God's kindness and mercy (*la benignità e la misericordia di Dio*) are so great that He would freely pardon them. After much weeping, Ciappelletto said it was that he once cursed his mother when he was a little boy. The friar agreed to pray for him and assured him God would forgive this sin, as He willingly pardons men who blaspheme Him every day if they repent and would forgive even one of those who placed Him on the Cross if he were so contrite. Finally, the friar absolved and blessed Ciappelletto, holding him to be a most saintly man and believing what he had said. Who wouldn't believe it, Panfilo asks, on seeing a man on the point of death speak thus? The friar offered to bury him in the monastery. Ciappelletto asked for the sacraments, so that if he had lived as a sinner, at least he might die as a Christian. The friar administered the sacraments to him, preached a sermon about his saintly life, and had him buried with pomp and ceremony in a marble tomb in a chapel in the church of the monastery. To this day, Panfilo reports, people light candles, pray to him, call him Saint Ciappelletto, and affirm many miracles God works through him.

Why is this so funny? Partly because it is surprising that Ciappelletto effects the result not by claiming to be without sin but by expressing great sorrow over minor sins. Partly because he manages to reverse roles and preach to the friar. Partly because we identify with and cannot help admiring the cleverness of a person who tricks someone less clever; and we find it funny.[8] In admiring Ciappelletto's cleverness we first admire the cleverness of Panfilo who created him and ultimately, of course, the cleverness of Boccaccio, who created both the fictional narrators and their characters. The Friar led a saintly and good life, and he was a great master of Scripture and a very venerable man,[9] but he was not wise in the ways of the world and was given to belief.

Panfilo and Boccaccio make us wonder why Ciappelletto made this remarkable confession. Would a habitual blasphemer care about getting a Christian burial? If he was moved by gratitude or compassion toward his hosts, then he might not be the worst man in the world after all. Or, like the ladies who laughed at parts of Panfilo's *novella*, Ciappelletto may simply have enjoyed a good joke. The brothers, eavesdropping on his confession, almost exploded with laughter and concluded that Ciappelletto, unmoved by fear of imminent death or divine judgment, was not turned from his wickedness[10] and wished to die as he had lived.

Panfilo says he does not wish to deny the possibility that Ciappelletto may have felt contrition for his wicked life at the last moment, and that God mercifully received him into His Kingdom.[11] But because this is hidden from us, Panfilo reasons instead according to what appears to us that Ciappelletto is rather in the hands of the devil in perdition than in

---

8. The stories of Days 7 and 8 are devoted to such tricks.

9. The brothers asked at the monastery for a saintly and wise man (*santo e savio uomo*), but the friar is not said to be wise.

10. In a footnote to this passage, Branca concludes that Ciappelletto therefore was not an atheist or skeptic.

11. Peterson notes that "there is no textual evidence to support the theory that confession reconciles the dying Ser Ciappelletto with God, nor was this ever presented as the goal of his confession." "Sins, Sex, and Secrets," 409.

Paradise. (Ciappelletto's confession expressed contrition only for fabricated sins, not for his actual wicked life.) This would still show God's kindness (*benignità*) toward us, which regards not our error in praying to Him through His enemy, believing him to be His friend, but the purity of our faith, as if we sought His grace by means of one who was truly saintly. Panfilo concludes that, in order that they by His grace may in the present adversity and in this merry company be kept healthy and safe, they should praise, revere, and commend themselves to Him in need, secure that they will be heard. Thus God's benevolence is vindicated whether He accepted Ciappelletto into heaven on the basis of last-minute contrition, or whether He accepts the prayers of those who sincerely pray to the worst man in the world as if he were a saint. Panfilo's *novella* itself, however, shows only that Ciappelletto came to be worshipped as a saint and that people affirm many miracles God worked through him, not that God granted His grace in response to prayers addressed through him. The ladies laugh at parts of Panfilo's *novella* but praise it in its entirety: it is *not* entirely ridiculous.

The Church, its saints, and its friars do not, however, come out as well as God Himself is said to do. God's ways are too mysterious, the human heart too dark, and the human tongue too deceitful, for the Church— even the most saintly and Scripturally-learned friar—to tell saints from sinners. If a merciful God listens to our prayers even if they are not mediated by genuine saints, we may wonder whether we need the Church and its saints at all.

The extreme case that manifests God's mercy may make one wonder about His justice. If God were not only kind and merciful, as Panfilo claims to show, but also just and omnipotent (which Panfilo does not assert), why would He not provide us with genuine saints to pray to? Or should such wonder be squelched by Panfilo's suggestion that such things are hidden from us (which does not prevent Panfilo himself from reasoning on the basis of evidence)?

As the worst man in the world who comes to be worshipped as a saint, Ciappelletto is the Christian equivalent of Glaucon's perfectly unjust man who gains the greatest reputation for justice and becomes dearest to the gods (Plato, *Rep.* 360e1–362c8). As the perfectly unjust man could escape divine punishment through pagan sacrifices and purifications, so

Panfilo's *novella* suggests it can also be done through deathbed Christian repentance.

Ciappelletto's confession takes Christian morality to the extreme. Christian morality, as Ciappelletto interprets it, demands that even a heterosexual man should abstain from acts of lust with women, that one should not only fast on bread and water but also not enjoy the water. The friar is forced to admit that no one can live up to these standards or avoid committing sins that he admits are "natural." He is open or vulnerable to Ciappelletto's confession because he is not only credulous but humane and respectful of human nature.

*   *   *

The second *novella* continues the theological theme of the first. Neifile tells it, she says, like Panfilo, to demonstrate God's kindness (*benignità*) in patiently enduring the faults of those who ought to bear witness to it in words and deeds but who do the opposite, an argument demonstrating His infallible truth, so we may believe it with more firmness of spirit.

Two merchants in Paris were friends, a Christian named Giannotto and a Jew named Abraham, both upright and loyal men. Giannotto, concerned that the soul of such an able, wise (*savio*), and good man as Abraham should go to perdition from lack of faith, began in a friendly way to plead with him to leave aside the errors of the Jewish faith and (re)turn to the Christian truth, which—he could see—being so holy and good, always prospers and increases, while his on the contrary diminishes to the point of nothing.[12] Abraham replied that he did not believe anything was holy or good outside of Judaism (*la giudaica*), in which he had been born and intended to live and die. Giannotto continued to argue crudely for the superiority of Christianity. Although Abraham was a great master of the Jewish law[13] and Giannotto an ignorant man (*uomo idiota*), nonetheless

---

12. In the *Summa Contra Gentiles* I.6, Aquinas offers the conversion of the world to the Christian faith as the clearest witness to the miracles performed on its behalf, which appear most clearly in their effect and need not be repeated, since for the minds of mortal men to assent to these things is the greatest of miracles.

13. Whereas Giannotto refers to the Jewish faith (*fede giudaica*), Panfilo calls Abraham a master of the Jewish law (*giudaica legge*), possibly illustrating the differences between Christian and Jewish understandings of religion. Abraham's *la giudaica* ambiguously could modify either *fede* or *legge*.

either his great friendship with Giannotto or, "perhaps" (*forse*), words the Holy Spirit put into his friend's mouth moved the Jew so that his friend's arguments began to please him, though he remained obstinate in his belief and did not abandon it.

We may note that one does not need Christian faith to be a wise and good man like Abraham, whereas an ignorant man like Giannotto can be a faithful Christian. Upright and loyal men of differing faiths can be friends, though their friendship may be troubled by a Christian's concern for his friend's soul. The Jew displays no corresponding worry about the fate of his friend's soul or any interest in converting him; Christianity differs from Judaism in its view of the perdition of those of other religions and consequent eagerness to convert them.

Finally, in response to Giannotto's persistence, Abraham announced he would go to Rome to examine the mores of the pope and cardinals, and if they showed his friend's faith to be superior to his own, he would become a Christian, but if not he would remain a Jew. Hearing this, Giannotto despaired, thinking that if Abraham saw the wicked and filthy life (*la vita scellerata e lorda*) of the clerics in Rome he would never become a Christian. He warned his friend of the expense and dangers of the voyage and claimed the prelates in Rome were just like those in Paris, only better; but he failed to dissuade him from going.

In Rome, Abraham, being a very perceptive man, observed that the pope, the cardinals, the priests, and their courtiers generally committed indecent sins of lust, not only natural but sodomitic (*non solo... naturale ma ancora... sogdomitica*) without restraint of remorse or shame, so that prostitutes and boys had no little power there. They were universally gluttons and drunkards, serving their stomachs like brute animals. He saw that they were so greedy for money they would sell human and even Christian blood[14] as well as divine things, whether sacraments or benefices, and that they acted as if God did not know their intentions and could be deceived. Being a sober and modest man, the Jew had seen enough and returned to Paris.

When Giannotto knew what he had seen, he had no hope Abraham would become a Christian. When he asked about the pope, the cardinals,

---

14. Abraham reverses the blood libel.

and their court, the Jew immediately replied that he wished God would punish them, as they had no sanctity, devotion, good deeds, or an exemplary way of life, but rather lust, avarice, gluttony, fraud, envy, and pride, a forge of diabolical rather than divine activities. It seemed to him that they were using every care, talent, and art to reduce the Christian religion to nothing and chase it out of the world.

The Jew concluded, directly contrary to the expectation of his Christian friend and probably of the reader as well, that since those who ought to be its foundation and support had despite their best efforts failed to destroy the Christian religion—but instead it continually grew and became more lucid and clear—that the Holy Spirit had to be its foundation and support as the most true and holy religion. Accordingly, he announced his decision to convert and they proceeded to Notre Dame for his baptism. As in the first *novella*, there is thus a funny double surprise, one in the plot and another in its purported theological lesson. The Jew unexpectedly converts to Christianity not despite but because of seeing the corruption of the Church in Rome, and this corruption is surprisingly offered by Abraham as proof of the truth of the Christian religion and by Neifile as a demonstration of God's patience. Neifile ends by reporting that Abraham, now baptized with the name Giovanni, quickly and completely mastered "our faith" (*nostra fede*) and was thereafter a good and able man of holy life. We were told, however, that as a Jew he was a good, able, and wise (*savio*) man. Had he become holy instead of wise?

As in the first *novella*, God is vindicated at the expense of the Church. Giannotto's argument from the prosperity of Christianity did not convert Abraham; only the combination of its prosperity with the corruption of its Church did so. We may wonder nonetheless whether this is a serious proof that Christianity is the true religion and why God did not keep His Church honest. Is it possible that the Christian religion prospered in this world *because of* rather than despite the worldly ways of its Church?[15] Montaigne, near the beginning of his *Apology for Raymond Sebond*, seems to refer to this story when he tells of someone who went to Rome to observe the sanctity of our morals but instead, seeing the dissoluteness of the prelates and people of that time, became all the more strongly estab-

---

15. Cf. Machiavelli, *The Prince*, ch. 11. Machiavelli seems to have admired Boccaccio.

lished in the Christian religion, considering how much force and divinity it must have to maintain its dignity and splendor among so much corruption and in hands so vicious.[16]

*　　*　　*

The third story is told by Filomena ("beloved" in Greek). We are told in the introduction to Day 1 that she was very prudent (*discretissima*), and at the beginning of her story on Day 2 that she was beautiful, tall, and had a more pleasing and delightful face than anyone else. In the *novella* she tells on Day 2 (which Shakespeare adapted for a subplot in *Cymbeline*), yet another just Muslim ruler brings about the happy ending, while her *novella* on the third day exposes the hypocrisy, stupidity, and avarice of the clergy, and her final *novella* on Day 10 is one of the three in the *Decameron* set in classical antiquity. Her perspective seems to transcend that of Christianity.

Filomena introduces her story by saying first that Neifile's *novella* reminds her of another about the precarious chance that befell a Jew. She then says that since much has already been well said about God and the "truth of our faith" (*verità della nostra fede*), she will descend to the events and acts of men and narrate a story that may make her companions more cautious in answering questions. She will show in particular how, just as there are many examples of how stupidity often takes one from a happy state into the greatest misery, so her little story (*novelletta*) will show that good sense takes the wise man (*il savio*) from the greatest dangers into great and secure tranquility. The contrast between her story and the two previous ones turns out, however, to be an act of misdirection on her part.[17] The two previous *novelle*, after all, also recounted the acts of men (e.g., those of Ciappelletto, the friar, Abraham, and Giannotto), and her *novella* turns out to address the question of the true religion most directly, which may be why Neifile's *novella* reminded her of it, as well as because both of them feature a Jew.

Filomena begins by saying Saladin's valor was so great that from a little man he became Sultan of Babylonia and had many victories over the Sara-

---

16. I owe this reference to Hillel Fradkin.

17. Cf. Pamela D. Stewart, "Tale of the Three Rings (I.3)," 99.

cen and Christian kings. (This reminds us that despite the claims of Giannotto for the prosperity and growth of Christianity relative to Judaism in Neifile's *novella*, it had suffered serious reverses at the hands of Islam.) Having spent all his treasure on various wars and great acts of munificence, and by some supervening accident needing a good quantity of money, Saladin decided to get it from a rich Jewish moneylender in Alexandria named Melchizedek, but he believed that the miserly Melchizedek would not give it to him voluntarily. Saladin did not wish to use force but instead resorted to "force colored by some reason" (*una forza da alcuna ragion colorata*). So addressing the Jew as one said to be most wise (*savissimo*) and advanced in the things of God, Saladin asked him which of the three laws (*tre leggi*) he reputed to be the true one, the Jewish, the Saracen, or the Christian. (Boccaccio's Muslims and Jews refer to religions as laws rather than faiths, whereas Lessing's Saladin, in his adaptation of this scene in *Nathan the Wise*, speaks of both *Glaube* and *Gesetz*, belief and law.) The Jew, being a truly wise man (*veramente ... savior uomo*), realized Saladin intended to trap him into praising one of the three more than the others. (If he replied that the Jewish law was the true one he could be punished for implying Islam was false; if he said the Saracen law was the true one he could be forced to convert or avoid doing so at a high price; Saladin may have included the Christian alternative to make the trap less obvious.) Instead he praised Saladin's question as beautiful, but to answer it he had to tell *una novelletta*, embedded within Filomena's *novelletta*.

Melchizedek's story was as follows. A wealthy man possessed a very beautiful and precious ring. Wishing to leave it in perpetuity to his descendants, he ordained that whichever son he left it to should be regarded as his heir, to be honored and revered by the others as the chief. This order was followed for many generations until the ring came to one father who equally loved his three sons, who were handsome, virtuous, and obedient to him. Each of the youths was eager to be the most honored, and begged their old father to leave the ring on his death to him. As the father did not know how to choose among them, he promised the ring to each of them, wishing to satisfy all three. So he secretly had a good master make two copies so similar to the first that even the ring-maker hardly knew which was the true one. Approaching death, he secretly gave one to each son. After his death each son, wishing to seize the inheritance and the honor

179

and deny it to the others, reasonably produced his ring as testimony. The rings were found to be so similar to each other that it could not be known which was the true one, and the question of the identity of the true heir of the father was left pending and remains pending.

Melchizedek concluded from this *novelletta* that of the three laws given by God the Father to the three peoples, each rightly believing it has the true inheritance, the true law and commandments, the question as to which of them has the true one, like that of the rings, remains pending.[18] Saladin recognized that Melchizedek had most excellently escaped the trap he had set and admitted what he had intended to do if Melchizedek had not responded so prudently (*discretamente*—the same quality ascribed to Filomena herself). Melchizedek lent the money to Saladin, who not only repaid it but gave Melchizedek very great gifts, held him always as his friend, and maintained him in great and honorable estate. (Saladin's generosity and interreligious friendship also figure prominently in Panfilo's *novella* on Day 10.)

We do not know whether Saladin became Melchizedek's friend only because he was impressed by the Jew's wisdom or because he was truly persuaded that the question of the true religion is unanswerable. At the risk of anachronism and tempted by Lessing's appropriation of the story, we might infer a lesson in favor of religious toleration; we hear, however, only of Saladin's friendship with Melchizedek, not of a general policy of toleration. More cautiously, therefore, we can regard the story as a demonstration of the possibility of friendship between wise men of different religions.

The element of surprise in this *novella* is different from that in the preceding two. The way in which Melchizedek escapes Saladin's trap is unexpected, but it is not as sharp a reversal as Ciappelletto's coming to be worshipped as a saint or Abraham's conversion to Christianity, and it is less likely to strike us as funny. While many of Boccaccio's *novelle* are funny in the way that stories about clever people tricking stupid people

---

18. It is not clear to me how the figure of the good master who made the rings fits into this allegory. The father who merely had the rings made and gave them to his sons could not tell which was the true one whereas their maker "hardly" (*appena*) could. What would it mean for God to be the giver but not the maker of the three religions and not to know which is the true one?

are funny, here a wise man escapes the trap of an intelligent man, and we may say that Melchizedek teaches Saladin rather than that he tricks him. Glenn Most has suggested to me that all three of the first *novelle* concern conversions: in the first the worst man in the world is converted into a saint or alternatively converts a saintly friar to a belief in his sanctity; in the second a Jew converts to Christianity; and in the third Melchizedek may convert Saladin to skepticism about the claims of his religion to be the true one.

Despite Filomena's introductory disclaimer, her *novella* obviously addresses questions about God and the true religion. Melchizedek suggests that his *novelletta* shows that God loves His three virtuous but contentious peoples equally, that He gave all three peoples their religions, and that those religions are basically similar. The *novelletta* itself suggests that, just as the oldest ring is the true one, so the oldest religion (the Jew's, of course) is the true one and the other two are later copies. Melchizedek's own conclusion instead is that we do not know which is the true one and that for all practical purposes they might as well all be simulacra of the truth. Filomena's Melchizedek is an implicit reproof of Neifile's Abraham, who thought he could, however oddly, determine the true religion. Unlike the first two narrators, Filomena presents her *novella* as an illustration of human wisdom; she does not claim it demonstrates God's kindness or strengthens our belief; on the contrary, it may make us wonder why God gave men three contending religions, leaving us skeptical about the claim of any religion to be true. There is a progression in the first three stories: Panfilo's suggests that the ways of God are hidden from us so that we cannot tell saints from sinners; Neifile's illustrates the perplexity of determining the true religion given the mysterious ways of God; Filomena's takes that a step further to the impossibility of determining the true religion.[19] Her Melchizedek's telling his *novelletta* may cast light on her telling her own *novelletta*, and even on Boccaccio's telling them all. As Melchizedek tells his *novelletta* to escape a trap and teach a lesson, so Filomena may tell hers to avoid having to affirm or deny that their religion is the true one and to teach her fellow narrators a lesson. Whereas Panfilo

---

19. Pamela D. Stewart shows how Boccaccio's version departs from previous ones in stressing the equivalence of the three religions. "Tale of the Three Rings (I.3)," 89–95.

tells his story about the difficulty of determining a true saint in a Christian context and Neifile puts hers about determining the true religion in a Jewish-Christian context, Filomena puts hers about determining the true religion in a Jewish-Muslim context, though she subtly makes her Saladin include Christianity in his question. Boccaccio himself tells his *novelle* not only to amuse but also to instruct while maintaining what we may call plausible deniability.

*   *   *

In his subtle interweaving of levity and gravity, Boccaccio's first three *novelle* lightly raise grave questions about the operations of divine grace, the implications of the corruption of the Church, and the true religion. Because these questions are raised in surprising stories whose diverse and competing narrators sometimes attribute questionable lessons to them, requiring us to think simultaneously on several levels—with the characters in the *novelle*, the characters telling them, and with Boccaccio, who is introducing and arranging them—we may be led to think about those questions more thoughtfully than we might by studying avowedly logical treatises. And when we are moved to laugh, we may ask why we do so and find wonder and insight in our laughter.

10

The Tyranny of Beauty:
On Art and Truth in Lessing's *Laocoön*

Richard Velkley

I. Lessing as Elusive Teacher

Laocoön: An Essay on the Limits of Painting and Poetry (1766), by Gotthold Ephraim Lessing, is an immensely complex work. A small book made up of short essays, it presents fundamental thoughts on art criticism, poetics, and philosophic inquiry into the nature of the arts. Beneath the surface lie profound ideas about human nature and metaphysics that are suggested rather than proposed in a straightforward argument. Of Lessing's writings Friedrich Schlegel says that they are a "labyrinth": easy to get into and extremely difficult to emerge from.[1] Søren Kierkegaard, one of Lessing's most appreciative readers, associates Lessing with Socrates, "who planned his entire form of communication artistically so as to be misunderstood."[2]

The original version of this essay was delivered as a Dean's Lecture at St. John's College, Santa Fe, on October 2, 2015. The wonderful conversations I have had over the years with Ronna Burger on the Platonic-Aristotelian treatments of poetry and beauty have helped me, in ways that are imponderable, with the reading of Lessing.

1. Schlegel, *Kritische Friedrich-Schlegel-Ausgabe*, ed. Ernst Behler, vol. 2, *Charakteristiken und Kritiken I, 1796–1801*, ed. Hans Eichner (Paderborn: Ferdinand Schöningh, 1967), 111. I owe this reference to Benjamin Bennett, *Beyond Theory: Eighteenth-Century German Literature and the Poetics of Irony* (Ithaca, NY: Cornell University Press, 1993), 119.

2. Kierkegaard, *Concluding Unscientific Postscript to the Philosophical Crumbs*, ed. and trans. Alastair Hannay (Cambridge: Cambridge University Press, 2009), 59; hereafter, *CUP*.

Lessing refuses to present a doctrine, as the intent of his work is to make one free. With paradoxical praise, Kierkegaard writes that Lessing lacks seriousness and reliability, as he mingles jest and earnestness and declines all partnership with the reader. He employs an indirect mode of communication arousing perplexity rather than a direct form seeking agreement (*CUP*, 63). His writing engages in "double reflection," as it addresses both the *what* of the inquiry and the *how* of communication (*CUP*, 63–64). Accordingly, Lessing rejects utterances that are "world-historical and systematic," addressed to all humanity, in the style of Hegel. But the effect of his writing is not merely confusion, since he leads the reader toward insights, albeit this is done often without the reader's notice. Johann Goethe, in his autobiography, *Poetry and Truth*, declares that "one has to be young to appreciate what an effect Lessing's *Laocoön* had on us, by lifting us up from the region of miserably limited observation into the wide spaces of thought."[3] But even as Lessing raises one's thoughts to an elevated plain of abstract reflection, in *Laocoön* he avows that his thoughts did not come together by a methodical development of general principles, and that "they are rather unordered *collectanea* for a book, than themselves a book."[4] This apparent defect contrasts sharply with a celebrated virtue of many modern writers, for of "systematic books there is no lack among us Germans. Out of a few assumed definitions to deduce most logically whatever one will—this we can manage as well as any other nation in the world" (29).

Indeed, Lessing allies his apparent disorder of writing to the spirit of the ancients, whose "prerogative in everything" is "to do neither too much nor too little" (26). We moderns with our systematic spirit "have considered ourselves their betters, when we transformed their pleasant little byways to highroads, even if the shorter and safer highroads shrink again to footpaths as they lead us through the wilds" (26). In place of methodical demonstration that extorts agreement, Lessing proceeds with mostly

---

3. *Goethes Werke*, vol. 27, *Dichtung und Wahrheit II* (Weimar, 1889), 164.

4. Lessing, *Laocoön: An Essay on the Limits of Painting and Poetry*, trans. W. A. Steel, in *Classic and Romantic German Aesthetics*, ed. J. M. Bernstein (Cambridge: Cambridge University Press, 2003), 29; page numbers in this edition are hereafter cited in the text.

implicit argumentation, especially through the use of examples, which demands the interpretative effort of an attentive reader. Kierkegaard takes note of this, as he says, "Altogether rare as it is these days for any thinker to call the beautiful Greek way of philosophizing to mind by cleverly concentrating himself and his thought-existence on something in a single, brief felicitous statement, Lessing reminds us vividly of the Greeks" (*CUP*, 84). Lessing makes other statements that have a less Greek and more modern ring about them. Thus he writes that nature has an infinite variety that is comprehensible only by an infinite intellect, and "in order for finite intellects to participate in the enjoyment of this spectacle, they had to be endowed with an ability to set limits to nature which nature herself does not possess."[5] I will argue that the problem of setting limits to nature's infinite fecundity emerges as a major theme in *Laocoön*.

II. Monumental Misreadings

Lessing begins with an account of three standpoints on the arts: those of the amateur, the philosopher, and the critic. The amateur makes the discovery that painting and poetry affect him in a similar manner, in that both present appearance as reality, and absent things as present (25). The arts deceive, and the deceptions are pleasing. The amateur is a person of "delicate perception," and although he does not investigate the causes of his pleasure, he notes a crucial common feature of what affords pleasure. It is the philosopher who seeks to penetrate to the source of the pleasure and finding one source, beauty, derives general rules, first by observing bodies and then applying them to actions, thoughts, and forms. Whereas the amateur finds a similar pleasure in diverse things, the philosopher uncovers a unitary ground and proceeds with subsuming particulars under it. The critic, the third standpoint, reflects on the philosopher's general rules, and sees a need for differentiation, as some rules apply more in painting, others apply more in poetry, even as painting and poetry still illuminate each other. Lessing presents these standpoints as though they form a temporal sequence: first the amateur discovers the common pleasure, the philosopher then uncovers its ground and establishes rules, then the critic differ-

---

5. *G.E. Lessings sämtliche Schriften*, ed. Karl Lachmann and Franz Muncker, 3rd ed., vol. 10, *Hamburgische Dramaturgie II, 1767–1768* (Stuttgart, 1894), 82. See Bennett, *Beyond Theory*, 140.

entiates in applying the rules. This suggests a natural course of discovery. Although the critic may seem non-philosophic, it is instead the case that criticism follows and corrects, and thus builds upon, the previous two standpoints. The critic brings the amateur's observations to a higher level of awareness, and turns the philosopher's abstract generalizations into nuanced judgments. This sequence puts Lessing's apparent disorder, his mere "collection" of thoughts, in a different light. The apparent lack of order masks the real movement of working rigorously through phases of inquiry. And although Lessing seems to disavow an association with the systematic philosopher and his methodical highroads, he is indebted to him. Indeed, as a philosopher, Lessing articulates principles. The path of discovery leads through general rules and arrives at disclosing their limitations. At the same time, Lessing as critic has an artful and deceptive procedure that cultivates the appearance of dilettantish treatment. The essay's discussion of art and poetry is itself artistic and poetic.

Good criticism is difficult, Lessing avers, for it involves the just application of feeling and rules to individual cases, wherein many critics go wrong. Lessing focuses on the antithesis of Simonides that painting is dumb poetry and poetry a vocal painting, which Lessing says was inspired and has some truth, but he laments its transformation into the crude correspondence of painting and poetry in modern critics. The ancients, Lessing claims, were not seduced by the comparison, and while admitting the similarity of the effect of the different arts, they did not omit to point out that they are distinct, both in their subjects and in their manner of imitation (26). But a modern critical attitude forces each art into the bonds of the other, engendering in poets a "rage for description" and in painters a "rage for allegorizing." The language of rage, or extreme willfulness, suggests something tyrannical. The idea of tyranny arises in several ways in the course of the essay and points to an underlying human tendency that embraces various phenomena the essay treats explicitly.

Lessing's prime example of questioning and questionable interpretation is the famous sculpture of late antiquity depicting Laocoön, the Trojan priest of Neptune, and his two sons struggling in the lethal coils of two serpents. This work, although not an example of the highest age of classical sculpture, is the focus of an argument Lessing has with the classical scholar and advocate of the imitation of the Greek ideal, Johann Winckelmann, concerning what is essentially classical.[6] The sculptor of the Laocoön group chose a moment of the story of Laocoön's attempt to warn the Trojans of the treacherous gift of the wooden horse that was brought into the gates of the city, for which action the priest is punished by Athena.[7] Lessing is in accord with Winckelmann on the beauty of the work. He cites Winckelmann's *aperçu* on the "noble simplicity and quiet grandeur" of the Greek masterpieces, and then quotes from that author's discussion of the Laocoön group: "Just as the depths of the sea always remain quiet, however the surface may rage, in like manner the expression of the figures of the Greek artists shows under all passions a great and steadfast soul" (28). The pain that is evident throughout Laocoön's body "expresses itself in the countenance and in the entire attitude without passion." Unlike the Laocoön in Virgil's *Aeneid*, the sculpted Laocoön "raises no agonizing cry," his mouth opened slightly only to suggest "an oppressed and weary sigh." Lessing agrees that the face of Laocoön does not disclose the passion one could expect, and adds that this restraint of the artist shows his wisdom. All the same, Winckelmann errs in his account of the reason for this restraint and in the universal rule he deduces from it.

Winckelmann's disdain for the Virgilian depiction of the hero's cries reveals a flaw in his conceptions of heroism and the classics. Lessing notes that the classical poets, Greek and Roman, allow their heroes and even their gods and goddesses to cry in pain, such that "suffering nature may have her rights." In respect of virtue, "Homer raises his heroes above nature, yet they ever remain faithful to her when it comes to the point of feeling pain and injury." Although beyond the human in their deeds, the heroes are in their sensibilities mere humans (30). The judgment of Winckelmann betrays a modern European prejudice, for the ancients did not have the modern shame of tears, and found no contradiction between fulfilling duty and expressing pain. The modern European is the heir of the barbarian who concealed all fear, grief, and expression of suffering as incompatible with virtue, and whose bravery, raging continually, con-

---

6. Johann Joachim Winckelmann, *Gedanken über die Nachahmung der griechischen Werke in der Malerei und Bildhauerkunst* (1755).

7. The story is also told in Virgil, *Aen.* 2.198–230. Lessing enters the controversy of whether the epic or the sculpture came first and favors the view that the sculptor was inspired by the epic.

sumed every other good quality (31). The restraint of the Laocoön sculpture cannot be due to the reason Winckelmann advances. Yet Lessing briefly notes that the ancient world saw the appearance of something akin to the barbaric attitude in Stoicism, which is unsuitable for the theatre since the drama calls for the evocation of pity (31). Lessing just hints at a connection between the rise of Stoicism and the decline of the public art of the drama, which went along with the decline of political liberty. There is a link between the free display of pain and political freedom.

But if tyranny is related to barbarism and suppression of feeling, it is more subtly linked to beauty and to the restraint that is deemed essential to its expression. This consideration, with political overtones, is the next step in Lessing's thought on the Laocoön group. Modern painters exercise wide latitude in their art's subject matter as they imitate bodies on plane surfaces, but the wise Greek, who Lessing says was following the prompting of Eros, limited the subject of plastic arts to the imitation of beautiful bodies (32–33). As the beautiful body was regarded as the perfection of beauty, this subject matter and its manner of treatment were so highly prized that laws existed to keep artists bound to their proper sphere. It was not merely the bungler who fell under penalty, but also the skillful artist who dared to exaggerate a less attractive aspect of the model. Lessing says that moderns will laugh when they hear that the ancients subjected the arts to municipal laws, but they fail to note that the law pertained to what gives pleasure, and that pleasure influences character. The plastic arts in particular exert this influence, and lawgivers perceived that beautiful statues have the effect of producing beautiful citizens. Laws of beauty that concern the character of the nation are not tyrannical, Lessing implies, as he states that laws usurping power over the sciences, whose purpose is truth, a necessity of the soul, are tyrannical in their violence to nature.[8] But Lessing subtly indicates that legislation of imitation that requires exclusion of truthful representation of the ugly is at odds with the need for truth, and that there is a tension between two competing goods, the demand of the city for formation of character and the need of the soul for truth.

---

8. "Wahrheit ist der Seele notwendig; und es wird Tyrannei, ihr in Befriedigung dieses wesentlichen Bedürfnisses den geringsten Zwang anzutun." *Sämtliche Schriften*, vol. 9, *Laokoon: oder über die Grenzen der Malerei und Poesie*, 13. See *Laocoön* (33).

In light of this reflection the Laocoön sculptural group is rich in significance, for Laocoön is a truth-teller who is punished by a goddess who seeks to defend her beloved Greeks from the consequences of his truthfulness.[9] It is remarkable that a work of plastic art, whose prime concern is the presentation of beauty, should portray in an allegory the punishment of truth-telling that threatens the victory of the particular people, the Greeks, who embody, above all others, the beautiful. And this portrayal is far from being wholly beautiful, for the terror of the serpents is an element of ugliness that is indispensable to the story of the punishment of the truth-teller. When Winckelmann and Lessing speak of the beauty of the sculpture, they focus on the priest and in particular his facial expression, and ignore the serpents. In an odd paragraph that follows this account of truth and laws of imitation, Lessing seems to correct his own abstraction from the serpents. He refers to ancient legends about pregnant women who gave birth to heroes after they looked at beautiful statues (Bacchus, Apollo, Mercury, et al.), usually adorned with a serpent, and then had dreams in which the serpent figured. Lessing says that he rejects the modest accounts of these dreams: "There must certainly be a reason why the adulterous phantasy was never anything but a serpent" (34). Does Lessing not humorously suggest that it was something other than the images of the beautiful gods that affected the mental and emotional state of the bearers of the city's heroes? Is he not suggesting that the city's laws exaggerate the role that the beautiful images have in producing beautiful citizens? The truth is that in the life of the city and its citizens serpents of all kinds loom large.

III. Beauty and the Need for Tyranny

Now one can ask if the two errors are related: first, Winckelmann's not seeing that classical poetry fittingly admits direct expression of feelings of pain, and second, modern perplexity over the imitation of beautiful bodies being regulated, even under penalties of law, due to its special character. In the first case Winckelmann misses the full humanity of the Greeks and

---

9. See Carol Jacobs, "Fictional Histories: Lessing's *Laocoön*," in *Telling Time: Lévi-Strauss, Ford, Lessing, Benjamin, de Man, Wordsworth, Rilke* (Baltimore: Johns Hopkins University Press, 1993), 118–19, 223n30. Jacobs observes that the serpents are sent to silence the speaker of truth, and further, that each passage on Laocoön in Virgil is followed by a scene involving truth and lies (Cassandra, *Aen.* 2.311; Sinon, *Aen.* 2.101).

Romans, imposing an abstract ideal of tranquil virtue on all things ancient. In the second case, moderns overlook the problem of the relation of theorizing, or the search for truth, to practical life, or the realm of opinion. What links these errors is the spirit of abstract systematizing that misses the complexity of the human.[10] This spirit is tyrannical, or has a tyrannical tendency, as it does not recognize that virtuous character has the rights of suffering nature, as Lessing puts it, and it rides roughly over the delicate tension between the ethos of beauty and that of free inquiry.

Lessing's observations on these features of the classical world prepare the way for the distinction for which the *Laocoön* essay is best known, the distinction between the media of the plastic and poetic arts, and how the different media are related to differences in subject matter and manner of representation. The distinction of media is between the art of bodily (two- or three-dimensional) representation, which must limit its imitative effort to a single moment, and the art of linguistic imitation of action, which has no temporal restriction. The plastic artists must choose for imitation a single moment with utmost discretion, for that moment has an unchanging continuance, and if it is an extreme state the imitation gives an unrelieved painful impression. The work of sculpture is made not "merely to be seen, but to be considered, to be long and repeatedly contemplated." The epic or dramatic poet, by contrast, can represent an extreme state as a moment in a sequence of moments, and its effect is muted by the imitation of other, less painful states that surround it. The extreme states are by their nature transitory (or at least they must be thought of as such) and to eternalize them in an image induces loathing (36–37).[11] The plastic

---

10. "Nothing is more fallacious than general laws for human feelings. The web of them is so fine-spun and so intricate that it is hardly possible for the most careful speculation to take up a single thread by itself and follow it through all the threads that cross it" (43).

11. Lessing implies that Winckelmann is unaware of these important distinctions. Late in *Laocoön* (ch. 26), Lessing suddenly praises Winckelmann's *Geschichte der Kunst des Altertums* (1763) as a work that has just appeared and that Lessing vows he must read. In this writing Winckelmann comments on the differences between the arts, and so it cannot be faulted with the oblivion that Lessing ascribes to the author in these early chapters. Jacobs discusses this as a case of Lessing's artful misrepresentation of history, arguing that Lessing read this work as well as the *Gedanken* before writing *Laocoön*. "Fictional Histories," 97–99. See also Henry Caraway Hatfield, *Winckelmann and His German Critics, 1755-1781: A Prelude to the Classical Age* (New York: King's Crown, 1943), 48–59.

artists are forced by their medium to concentrate on bodily beauty in a way that does not hold for poets. Accordingly, the moment chosen by the plastic artist cannot be the supreme moment of an action, but rather a moment suggestive of the supreme moment. The sculptor of Laocoön does not depict the ultimate death throes of the hero, but rather a moment of struggle that is pregnant with that inevitable outcome.

But Lessing gives another reason for avoiding visual depiction of the final ruination that seems quite different. I quote the passage:

> It is certain that the single moment ... can never be chosen too significantly. Now that alone is significant and fruitful which gives free play to the imagination. The more we see, the more must we be able to add by thinking. The more we add thereto by thinking, so much the more can we believe ourselves to see. In the whole gamut of emotion, however, there is no moment less advantageous than its topmost note. Beyond it there is nothing further, and to show us the uttermost is to tie the wings of fancy and compel her, as she cannot rise above the sensuous impression, to busy herself with weaker pictures below it. (37)

This seems to be a different consideration from the first, which was the avoidance of an unbearably painful image that offers no relief. It seemed before as though what one wants from the sculpture is to rest in contemplation of a beautiful image. Now the point is that the imagination rebels against the compulsion to stop in a single moment, and wants the freedom to think beyond it. It cannot accept finality at all, not just a painful finale. At this point one should recall the opening description of the amateur who takes pleasure in the representation of appearance as reality, and absent things as present. The mind enjoys not only the contemplation of the present image, but the presentation of the absent through the present. The image is not fully enjoyable if it does not suggest what lies beyond the present. The free play of the imagination is the play with the absent as well as the present. If constrained to think only about the present, the mind is denied its freedom, or subjected to the tyranny of the present against its nature. One could say, however, that Lessing is suggesting that the two needs of the spectator are not exclusive, but that they are in fruitful tension. To rest in contemplation of the present beautiful image is a need that is opposed, at the same time, by a need to imagine freely beyond the present. It is not the case that through the beautiful work of art, one can satisfy only one of the two needs at a time, at the expense of the other, but that both needs are satisfied, and that the tension between them is an essential part of the pleasure. I believe that the entire essay is a reflection on the two needs, and what it means for human beings to have them. It is worth noting that there is a related reflection in Kant's account of the judgment of beauty, more than twenty years after *Laocoön*, in which he describes the free play of the imagination with forms judged to be beautiful, and writes of a combination of lawfulness and free association as central to the pleasure in the judging.

But I would maintain that in Lessing's view the demand for beautiful form has something tyrannical about it all the same, and that the human mind has a need for this tyranny, even as it also has a need to transgress this tyrannical rule. The accomplished artist has an understanding of this, even if it is not articulated theoretically.[12] Nevertheless, there is also a human tendency to miss this complexity, and thus for lawgivers, pseudo-philosophers, and bad critics simply to take the side of contemplation of the present beautiful form, and to regard it as wholly satisfying. For they in effect treat the beautiful only in its relation to law, or to the formation and ruling of the human. If I understand Lessing correctly, the problem is not that the city or law dictates what is beautiful, but that beauty, the city, and law are all results of the human need to place limits on nature. And just as humans must set such limits, they must also transgress them, at least in thought. The arts offer the enjoyments of transgression even as they also provide a pleasing sense of order.

IV. Poetry and the Need for Freedom

Turning from Winckelmann on ancient sculpture to certain modern critics on painting, Lessing notes that they assume that visual art is capable of treating all the subjects of poetry: "Art in these later days has been assigned far wider boundaries. Let her imitative hand, folks say, stretch out to the whole of visible nature, of which the beautiful is only a small part. Let

---

12. For a closely related thought see Friedrich Nietzsche, *Beyond Good and Evil*, no. 188.

fidelity and truth of expression be her first law, and as nature herself at all times sacrifices beauty to higher purposes, so must the artist subordinate it to his general aim and yield it no further than fidelity of expression permits" (36). If Winckelmann would constrain poetry by the standard of beauty in sculpture, modern critics of painting would expand painting's range by the standard of expression in poetry. Lessing proceeds to expound on the greater freedom of poetry: "Nothing requires the poet to concentrate his picture on one single moment. He takes up each of his actions, as he likes, from its very origin and conducts it through all possible modifications to its final close. Every one of these modifications, which would cost the artist an entire separate canvas or marble-block, costs the poet a single line" (39).

Lessing says that a modern English critic, Joseph Spence, appears to have no notion "that poetry is the more comprehensive art, that beauties are at her command which painting can never attain, that she may frequently have reason to prefer unpicturesque beauties to picturesque" (60). Indeed, Lessing claims that the poet alone can make the ugly pleasing, for "to the poet alone belongs the art of depicting with negative traits, and by mixing them with positive to bring two images into one" (63–64). And more strikingly, he writes of Homer's freedom to make the invisible present, invoking again the free play of imagination: "When at last the divided gods come to blows among themselves over the fate of the Trojans, the whole struggle passes with the poet invisibly, and this invisibility permits the imagination to enlarge the stage, and leaves it free play to conceive the persons of the gods and their actions as great, and elevated as far above common humanity as ever it pleases. But painting must assume a visible stage, the various necessary parts of which become the scale for the persons acting on it, a scale which the eye has immediately before it" (73).

Lessing seems to regard poetry as having no limits to its expression, but this impression is corrected when he announces that he "will turn to the foundations and try to argue the matter from first principles" (80–81). At this point Lessing sounds like a systematic philosopher. He notes that painting and poetry employ quite different signs in their imitations: figures and colors in space in the one case, articulate sounds in time in the other, and these different signs are suited for expressing different subject matters. Signs arranged together side by side can express only subjects whose parts exist thus side by side, and signs which succeed each other can express only subjects whose parts succeed each other. Subjects whose parts exist side by side "may be called bodies" and these with their visible properties form the proper subjects of painting. Subjects whose various parts succeed each other "may in general be called actions," and these form the proper subjects of poetry. But immediately there is an important acknowledgment of interdependence between bodies and actions, for "all bodies exist not in space alone but also in time." In the painting or sculpture one beholds a momentary appearance that stands in relation to other momentary appearances that precede and follow, and the depicted moment lies within an action. Thus visual arts can imitate actions, but only by way of suggestion through bodies. This thought was already raised in the account of the sculptor's choice of the fruitful moment. But now Lessing makes a symmetrical point about a limitation of poetic art, for "actions cannot subsist for themselves, but must attach to certain things or persons.... In so far as these things are bodies or are regarded as bodies, poetry too depicts bodies, but only by way of suggestion through actions."

The arts, in other words, address a common realm, that of bodily beings in action, but their differing media, spatial signs, and temporal signs, allow them to depict directly only one aspect of the whole phenomenon, and compel them to suggest the other aspect. To put this in other words, the humanly available means of imitation compel the visual artist and the poet to perform different abstractions from the whole phenomenon of bodies in action. At the same time, the abstractions must point toward what they fail to present directly, or what is present through signs must point to what is absent. If this were not done, and bodies were presented without relation to actions, and actions presented without relation to bodies, then both bodies and actions, thus imitated, would be unintelligible. This reflection brings forward the question whether one might not be in the happiest position with an art that combines visual images and poetry, presenting thereby directly the whole phenomenon of bodies in action. Of course the staged performance of dramatic art comes to mind.

But the expressive power of drama does not alter the reality that poetic language and visual images each have limits to their representative power. As for poetry, it can use in its continuous imitations "only one single property of bodies, and therefore must choose that one which calls up the most living picture of the body on that side" from which the poet regards it (81). Here "we find the origin of the rule which insists on the unity and consistency of descriptive epithets, and on economy in the delineations of bodily subjects." Lessing adduces the example of Homer, whose prac-tice contrasts strongly with the tendency of modern poets to emulate painters. "Homer... paints nothing but continuous actions, and all bodies, all single things, he paints only by their share in those actions, and in gen-eral only by one feature.... A ship is to him now the black ship, now the hollow ship, now the swift ship, at most the well-rowed black ship. Beyond that he does not enter on a picture of the ship" (82). Lessing notes that Homer sometimes dwells on a single corporeal object, but he presents it in a succession of moments in which it assumes different appearances, and the image that the painter could imitate arises only at the end, after the poet has run through all the appearances. Lessing takes up a famous example, the Shield of Achilles. (See Section V below.)

Looking at this comparison of arts and their media at a distance, one is tempted to propose a metaphysical observation. Although Lessing holds back from stating this directly, I would say he suggests it. The spatial arts that use co-existing signs are more closely related to body. This Lessing says. The temporal arts that use successive signs are more closely related to actions. Lessing says this, too. But the successive signs of temporal arts are linguistic, and language in conveying action is performing an action. The primary action of language is to convey thought, as the actions it con-veys are not present in body but only in thought. Action itself is not simply a bodily reality but exists crucially in the thought of the actor and in the thought of observers. In the linguistic expression of thought one can make present many things that are not presentable in visual images. Moving beyond actions, one can deal with entirely invisible and abstract things, in the first place gods, as Lessing notes, but also abstract discourse about things divine, natural, and human. One can sum this up and take it a bit further. Humans have different capacities for knowing, and some capa-cities are better suited for apprehending bodies, others for apprehending action and thought. Remarkably, there is no human power of knowing able to make things fully present in their wholeness. This suggests that the human experience of bodies is not strictly in harmony with the human experience of thought and action.

It is interesting, at this point, to ask why Lessing does not directly state all the conclusions that seem to follow from his observations. An answer comes from Lessing's own words about the good poet and the good critic, for these apply to Lessing the philosopher-poet-critic. The good poet and good critic do not attempt to say everything directly. Indeed, every writer who thinks seriously about writing must realize that the effort to give an account of anything is necessarily by way of abstractions, and the best writer will try to suggest what is left out of the abstractions through a deft use of language. In Lessing's terms, this means to allow freedom to the imagination, and accordingly not to be a tyrant who tries to say everything in a completed doctrine (87).[13] Although Lessing in this passage on signs comes close to sounding like a systematic thinker, he still leaves much unsaid.

V. The Illusion of Presence

Soon after introducing his "foundations," Lessing responds to an objection that the poet can use linguistic signs that succeed one another in time to represent spatially figures whose parts are side by side. The tradition calls such representation *ekphrasis*. It can be done because linguistic signs are arbitrary signs, and as such they are not limited in their capacities as are figures, shapes, and colors. They can be interpreted, therefore, as representations of side-by-side figures. Lessing illustrates this by an account of the famous passage in *Iliad* 18 that describes the shield that Vulcan (Hephaestus) made for the hero Achilles. The description, in over 100 lines, is an elaborate representation of urban and rural life with indications of cosmological ideas, as these are imitated on the shield. Lessing says "we have only to remember the Shield of Achilles in order to have the most decisive example in how detailed and yet poetical a manner some single thing can be depicted, with various parts side by side" (87). What is more, Homer describes the shield in his characteristic way of giving it a sense of continuous action, and not simply as a representation of a static

---

13. Here and in other references to the tyrannical the intent is not to speak of something irrational; only rational beings can be tyrannical. Nor, on the other hand, is freedom of the imagination contrary to reason. Lessing sees in it the presentiment of the infinite wealth of being that only a rational creature can have. His discussion of competing tendencies relates to possibilities within the rational life of humans.

thing. As Lessing puts it: "The poet is not concerned merely to be intelligible, his representations should not merely be clear and plain, though this may satisfy the prose writer. He desires rather to make the ideas awakened by him within us living things, so that for the moment we realize the true sensuous impressions of the object he describes, and cease in the moment of illusion to be conscious of the means—namely, his words—which he employs for his purpose. This is the substance of what we have already said of the poetic picture. But the poet should always paint" (87).

The poet does paint in a special way, namely that of temporal succession. This analysis of Homer's shield brings forth the question that arises early in the essay of how poetry might be different from science, and how poetry's concern might differ from the concern with truth. Now Lessing says that poetry does not seek just to make things clear, plain, and intelligible, but to awaken ideas within us as living beings. Poetry should make present to us sensual impressions that have the illusory effect of reality. Lessing characterizes how Homer's accomplishment of this contrasts with the visual representation in the plastic arts. In the visual work of art the observer takes in all the parts rapidly; they are regarded singly and then in combination as a whole. These operations are performed with "so astonishing a swiftness that they seem to us but one, and this swiftness is imperatively necessary if we are to arrive at a conception of the whole, which is nothing more than the result of the conception of the parts and their combination." The poet in imitating a spatial figure must do something comparable, moving from one part to another, but the time taken for this is different with the poem:

> What the eye sees at a glance, [the poet] counts out to us gradually, with a perceptible slowness, and often it happens that when we come to the last figure we have already forgotten the first. Nevertheless, we have to frame a whole from those features: to the eye the parts beheld remain constantly present, and it can run over them again and again; for the ear, on the contrary, the parts heard are lost if they do not abide in the memory. And if they so abide, what trouble, what effort it costs to renew the impressions, all of them in due

order, so vividly, to think of them together with even a moderate swiftness, and thus to arrive at an eventual conception of the whole. (87–88)

Lessing points out that this poetic movement through a complex whole with many parts that coexist can fail to be effective, as in the case of the description of the Alps (*Die Alpen*) given by the natural scientist-poet Albrecht von Haller. Lessing says, "Here are weeds and flowers which the learned poet paints with much art and fidelity to Nature. Paints, but without any illusion whatever.... It remains infinitely below that which lines and colours on canvas can express, and the critic who bestows on it this exaggerated praise must have regarded it from an utterly false point of view" (89). The linkage of blossoms, stems, twigs and so forth; of this Lessing claims that it can hardly compete with the representation by a Dutch painter, Jan van Huysum. In Haller Lessing hears "in every word the toiling poet, and I am far enough from seeing the thing itself." This comparison of Homer and Haller brings out the challenge the poet confronts, namely to convey a certain vivid effect of wholeness while moving through a continuous series of parts, and to do so in a way that is engaging. This is difficult for the poet because the whole is more elusive than it is in visual art, because the whole has to emerge from our active reconstruction, from a movement of thought through the parts. Homer's solution to the part-whole problem is characteristically Homeric, namely that of not burdening the parts with much description. And, moreover, Homer presents the shield as though it is being produced by Vulcan, as a work in progress emerging from an artificer. What would otherwise be just spatial becomes a continuous action. It has the quality of action, the action of being made. But why must poetry resort to this?

The point seems to be that poetry is not just concerned with intelligibility, because a thorough description, a kind of catalog, would achieve this end. Poetry is not concerned solely with truth, although it has a greater range of possible subjects than visual art and does not limit itself to presenting the beautiful. However, it is concerned with the "illusion of presence"—of making a whole seem to be a living thing, and therefore it must move through the parts so that the whole is alive. The whole must have a certain vividness of presence and not be merely the summation of parts, not something we realize we have gone through, being attentive to the various parts, which we could do in a treatise or catalog or some prose-writing where we are not concerned with poetic illusion. Instead, as Lessing states in the Preface, in poetry the concern is with "appearance as reality" and with the absent being made present. Painting and sculpture make immediately present the given body or group of figures, and poetry tries to make immediately present an action or a series of actions or temporal events that belong to things. But actions are less amenable to being presented as whole. To the actors themselves they have anticipated outcomes that depend on factors beyond human control. All action begins in the vivid present and fades into the indeterminate future—into absence. Whereas actions depicted by poets are completed wholes with determinate outcomes, their representation unfolds in time and for the reader or listener this has a sense of indeterminacy as the story unfolds.[14]

In Lessing's view, Virgil's description of Aeneas' shield in the *Aeneid* does not succeed in achieving poetic illusion of presence. That is, he characterizes Virgil as proceeding more in the way of a cataloguer than a poet, as someone who, as he puts it, is more like a courtier attempting to impress his patrons with his knowledge of heraldry—knowledge of the elaborate insignia on shields. Homer by contrast produces a shield that is the "natural outgrowth of the fertile soil" (97). This sounds like a Romantic characterization of the shield as autochthonic, but Lessing corrects this by stressing how it is an artifact, albeit one produced in a way analogous to the growth of a living being. It is something made by the poet, but by a poet who has the ability to generate an artifact naturally rather than mechanically. Of the two shields in the ancient epics, Lessing says:

> The Shield of Aeneas is consequently a sheer interpolation, simply and only intended to flatter the national pride of the Romans, a foreign tributary which the poet leads into his main stream in order to give it a livelier motion. The Shield of Achilles, on the other hand, is a rich natural outgrowth of the fertile soil from which it springs; for a Shield had to be

---

14. See the discussion of action and its imitation in Michael Davis, *Aristotle's "Poetics": The Poetry of Philosophy* (Lanham, MD: Rowman & Littlefield, 1992).

made, and as the needful thing never comes bare and without grace from the hands of the divinity, the Shield had also to be embellished. But the art was, to treat these embellishments merely as such, to inweave them into the stuff, in order to show them to us only by means of the latter; and this could only be done by Homer's method. Homer lets Vulcan elaborate ornaments because he is to make a Shield that is worthy of himself. Virgil, on the other hand, appears to let him make the Shield for the sake of its ornaments, considering them important enough to be particularly described, after the Shield itself has long been finished. (97)

This is a theme important in later writers on art and aesthetics: productions by poetic genius are compared to living nature or organisms. Lessing seems to be stressing that poetry and visual art convey in their distinctive ways the sense of the presence of wholeness that is an illusion, an illusory sense of the vital presence, and this is something that is not available or comes not easily to science and philosophy. So it would take a poetic form of philosophy to do something comparable—perhaps he might consider the Platonic dialogues as a candidate for that. In other words, even the philosophic writing that is concerned with the truth also entails abstraction and therefore is confronting the fact that it must exist in a realm of partiality or falsity. The different forms of art create these illusory senses of the presence of wholeness and each does so with a certain tendency toward abstraction. The visual art can make immediately present the wholeness of a visual figure as agent but it does not make immediately present the wholeness of action, which belongs to the realm of the suggested. Conversely, the poetic imitation can convey the immediate presence of temporal events—the moments of action—but more difficult for it is to convey the wholeness of the actor. To summarize, what is difficult to do in all the arts is to bring together as vividly present, as a form of immediate presence, the wholeness of beings, bodies and figures, and the wholeness of actions. One could say that if these could be brought together it would constitute *intuitive knowledge*. Perhaps this is what the Aesopic fable (a subject of great interest to Lessing) approaches, because it uses figure in a relatively simple way, but it conveys, on a more abstract level, a teaching or rule concerning action. It thus offers some experience of how action makes sense, or forms a whole.[15]

VI. The Rights of Laughter

Having considered these strengths and limitations of the arts, it might be timely to return to the earlier moral observations concerning how painting and sculpture are more closely tied to custom and to law than poetry. Because the primary emphasis in visual art is on beauty, one must ask: "What is beauty?" Beauty is the immediate presence of something whose parts form a harmonious *whole*. The figure or the group of figures is something the eye can take in rather easily and quickly as a whole. Lessing said that the cities of Greece had a certain concern with rules or laws concerning the production of art with a view to maintaining standards of beauty. But why would there be a closer tie between law or custom and the way visual art makes wholes present to us? It is characteristic of political life or the realm of law and custom that some form of wholeness must be immediately present. In other words, it is in the interest of a city, which demands full allegiance of its citizens, that the citizens be not left to themselves to find or form a whole. The laws, with their divine sanction, define the whole for the citizens. For the poetic art, even with a brilliant poet like Homer who goes through a complex series of actions to convey a whole—as the shield example illustrated—the whole is still, nevertheless, only an accomplishment. As unfolding in time, it cannot be immediately present. The whole that poetry presents is not concerned solely with the beautiful. It is tolerant of a kind of complexity of parts that can even be discordant or at odds with one another. From this perspective one can see why there would be a tendency for political life to be more attentive to the less problematic kinds of wholeness. Political life would tend to stress beauty and to favor it, to make sure that there are laws that maintain it because it is concerned with forming a kind of wholeness in its citizens. With respect to the human need for truth there is an element of the tyrannical in this.

Of course the spirit of Greece cannot be described as simply tyrannical. For one thing, it is clear that the age of flourishing of the arts in Greece

---

15. See Lessing, *Abhandlung über die Fabel* (1759).

(Athens in particular) is a flourishing of poetry as much as the plastic arts, with tragedies and comedies presenting more complex forms of wholeness alongside the beautiful wholes of sculpture. This is not to mention the works of the philosophers. *Laocoön* has one citation of poetic writing about a philosopher. This occurs in the rather strange concluding chapters of the essay, which treat the ugly, the laughable, and the disgusting. Lessing gives examples of how the disgusting is able to enhance the laughable. The prime example, significantly, is from Aristophanes' *Clouds*, where the subject is Socrates, who is the object of the poet's mockery (124–25). In a passage Lessing quotes from the play, a student of Socrates describes Socrates as having an unpleasant encounter with a lizard. The student is speaking to Strepsiades, an angry parent who has accused Socrates of being a trouble-maker and corrupter of the youth. Note that once again a serpent is attacking a truth-teller or truth-seeker:

> *Student*
> And yet last night a mighty thought we lost
> through a green lizard.
> *Strepsiades*   Tell me, how was that?
> *Student*
> Why, as [Socrates] Himself, with eyes and
>   mouth wide open,
> Mused on the moon, her paths and revolutions,
> A lizard from the roof squirted full on him.
> *Strepsiades*
> Hee, hee, hee, hee. I like the lizard's spattering Socrates.
> (*Clouds* 169–74)

Why is the prime example of the laughable and disgusting taken from a text that is humbling a philosopher? Is Lessing's purpose only to show the poetic mocking of philosophy, or is it also to suggest that the poetic and comic treatment of philosophy is itself something akin to philosophy? Strikingly, in none of the other writings or works of art treated in the essay is philosophy itself a subject or directly pointed toward.[16] Perhaps a more

---

16. See, however, the brief statement about a painting and engraving of the French physician and philosopher Julien Offray de La Mettrie (1709–1751), "a second Democritus" (37).

philosophic spirit exists in comedy, with its mixing of the disgusting and the laughable, than in any of the other forms of art that Lessing examines. Its freedom, one might suggest, is most remote from the tyranny of beauty.

III.

The Bible, Divine Law, and Interpretation

11

Elohim: Knower of Good and Evil

Roslyn Weiss

This paper explores the theological implications of taking the Torah at its word when it tells us explicitly that God is a knower of one thing in particular—*tov* and *ra'*, good and bad or good and evil.[1] By contrast, the Torah does not affirm, explicitly or otherwise, that God knows all things.

Having the opportunity to read and study Ronna Burger's work—in particular, her work on Plato and on the Hebrew Bible—has been a source of pleasure and a great privilege. Her exquisite analysis of profound texts has a unique sparkle that delights and inspires even as it uncovers depths of wisdom in the classic works to which she has devoted her life. My wish for Ronna is that she may continue to enrich the lives of those she teaches and mentors even as her own work flourishes well into the future.

1. "Good" is not a narrowly moral term, but nor is it a narrowly utilitarian one. I take *tov* to be something akin to what Plato meant by good, something that represents the best state of things—tout court. It conveys a sense of things being "as they should be." The first *ra'* that we find in the world according to Genesis is moral evil or the inclination to it: see 6:5 and 8:21. And certainly the "well" in God's saying to Cain at Gen. 4:7, "If you do well, will you not be accepted? And if you do not well, sin crouches at your door, and its desire will be to you," has moral connotations. It is difficult to articulate the way in which "good" need not be viewed as "good for something" or as the suitable means to an end. Yet, that appears to be what is intended by, for example, God's judgment of Creation as good. There is in this case no further end. When Socrates speaks to Glaucon of the Good in book 6 of Plato's *Republic*, Glaucon responds: "An inconceivable beauty you speak of, if it is the source of knowledge and truth, and yet itself surpasses them in beauty. For you surely cannot mean that it is pleasure." No; that is surely not what Socrates means. All Socrates can then say in response is: "Bite your tongue!"—*euphēmei* (*Rep.* 6.509a9).

In light especially of Maimonides' well-known contention that, as a result of their sin, Adam and Eve were demoted from being knowers of fact, of true and false, of what is, to being moral knowers of accepted norms, that their *punishment* consisted in their plummeting to the level of *elohim*—in the (tendentious) sense not of God (who is *not*, for Maimonides, a moral knower) but of human judges[2]—we shall consider the theological implications of reading the Torah straightforwardly, as viewing God as being indeed a *moral* knower, a connoisseur, as it were, of the goodness and badness of things.

The Torah, I shall argue, points beyond God to a *standard* of good and bad, to a higher authority to which God himself is answerable.[3] What it affirms is that there is a standard, a measure, an objective moral truth. One cannot but think in this context of Plato's *Euthyphro*. The holy is holy not because God loves it; God loves it because it is holy (10e2–3). The Torah, I will argue, is not to be seen as teaching us first and foremost about God, is not primarily offering a lesson in theology; rather, its teaching is moral. Specifically, its teaching is that there is objectivity in morality, a standard to be known.[4] *This*, I shall argue, is the implication of God's

---

2. Maimonides (in *Guide of the Perplexed* 1.2) asks rhetorically how Adam and Eve could be rewarded for sinning; how, as a result of their sin, they could achieve a state *higher* than their original one. Yet, the Torah does not present the acquisition of knowledge of good and evil as either a reward or a punishment; Adam and Eve's punishments are explicitly issued later (Gen. 3:15–19). The opening of their eyes is but the natural consequence of their eating the fruit of the tree of knowledge of good and evil. That can no more be avoided than a bank robber's having more money after he robbed the bank than he had before. That newfound wealth is not a reward. The authorities can certainly punish him by compelling him to return the money he stole as well as by imprisoning him, but it is inaccurate to say he could only have become poorer as a result of his robbery because, after all, it was an illegal act.

3. One might say that the famous midrashic/kabbalistic view that God used the Torah as a blueprint for creating the world (*Zohar* II:161a) is a way of saying that there is something—perhaps morality itself—to which God looked in fashioning the world, such that He was thus not morality's author. Another way one might go is to say that in the very creation of the universe, its laws—whether physical, mathematical, logical, *or moral*—were created as well, such that God, although He is the universe's Creator, is, post-Creation, *subject* to them.

4. I would claim that this is precisely the point of the *Euthyphro*: that there is a standard beyond the gods. The only way to manifest holiness is to conform to that standard. It

knowing good and evil: it is not so much that *God* knows them but that *they* are there to be known by God—and, eventually, by us.[5]

This paper is an exercise in *peshat*, in reading the Torah straightforwardly. It is not an argument for the superiority or preferability of *peshat* to more nuanced midrashic or philosophic readings, but for its priority: one ought to understand what one is deviating from before one deviates. Needless to say, every reading is an interpretation. Some would go so far as to say that there is no *peshat*. But, it is surely possible to aim at *peshat*, to *attempt* to hew as closely as possible to the plain meaning of the text.[6]

Let us begin with an example, one that will soon become central to the argument of this paper. Genesis 3:5 reads as follows: "For *elohim* knows that on the day you eat from it your eyes will be opened and you will be like *elohim*, knowers of good and bad." I would argue that *peshat* cannot countenance a drastic change in the meaning of a term from its first appearance to its second within the same verse, as occurs, for example, in Onqelos' translation of this verse. Onqelos renders the first *elohim* as God, but the second as *ravrevin*: noblemen. Indeed, Onqelos frequently strays from *peshat* in order to sanitize the text. Maimonides, applauding him and following him, renders the second *elohim* as judges. Less radical are those translations that take the first *elohim* as God but the second as "divine

---

is in that way—and in that way alone—that we show reverence to the "gods." We are the gods' assistants when we encourage virtue and justice on earth.

5. Rashi on Gen. 1:1 asks, in the name of R. Yitzhaq, why the Torah does not begin with "This month shall be for you the first of the months" (Exod. 12:2), that is, with the first commandment that the Israelites received as a nation (*Tanhuma Yashan* on Gen. 11; *Yalqut Shimoni* on *Bo* 187). One answer might be that the Torah is first and foremost a book of morality, and that, as many thinkers have said, referring to Mic. 6:8 and Jer. 7:21, basic morality must precede ritual commandments. See, for example, Yehudah Halevi, *Kuzari*, II §48. Another relevant text is Isa. 1:12–14: "When you come to appear before Me, who has required this at your hand, to trample My courts? Bring no more vain offerings; incense of abomination they are to Me. As for New Moons and Sabbaths and the calling of Assemblies, I cannot bear iniquity along with solemn meeting. Your New Moons and your festivals My soul hates: they are a trouble to Me; I am weary of enduring them."

6. One reason reading the Torah as *peshat* is problematic is that one is easily led in this way to doubt the narrative integrity of the Pentateuch. Midrash unifies the text (and perhaps philosophic interpretations do as well). Arguably, without narrative integrity, the moral thrust of the narrative is undercut.

beings" (Etz Hayim, 1985) or "gods" (Koren, 1969; also King James). This latter sort of deviation may be appropriate—and necessary—on occasion; but why here? The speaker in this verse is the serpent. Why should we suspect the serpent of changing the sense of *elohim* midstream?[7] Moreover, the only divine being with whom Adam—and Eve through him—has any familiarity is surely God himself.[8]

In taking the Torah at its word, in taking it quite literally where it identifies God as a knower of good and evil, we rely on two verses. The first is, of course, the serpent's assertion in Genesis 3:5, just quoted. The second, Genesis 3:22, is a perhaps more problematic text for those who would deny God's knowledge of good and evil—since it records *God's* words rather than the serpent's. When read straightforwardly, it has *God* (*adonai elohim*) saying: "Behold the human being (*ha'adam*) has become as one of us, knowing good and evil."[9]

I. God as Knower of Good and Evil

Virtually the first thing we learn about God after being told of His creative activity in fashioning the universe is His judgment that what He has created is *good*, *tov*. Genesis begins with God's pronouncing His individual creations good and the whole of Creation very good. God thus *judges* the

---

7. Hertz, who uses the JPS 1917 translation, is more troubled by "good and evil" than by *elohim*. Why would God deprive the human being of knowledge of good and evil? For this reason he says, in his commentary, that "good and evil" means "all things." He argues further that, without knowledge of good and evil, Adam could not be said to have been made "in the image of God." Moreover, Adam's obedience or disobedience would have no moral significance without his having knowledge of good and evil. Joseph H. Hertz, *The Pentateuch and Haftorahs*, 2nd ed. (London: Soncino, 1960), 10.

8. One *could* take the expression "knowers of good and evil" to apply to these gods or divine beings, in which case it would be especially reasonable to see in this verse a shift to the plural. And at 3:22 it is surely implied that there is a plurality of divine knowers of good and evil. Yet, since the serpent is the speaker and the human couple knows no divine being other than God, there are rather weak grounds for permitting a shift in the interpretation of *elohim* in 3:5.

9. See the extreme liberties taken with this text in *The Stone Edition Chumash* (*Art Scroll*), ed. Nosson Scherman (Brooklyn, NY: Mesorah, 1993), 19: "Man has become like the Unique One among us"; see, too, Rashi, whom Art Scroll follows: "He will be unique among those below, as I am unique among those above"; and Onqelos, whom Rashi follows: "The human being is unique in his world."

goodness of what He has made. Unlike in the case of God's activities of bringing things into existence or conferring names on them, and certainly those of blessing and sanctifying, of speaking and planting and infusing breath (or soul) and commanding, in the case of His "seeing that" the results of His efforts are good, a standard is required, against which or in light of which God so judges.[10] Once again one is put in mind of the *Euthyphro*, where Socrates says (6d9–e6):

> Do you remember that I did not bid you to teach me some one or two of the many holy things, but that *eidos* (form) itself by which all the holy things are holy? For surely you were saying that it is by one *idea* (form) that the unholy things are unholy and the holy ones holy.... Then teach me what this *idea* is, so that by gazing at it and using it as a pattern, I may declare that whatever is like it, among the things you or anyone else may do, is holy, and that whatever is not like it is not.[11]

That a thing is good is something God recognizes or understands or appreciates or, biblically speaking, "sees"—not something He causes, not something He initiates. I would argue that every occurrence of *vaya'ar ki*, "He saw that," found in the Pentateuch has the sense of judging or assessing; it is not a visual but an intellectual act. (This is the case as well

---

10. It is not possible, in my view, for the original formulation of the verse Isa. 45:7 to be, as we now have it: "I form the light and create darkness, I make peace and create evil," implying that God creates bad or evil. Creation is, as God himself proclaims, "very good." The first appearance of "bad" is in connection with the tree of knowledge of good and evil, but it is only *knowledge* of bad that is associated with the tree. Naeh contends, for his own reason, namely, that *shalom*, here rendered as "peace," is an all-encompassing word whose parallel could not be "evil" or "bad," that this could not be the correct, original formulation of the verse. See Shlomo Naeh, "The Role of Biblical Verses in Prayer according to the Rabbinic Tradition," in *Prayers that Cite Scripture: Biblical Quotation in Jewish Prayers from Antiquity through the Middle Ages*, ed. James L. Kugel (Cambridge, MA: Harvard University Press, 2006), 43–59.

11. Adapted from *Four Texts on Socrates: Plato's "Euthyphro," "Apology," and "Crito" and Aristophanes' "Clouds,"* trans. and ed. Thomas G. West and Grace Starry West (Ithaca, NY: Cornell University Press, 1984), 48. The most significant modification is the rendering of *hosia* as "holy things" rather than as "pious things."

with the expression *vaya'ar... vehinei*—"He saw...and behold.") Inter-estingly, when Onqelos encounters expressions of God's seeing—without the *ki* or *vehinei*, without the "that" or the "and behold"—his commit-ment to removing from God all traces of anthropomorphism kicks in and he translates: *ugeli qodam*, "it was revealed before Him" (lest it seem as if God literally sees). But when there *is* a *ki* or *hinei*, he translates *vehaza arei* or *vehaza... veha* ("He saw that" or "He saw...and behold").[12] He does not worry that the "He saw" in these cases might suggest exercise of the sense of sight. In ascertaining the goodness of things, God indeed judges. What He judges is that the thing in question meets the relevant standard.[13] Using that same standard God can recognize when something falls short. Although His overall assessment of Creation is that it is very good (*tov me'od*), He does notice something in Creation that is "not good": "It is not good (*lo tov*)," God observes, "for man to be alone" (Gen. 2:18).

The first occurrence, however, of *ra'*, bad or evil, is found between, on the one hand, God's pronouncement that each of the elements of Cre-ation is good and Creation as a whole very good and, on the other, His recognition of the one thing in Creation that is "not good." It appears in connection with the tree of the knowledge of good and evil, and so with what is at first only a human potential to do wrong. God causes this tree to grow in the garden but, unlike the other trees in Genesis 2:9 that are said to be *nehmad lemareh vetov lema'akhal*—pleasing to sight and good

---

12. Maimonides speculates that Onqelos translates "saw" as *geli* when the things God sees are bad (see *Guide* 1.48). He then admits to being puzzled by the few cases (he says there are three) of God's seeing bad things in which Onqelos translates "saw" as *haza* rather than *geli*. The solution, however, is clear: Onqelos is careful to avoid *haza* only when there is danger of *vaya'ar* being taken to imply visual seeing. But, in all cases where the seeing is paired with "that" or "and behold" it is evidently intellectual and so no precaution need be taken. Whether the things seen are good or bad is irrelevant. See my "See No Evil: Maimonides on Onqelos' Translation of the Biblical Expression 'And the Lord Saw,'" *Maimonidean Studies* 4 (2000): 135–62. An interesting instance of Onqelos' wariness occurs in the matter of Sodom and Gomorrah; when God says He will go down and "see" (Gen. 18:21), Onqelos translates: "I will go out and *judge*." Onqelos thus protects against taking this seeing as visual.

13. Similarly, Moses' mother's pronouncement regarding Moses (Exod. 2:2): "She saw that he was good." She proceeds to name him, as God names the light "day" and the darkness "night." See Menachem Kasher, *Torah Shelemah*, Torah Shelemah Institute 3 (Jerusalem, 1952), 56n16, on the connection between Moses' birth and Creation.

for eating—the tree of life and the tree of knowledge of good and evil are not (yet) characterized in this way. The full verse reads as follows: "And the Lord God caused to grow from the ground every tree pleasing to sight and good for eating; *and* the tree of life in the midst of the garden and the tree of the knowledge of good and evil." Judgments that things are delicious or aesthetically pleasing do not require a standard, even if they involve assessment. Assessment in these cases is subjective, and is relative to something—to eating or to sight. By contrast, the judgment of *tov* that God pronounces on each day of Creation is of goodness absolutely and *simpliciter*—not goodness relative to something.[14] Indeed, when God identifies for Adam the tree of the knowledge of good and evil (as well as the tree of life), He withholds subjective evaluation both of the tree itself and of the good and evil of which the tree provides knowledge.[15]

Significantly, the serpent also refrains from representing the fruit of the tree of the knowledge of good and evil as good *for eating* or desirable *from the perspective of sight*; he does not recommend it for its subjective appeal.[16] He says only that it will open the human beings' eyes and they will be as God, knowers of good and evil. He thus entices the woman with the promise of *knowledge* ("you will become *knowers* of good and evil," *yode'ei tov vara'*), and hence of something that is objective, which is the only sort of thing of which there *can* be knowledge. Indeed, it is no accident that the serpent says *ki yodei'a elohim*—because God *knows*. Knowledge is a commodity whose value the serpent expects Eve to appreciate. Knowledge is what will raise the human being to the level of God. It is not, however, just any knowledge that will raise human beings to the level of God. It is, specifically, knowledge of good and evil that will do so. Note

---

14. In explaining why there is no pronouncement on the second day of Creation that "it was good," Maimonides explains that the expression indicates "that the thing in question is of externally visible and manifest utility for the existence and permanence of that which exists" (*Guide* 2.30:354). The matter of the firmament and the water above it is an esoteric one and there is therefore with respect to them no pronouncement of goodness.

15. There appears to be one place where *tov* alone clearly means "pleasing to sight," and that is in the incident of the sons of the *elohim* taking human wives because they are beautiful (Gen. 6:2, "for they were good").

16. The serpent certainly seems to be wiser (or more clever, at least) than the innocent (or naïve) man and woman.

that when the woman appraises the fruit of the tree of knowledge of good and evil, she checks first to be sure that it is good as a food (*tov ha'eitz lema'akhal*) and that it is visually charming (*ta'avah hu la'einayim*)—we recall that this tree, along with the tree of life, was excluded initially, in Genesis 2:9, from this characterization—but it is not until she is struck, too, by its appeal as a source of enlightenment (*neḥmad lehaskil*) that she actually takes the fruit and eats it: "And the woman saw that the tree was good for eating and that it was attractive to the eyes and that the tree was pleasing for becoming wise, and she took of its fruit and did eat" (Gen. 3:6). Of course, she would have no reason to eat the fruit of this tree in disobedience to God if it were merely good to eat and visually alluring. After all, all the fruits of all the trees in the garden are nutritious and sensually attractive. She could just as easily have eaten the other fruit to satisfy those appetites. The unique seductiveness of the fruit of the tree of knowledge of good and evil was its ability to enlighten.

As a consequence of eating of the fruit of the tree of the knowledge of good and evil, the eyes of the woman and man were opened and they became aware of their nakedness. Here, too, the term is "knew," *vayeide'u.* The verse's intent cannot be that they discovered the fact of their nakedness; surely what they discovered was the moral import of their nakedness, its shamefulness. As the Torah tells us, initially Adam and Eve, although they were naked, experienced no shame (Gen. 2:25). One can only conclude that they now know an objective moral truth of which they were formerly ignorant. It is thus apparently the case that nakedness is not bad simply by convention; it is bad by nature, objectively bad. There is as yet, after all, no convention or societal norm to be upheld. The reason they can *know* that they are naked is that the objective wrongness of nakedness is something that *can* be known. This is their first awakening to evil. It is a new intellectual acquisition. To know objective morality is no less an act of intellect, an act of cognition, a matter of enlightenment (*haskalah*), of opened eyes, than any knowledge of true and false. In fact, morality—as something objective—*is* a matter of true and false. This is not to say that there are no difficult questions, or even that there are no gray areas. But it is to say that the Torah opposes all forms of moral relativism. Morality is not conventional. Indeed, the *basics* of morality are not only fixed and factual, but are known to all. We have all eaten of the tree.

214

God's original intent, it would seem, was for human beings to live indefinitely, possibly forever. Although the tree of life was not recommended to Adam and Eve as one of the trees pleasing to sight and good for eating, neither was it forbidden to them. Even if they were to eat of its fruit and live forever, however, there is no danger of their being by their nature eternal beings, and being in this respect like God. And this for two reasons: first, they did not always exist but were created; and, second, their indefinitely continued existence could be curtailed—if they were for some reason prevented from eating from the tree of life.

It would appear that it was also God's initial intent that human beings live in innocence of good and evil, that they live as obedient children.[17] He clearly does not wish to share His knowledge, for He forbids the eating of the fruit of the tree of the knowledge of good and evil. Adam and Eve's original state of childlike innocence is best captured by their initial obliviousness to their nakedness. Like children, they have no shame. Like children, they have no modesty or appreciation for the virtue of modesty.[18] God knows that Adam and Eve's awareness of the import of their nakedness can only have come from their eating of the tree that was forbidden to them; for, otherwise, why would their awareness of their nakedness cause them immediately to fear God and hide (Gen. 3:10)?; how would they know that it is shameful to be naked? Their moral innocence is thus another way in which the man and woman are not like God. Just as God is eternal by His nature—such that His eternality does not require that He eat of the fruit of the tree of life—so He is by His nature a knower of good and evil, without His having to eat of the tree of the knowledge of good and evil. Once the man and woman lose their moral innocence by eating of the tree of the knowledge of good and evil, God is no longer sanguine about their existing indefinitely into the future and perhaps forever. They must be permanently evicted from the garden. Apparently, once they know good and evil, their inclination to evil has the potential to dominate (Gen. 6:5, 8:21).

---

17. See Strauss: "While not being a child he was to live in child-like simplicity and obedience to God." Leo Strauss, "Jerusalem and Athens," in *Studies in Platonic Political Philosophy*, ed. Thomas L. Pangle (Chicago: University of Chicago Press, 1983), 147–73; see 155.

18. The man and the woman are skilled; they sew fig leaves to make garments for themselves.

The Torah thus provides two ways that human beings might do good and avoid evil. One is via direct obedience to God, represented by God's requiring of Adam and Eve in the garden that they obey a single command. But that they disobeyed and ate of the fruit of the tree of the knowledge of good and evil suggests the nonviability of this model for human beings. Even though what God asked of Adam and Eve was hardly onerous, they could not be simply obedient. They insisted on having in addition to divine guidance their own direct access to good and evil. This, then, is the second way in which human beings might do good and avoid evil— namely, by judging good and evil for themselves.[19]

If we, like God, are knowers of good and evil, then it becomes possible to understand in this sense [20] the idea that the human being is created "in God's image" (Gen. 1:27).[21] And this is so despite the fact that the woman at first seems really not to know that eating of the tree is evil and knows only that it is forbidden; and despite the fact that there is no way to account for the "opening of the eyes" experienced by Adam and Eve as a *result* of their eating this fruit if they were created with open eyes. We may, however, look at the matter of the human being's knowing good and evil on analogy with the human being's being created male and female. (Indeed, both appear in the same verse, Genesis 1:27, "And God created the human being in His image, in the image of God He created him; male and female He created them.") As soon becomes clear from the Torah's text, the dual-genderedness of the human race is not God's first thought but His final one. What is recorded in Genesis 1 is the end of the story, not its beginning. As the account of creation unfolds we find that the male is complemented by the female only once God realizes that it is "not good" for the man to be alone. God thus alters His original plan. Similarly, in our case, the initial divine plan was to have an obedient child. This plan, too, is reversed—this time, however, not at God's initiative but at man's. Nevertheless, the end of the story—what eventually happens—is indeed

---

19. Adam must have been alongside Eve at the time of the seduction: "And she gave also to her husband *with her* and he did eat" (Gen. 3:6).

20. See the commentator Seforno on Gen. 3:22.

21. To be created in God's image is to be like God but to be ontologically one step removed, as is the case with all images and that of which they are images. God, as we have seen, does not need to eat from the tree in order to be a knower of good and evil.

that the human being is created in God's image: he knows good and evil. In other words, until the human being has eaten of the tree and has acquired knowledge of good and evil, it cannot be said of him that he is created in God's image. Once Adam and Eve's eyes are opened, they, like God, have direct access to the standard; and they have no excuse for not conforming their behavior to it.

As the biblical narrative continues, the one constant is that there is a right and wrong that is available to human beings and to God. In the Cain and Abel incident, God's understanding is of good and evil. He distinguishes for Cain between doing well (*im teitiv*) and its consequences, and not doing well (*im lo teitiv*) and *its* consequences; indeed, we have the first explicit mentions of sin in connection with Cain's doing not-well ("sin croucheth at the door"—*lapetah hatat roveitz*—Gen. 4:7; and "my iniquity is too great to bear"—*gadol 'avoni minneso*—Gen. 4:13). There is no suggestion that Cain is unaware that what he does is wrong.[22] A bit later on in Genesis, God sees—that is, knows—that "the wickedness of man was great in the earth and that every imagination of the thoughts of his heart is only evil (*ra'*) continually" (Gen. 6:5). Men sin so audaciously that God repents of having created them (Gen. 6:6). The Torah thus takes something akin to a natural law position. There is a standard; it is objective; it is knowable. Furthermore, all are subject to it—both God and people.

It is because there is a standard to which God, too, is subject, that Abraham, in the incident of Sodom and Gomorrah, can say to God, "Will not the judge of all the earth do justice?"[23] Justice is the measure to which Abraham holds God. That men, too, are held to this standard of justice is clear, for otherwise the terms *tzaddiq* and *rasha'*, "righteous" and "wicked," would be without meaning. It is a standard that Abraham knows, without God's having to convey it to him. That there is a standard common to both God and men is implicit, too, in the judicial system Jethro proposes to his son-in-law Moses (Exod. 18:19–23). Although some matters to be adjudicated

---

22. Perhaps God protected Cain because God did not directly tell him that murder is forbidden. Even with sin crouching at the door, however, there is no reason that Cain could not conquer it.

23. For further discussion of the Abrahamic challenge to God's justice in the matter of Sodom and Gomorrah, see Section III of this essay.

would surely have been religious or ritualistic in nature, some would certainly have been civil. It would have been up to a judge to render the correct (or best) determination. In most cases the appointed judges would have been sufficiently competent to discover the answer on their own. Occasionally, they would have needed to turn to Moses. And even more occasionally, Moses would have needed to turn to God. The only reason the judges would turn to Moses and Moses to God is because of the difficulty of the question. Moses does not seek a divine fiat: God's answer is not the right one because God makes it so; His answer is right because He *knows* best. Even though two of the recorded instances in which God had to step in were matters of religious law, namely, the matter of the blasphemer in Leviticus 24, and of the violator of the Sabbath in Numbers 15, there nevertheless remains a third case, that of the daughters of Zelophehad in Numbers 27 (cf. Num. 36), that is a civil matter. In this third case, what God affirms is that the women "spoke *correctly* (*ken*)" (Num. 27:7).

When God, then, in Deuteronomy 30:15, places before the people the good and the bad and urges them to choose the good, He is not making the news but reporting it. He prefaces the choice with the famous assurance that the commandments are "not far away from you," "not in the heavens," and, most importantly, not such that someone has to be delegated to go up to the heavens, seize the commandment for us and "tell it to us and we will do it" (Deut. 30:11–12). In other words, the commandments are not decrees that have simply to be obeyed; on the contrary, they are within human reach, accessible and knowable.

II. *Beyond the Standard*

If there is a standard of right and wrong that is open to all "knowers of good and evil"—even if some are more proficient than others at determining the particular rulings that derive from the standard—is there nothing to distinguish God from people in the moral realm? Is there nothing in morality that remains hidden from people, or mysterious?

Despite the common standard to which we and God are answerable, we know from Exodus 33–34 that there is something about God that must remain unknown and unknowable. Here Moses asks to have God's way made known to him and to be shown God's glory. It is evident that Moses, even more than other people, knows justice and implements it. He is the judge par excellence. When he asks, then, to know God's way and to see God's glory, he surely does not wish to know about justice, the standard common to God and to us, the standard he has already mastered. He is asking about something else, some other way in which God operates, something that reveals the divine essence in a way that justice does not. In other words, what Moses wants to do is to penetrate the familiar aspect of God as "knower of good and evil," and to see something deeper, something essential, perhaps something unique, something distinctive about God.

I would suggest that the thirteen divine attributes—known in the rabbinic tradition as the thirteen *middot*—enumerated in Exodus 34, attributes that God revealed to Moses as He passed before him and covered him with His hands, permitting him to see only His back, introduce a moral dimension distinct from the justice, the *mishpat*, to which God may be held just as people are, and to which both people and God have access. Indeed neither the term *mishpat* nor the term *tzedeq*, another term for justice, appears in this list of divine attributes. The verses in which the divine attributes are listed read as follows (Exod. 34:5–7):

> And the Lord passed before him and called out the Lord, the Lord, God mighty, compassionate and gracious, slow to anger, and abundant in kindness and faithfulness, keeping kindness to the thousands, forgiving iniquity, and transgression, and sin, but who will by no means clear the guilty; visiting the iniquity of the fathers on the children, and on the children's children, to the third and to the fourth generation.

These *middot*, I would argue, do not constitute a standard to which God is *held*, one which we, too, recognize, understand, and are held to, but instead in fact *set* a standard. It is here that God does not look to a standard of right and wrong that is above Him, but rather provides by example the standard to which we look. If there is a sphere in which the notion of *imitatio dei* operates, it is with respect to these *middot*. For, whereas with respect to straightforward right and wrong—justice—we do not imitate God, but instead look directly to the standard that is, so to speak, above both God and us, with respect to the special kind of morality that is not a manifestation of justice, we look not past God but directly at Him.

Consider the following passage from Anselm's *Proslogion*.

> For on the one hand it is from plenitude of goodness that
> You are gentle with those who sin against You; and on the
> other hand the reason why You are thus is hidden in the
> depths of Your goodness. For although from Your goodness
> You reward the good with good and the bad with bad, yet
> it seems that the very definition of justice demands this.
> But when You give good things to the wicked, one both
> understands that the supreme Good has willed to do this
> and one wonders why the supremely just One could have
> willed it.[24]

Several things are striking about this passage. First, Anselm finds nothing puzzling in God's requiting good with good and bad with bad: that is justice, and, as such, it is nothing less than one would expect from a just God. Note that in recognizing that this is what justice, by definition, demands, Anselm acknowledges that justice can place demands on God. In that sense, justice is something to which God is answerable. Second, what Anselm does find puzzling is God's requiting bad with good. Not only is this not what justice requires; one wonders how someone who is just could will it—that is, is not such an act inconsistent with justice? Third, Anselm observes that the requiting of bad with good is "hidden in the depths of Your goodness." To put it differently, this is a *middah* that is hidden, that is mysterious, in a way that justice is not. But, fourth, and perhaps most significantly, it is only in relation to the notion of "giving good things to the wicked" that Anselm speaks of God's willing. It is here, in the gentleness displayed toward the wicked, that we encounter God's will, that we see God *being* the standard rather than being answerable to it.

It is notoriously difficult to identify, to count, the thirteen *middot*. And, complicating the count still further is the fact that the *middot* are sometimes called "the thirteen *middot* of mercy": if they are all *middot* of mercy then are there not two *middot* that are excluded—the *middah* that God will surely not acquit (*venaqqeh lo yenaqqeh*), and the *middah* that He visits the

---

24. *Anselm of Canterbury: The Major Works*, trans. M. J. Charlesworth, ed. Brian Davies and G. R. Evans (Oxford: Oxford University Press, 1998), 92 (question 9).

iniquity of the fathers on the children (*poqed 'avon avot*)? Among the points of contention in determining which constitute the thirteen are (at least) the following: (1) whether to count the first of the two adjacent occurrences of the term "the Lord" as one of the *middot* or to regard it as referring to the proclaimer who is calling out in God's name. To repeat the relevant verse (Exod. 34:6): "And the Lord passed before him [Moses] and called out the Lord, the Lord, God, merciful. . . ." Depending on where one places the commas, this verse could mean either that the Lord called out, in which case only one instance of "the Lord" is in the count of thirteen, or that [He] called out, "The Lord, the Lord," in which case both instances of "the Lord" are in the count; (2) whether or not *venaqqeh lo yenaqqeh*, normally rendered, "He will surely not acquit," should be split, so that *venaqqeh* is taken to mean that God does acquit those who are worthy of acquittal, and *lo yenaqqeh* is taken to mean that He does *not* acquit those who are not (this is Onqelos' solution); and (3) whether visiting the iniquity of the fathers on the children until the fourth generation is in the count or not (Maimonides includes it, but he thinks, therefore, that there is one attribute that is not an attribute of mercy—see *Guide* 1.54). Of course, the Torah itself does not specify that the number of *middot* is thirteen, so perhaps we can set this particular problem aside. What we have, then, is God, in response to Moses' request to have God's way made known to him and to have God's glory shown to him, parading "all His goodness" (*kol tuvi*—Exod. 33:19), or His glory (Exod. 33:22), or Himself (Exod. 34:6), before Moses, while shielding Moses from the sight of God's face (Exod. 33:20, 33:23), which cannot be seen by a human being.

What God parades before Moses is not ordinary justice, which is and can be known by human beings, but aspects of God that cannot be known—even by Moses. These are God's goodness, God's glory, or God Himself. The sense in which these cannot be known is that no one can know the way in which God deploys them. This mystery is captured in the verse, "and I shall be gracious to whom I shall be gracious and I shall be merciful to whom I shall be merciful" (Exod. 33:19), reminiscent, of course, of the equally opaque, "I shall be what I shall be" (Exod. 3:12). In other words, the divine calculus that determines who it is to whom God will be gracious or merciful and when He will be so is unknowable; it remains hidden from human beings. It is not the case, however, that we do not know what it means to be gracious and merciful, or, for that matter, what it means to be slow to anger and forgiving of iniquity. Yet, in conducting ourselves in any of these ways, we are not adhering to a standard outside of God but are instead imitating God. Moses could not see God's face, but His *middot* were nevertheless paraded before him as a model to be emulated, as a way of being moral that is not reducible to an objective standard.

The Torah contains not only the moral laws whose intent is to inculcate justice, but, in addition, moral laws that require of us mercy, compassion, and kindness. It is these laws that reflect the standard that God *sets*, rather than a standard to which both He and we are subject. It is in observing these laws that we emulate God, that God *is* the standard for us. This is not to say that there are no people who are kind and compassionate without reference to God; of course, there are. But, insofar as they look to a standard, that standard is found not *in* the natural course of things but beyond it—and it is found in the Torah. Prior to the revelation at Sinai the moral failures for which human beings were held accountable in the Torah's narratives were failures with respect to justice. Only once the Torah was given do failures of compassion count as sins—indeed, as ugly sins of cruelty. Neglect of the stranger, the orphan, the widow, and the poor, and mistreatment of a slave or animal are serious violations of God's standard.

To summarize the first two sections: The Torah offers in total three ways for us to know what morality requires. First, God tells us what is right and wrong, what is just and unjust, what is good and evil, and we can do as He commands. This is what is meant by listening to God and walking in God's ways,[25] walking in His statutes,[26] and keeping His commandments and statutes. In this way we reproduce our original innocence in the Garden of Eden. The second is through our own direct access to natural, objective justice, access which we gained, symbolically, through our eating of the fruit of the tree of knowledge of good and evil. We wanted to be enlightened, and we were. That enlightenment, however, confers on us the burden of morality: we are expected to live justly in accordance with our own direct access to the standard of justice, and we

---

25. See, e.g., Deut. 13:19, 26:10, 28:22, 28:45, 30:8, 30:10, 30:20; and also several references in Leviticus.

26. See, e.g., Deut. 8:6, 19:9, 28:9.

incur God's wrath to the extent that we murder, steal, and are otherwise corrupt. The third is through imitation of God's mysterious attributes of compassion, graciousness, slowness to anger, and abundant kindness and faithfulness.[27] Although God's visiting of iniquity on the second, third, and fourth generation is not something we would recognize as just, nevertheless, by including this attribute among the divine attributes, the Torah opens up the possibility that, under certain circumstances, human dealings of this kind, in imitation of God's attribute, may be appropriate. One such case might be the matter of idolatry, as Maimonides contends in *Guide* 1.54.

III. Is God Always Just?

There are clearly events in the Torah that strike the reader, certainly at first glance, as instances of divine injustice. The favoritism that God shows one brother over another, for example—a disastrous favoritism replayed in the relations between biblical fathers and mothers and their sons, all of which are then the source of so much trouble and difficulty between the siblings—makes one suspect that the biblical God, unless the text is subjected to midrashic or philosophic departures from the *peshat*, is not fully just. His preference for Abel over Cain and, perhaps worse, His favoring of Isaac over Ishmael (possibly in opposition to Abraham's own preference), His privileging of Jacob over Esau (in this case in clear contradiction to Isaac's sentiments), and His singling out of Joseph (here in line with Jacob's feelings)—all have calamitous consequences. At least to the extent that justice requires, at a minimum, fairness, it is difficult to regard this God as fully just. Moreover, it might be said that the Torah alerts us to the wrongness of God's favoritism by showing us the misery that unfailingly follows in its wake.[28] Significantly, however, in

---

27. This is perhaps captured in the injunction: "Be ye holy, for I, the Lord your God, am holy" (Lev. 19:2).

28. If the Torah could not count on us to have access to the objective standard of justice, it could not risk relating the stories it relates about its oversized personalities and about God. And because we do exercise our knowledge of the standard, we know we have two choices: either to censure the immoral activities we see, believing we are meant to do so, or to interpret the Torah figuratively. The Torah's intention is certainly not to teach us to behave badly.

none of these instances does the Torah itself or any character in the Torah suggest that God is at fault. Perhaps God has His reasons.

Other moral failings that have been attributed to God need not be seen that way. Some have regarded God's anger as excessive, His vengefulness as out of bounds. Yet God's burning anger, for example, may well be fully appropriate to the various situations in which it is made manifest. The sinfulness and ingratitude of a nation may well merit God's reaction—or worse. Perhaps we are simply not in a position to judge.

Even if God is not unjust in any of these cases—perhaps His unfairness (or worse)[29] is either merely apparent or fully legitimate—nevertheless, the Torah seems to permit human beings to challenge God in the court of justice; indeed, God himself does not rebuke the challenger. Is it then correct to conclude, even if God turns out in every case not to be unjust, that divine injustice is not unthinkable, not unimaginable?

The locus classicus of the human challenge to God's justice is Abraham's challenge in the matter of Sodom and Gomorrah. As we have seen, Abraham says to God, "Will not the judge of all the earth do justice?" (Gen. 18:25). In effect, Abraham accuses God of a patently unjust intention to destroy the righteous along with the wicked. Such an act is so uncontestably unjust, so clearly violative of any objective moral standard, that Abraham goes so far as to say, *twice within a single verse*, "Far be it from You"—in the rather benign rendering into English of the exclamation of horror, *ḥalilah lekha*. Were that very expression used in association with anyone but God, the most apt translation of it would be something like "God forbid!" The single verse (18:25) reads as follows: "Far be it from You to do such a thing—to kill the righteous with the wicked so that the righteous and the wicked would fare alike—far be it from You!" What is striking about this passage is that the expression, *ḥalilah lekha* (or *lakh*), applies specifically to blatant injustice: to the killing of the righteous with the wicked, to treating both equally badly. It is thus the objective standard of justice to which God, though judge of all the world, is held no less than are men.

---

29. Nor are these the only troubling cases: Is it not cruel for God to force Abraham to send Ishmael away? Is God's demand that Abraham sacrifice his beloved son Isaac not cruel?

Closer examination of the text, however, reveals that God's intention could never have been to violate the standard of justice. Moreover, it is fairly evident that Abraham never suspected that it was. What Abraham did was conceal his request for mercy, for compassion, within a putative demand for justice. Mercy and compassion cannot, of course, be demanded, and Abraham shows his recognition of the difference when he humbly says, in asking for compassion: "Behold, I venture to speak to my Lord, I who am but dust and ashes" (Gen. 18:27). Abraham relinquishes the brazenness of the demand for justice and instead beseeches God for an act of kindness to which no human being has any claim. The prize Abraham is after is not that the righteous not be killed along with the wicked, but that the wicked be spared on account of the righteous— whether there be fifty righteous, or but forty-five, or forty, or thirty, or twenty, or only ten. In fact, Abraham *wants* God to treat the righteous and the wicked alike—but by treating them equally *well*. What Abraham wants, in Anselm's terms, is that God be "gentle with those who sin against You," that He "give good things to the wicked." This is hardly a matter of justice. Abraham, then, is actually asking God to be true to God's own standard, to the standard that God sets—not one to which He may be held. Abraham's initial challenge is, it appears, no more than rhetorical. God does not even dignify it with a response. All God does is assure Abraham that if there are righteous men to be found—even if they number as few as ten—He will indeed spare the wicked for their sake.

The closest parallel in the Torah to Abraham's challenge occurs in Numbers 16, where Korah and his followers impugn Moses' and Aaron's authority. God becomes enraged, and Moses and Aaron "fell upon their faces and said: 'O God, the God of the spirits of all flesh, shall one man sin and You be wrathful against all the congregation?'" (Num. 16:22). We may observe that here, as in the case of Abraham, God does not respond. He simply continues with what may be assumed to be His original plan. In v. 21 he had told Moses and Aaron to "separate yourselves from among this congregation that I may consume them in a moment." And in vv. 23–24, after Moses' and Aaron's outburst, He resumes: "Speak unto the congregation, saying: Get up from about the dwelling of Korah, Dathan, and Abiram." It appears that Moses and Aaron jumped the gun, and their rude interruption was not to be accorded validation by a divine response. Indeed, the passage provides no indication that God approved of their challenge or that He acted because of it.[30] Their words are simply ignored.

We may usefully compare Abraham's supplication to Moses' two similar petitions—the first following the sin of the Golden Calf, the second following the sin of the spies. In neither case does Moses hold God to a standard of justice. In the first of these, found at Exodus 32:11–14, Moses appeals to God on two grounds. The first is God's love for His people: why should the Egyptians be able to say that God's intentions were malevolent in taking the people of Israel out of Egypt, that He wished only to destroy them? The second is God's promise to the Patriarchs, the promise to make their progeny as numerous as the stars in the sky. This second reason is designed to trigger God's love for Abraham, Isaac, and Jacob, and hence His compassion for their descendants. He asks God to relinquish His (rightful) anger and renounce the evil He wished to visit on them. And so God did.[31]

In the second instance, Numbers 14:13–20, Moses first warns God that the nations will say that it is because God lacked the power to bring the people to the land He had promised them that He slaughtered them in the wilderness.[32] It would therefore be appropriate for God to show His power in line with the divine attributes of which He had spoken—

---

30. Cf. God's response to Moses after his petition in Num. 14:20, "I have forgiven in accordance with your word."

31. We may compare with this passage the one in which Moses recapitulates for the new generation, in the fortieth year of the wandering in the desert, his supplication before God on the Israelites' behalf after the sin of the Golden Calf. In this account (Deut. 9:26–29), Moses mentions his having invoked God's promise to the Patriarchs, as well as his having warned that the Egyptians would draw the unwelcome conclusion that God hates the Israelites and took them out of the land of Egypt only because He wished to kill them in the desert. He reports in addition, however, that he had given God yet a third reason at that time, namely, "lest [the inhabitants of] the land from which You took us out say that because the Lord lacked the power to bring them to the land that He had promised them." In light of God's professed interest in having the Egyptians witness His might (see, for example, Exod. 7:3, 5, 9:16, 11:9), this third argument is a rather strong one.

32. See n. 31. The additional argument that Moses in Deut. 9 reports having used after the incident of the Golden Calf is one he actually used after the incident of the spies.

that is, of the high standards He sets rather than to a standard with which He must comply. As noted above, there is in this recapitulation of the thirteen attributes no mention of justice—of *mishpat* or *tzedeq*—and, perhaps significantly, even the word for truth, *emet*, is absent, perhaps because of its association with what is fitting or deserved. Moses asks God to pardon the people's transgression in accordance with the magnitude of His kindness just as He has forgiven them from the time they left Egypt until the present. And God indeed forgives—in accordance with Moses' word.

In neither of these instances is there any implication that God might commit injustice. Indeed, were God to be strictly just, His wrath would surely burn against this rebellious, stiff-necked people. Moreover, as we have seen, there was never any real possibility, either in the matter of Sodom and Gomorrah or in the Korah incident, that God would smite the innocent along with the guilty.

IV. Theological Implications

The God of the Torah is first and foremost a God of justice. Indeed, the biblical God might even be said to be hyper-just in His almost obsessive concern with human justice.[33] He is a judge and an enforcer of justice, a God whom Abraham can call "the judge of all the earth" (Gen. 18:25), a God who can be relied upon because He is reliably just. Moreover, His justice is not voluntaristic: as the primary *knower* of good and evil He sees justice with His mind's eye and answers to it. He is the consummate discerner of what justice demands—not its author.

As we have seen, however, human beings can be just, must be just, God or no God. In knowing good and evil, we have, the Torah tells us, become *like* God; we are capable of *choosing* justice, of moving beyond a child's

---

33. The Torah's God is not the God of the philosophers. Indeed, the God of the philosophers is not a God of relation. How can a God who is Intellect or who is wholly other (as Maimonides' God is) care about human justice? Buber, for one, was troubled by the notion of a God who is only transcendent. As he so memorably expressed it: "And if He was not a person in Himself, He, so to speak, became one in creating man, in order to love man and be loved by him—in order to love me and be loved by me." See Martin Buber, *The Way of Response*, trans. and ed. Nahum Glatzer, 2nd ed. (New York: Schocken, 1966), 26.

simple obedience. We do, however, need God to serve as a paradigm for us, to take us, by His example, beyond justice—to generosity, love, care, and forgiveness.[34]

We are left, however, with a puzzle. Even if Abraham's challenge to God in the matter of Sodom and Gomorrah as well as Moses and Aaron's challenge in the Korah incident, are, as we have noted, wholly without merit, we must wonder why the Torah nevertheless saw fit to record them. The tentative answer to this question proposed in this essay has been that the Torah's intent is to make clear that the standard of justice—unlike that of mercy and compassion—is independent of God. If it is even thinkable for someone to say to God, "How could You commit an injustice?" we can preserve the objectivity and perfection of the standard, and thus maintain the separation between it and even its perfectly successful adherent. Moreover, so long as the standard stands apart from God, *we* have no excuse for not adhering to it; atheism is no excuse nor would it matter that we had not been informed of the requirements of justice by way of the Torah.

Once we move beyond justice, however, and enter the realm of the divine attributes, we no longer have even the theoretical possibility of God's falling short. In the matter of graciousness, compassion, forgiveness, restraint, and kindness, God is not a *knower* of the standard but rather constitutes the standard in himself. The only way we know of an obligation on our part to cultivate these virtues is through God as model and through the Torah's injunctions with respect to caring for the stranger, the widow, the orphan, the poor, the slave, and animals. It is not surprising then that the rabbinic tradition teaches not that, as God is just so ought we to be, but rather that, "as He is gracious, so you be gracious; as He is merciful, so you be merciful" (Babylonian Talmud, *Shabbat* 133b).

---

34. It is only with respect to these virtues and, I would argue, not with respect to justice that God may be said to be, as Buber contends, the indispensable ground for our ethics. See Buber, 65.

12

The Problem and Paradox of Politics: The Expulsion from Eden and the Oven of Akhnai

Jacob Howland

Among her friends, including students and colleagues across Europe and North America, Ronna Burger is cherished for her philosophical charm and intellectual generosity. She is a philanthropist when it comes to her *ousia*, the wealth of her mind and soul. Her teaching and scholarship have been distinguished by a deep and continuous engagement with the political philosophies of Plato, Aristotle, Maimonides, and the Hebrew Bible. Finely attuned to Greek and Jewish variants of the philosophical art of writing, her interpretations unfailingly unlock fresh meanings. It seems fitting to honor Ronna's remarkable career with an interpretation of a famous Talmudic narrative of political crisis, one that takes its bearings by her most beloved authors and texts.

*   *   *

Although the intellectual traditions of Athens and Jerusalem begin from the radically different experiences of philosophical wonder and the fear or love of God,[1] a family resemblance unites the ancient tribes of Greeks

---

1. Leo Strauss, "Jerusalem and Athens: Some Preliminary Reflections," in *Jewish Philosophy and the Crisis of Modernity: Essays and Lectures in Modern Jewish Thought*, ed. Kenneth Hart Green (Albany: State University of New York Press, 1997), 379–80.

and Jews. The Israelites that Joshua led into the Jordan Valley were pious, law-abiding, and capable in war; not for nothing did the Spartan King Areus claim that the Spartiates and the Jews "are brothers... from the race [*genos*] of Abraham" (1 Macc. 12:20–23). Areus doubtless understood that Jews, like Spartans, were *made*, not born: their identity as a people was fashioned, and their virtues cultivated, by laws and customs governing every sphere of life. The word *politeia* ("regime") first appears in Herodotus in connection with Sparta (9.33–35), and designates not simply the structure of political power in a community, but, more broadly and fundamentally, "the one way of life of a whole *polis* ['city']."[2] While the Spartans trace their regime to the lawgiver Lycurgus, it is God who gives the Jews their distinctive political culture or "way of life": a comprehensive regimen of habits and practices sustained by a shared education that weaves disparate natures into a tightly-knit social fabric. The Hellenized Jew Josephus accordingly grasped a deep truth when he spoke of the *politeia* born at Sinai (*AJ* 3.84, 213). Thinkers in both the Greek and Jewish traditions furthermore attempt to explain the origin of politics, and to determine the necessary conditions and limits of its specific work: reasoned deliberation by an authoritative body on matters bearing on the life and welfare of the community as a whole.[3] And it is in this area that one discovers a rich vein of shared insight and a striking convergence with respect to what I am calling the *problem* and *paradox* of politics.

Philosophers and Rabbis on Truth and Politics

The political problem, as the Greeks and the Jews of antiquity agree, is our ignorance of how to live good and peaceful lives in community, and more fundamentally, how to negotiate answers to this question without serious conflict. According to the tales of the Golden Age of Cronos in Hesiod's *Works and Days* and of the Garden of Eden in Genesis, the political problem arose when human beings ceased to live in the company of God or the gods. We initially dwelt in heavenly ease and peace; separation from the divine bosom subsequently burdened us with the difficult and fractious business of preserving life and providing for the good life on our

---

2. See the scholium on Plato, *Laws* 625b.
3. Cf. Arist., *Pol.* 1253a7–18 with 1275b17–21.

own. The Bible attributes this separation to the free choice of Adam and Eve; Hesiod, to the vengefulness of Zeus (*WD* 42–120). Plato's retelling of Hesiod's tale in the *Statesman* (268e4–274e4) offers yet another explanation: our ejection from the care of the gods follows from a combination of natural necessity and divine intervention. This traumatic separation from the living presence of a Truth we need not strain to know because *it* knows *us* (whether literally or figuratively, e.g., in the way animals are enfolded by natural instinct) necessitates the fractious and onerous self-management of politics. It also gives rise to the search for practical wisdom (*phronēsis* or *ḥochmah*) through philosophical inquiry, dialogue, and the interpretation of sacred traditions and texts, including written and oral Torah.

Strange as it may seem, however, the decisive achievement of wisdom by one or a few human beings—and no ancient thinker could imagine anything beyond this—is politically undesirable. For both the philosophers and the rabbis, *the* political paradox is that communities may be destroyed not only by ignorance, but by the immediate presence of Truth in the form of the perfected sage or wise man. Aristotle makes the point succinctly in the *Politics*. Because a *polis* is a partnership in which citizens share in ruling and being ruled under law, one whose excess of virtue is so great as to be incommensurable with the virtue and political capacity of others "can no longer be counted as part of the city." For people of this sort "there is no law [*nomos*], for they themselves are law"; in this, they resemble "a god among human beings" or "lions" among "hares." And while it would be unjust to make individuals of godlike wisdom submit to the city's law, it would be no less unjust to make the other citizens submit to them. For they would occupy the entirety of the public, political space, obliterating the middle ground where citizens structure their shared existence through debate and deliberation. The survival of the community as a political partnership therefore requires their eviction. This is, more or less, Aristotle observes, why democracies have instituted the practice of ostracism (*Pol.* 1284a3–19).

This article focuses on the understanding of the problem and paradox of politics developed in two well-known Jewish texts whose dramatic and thematic complementarity has not, to my knowledge, been previously recognized. The first, the Bible's tale of the expulsion of Adam and Eve from

Eden, particularly as interpreted by Maimonides, illuminates the political problem. The other is the Babylonian Talmud's reversal of the Eden narrative in the story of the Oven of Akhnai (BT Bava Metzia 59a–b), which tells of the exclusion of God and the eviction of the greatest of sages from the Academy at Yavneh, and illuminates the political paradox. Considered as a whole, this mythical/historical diptych teaches the necessary yet noble imperfection of politics as such. For it is the rabbis' recognition of the paradox that leads them decisively to cement the identity of the Academy as an authoritative body independent of the judgment and will of God.

The Political Problem in Genesis

Perhaps the earliest and most fundamental statement of the political problem is contained in the Eden narrative of Genesis. Life in the Garden is pre-political. Its structure arises from the direct paternal governance of God, who gives a few simple imperatives to *ha'adam*, the human being created in His image (1:27): Tend the Garden, Be Fruitful and Multiply, Don't Eat of the Tree of Knowledge. But even God's immediate presence cannot keep man and woman from going astray. The problem is that human intelligence is profoundly susceptible to the distortions of powerful desire. The first instance of such distortion is the sexually-awakened male's confusion, on rousing from deep slumber, about the origin of the female. He calls her "woman" (*isha*), claiming that she was taken from "man" (*ish*), that is, from himself (2:24). This is false, for man is merely what is left over when woman is separated from the (somehow male *and* female) whole of *ha'adam* (cf. 1:27). The next instance also reflects a tendency to self-inflation, this time on the part of the woman. It involves the serpent, who according to the great medieval commentator Rashi is himself motivated by desire for the woman and rivalry with the man.[4] The woman subtly alters God's prohibition even as she corrects the serpent's misstatement of the same; God did not forbid merely touching the tree (3:3; cf. 2:16–17). The serpent impregnates Eve in soul, at least; his cunning assertion that "God knows that ... you will become as gods knowing

---

4. See *The Torah: With Rashi's Commentary*, trans. Rabbi Yisrael Isser Zvi Herczeg (Brooklyn, NY: Mesorah, 1995), on 3:1 and 3:15.

good and evil" arouses a fatal attraction, drawing the woman to the tree of knowledge as "lust to the eyes" (3:5–6).[5]

The point of this story is clear enough. Shot through with dynamic configurations of interpersonal desire, the speech of intelligent animals is *itself* a slippery snake. Aristotle acutely observes that what makes us political animals is sharing in discussion and deliberation (*logos*) about "the advantageous and the harmful, and therefore also the just and the unjust" (*Pol.* 1253a1–18). This primal birth-scene nevertheless reveals that politics-as-speech originates in powerful passions, and is in the first instance the public justification of the same.

Maimonides on the Political Problem

Maimonides develops this perspective on politics in the second chapter of *The Guide of the Perplexed*,[6] where he illuminates the poisonous ambiguity of the serpent's assertion, "God knows that on the day you eat of it your eyes will be opened and you will become as gods knowing good and evil" (3:5):

> Every Hebrew knew that the term *Elohim* is equivocal, designating the deity, the angels, and the rulers governing the cities. *Onqelos the proselyte*, peace be on him, has made it clear, and his clarification is correct, that in the dictum of Scripture, *And ye shall be as Elohim, knowing good and evil*, the last sense is intended. For he has translated: *And ye shall be as rulers*.

Expelled from Eden, human beings must work for a living, culturally as well as materially. They must find ways to produce and transmit, through their own defective devices, something like the material conditions and psychological and ethical order of life in the Garden. God reveals the nature and cost of this necessary political work in fashioning clothes for Adam and Eve from the skins of animals with which they had formerly lived in peace; *nomos* ("custom, convention, law") is also a protective cov-

---

5. *The Five Books of Moses*, trans. and ed. Robert Alter (New York: W. W. Norton, 2004).

6. Maimonides, *The Guide of the Perplexed*, trans. and ed. Shlomo Pines, 2 vols. (Chicago: University of Chicago Press, 1963), 1:23–26.

ering for human beings in our thorny, cursed world, one that requires a degree of controlled violence against souls as well as bodies. Cain's murder of Abel, tellingly provoked by wounded pride (Gen. 4:3–6), underscores both the urgency and the difficulty of the political project. It leaves no doubt that the knowledge won through transgression—the terrible knowledge at the root of politics—consists not in wise comprehension, but in the direct experience of human depravity.

In brief, we are diminished rather than perfected by the bitter fruit of knowledge, and especially by the obligation to assume God's ruling responsibilities while lacking His wisdom. For not the least part of our punishment for eating the forbidden fruit consists in the ceaseless and burdensome exercise of self-governance that is needed to keep moral chaos at bay. Man, Maimonides intuits, was originally free to delight in the intellectual apprehension of God's creation; ejected from the Garden, however, "he became absorbed in judging things to be bad or fine. Then he knew how great his loss was, what he had been deprived of, and upon what a state he had entered." Maimonides knew this all too well; his labor as a doctor, a judge, and an advisor to Jewish communities in the Muslim world left him little leisure for philosophical reflection. Onqelos grasped the deceptive equivocality of *Elohim* from the other side: a nephew of the emperor Hadrian, he happily exchanged rank and power for what he regarded as the inner peace and nobility of Judaism.[7]

Maimonides delivers his interpretation of Genesis 3:5 with astonishing *ad hominem* vitriol. His target is an anonymous "learned man" who posed to him the question why the disobedience of Adam and Eve "procured ... as its necessary consequence the great perfection peculiar to man, namely, his being endowed with the capacity that exists in us to make this distinction [between good and evil]." "When in some of your hours of leisure," he rebukes the poor fellow, "you leave off drinking and copulating: collect yourself and reflect, for things are not as you thought following the first notion that occurred to you." Such a debauched individual as he

---

7. See Maimonides' letter to Samuel ibn Tibbon, in *The Sacred Books and Early Literature of the East*, ed. Charles F. Horne, vol. 4, *Medieval Hebrew*, trans. Dr. W. Wynn Westcott et al. (New York: Parke, Austin, and Lipscomb, 1917), 375–80, with Shulamis Frieman, *Who's Who in the Talmud* (Northvale, NJ: Jason Aronson, 1995), s.v. "Onkelos (Aquilas)."

describes could have no idea of genuine virtue and happiness, and therefore no appreciation of the perfected politics of Mosaic Law: the cultivation of wholesome habits and characters, healthy souls and bodies. Maimonides seems to regard his nasty polemic as a necessary antivenin for his readers, meant to counteract the prideful intoxication inevitably induced by the political speech of intelligent animals: the confusion of spurious and real divinity.[8]

The Political Paradox in Bava Metzia

For the Greek philosophers, the supreme form of practical wisdom is exhibited in the architectonic art of lawgiving (*nomothetikē*).[9] The foundational act of legislation, invariably memorialized in myth, calls into being a distinctively structured, unified way of life: a regime. *Nomos* encompasses usages as well as binding laws; the lawgiver encodes the constitutive identity of a political community in a broad range of practical idioms—ritual, myth, music, exercise, military training, and so forth. The same expansive conception of law is operative in the Jewish tradition, with one major difference: the lawgiver who constitutes the people and polity of Israel is God, whose Law is laid down in the comprehensive teaching of Torah. The practical wisdom of the rabbis accordingly manifests itself not in legislation, but in the interpretation of the literary and legal code of the Bible. And it is in the context of the public, communal activity of interpretative inquiry and debate—a rational activity and regimen structured by its own distinctive traditions and practices—that the Talmud locates the political paradox.

The Bible teaches the political problem in a story of separation and expulsion from the presence of God. The Talmud teaches the political paradox in a tale that answers the expulsion from Eden point for point. In the Oven of Akhnai, another, metaphorical snake poisons the rabbinical

---

8. My reading of the second chapter of *The Guide of the Perplexed* remains on the surface of the text. Ronna Burger delves deep, and retrieves significantly different insights, in "Maimonides on Knowledge of Good and Evil: *The Guide of the Perplexed* I 2," in *Political Philosophy Cross-Examined: Perennial Challenges to the Philosophic Life*, ed. Thomas L. Pangle and J. Harvey Lomax (New York: Palgrave Macmillan, 2013), 79–100.

9. Cf. Arist., *NE* 1141b26 with Plato, *Laws* 678e6–688b4.

Academy at Yavneh, a group of scholars and judges that constituted the leadership of the Jewish community of Palestine; Rabbi Eliezer, the one perfectly wise man among them, is excommunicated; and the living God is excluded from all discussion of the meaning of the Law. Yet while the Talmud recognizes the necessity of these ostracisms, it also makes clear their great cost. For the Oven of Akhnai is shot through with violence and suffering, the unavoidable consequences of rejecting Truth in favor of falsehood.

Understanding the Story

The Oven of Akhnai is arguably the most famous narrative in the Talmud. The text is extraordinarily rich, and supports multiple interpretative approaches. The bitter and bloody conflict between Eliezer and his colleagues has been closely studied from legal, historical, theological, and literary perspectives.[10] In a landmark article, Daniel J.H. Greenwood has even identified the political paradox at the heart of the story.[11] Yet its fundamental political meaning remains largely unexplored.

Here the Greeks furnish yet another useful point of reference. In one of the best recent studies, Charlotte Elisheva Fonrobert observes that the Oven of Akhnai, "a foundation myth about establishing the collective identity of the rabbinic *beit midrash* [Academy]," does for the Academy what Aeschylus' foundational trilogy *Oresteia* does for the Athenian *polis*.[12] This comparison is perhaps more inspired than Fonrobert realizes. Both myths narrate the dramatic moment when a human court comes into being as a sovereign body with independent authority to adjudicate even disputes in which God or the gods have a stake. Aeschylus' trilogy tells

---

10. See the studies cited in Jeffrey Rubenstein, "Torah, Shame, and 'The Oven of Akhnai' (Bava Metsia 59a–59b)," ch.2, in *Talmudic Stories: Narrative Art, Composition, and Culture* (Baltimore: Johns Hopkins University Press, 1999), 34–63, and in Nachman Levine, "The Oven of Achnai Re-Deconstructed," *Hebrew Studies* 45 (2004): 27–47.

11. "Only by excluding his [Eliezer's] claim to special privilege could the community continue. But only by respecting his claim to truth can the world endure." Daniel J.H. Greenwood, "Akhnai: Legal Responsibility in the World of the Silent God," *Utah Law Review* 1997, no. 2, 309–58; see 354.

12. Charlotte Elisheva Fonrobert, "When the Rabbi Weeps: On Reading Gender in Talmudic Aggadah," *Nashim: A Journal of Jewish Women's Studies and Gender Issues* 4 (2001): 56–83.

the story of the crime and trial of Orestes. In the *Agamemnon*, Clytemnestra murders her eponymous husband, putting her lover Aegisthus, Agamemnon's cousin, on the throne of Argos. In the *Choephoroe*, Agamemnon's son Orestes slays the adulterous couple and, polluted with his mother's blood, is immediately pursued by the Erinyes or Furies. In the *Eumenides*, Orestes seeks refuge in Athens and stands trial for his deeds before a jury of citizens that hears testimony from the Furies and from Apollo (who, in taking Orestes' side, invokes the authority of Zeus). The Areopagus or homicide court is founded and the jury convened by Athena, who declares that even she—the city's patron goddess—does not have the right to render judgment on this great dispute between the chthonic deities and the Olympians (470–72). The Oven of Akhnai, by comparison, relates not the birth of a court, but its momentous passage from youthful subservience to mature adulthood. The Academy achieves its independence from an interfering God and His favored son by a kind of judicial fiat. The rabbis accept the law of God, but in ostracizing Eliezer, they reserve for themselves the power of deciding what the law *means* and how it should be applied.

The trial of Orestes gives birth to two Athenian institutions: the Areopagus, which functions according to the democratic principle of majority rule (the very principle upheld in the Oven of Akhnai), and the religious cult of the Eumenides, which controls and channels the furious forces unleashed by violations of sacred order, including parricide. But Orestes' acquittal exposes the city to a new danger, for the aggrieved Furies themselves threaten to pollute the motherland. They express the open wound of righteous indignation in words that could just as well have been spoken by the spurned Eliezer:

> Oh! Younger gods [Olympians], you have trampled the
>   ancient laws,
> and torn them out of my hands.
> And I, dishonored, wretched, heavy in wrath,
> shall let loose from my heart
> poison, vindictive poison,
> dripping blight on the land.
>   (778–84; repeated at 808–14)

In the end, Athena assuages the Erinyes with the offer of an honored position in the *polis*: cultic worship as powerful household deities. Their rage for justice contained but not entirely defanged, they are blessed with the new name of Eumenides, "Well-Disposed Ones."

The crisis of Akhnai also leads to bloodshed, and its ultimate resolution involves a similarly blessed outcome (albeit one mediated by a mortal female, not an immortal one). Fonrobert rightly intuits that the Oven of Akhnai is a political tragedy; like other scholars, however, she supposes that "the point of the story...is the mistreatment of Rabbi Eliezer by his colleagues and their excessive reaction to and repression of his dissenting opinion."[13] This approach implicitly assumes that the crisis and its "tragic consequences" were avoidable—that the rabbis could and should have behaved otherwise. Yet it fails to explain their supposed excesses. With Maimonides in mind, should we not ask what good reason they might have had for their *ad hominem* venom? In tragedy, fundamental tensions make conflict and suffering unavoidable. I propose that the Oven of Akhnai describes just such a situation, and that its tragic tensions and paradoxes are intrinsic to politics as such.

There is, however, another deep point of contact between the Oven of Akhnai and the *Oresteia*: neither is *simply* tragic. Orestes' matricide sets the gods at odds, and strains every significant bond in the web of relationships that binds parents with children, men with women, and mortals with immortals. But the badly fraying fabric of the Whole is repaired by Athena, who as a virgin female goddess, a weaver, and a warrior, is simply representative of neither femininity nor masculinity, family nor city, but unites these elements of the social and cosmic whole in her person. The Yavneh Academy and its leading family—Eliezer is the brother-in-law of Rabban Gamliel, the Academy's Nasi or head—are internally torn in similar ways, and the rabbis' relationship with God is implicitly jeopardized. There is violence here as well: death and hurt feelings. The hurt feelings are healed on the level of the divine by the good humor of God, who accepts rejection with fatherly grace. Even deeper wounds of mortal loss

---

13. Fonrobert, "Reading Gender in Talmudic Aggadah," 62; cf. 58. Greenwood asserts that the story's "ultimate implication [is] that it was wrong to excommunicate Eliezer." "Akhnai: Legal Responsibility," 355. Cf. Rubenstein, "Torah, Shame, and 'The Oven of Akhnai,'" 42: "The [sages'] punishment far outstrips the crime."

are healed by a wise and good woman with a name of mythical proportions, Imma Shalom ("Mother Peace")—in this respect, a kind of Jewish Athena. As the wife of Eliezer and sister of Gamliel, Imma Shalom stands on both sides of the conflict; as a Mother of Peace, she absorbs its violence and pain, and so suffers to hold together her family and community. The pivotal role of females in the denouements of both historical myths points toward the primal womb or Edenic ground of unity to which all communities must ceaselessly aspire if they are to withstand the disintegrative forces of exile, the essential condition of human existence.[14]

Who Is Eliezer?

Pirke de-Rabbi Eliezer ("Sayings of Rabbi Eliezer"), a rabbinic text of late antiquity, relates Eliezer's origins in a remarkable story of filiation, disinheritance, and metaphorical parricide that offers an essential prelude to the Oven of Akhnai. The story establishes Eliezer's *bona fides* as a uniquely gifted and favored interpreter of the Word of God. More, it introduces the theme of public shame and wounded feelings that the Oven of Akhnai is particularly intended to illustrate.

Eliezer is the son of Hyrcanus, a wealthy Palestinian landowner who gives him no Jewish education and consigns him to work "a stony plot" while his brothers plough arable ones.[15] Eliezer weeps because he wishes to learn Torah, but his father refuses to send him to school, regarding him, at twenty-eight, to be too old. The prophet Elijah then miraculously appears to him and instructs him to go to Jerusalem to study with Rabbi Yochanan ben Zakkai. Eliezer does so, and lives in abject poverty until Yochanan discovers his condition; thereafter he is nourished in body and soul alike. Yochanan becomes a surrogate father to the young man, whom he takes to calling "my son."

When the aggrieved Hyrcanus eventually arrives in Jerusalem to disinherit his disobedient child, Eliezer and his teacher are dining with the

---

14. Levine observes the remarkable fact that everyone in the Oven of Akhnai "was himself once banished or banned...*even those* appearing *as commentators* in the text." "Oven of Achnai Re-Deconstructed," 33 (emphases in original).

15. I quote from the translation of Gerald Friedlander, reprinted in Jacob Neusner, *Eliezer Ben Hyrcanus: The Tradition and the Man*, pt. 1, *The Tradition* (Leiden: E. J. Brill, 1973), 442–45.

wealthiest men of the district. Informed that Hyrcanus has come, Yochanan, who elsewhere describes Eliezer as "a plastered cistern that loses not a drop" (Mishnah Pirke Avot 2:8), invites his student to "tell us some words of the Torah." Eliezer modestly demurs; "like a well which cannot yield more than the amount which it has drawn," he protests, "I [am] unable to speak words of Torah in excess of what I have received from thee." Yochanan generously replies that Eliezer is a bubbling fountain "able to speak words of the Torah in excess of what Moses received at Sinai," and he withdraws to join Hyrcanus in the anteroom, "lest thou shouldst feel ashamed on my account." Told a bit later that Eliezer is "sitting and expounding, his face shining like the light of the sun and his effulgence beaming like that of Moses, so that no one knows whether it be day or night," he and Hyrcanus come in to hear him. "Happy are ye, Abraham, Isaac, and Jacob, because this one has come forth from your loins," Yochanan proclaims. But Hyrcanus, now eager to bask in his son's reflected light, objects: Yochanan should have said, "Happy am *I* [Hyrcanus] because he has come forth from *my* loins."

It is Eliezer who settles the question of his paternity. "Now that I have come and I have witnessed all this praise," Hyrcanus proclaims, "behold thy brothers are disinherited and their portion is given to thee as a gift." But in a stunning reversal, Eliezer rejects his earthly father and inheritance, claims the divine legacy of Torah, and effectively declares himself to be not simply a descendant of the patriarchs, but an adopted son of God:

> [Eliezer] replied: Verily I am not equal to one of them [his brothers]. If I had asked the Holy One, blessed be He, for land, it would be possible for Him to give this to me, as it is said, *The earth is the Lord's, and the fulness thereof* (Ps. 24:1). Had I asked the Holy One, blessed be He, for silver and gold, He could have given them to me, as it is said, *The silver is mine, and the gold is mine* (Hag. 2:8). But I asked the Holy One, blessed be He, that I might be worthy to learn the Torah only, as it is said, *Therefore I esteem all precepts concerning all things to be right; and I hate every false way* (Ps. 119:128).

Eliezer has no need of anything his father offers—land, money, belated recognition. He is wholly at home in Jerusalem, where he is supported by philanthropists and cherished by Yochanan. What is more, his father has no claim to the land and gold with which he clumsily wants to redeem their broken relationship, for these things belong to God. Hyrcanus had wanted to disinherit him, but Eliezer uses his claim on the divine patrimony of Torah effectively to disown his father—whose ways, as he makes abundantly clear, are in his view false and hateful. And in publicly rejecting and humiliating his father, Eliezer also disowns his brothers—to whom he manifestly feels, "not equal," but immeasurably, incommensurably superior.

What Is Akhnai?

The Oven of Akhnai is told in a section of tractate Bava Metzia that concerns verbal wrongdoing (*ona'ah*), including words that publicly shame another.[16] It takes place at Yavneh in a time of exile, after the destruction of Jerusalem and the expulsion of the Jews. When the Jews were starving during the Roman siege, Eliezer helped to smuggle Yochanan out of the city in a coffin so that he might negotiate with Vespasian at his camp. From death came life: having become emperor as Yochanan prophesied, Vespasian granted him the lives of the sages and a scholarly and judicial center on the coast (BT Gittin 56a–b). The Yavneh Academy was the bark on which Judaism was saved, but stormy seas lay ahead. The Oven of Akhnai relates a terrible crisis that almost destroyed the Academy, but ultimately made it stronger.

The story is prefaced by the following passage in Mishnah Kelim (5:10):

> If he cut it [a clay oven] [into] segments and put sand between segment and segment, Rabbi Eliezer declares it ritually pure and the sages declare it ritually impure.

Palestinian Jewish communities used large communal ovens. Such an oven could be rendered impure and might have to be destroyed if, for example, a serpent or scorpion entered it and died. Because only whole objects are

---

16. Translations are drawn from *The Talmud: The Steinsaltz Edition*, vol. 3, *Tractate Bava Metzia*, pt. 3, trans. and ed. Adin Steinsaltz (New York: Random House, 1990), 59a–b.

susceptible to impurity, Eliezer advocates a practical solution that neatly avoids what must have been a fairly common inconvenience and expense. He argues that an oven cut horizontally and reconstructed of stacked rings of earthenware cemented by mortar is no longer whole, and therefore incapable of contracting impurity.

The Gemara (commentary on the Mishnah) now asks: "What is Akhnai?" Why is this the name of the oven in question? Because, Rav Yehudah answers in the name of Shmuel, "they [the sages] encircled [Eliezer with] words like a snake [*achna*], and declared it ritually impure." The snake is a biblical symbol of transgressive desire and venomous speech; we are on notice that Eliezer's struggle with the sages turns on something other than logical cogency. The story will certainly involve violence, possibly the deadly sort; it will also require a catharsis of political and psychological poison. But why would a rabbinic dispute over laws of purity turn into a life-and-death battle that pollutes all parties? If we are to learn what Akhnai really is, we must try to answer this question.

The Battle for the Academy

The expulsion from Eden, the escape from Egypt, the eviction from Jerusalem: these are the archetypes of Jewish history. In each case, fundamental relations of God and human beings are unsettled and need to be renegotiated. In each case, a new order must be established, and it is paradoxically the act of transgression that makes this possible. For only when borders are manifestly breached does it become clear where they must be drawn.

This archetypal story, the one called the Oven of Akhnai, is told in two *baraitot*, teachings from the era of the Mishnah. The first begins as follows:

> On that day, Rabbi Eliezer used all the arguments in the world, but they did not accept [them] from him.

How could Eliezer fail to convince his colleagues? The obvious answers are entirely unsatisfactory. Perhaps Eliezer's arguments are poor ones. This is highly unlikely. Rabbinic debate on matters of *halakha* ("law") involved the interpretation and application of written and oral Torah; no one knew the sacred tradition better than Eliezer, or was more able to

242

extend this knowledge in new and creative ways. Perhaps the sages are incapable of grasping the cogency of Eliezer's arguments. This is equally unlikely. We are forced to conclude that their opposition to Eliezer has nothing to do with the matter of the oven, and everything to do with *him*. Yochanan used to say that Eliezer outweighed all the other sages put together (Pirke Avot 2:8); his colleagues seem to have found this imbalance intolerable.

The sages are of course under no obligation to accept Eliezer's arguments. And it must be said that it is Eliezer who, in his frustration, violates the implicit rules of rabbinic debate.

> He said to them: "If the *halakha* is in accordance with me, let this carob tree prove [it]." The carob tree was uprooted from its place one hundred cubits—and some say four hundred cubits. They said to him: "One does not bring proof from a carob tree." He then said to them: "If the *halakha* is in accordance with me, let the channel of water prove [it]." The channel of water turned backward. They said to him: "One does not bring proof from a channel of water." He then said to them: "If the *halakha* is in accordance with me, let the walls of the House of Study prove [it]." The walls of the House of Study leaned to fall. Rabbi Yehoshua rebuked them, [and] said to them: "If Talmudic sages argue [lit., 'contend for victory,' *menatzhim*] with one another about the *halakha*, what affair is it of yours?" They did not fall, out of respect for Rabbi Yehoshuah; but they did not straighten, out of respect for Rabbi Eliezer, and they still remain leaning.

In his mysterious closeness to God, Eliezer is favored with supernatural powers. But miracles have no evidentiary force with respect to the determination of the *halakha*; as the sages observe, they are irrelevant in the context of academic debate on matters of law. These particular miracles are furthermore shot through with combative hostility. Carob was a staple in the diet of the poor Jews of Palestine; in uprooting the tree and turning back the water, Eliezer implicitly threatens basic conditions of the community's existence. Much more serious is the matter of the study house walls; had they fallen, many would have been killed or injured. Eliezer's message is clear: the Academy does not deserve to exist if he cannot prevail, and if necessary, he is willing to destroy it. The stakes of the conflict could not be higher.

Eliezer's last miracle is the most impressive of all: he gets God to weigh in on his side.

> He then said to them: "If the *halakha* is in accordance with me, let it be proved from heaven." A [heavenly] voice [*bat kol*] went forth and said: "Why are you [disputing] with Rabbi Eliezer, for the *halakha* is in accordance with him everywhere?"

What better proof could one ask for? But instead of winning the day for Eliezer, this miracle escalates the crisis and brings it to a head. For it is now simply impossible for the sages to capitulate to him: were they to do so at this point, Eliezer's mere presence would suffice to destroy the Academy. The heavenly voice declares that he is *always* right on matters of law. If so, he himself *is* the law; the opinions of others are irrelevant. There is no need for debate and deliberation, interpretation and argument—no need, in a word, for the community of sages or the house of study. What is to be done?

The sages' response to the heavenly voice is dignified, unwavering, and utterly remarkable:

> Rabbi Yehoshuah rose to his feet and said: "It is not in heaven" [Deut. 30:12]. What does "it is not in heaven" [mean]? Rabbi Yirmeyah said: That the Torah was already given at Mount Sinai, [and] we do not pay attention to a [heavenly] voice, for You already wrote in the Torah at Mount Sinai: "After the majority to incline" [Exod. 23:2].

Yehoshuah's declaration of intellectual independence is a revolutionary and foundational deed. It draws bright borders around the Academy, and effectively calls it into being as a self-sufficient community. But in standing up to God, in telling Him that *He* has *no* right *ever* to intervene in the sages' work, Yehoshuah does not exactly speak truth to power. Quite the opposite: he speaks power to Truth. Like Eliezer's miracles, his declaration has no evidentiary force with respect to the question at hand. It is purely political; indeed, as Yirmeyah immediately illustrates, it is essentially an assertion of the inviolable right of the sages to be *wrong*. Yehoshuah supports majority rule by quoting from a passage whose plain sense is not that God has no authority to interpret the law He Himself has established, but rather that the Israelites are fully capable of *obedience*: "[God's] word is very close to you, in your mouth and in your heart, to do it" (Deut. 30:14). And Yirmeyah's explanation of "it is not in heaven" still more radically distorts the plain sense of a divine commandment: inveighing against giving false witness, Exodus 23:2 explicitly states that one must *not* incline after the majority![17]

Who Is God?

While Yehoshuah's bold words elicit no heavenly reply, the sages learn indirectly how God received them:

> Rabbi Natan met Elijah [and] said to him: "What did the Holy One, blessed be He, do at that time?" He said to him: "He smiled and said: 'My sons have defeated Me, My sons have defeated Me.'"

This anecdote is more than a fanciful aside. God has every reason to be angry at being excluded from a community constituted for the purpose of ensuring that human affairs are structured in accordance with divine Truth. He nevertheless takes his defeat with no hard feelings. Like Aristotle's *epieikēs*, the equitable person who demands less than his due of strict justice, God is free of righteous indignation.[18] The forbearance with which He allows Yehoshuah to put Him in His place is an essential step in the reestablishment of moral order after the sages' revolution. But, God's smile to one side, His otherwise unnecessary repetition of the phrase "My sons have defeated Me" suggests ambivalence—a mixture of pride in his now grown-up children and sadness at the adult sufferings

---

17. Cf. Daniel Boyarin, *Intertextuality and the Reading of Midrash* (Bloomington: Indiana University Press, 1990), 34–36.

18. Arist., *NE* 1137a31–1138a3.

that await them.[19] The victory of the sages is in any case Pyrrhic: as the sequel makes clear, no community can separate itself from Truth without paying a steep price.

Purging the Academy

There is blood on the floor after the battle for the Academy, and a comprehensive purification is needed.

> They said: "That day they brought all the objects that Rabbi Eliezer had declared ritually pure and burned them in a fire, and they voted [lit., 'were counted'] about him and they excommunicated [lit., 'blessed'] him."

Because Eliezer has been proved wrong—erroneously in God's view, and in any case not by rational argument but by imputation and communal fiat—his rulings on purity are retroactively suspect. Fire solves this particular problem, either by destroying the objects entirely or by ritually cleansing them. But the problem of Eliezer goes far beyond his legal record. It consists in his superior nature, whose very presence radically destabilizes the Academy. This fundamentally political poison must be cut out at the root by a political deed. The euphemism "blessed" masks the despair Eliezer must feel in exile. But it also expresses the sages' hope for a transformation akin to that of the Erinyes at the end of the *Oresteia*, the hope that Eliezer's righteous fury might somehow be limited and contained.

The sages face an immediate problem: who will inform Eliezer of the vote? The question is answered by his most famous student.

> Rabbi Akiva said to them: "I will go and inform him, lest someone who is unsuitable will go and inform him, and as a result he will destroy the entire world."

The eponymous hero of Sophocles' *Ajax* attempts to slaughter the entire Greek army when its leaders conspire to deprive him of the honor that is his due as the greatest of the Achaean warriors. The academic warrior

---

19. "So God laughed. Why? The Father saw that his education had worked. Akhnai marks the end of the childish Israelite people." Greenwood, "Akhnai: Legal Responsibility," 357.

Eliezer is also dishonored by manifestly inferior peers, and his indignation is potentially even more destructive than Ajax's. Akiva's sympathetic and forgiving character uniquely qualifies him for the task of softening his intellectual father's potentially world-destroying rage. A story elsewhere in the Talmud tells of the time Eliezer's fasts and prayers brought no relief from a drought; Akiva's plea for mercy, however, produced rain. A *bat kol* explains that Akiva is no greater than Eliezer, but that he alone "forbears to retaliate" (BT Ta'anit 25b).

Akiva approaches his teacher with extraordinary respect and deference:

> He dressed in black [garments] and wrapped himself in black, and sat before him at a distance of four cubits. Rabbi Eliezer said to him: "Akiva, what is the difference between today and any other day [lit., 'what is one day from two days?']?" He said to him: "Rabbi, it seems to me that [your] colleagues are staying away from you." He [Eliezer], too, rent his garments and took off his shoes, and he slipped down and sat on the ground. His eyes streamed with tears.

Akiva feels Eliezer's loss personally and immediately. He behaves like a man in the period of mourning (*shiva*): he tears his clothes, removes his shoes, and sinks to the ground, separated from the excommunicant by the prescribed distance. It is in some sense Eliezer he is mourning, for he will no longer hear his teacher's living voice in the Academy. Yet Eliezer joins him on the ground when he learns the news. Like a father and his son, they both now seem to mourn God, the heavenly Grandfather, who has been expelled from the community along with the one sage who speaks pure Truth in matters of law.

But that is not the whole story. Eliezer echoes the question asked every year at Passover, a holiday commemorating the end of the Egyptian enslavement of the Hebrews and the birth of the people of Israel: "Why is this day different from all others?" It is as though the Academy, rejecting the yoke of Pharaonic oppression by an infallible exponent of God's legislative will—a miracle-working, *bona fide* son of God—has finally come into being as an independent Jewish community. And the natural order itself convulses with its birth-pangs:

247

> The world was smitten: one third of the olives, and one third
> of the wheat, and one third of the barley. And some say [that]
> even the dough in a woman's hand swelled.

Just as the rejected Furies threaten to leak poison from their hearts to
blight the land, Eliezer, shamed and rejected by his colleagues, leaks tears
from his eyes that cause crops to wither. But there is another way to interpret this episode. Having made it clear that the living God is no longer
the measure of all things, the Jewish community of Palestine must be prepared for the consequences of structuring its existence in accordance with
something less than divine Truth. Famine is today widely understood to
be rooted in political disorder; similarly, in the Bible, it is the predictable
consequence of straying from the *halakha*, the way of God.[20] It is little
wonder that the refusal of heavenly sustenance causes a shortage of the
earthly sort.

A Family Tragedy

As Greenwood observes, Akhnai is a "family dispute" that "centers on a
struggle between generations, the children overthrowing the father of the
generation and the Father himself"; it is "the parricide, parallel to
Eliezer's own rejection of his own (natural) father, that mythologically
marks the coming of age of a new nation."[21] The story is told in two for-
mally analogous parts, as if to underscore the deep doubleness of the political paradox. The second, much shorter *baraita* that concludes the Oven
of Akhnai relates Eliezer's revenge against the Academy. As Eliezer has
now been shut out of the life of the sages, this conclusion plays out within
the sphere of his family. But his family intersects with the rabbinic community, and in some manner includes God, his adoptive father. The main
elements of the earlier story are furthermore repeated in the sequel. Once
again, Eliezer's destructive fury threatens to turn deadly; once again, a
sage stands up to God, and a loved one attempts to avert disaster.

The second *baraita* begins as follows:

---

20. See, inter alia, Deut. 11:13–17 and Lev. 26:3–4.

21. Greenwood, "Akhnai: Legal Responsibility," 347, 356.

There was a great calamity that day, for every place upon which Rabbi Eliezer laid his eyes was burnt. And Rabban Gamliel, too, was coming on a ship, [and] a wave rose up against him to drown him. He said: "It seems to me that this is only because of [Rabbi Eliezer] ben Hyrcanus." He rose to his feet and said: "Master of the Universe, it is revealed and known before You that I did not do [this] for my own honor, nor did I do [it] for the honor of my father's house, but for Your honor, so that controversies will not multiply in Israel." The sea rested from its wrath.

As the ultimate source of miracles, God stands on both sides of the divide between Eliezer and the sages. For while he graciously accepts being banished from the Academy, it is He who makes possible Eliezer's supernatural channeling of elemental powers of destruction. Gamliel is well aware of this fact. Like Yehoshuah, he rises to confront his Maker—the wording is in both cases identical (*amad al raglaiv*, "he stood on his feet")—and his appeal is successful. Yet he manages only to delay the day of reckoning.

The conclusion of the Oven of Akhnai exhibits cosmically symmetrical justice:

Imma Shalom, Rabbi Eliezer's wife, was Rabban Gamliel's sister. From that incident onward she did not let Rabbi Eliezer fall on his face. One day it was the New Moon, and she mistook a full [month] for a short one. Some say: A poor person came and stood at the door, [and] she brought out bread for him. She found him fallen on his face, [and] she said to him: "Rise! You have killed my brother." Meanwhile the sound of a horn came from Rabban Gamliel's house that he had died. He said to her: "From where did you know?" She said to him: "I have this tradition from my grandfather's house: all the gates are locked except for the gates of *ona'ah*."

Gamliel's end recalls the first act of human bloodshed, Cain's murder of Abel. Heard by God, Eliezer's prayer indirectly causes the death of *his* brother by marriage, and in this case, too, wounded feelings are fueled by God's apparent preference for a sibling. But in a more important way,

Imma Shalom reverses the Eden narrative. For while Eve is a mother of war, Imma Shalom, despite appearances, really is a mother of peace.

Mother Peace

Like her counterpart Akiva, Imma Shalom mediates between opposing parties with strong claims on her love. But she fails to prevent the death of her brother. She either miscalculates the calendar, a theoretical mistake, or tends to the hungry stranger instead of keeping an eye on Eliezer, a practical one. She may have thought it was the first day of the new month when in fact it was the last day of the old one—apparently an especially propitious time for prayers of supplication, which were offered in the prone position. (We are reminded of Eliezer's question, "What is one day from two days?" The death of Gamliel marks yet another epochal turning-point in Jewish history, the last gasp of the old era and the beginning of the new one.) Or she may have been forced to choose between caring for the stranger and protecting her brother, a truly tragic alternative. Significantly, she chooses to help the stranger.

The ending of the Oven of Akhnai involves tragic suffering, but crucially, it *is* an ending: Imma Shalom's acceptance of Gamliel's death marks a permanent cessation of hostilities. One can only imagine her suffering—her husband has killed her brother!—yet incredibly, she exacts no retribution; she exercises blessed forbearance for the sake of peace. But how, exactly, will their marriage survive? We cannot be certain, because the narrative curtain drops at the moment when the bonds that had attached her to the Academy through its two leading figures are severed—the moment when she, too, is effectively excommunicated. Yet Fonrobert furnishes a crucial hint when she suggests that Eliezer's question to Imma Shalom indicates that he did not know his prayers would be heard. He is surprised at the news of Gamliel's death, because (astonishingly) he is ignorant of the tradition she cites.[22] This, too, is a dramatic reversal. Free at last from the strife of politics, the sage becomes a student, and bitterness gives way to wonder. In our last image of them, Imma Shalom and Eliezer are teach-

---

22. Fonrobert, "Reading Gender in Talmudic Aggadah," 80n33. Could "the father of my father" (*avi aba*) from whom (according to Imma Shalom) this tradition derives be God, the Grandfather?

ing and learning Torah within a community of study animated purely by the erotic love of wisdom. Following Maimonides, we may say that this ending promises a return to something like the peace and happiness of Eden. In spite of everything, Eliezer has indeed been blessed.

The Last (and First) Word

When God came to create Adam, the rabbis teach, the heavenly polity was split: "the ministering angels formed themselves into groups and parties, some of them saying, 'Let him be created,' whilst others urged, 'Let him not be created.'" God has nothing to say on the matter. Rather, He resolves this debate by main force:

> Love said, "Let him be created, because he will dispense acts of Love"; Truth said, "Let him not be created, because he is compounded of falsehood"; Righteousness said, "Let him be created, because he will perform righteous deeds"; Peace said, "Let him not be created, because he is full of strife." What did the Lord do? He took Truth and cast it to the ground.[23]

Thus transposed to the primal scene of creation, the suppression of Truth in the context of politics reveals itself to be nothing less than the metaphysical precondition of human existence.

---

23. Genesis Rabbah 8.5, in *Midrash Rabbah*, trans. Rabbi Dr. H. Freedman, ed. H. Freedman and Maurice Simon, vol. 1, *Genesis I*, 3rd ed. (London: Soncino, 1983), 58.

13

The World-to-Come in Maimonides' *Introduction to Pereq Ḥeleq*

Seth Appelbaum

A major obstacle to making sense of Maimonides' teaching about the Messianic Age is that he addresses it in different ways in different places, sometimes explicitly and sometimes less so. In this paper, I will compare the explicit account found in the *Commentary on the Mishnah* (*Commentary*) with a more implicit account found in *The Guide of the Perplexed* (*Guide*). The *Commentary* is one of Maimonides' earliest works, completed in 1168, when he was 30. By contrast, the *Guide* was completed in 1191, when he was 53. Like the *Guide*, the *Commentary* was written in Arabic, and consists mainly of commentaries meant to explain the Jewish legal text known as the Mishnah, which forms the backbone of the Talmud, the traditional Jewish legal source text. In general, the *Commentary* was superseded by Maimonides' so-called "great compilation"—the Hebrew-language legal code known as the *Mishnah Torah* (1177).

However, one element of the *Commentary* has remained in wide circulation even after most of the book was supplanted by the *Mishnah Torah*— the special essays Maimonides wrote as introductions to some of the sections of the *Commentary*. For someone interested in Maimonides' treatment of the Messianic Age, the best place to look happens to be in one of those special introductions. The treatise, known as the *Introduction to Pereq Ḥeleq*, is Maimonides' introduction to a certain chapter in the portion of the Talmud that addresses the establishment of courts. This chapter's title means "the chapter regarding the portion," so named because it begins with the phrase, "all of Israel have a portion in the World-to-Come except for these," i.e., the ones guilty of some kind of heresy. This text is a major source for Maimonides' views about the Messianic Age.[1]

Maimonides starts the work off in an Aristotelian fashion, surveying the *doxai* or opinions about reward and punishment for obedience or disobedience to the Torah. There are five opinions: First, there are those who believe straightforwardly that the good one receives from obedience is the Garden of Eden, a paradise where one eats and drinks and is free from toil, while disobedience is punished with the fires of Gehinnom, a kind of hell. Second, there are those who believe the good will be the Days of the Messiah—all men will be kings forever, immortal. The rule of the Messiah will last as long as God rules the world; earth will be miraculously transformed, and impossible things will take place such as bread and garments springing ready-made from the earth. The third opinion believes that the reward will be the Resurrection of the Dead, who will be returned, together with family, to eternal physical life. The corresponding punishment is to never be resurrected. The fourth opinion holds that the reward is to live a prosperous life under a good king. The punishment is the life of exile we currently lead. The fifth and final opinion, which is the most widespread, is said to combine the other four, including "the coming of the Messiah, the Resurrection of the Dead, their entry into the Garden of Eden, their eating and drinking and living in health there so long as heaven and earth endure" (*JQR*, 29–30).[2]

The second and third opinions, the Age of the Messiah and the future Resurrection of the Dead, are said to come from a literal reading of the

---

1. In this paper, I will reference the *Introduction to Pereq Ḥeleq* from two sources: J. Abelson, "Maimonides on the Jewish Creed," *Jewish Quarterly Review* 19, no. 1 (Oct. 1906): 24–58 (cited as *JQR*); and "The Days of the Messiah," in *Ethical Writings of Maimonides*, trans. and ed. Raymond L. Weiss and Charles E. Butterworth (New York: Dover, 1983), 165–68 (cited as *EWM*). Other citations are from *The Guide of the Perplexed*, trans. and ed. Shlomo Pines, 2 vols. (Chicago: University of Chicago Press, 1963).

2. It seems to me that this fifth opinion does not include the fourth opinion, which was that rewards and punishments took place entirely within this world.

words of the Sages and the Scriptures. The first opinion, the bodily pleasures of the Garden of Eden and the bodily punishments of Gehinnom, is attributed to a literal reading of the words of the Sages alone—Maimonides does not mention the Scriptures as a source for this opinion. Presumably this is because the Scriptures barely make mention of the afterlife. The fourth opinion, the this-worldly account of prosperity and security or miserable exile, is attributed solely to the Scriptures. The belief in a world-to-come, the Messiah, and the Resurrection of the Dead, are elaborated most of all by the Sages. Perhaps Maimonides is indicating that these doctrines are not as literally present in the Scriptures as they would later become in the Talmud. Maimonides might be giving us an indication that the Sages' understanding in some respects surpasses that of the original recipients of the Torah.

After laying out the different opinions, Maimonides complains that virtually no one makes a serious investigation of the world-to-come. In the first place, all but a few beg the question—they do not inquire into whether or not a new world is a genuine possibility but rather they wish to know what the putative new world will be like. This has some bearing on the direction of the *Introduction* because Maimonides will eventually present us with a naturalized Messianic Age that is quite different from the radically new world that many expect. Rather than consider the truth about this matter of the world-to-come, or determine which of these opinions is correct, most people, both the vulgar and the elite, are concerned only with very particular questions about the world-to-come: "In what condition will the dead rise to life, naked or clothed? Will they stand up in those very garments in which they were buried, in their embroideries and brocades, and beautiful needlework, or in a robe that will merely cover the body? And when the Messiah comes will rich and poor be alike, or will the distinctions between weak and strong still exist?" (*JQR*, 30–31).

His other complaint is that most people fail to distinguish between "ends and means" in this matter. From the context, it is clear that he means that the belief in the Messianic Age should be seen as a means to some other purpose. To explain how this belief might be a means to an end, Maimonides employs a simile and advises us: "O reader, understand the following simile of mine, and then you will make it your aim to grasp my meaning throughout." This passage is crucially important for our understanding of the aim and meaning of Maimonides' project in this text. He has us consider the example of a teacher who, in educating a small child, entices him with candies into diligently pursuing his studies. Just as the teacher bribes the student with candy, so too are adults bribed into good behavior with the promise of a world-to-come that is based on our deserts.

The simile is not static; as the student matures his motivations develop the capacity to shift away from treats. Gradually, the teacher must vary the reward according to the maturing desires of the pupil—first candy, then a few coins, then beautiful garments and shoes, and finally the promise of honor in life and after death. Maimonides notes that at no point does the student pursue the knowledge for its own sake. These methods are thus not good in themselves, but are necessary only because of the weakness of human beings. Maimonides sums up the proper approach thus: "The aim of one's study of truth ought to be the knowing of truth. The laws of the Torah are truth, and the purport of their study is obedience to them. The perfect man must not say, 'If I perform these virtues and refrain from these vices which God forbade, what reward shall I receive?'" (*JQR*, 31). Maimonides tells us the Sages called disinterested obedience "service out of love." It is important to note that the purport of these remarks has switched from *knowledge* for its own sake to *action* for its own sake, a switch that will be quite important later.

To return to our subject, why, then, do we bribe children, if it's so blameworthy to study the Torah and perform commandments for the sake of reward? As the grounds for this practice, Maimonides cites Proverbs 26:5, "Answer a fool according to his folly," meaning that the child's intellect is not yet able to understand the concept of service out of love. However, Maimonides says that the Sages did not in fact expect the majority of human beings to study and to act out of love. The Sages were aware that human nature is fundamentally oriented towards acquiring what is beneficial and avoiding what is harmful. When faced with the highest form of obedience, service out of love, it is natural to respond with, "What's in it for me?" The Sages believed that this skepticism would be present even in "refined individuals," so that it is not possible to tell even one who was "learned in the Law" to act without fear of punishment or hope for reward. In light of this human tendency, and "in order that the common folk might be established in their convictions, the Sages permitted them to perform meritorious actions with the hope of reward, and to avoid the doing of evil out of fear of punishment" (*JQR*, 33–34).

Although the Sages took a dim view of human nature, Maimonides says that they nevertheless held out hope that over time the most intelligent among the multitude would become habituated to acting properly and thus would somehow become open to the possibility of serving out of love. Since the doctrine of reward and punishment is permanently necessary for most and temporarily necessary for a few others, the Sages were protective of this doctrine. Maimonides mentions that the other Sages blamed a certain rabbi, Antigonus of Socho, who was known to say, "Be not like servants who minister to their master upon the condition of receiving a reward; but be like servants who minister to their master without the condition of receiving a reward." Although Maimonides says that Antigonus of Socho was a "distinguished and perfect man who understood the fundamental truth of things," the Sages rebuked him for speaking in a manner unsuited to the goal of habituating the multitude to obedience, warning him and anyone else who might want to spread the message of service out of love: "Oh, wise men, be cautious of your words." Rather than the openness of Antigonus, the Sages preferred the following dictum: "Man should ever engage himself in the Torah, even though it be not for the Torah's sake. Action regardless of the Torah's sake will lead on to action regardful of it" (*JQR*, 33–34).

So far, Maimonides has presented us with opinions about the world-to-come, followed by a parable that seems to debunk the very idea of the world-to-come. Notions of reward and punishment are concessions to the narrow-minded practicality of the great run of human beings. However, he has also brought forward passages from the Sages that indicate that these ideas are not simply fairy tales but are meant to be a ladder that at least some might ascend toward a purer form of service to God. What this service consists in seems to already transcend deeds or actions, insofar as the perfect man who acts out of love is characterized above all as one who possesses knowledge. Recall that the parable that introduced the idea of service out of love had to do with study rather than action. Ultimately, the good conferred by study is some form of understanding, which does not necessarily indicate one particular way of life.

However, Maimonides does not wish to detract from the social utility of the ideas of reward, punishment, and the world-to-come, and he does not want to interfere with the educative process by moving too quickly to its conclusion, as Antigonus of Socho did when he stated bluntly that we should obey the Law without hope of reward. Having revealed that the Sages agree with Antigonus' position but did not think it politic to state that position bluntly, Maimonides now discusses the correct mode of interpreting the words of the Sages and of the Scriptures as well.

Once again, Maimonides begins by sketching out common opinions, this time enumerating how the words of the Sages are understood by three types of readers.

First, there are those who understand the Sages literally. This is the majority—they have no training in the sciences and accept all the statements of the Sages, no matter how preposterous, as literally true. They think they are honoring the Sages, but in truth they are degrading them by attributing nonsense to them. The Torah is supposed to be "your wisdom and your understanding in the sight of the nations, which shall hear all these statutes and say, 'Surely this great nation is a wise and understanding people.'" Maimonides quips that it is about this group that the nations will say, "Surely this small nation is a foolish and untutored people" (*JQR*, 34–35). Second are those who, like the majority, understand the Sages literally, but unlike the majority, mock the Sages for their absurd sayings. They think themselves to be Sages and philosophers, but Maimonides says they are more foolish even than the majority who piously accept the absurdities of the Sages. About this group, Maimonides says they will not be in a position to judge the wisdom of the Sages unless they understand "how necessary it is to use the appropriate speech in theology and in like subjects which are common to both the uneducated and the cultured, and to understand also the practical portion of philosophy." This second group might be capable of understanding recondite subjects such as theology. However, they naively fail to see that the Sages have adjusted their manner of speech to the conception of the multitude. If the scoffers understood "the practical portion of philosophy," they would see how necessary it is to promote certain preposterous beliefs about the highest beings that are nonetheless salutary. Thus, the absurd sayings of the Sages do not represent their own beliefs but are rather for the consumption of the multitude, just as Maimonides pointed out in his explanation of the parable of student and teacher (*JQR*, 35–36). The third and final class is the smallest—Maimonides implies that it might only include a single member, just as the class to which the Sun belongs has only a single member. This last group is well versed in physics, i.e., the nature of the possible and impossible. Because they trust that the Sages were men of understanding who knew these things as well, they assume that the Sages spoke in riddles and parables, and that the words of the Sages had an inner and an outer meaning (*JQR*, 36–37).

Having set up these three classes of interpreters, Maimonides now turns to the question of how we ought to read his own writings. He warns off any readers who belong to the first two groups, the pious literalists and scoffing literalists. His own work is for the third group alone—those who are versed in the sciences and who are aware that the words of the Sages convey a true inner teaching and a false yet salutary (or pedagogically necessary) outer meaning. A reader who is in the habit of pondering the words of the Sages to find their inner meaning will profit from Maimonides' book as well.

Although the third group of readers seems to be the most important one, Maimonides nevertheless does not regard the second group as totally lost. They see the insufficiency of literal understandings, and they have some knowledge of the sciences, enough to see that the plain meaning of the Sages' words are impossible for a rational person to accept. Maimonides phrases their deficient understanding as a conditional—they will learn whether or not the Sages are wise when or if they learn practical science and how to interpret speeches of the wise about subjects in which the vulgar have a vested interest. Perhaps the second group is not incorrigible, now that Maimonides has clued them into the Sages' careful manner of expression and the political reasons for their caution.

Having given an indication about his manner of writing, Maimonides returns to his original subject, reward and punishment and the world-to-come. Reward is to be understood purely as spiritual pleasure, which is a natural consequence of cultivation of the intellect. Maimonides argues for this by making the commonsensical point that virtually all human beings have some experience of non-corporeal pleasure—reputation. We seek after honor or revenge, or shun pleasure out of fear of a bad reputation or desire for a good one. On the basis of this common experience, Maimonides argues that the soul, unhindered by the body, can experience spiritual pleasures of a very high order. In effect, Maimonides begins to revise the traditional understanding of the meaning of reward and punishment in the world-to-come on the basis of this narrow point of agreement between the philosophic position and ordinary human belief, i.e., that there are at least some goods experienced chiefly by the soul. Apparently, the argument is that because when we desire revenge we desire it in our soul, all human beings have some inchoate awareness of the bliss that arises from the union of the soul with the intellectual sphere and the comprehension of the highest beings. This intellectual bliss comes to be identified with reward in the world-to-come. Punishment, on the other hand, is redefined naturalistically as the dissipation of the soul when the corporeal matter of the body disappears, and is described as a necessary consequence of failing to attain union with the intellectual sphere (*JQR*, 38–40).

Maimonides admits that this version of spiritual reward and punishment comes from the philosophers, but he claims that it was alluded to in the Torah. For instance, he interprets Deuteronomy 22:7, "In order that it may be well with thee and that thou mayest prolong thy days," as a reference to the union of the soul with the intellectual sphere, and he interprets Numbers 15:31, "That soul shall surely be cut off," as a reference to the dissipation of the soul. Neither of these lines immediately appears to justify what Maimonides hangs on them here. In fact, his attempt to identify the opinion of the philosophers with the traditional opinions seems to only highlight the distance between the philosophers' beliefs and the opinions about reward, punishment, and the world-to-come that Maimonides enumerated at the outset. The new philosophic account of the world-to-come more or less eliminates any connection between the possession of moral virtues or acts of obedience and the fate of the individual after death. The only factor that determines the fate of the soul is whether an individual attained theoretical knowledge in life. In what follows, I will try to evaluate the plausibility of the reconciliation that Maimonides attempts between these two accounts of the soul's fate.

Maimonides starts by revisiting the opinion that came last in his original enumeration, that divine reward and punishment are purely phenomena of this world. The worldly success that comes from obedience to the sacred law has one purpose—to create quietude in order to allow a human being to attain "perfection of knowledge and be worthy of the life of the world-to-come." Failure to obey the law is punished only inasmuch as disobedience leads to poverty and civil strife, which in turn present even greater obstacles to obedience. A disordered society and a disordered individual soul are both obstacles to the development and exercise of the intellectual virtues, or for that matter the success of commerce and industry. Maimonides does not specify whether worldly success supervenes miraculously on obedience or if the law is a source of practical good counsel. In the latter case, law would for the most part contribute to peace within society and within the soul and may help to secure the conditions for the development of the intellectual virtues or worldly success. However, there is no guarantee that possession of the condition results in actualization of those ends. If it is indeed the case that law should be understood as prudent counsel, then in this respect, too, Maimonides has naturalized his account of reward and punishment (*JQR*, 40).

Having explained how it might be possible for earthly reward and punishment for obedience to law to take place without miraculous intervention, Maimonides addresses the more recalcitrant beliefs in the Garden of Eden and Gehinnom. He asserts without offering any proof that Eden is a real place, and that at some point God will permit human beings to rediscover it. This is already a major step toward a naturalistic interpretation—surely there are natural places on earth that are lovely or horrific. While he notes that Eden is clearly mentioned in the Torah, Maimonides does not mention whether Gehinnom appears in the Torah and even admits that the term's precise signification is unclear in the teachings of the Talmud, where the term first enters the Jewish tradition. It is some kind of fiery punishment that sinners endure, but he does not say when or where this might occur. By contrast, Maimonides claims that the belief in the existence of Eden might be possible even without revelation. How come Maimonides downplays Gehinnom? Perhaps he wants to remind the reader that death either allows the soul to be united with the active intellect or to dissolve, but does not allow for some kind of eternal punishment (*JQR*, 41–42).

Hitherto, Maimonides has been trying to provide naturalistic reinterpretations of the common opinions about the afterlife. Of these opinions, the belief in resurrection of the dead presents the most stubborn resistance to such a procedure. This doctrine is a fundamental root of the sacred law. It should be clear at this point that Maimonides has cast serious doubts on the possibility of a bodily resurrection of the dead. Whether the dead are righteous or wicked, learned or ignorant, it's hard to see how his discussion of the world-to-come is compatible with any kind of resurrection. On the one hand, there would be no reason to re-embody those who have achieved union with the intellectual spheres; they might not even persist as individuals in that state. On the other hand, the wicked are said by Maimonides to be dead even when they are alive, and after death they disintegrate and return to the elements. So either way, it's hard to see how Maimonides can hold on to the belief in resurrection (*JQR*, 42).

After discussing the truth about worldly reward and punishment, Eden, and the Resurrection of the Dead, Maimonides describes the Messianic Age at great length. Just as he presented a naturalistic view of the afterlife, he does the same with the Messianic Age, stating that "nothing at all in existence will change in the Messianic Age except that Israel will have a kingdom" (*EWM*, 166). The prosperity of the new era will be concrete; livelihoods will be more easily attained because the Messianic Age will bring political stability that will allow for economic prosperity. The primary benefit of the political restoration of Israel is that freedom from exile means the Jews will no longer be "hindered from acquiring all the virtues."

However, Maimonides is not really interested in the acquisition of "all the virtues," meaning the moral ones as well as the intellectual ones. The principal virtues on Maimonides' mind are the intellectual virtues, for he goes on to emphasize that "knowledge of God will fill the earth." Indeed, the Messianic Age should not be desired because "crops and wealth will increase" or "so that we ride fine steeds and drink wine accompanied by music." Rather, what is desirable is that the virtuous community will come to be: "In the virtuous community, there will be a noble way of life, knowledge, and a just king who will be great in knowledge and close to the Creator" (*EWM*, 167).

Totally absent from this discussion is any mention of the Restoration of the Temple, a fundamental part of the traditional doctrine of the Messiah. Apparently the goodness of the Messianic Age is not connected to the rebuilding of the Temple, although traditionally that restoration is understood to be its chief benefit. Rather, what is important for Maimonides about the Messianic Age is that knowledge of God will flourish to some extent. To prove this, Maimonides quotes a verse from Jeremiah (31:34), "A man shall not teach his neighbor . . . for they shall all know me, from the least of them to the greatest." In the "world-to-come," or Messianic Age, "the equitable man," believing that the prophets have received true knowledge of the virtues and vices from God, will pursue the virtues and shun the vices. Thus, he will attain perfection in respect of the "meaning" or essence of a human being. As a result, his soul will permanently abide with its knowledge. This is the true meaning of "world-to-come" (*EWM*, 167).

To emphasize the intellectual perfection attendant on the Messianic Age while de-emphasizing the potential Restoration of the Temple is tantamount to denying the uniqueness of the Messianic Age as an epoch. It is almost as if Maimonides is attempting to show that the Messianic Age is best understood as one epoch among many, albeit one that has some features that make it more conformable to the quest for wisdom, but not uniquely so. Perhaps, in the final analysis, the Messianic Age might help certain individuals in the quest for the perfection of the soul, but such perfection is at least available in other eras. Nothing in what Maimonides has said has contradicted the belief that the felicity that comes from knowledge of God is in principle always available. The advent of some kind of Messianic Age, a period of universal peace and prosperity, would remove some of the distractions that hinder the pursuit of perfection in other eras. However, even in our time it's possible for one who is fortunately situated and has a suitable nature to acquire knowledge of God. And in fact, as Maimonides presents it, the Messianic Age is no panacea. Even in the Messianic Age the limits on the attainment of knowledge will still exist because there will still be strong and weak, rich and poor. All of the divisions within human life will continue, and these divisions will continue to present obstacles to the attainment of knowledge. If human nature will not change, then some will simply not be suited or able to pursue knowledge. Others might have the capacity but lack the leisure for it.

One might argue that the statement "knowledge of God will fill the earth" implies some kind of large-scale enlightenment. And yet, insofar as there will still be kings and rulership, then political life as we know it will continue, and there will still be a need for the salutary but untrue teachings about reward and punishment. In other words, the Cave, as Socrates described it, will continue to exist even in the Messianic Age—it will persist as long as political life and human diversity continue to exist. Since some, even many, humans will require extended or permanent tutelage, it will still be inadvisable for would-be enlighteners to spread the message that God ought to be served in a disinterested way without hope for reward.

Maimonides alludes to the deficiencies of the Messianic Age through the oblique way in which he indicates that this state of affairs will not be permanent. "The men of knowledge [a term that ambiguously refers to philosophers or rabbis] have said that the virtuous community will not easily fall apart." But even if it will not "easily" fall apart, it will nevertheless fall apart. Although Maimonides does not say why the Messianic Age will eventually decline, we might be able to infer the reason from his statement that the Messiah will die, his son will succeed him, and his grandson in turn will succeed his son. Insofar as the Messianic Age will share a nature with our own, there is no reason to think that an infinite succession of just, wise, and pious kings will come to be (*EWM*, 167).

If the Messianic Age can decline and eventually disintegrate, then we must regard universal enlightenment as incomplete and doomed to be rolled back at some point. The most obvious sign of the defective character of the enlightenment of the Messianic Age is that this era would involve a restoration of the sacrificial rites and the Temple service. Maimonides has made it abundantly clear that these rites have already been improved upon, whether by prayer or by intellectual apprehension of the divine. After the development of more rational means of approaching the divine, it would be a step backwards to return to the Temple service. Now, as I mentioned earlier, Maimonides never mentions this restoration, precisely because if he did we would notice how greatly his vision of the Messianic era differs from the traditional one.

To understand why the restoration of the Temple service is incompatible with an age of enlightenment, we have to look at Maimonides' explanation in the *Guide of the Perplexed* for why the Temple service existed at all. Much of the *Guide* is devoted to demonstrating that the Scriptural references to God's corporeality are exoteric statements adapted to the limited understanding of the multitude of ancient Hebrews. The original recipients of the Scriptures were steeped in a pagan religion Maimonides called "Sabianism." To eliminate this worship, the Mosaic legislation adopted many of the Sabian practices but reconfigured them so they now referred back to the one God. Thus, the Sabians sacrificed animals in their temples to all the stars, and represented the moving spirits of the heavenly bodies as idols. The Mosaic legislation kept the sacrifices but directed them towards God, and performed these rites in a room symbolically empty, the Holy of Holies, to indicate that God has no physical presence (*Guide* 3.29–30).

The Scriptural co-optation of Sabian rituals and materialistic language about God is termed a "gracious ruse" in the *Guide*, a concession to the natural limits of human understanding. To illustrate the impossibility of ending idolatry by fiat, Maimonides invites the reader to consider a highly provocative simile:

> One could not then conceive the acceptance of [such a Law], considering the nature of man, which always likes that to which it is accustomed. At that time, this would have been similar to the appearance of a prophet in these times who, calling upon the people to worship God, would say "God has given you a Law forbidding you to pray to Him, to fast, to call upon Him for help in any misfortune. Your worship should consist solely in contemplation without any works at all." (3.32, 526)

Just as the sacrificial cult was a concession to the understanding of our forefathers, prayer and the belief in a particular providence are a concession to us. In that case, could we envision that a further development is possible, away from prayer and towards "contemplation" without any rituals or ceremonies, perhaps even without charitable actions? That would map on to the Messianic Age, when knowledge of God will fill the earth, and even the uneducated multitude would have some access to the truth about divine things. Perhaps Maimonides' works would fulfill a decisive role in this evolution. Just as the destruction of the Temple and the exile of the Jews were a kind of providential disaster that allowed the Jews to be weaned off the last Sabian relics, so too the exile allowed the Jews to encounter Greek modes of thought. Maimonides' works would then be the culmination of that encounter.

The description of the Messianic Age as found in the *Introduction to Pereq Heleq* would be in tune with this possibility. However, if the Messianic Age is like our own age, insofar as all human beings will come to grasp the truth about the divine to the best of their ability, then there is every reason to expect that the human beings of that age would share our need for Temple sacrifices or prayers. At the most, peace and prosperity might reduce the dangers that accompany human life and thus reduce the amount of uncertainty and fear that the sacrificial rites are supposed to remedy. If there were less strife and poverty in the world, there would consequently be few reasons to sin, hence less guilty regret or fear about the consequences of sin. Likewise, there would be less to hope for, hence fewer sacrifices intended to acquire divine grace. But the difference between rich and poor, mighty and weak would persist, and thus efforts to overcome the personal injustice of this state of affairs would continue, as would fears that one's own unfortunate state of affairs is a result of some kind of sin, perhaps an unintentional sin. The perennial existence of human difference and good and bad fortune would provide the centrifugal forces to allow idolatry to manifest again and the end of the Messianic era to eventually occur.

IV.

Moderns: Nature,
Self-Knowledge, and God

14

Physics and "Normal Life" in Descartes' First Meditation

Peter Vedder

The First Meditation initiates Descartes' attempt to establish certain and indubitable foundations of the sciences. This attempt requires him to demonstrate the dubitable character of the foundations of traditional science. Descartes' foundational argument has therefore both a negative or destructive and a positive or constructive aspect. The skeptical challenges to the traditional foundations disclose what must be the character of the foundations being sought. The "reasons to doubt" the traditional foundations appear however to be traditional, for they seem to be taken from standard positions of premodern skepticism.[1] Indeed, the very search for foundations, first principles, or first causes of human knowing seems to be a traditional inquiry. Descartes' argument does not however culminate in the recognition of first

---

1. This appearance led Hobbes to wonder why Descartes wished to publish this "ancient material" (Third Set of Objections, AT VII.171, CSMK II.121). I have used the standard Cottingham translation of the *Meditations* in *The Philosophical Writings of Descartes*, trans. and ed. John Cottingham, Robert Stoothoff, Dugald Murdoch, and Anthony Kenny, 3 vols. (New York: Cambridge University Press, 1984–91). In citations from this text, the Meditation and paragraph number are given first, followed by the volume and page number of *Oeuvres de Descartes*, ed. Ch. Adam and P. Tannery, rev. ed., 11 vols. (Paris: Vrin/C.N.R.S., 1964–76), followed by the volume and page number of *Philosophical Writings of Descartes*. In the body of the paper, the numbers in parentheses correspond to the page and line numbers of the seventh volume of the Adam and Tannery revised edition of the works of Descartes.

causes or principles of either being or nature, but in certain knowledge of the existence and "nature" of the human mind. His argument for mind or consciousness comes to light however only with the recognition of the "well-considered" and "valid" reasons to doubt that are contained in the apparently traditional skeptical challenges to the foundations of the traditional sciences. These valid reasons to doubt are based on his novel science of nature. The way to the foundations and the foundations sought are both modern.

Descartes' foundational argument is an argument for mind or consciousness. Descartes' theory of the human mind is established in explicit opposition to the soul doctrine of the tradition.[2] According to the dominant premodern understanding, the human soul has two primary functions, as both the principle or cause of the life and motions and of the perceptions and thinking of human beings.[3] For Descartes, the human soul is exclusively a mind or "thinking thing." The understanding of the human soul as mind proves to be just that understanding of the human soul that is compatible with the new physics.[4] The human soul regarded as consciousness, however, cannot feel sensations, have desires, or experience passion without becoming a cause or principle of the motions of human beings. Descartes is therefore compelled to broaden his conception of mind to accommodate the mind of real human beings. This comprehensive sense of mind proves to be the foundation of another novel science, namely, the science of the nature of man as a "combination of mind and body."[5] The composite nature of the human mind is the ground of its capacity to feel sensations that, in turn, direct human beings toward what is advantageous and away from what is disadvantageous to their

---

2. II.5–6, AT VII.25–27, CSMK II.17–18.

3. Arist., *De An.* 413a22–25; Plato, *Ph.* 83a1–c3, 105c9–d4. The argument of the *Phaedo* seems to show that the two functions are inseparable albeit in tension with one another. See Ronna Burger, *The "Phaedo": A Platonic Labyrinth* (New Haven, CT: Yale University Press, 1984), 96–100, 171–74.

4. "The peculiar feat of *Meditations* 1–2 is to gain indubitable access to the soul as exclusively a mind independently of responsibility for motion, and thus to avoid all jeopardy to the integrity of the object of physics." Richard Kennington, "The 'Teaching of Nature' in Descartes' Soul Doctrine," in *On Modern Origins: Essays in Early Modern Philosophy*, ed. Pamela Kraus and Frank Hunt (New York: Lexington Books, 2004), 161–86; see 178.

5. VI.23, AT VII.88, CSMK II.61.

health and preservation.[6] The challenge of the *Meditations* is to discover the authentic argument that unites the precise sense of mind as consciousness with the comprehensive sense of mind as the cause of man's pursuit of the beneficial and his avoidance of the harmful.

The problem of the foundations of the sciences is introduced by Descartes' recollection that he had noticed, already "some years ago," the many false things he had "accepted" as true in his youth and the "doubtful nature" of the "edifice" he had afterwards built on them. He implies that the foundations of the traditional sciences are identical to the false beliefs he accepted as true in his youth and that the dubitable things he had built on them correspond to the sciences proper. Based on this identity and correspondence he proposes to demolish the traditional sciences and their false foundations on the way to establishing something "stable" in the sciences. His procedure seems to assume that the sciences must be based on certain foundations if they are to be made free of the dubious. Since the false foundations of the traditional sciences are the senses and the primary science at issue is physics, he implies that the traditional physics is based on the false beliefs about the world acquired by means of "childhood" experiences.[7]

Descartes draws a far-reaching conclusion from his observation concerning the many false things he had accepted as true in his youth. He says that it is necessary, once in life, to demolish all things and to begin again from the first foundations (17, 4–6). The proper response to the defective character of the mind's cognitive powers is not to correct them by means of the traditional sciences but to reject these sciences in their entirety and to begin again from the very first foundations of the sciences. Descartes' discovery that the many false things he had accepted as true in his youth were false, however, can only have been accomplished by means of the new physics. It is the new physics that supplies the "powerful and well-thought-out reasons" to doubt the traditional sciences.[8] To begin again from the first foundations means to elaborate the theoretical justification of the new physics.

---

6. VI.22, AT VII.57, CSMK II.60.

7. Physics leads the list of the sciences of "composite things" (I.8, AT VII.20, CSMK II.14).

8. I.10, AT VII.22, CSMK II.15. Consider the claim that the simple universals of physics are the material out of which the mind forms "all the images of things, whether true or false, that occur" in human thought (I.6, AT VII.20, CSMK II.14).

The announced goal of the argument from doubt is to find "just one thing, however slight, that is certain and unshakeable."[9] Descartes is compelled by the argument from doubt to recognize that it is impossible for one who is doubting to doubt that he is or exists. He concludes that the "proposition, *I am, I exist*, is necessarily true."[10] The Second Meditation proceeds to demonstrate that the "I" that is known with indubitable certainty to exist is a "thinking thing" or mind.[11] The argument from doubt establishes the existence of the human mind. In the context of the doubt of all things the human mind comes to light as a consciousness or power of awareness. Sensory perception in the "precise sense" is for example nothing other than the mind's awareness of its perceptions.[12] The understanding of the human mind as consciousness is however simultaneously a repudiation of the Aristotelian cognitive soul doctrine, according to which the human soul is "in a certain way all beings" and the human intellect is the "place of forms" or natures of the beings.[13] The determination of the "nature" of mind prior to the demonstration of the existence of body implies that the Cartesian mind or consciousness is not epistemically bonded or even cognitively related to any being that exists outside of the human mind.[14]

Descartes seeks to establish "certain and unshakeable" foundations of the sciences to leave to posterity something "firm and lasting in the sciences." He suggests that his contributions to the science of the "laws of nature" will be superseded by future advances in physics, but his placing of this physics on the foundation of his novel doctrine of mind will never be overturned or abandoned. He implies that the new physics and doctrine of the human mind stand or fall together. What they share is the denial that the beings are constituted by "forms" or natures and that first causes

---

9. II.1, AT VII.24, CSMK II.16.

10. II.3, AT VII.25, CSMK II.17.

11. II.6, AT VII.27, CSMK II.18.

12. II.9, AT VII.29, CSMK II.19.

13. Arist., *De An.* 431b20, 429a27.

14. II.7, AT VII.28, CSMK II.19: "I know for certain both that I exist and at the same time that...everything relating to the nature of body could be mere dreams." See Jacob Klein, *Greek Mathematical Thought and the Origin of Algebra*, trans. Eva Brann (New York: Dover, 1968), 298.

or principles of nature exist.[15] The material simple universals or concepts of physics are not forms or "essences" of the beings nor deductions from first principles or causes of nature, and the principles or foundations of human knowing are identified by Descartes with the mind's cognitive powers or faculties.[16]

Descartes turns from his account of what he is pursuing in the *Meditations* to an account of the nature of his own mind. He says that the task he had proposed for himself appeared to him to be an enormous one and that its enormity led him to put it off until he had arrived at that age in which none more "suitable" for such "inquiries" would follow (17, 8–10). Descartes wished to be at the peak of his cognitive powers when he set out to demolish his opinions. The doubt of all things takes place within the context of a past known to be constituted by falsehood and of a future characterized by cognitive decline.

The action of the *Meditations* must be understood to be taking place in the present. This present, however, is not a moment or an instant of time but an indeterminate span of duration that is saturated with memorials of the past and anticipations of the future.[17] Descartes says that he is running out of time. He runs the risk of incurring "blame" by deliberating about the demolition project and thereby wasting the time still needed to carry it out (17, 10–13). The finite and temporal nature of the human mind compels it to become aware of and to take an interest in its own interests. The mind that Descartes comes to know with indubitable certainty to exist, however, does not have any interests, cares, or concerns. It is ignorant of having a beginning or a possible end and exists exclusively in a present devoid of both a past and a future.[18] Descartes' argumentative strategy

---

15. Both claims are objects of the method of doubt. The forms or natures of the beings are doubted in I.6, and the existence of first causes or principles of nature are doubted in I.10.

16. A thing that thinks is a thing that "doubts, understands, affirms, denies, is willing, is unwilling, and also imagines and has sensory perceptions" (II.8, AT VII.28, CSMK II.19).

17. In the Third Meditation, Descartes defines time as constituted by an infinite number of moments, "each completely independent" of one another. This definition of time effectively denies the reality of human temporality. III.31, AT VII.49, CSMK II.33.

18. In the second proof of God's existence, Descartes investigates the cause or causes of the existence of the mind. He says that it is impossible to escape the force of the argu-

permits him to say that his mind and the mind he discovers necessarily exists are one and the same mind because both are demonstrated to be thinking things. It is however impossible for these two minds to be one and the same, for the non-temporal character of consciousness deprives it of any concern for its well-being or even any interest in its existence.

Descartes says that his mind must be free of cares, at leisure, and in solitude if he is to bring about the general demolition of the existing sciences and to free his mind of all opinions. The project therefore requires that he conform his mind as closely as possible to the nature of consciousness (17, 13–18, 3). Descartes cannot be the master of his thoughts if they are being determined by "unknown and foreign" causes.[19] The requirements necessary to pursue the doubt raise the question whether there are some things that cannot be sincerely doubted. Is it the case, for example, that Descartes really doubts the existence of the world? Has he succeeded in assimilating his mind to the pure mind of consciousness? Descartes' account demonstrates that his resolution to render his mind opinion-free cannot be fully achieved because, despite his efforts to the contrary, his "habitual opinions" constantly return and capture his belief (22, 4–5). His opinions are doubted in one sense, but in another they remain unaffected by the doubt. Descartes finally concedes that the doubt of the existence of the world is an "exaggerated" doubt, i.e., not something that is sincerely doubted.[20] Doubt of the existence of the world appears to be necessary, however, to achieve the clear and distinct or precise understanding of the human mind.

Descartes brings a method to the project of rejecting his opinions. The method consists of three rules that are deductions of reason drawn from the goal of the doubt. The first rule demands that a "reason to doubt" be supplied for every opinion that is doubted. Descartes seems to say that "any reason for doubting" is sufficient to reject an opinion. The reason for doubting, apparently, does not have to be a strong or an assent-com-

---

ments that prove that the mind cannot be the cause of itself by supposing that it has "always existed" as it does "now, as if it followed from this that there was no need to look for any author" of its existence. III.31, AT VII.48–49, CSMK II.33.

19. II.10, AT VII.29, CSMK II.20.

20. The doubt of the existence of body "should be dismissed as laughable" (VI.24, AT VII.89, CSMK II.61).

pelling reason; it may even be extravagant or unreasonable. The claim that the method sanctions an unreasonable reason to doubt is however incompatible with the goal of the doubt. The rejection and possible removal of an opinion from the mind requires that the opinion be "sincerely" doubted. The reason to doubt an opinion that is sincerely doubted must be "powerful and well-thought-out" and not based on "flippant or ill-considered" conclusions (21, 27–30).

The second rule of the doubt defines what is subject to doubt. Descartes says that "reason already persuades" him that "assent is to be withheld" from opinions that are "not completely certain and indubitable" just as carefully as the mind now withholds its assent from those that are "patently false" (18, 6–9). The rule demands that the mind not assent to any opinion not known to be necessarily true. Every belief or proposition whose denial does not imply a contradiction or has the character of being a contingent proposition is an "opinion" and is therefore something that is subject to doubt.

Descartes defines doubt as assent-withholding. To withhold one's assent means not to make a judgment about the truth or falsity of a belief or proposition. An opinion, therefore, is something one holds to be true or false without knowing it to be either necessarily true or necessarily false. Since a certain and indubitable proposition is one known to be necessarily true, all truths of reason and all a priori propositions of "pure mathematics" are certain and indubitable propositions. The search for at least one thing that is "certain and unshakeable" appears, from the standpoint of pure mathematics, to be a fool's errand. It therefore seems necessary to understand the "doubt of all things" quite literally, for the method of doubt excludes the principles of reason from doubt. The doubt of the epistemic legitimacy of the principle of non-contradiction, for example, is clearly incompatible with the "nature of doubt."[21] The doubt must be the search for at least one thing that is known with indubitable certainty to exist.

The third and final rule of the doubt guarantees that the demolition project is a finite task. It is not possible but also not necessary to doubt all of the mind's opinions individually. To successfully doubt all of the mind's opinions it is only necessary to doubt the "foundations" or "principles"

---

21. *Regulae*, Rule 12, AT X.421, CSMK I.46.

on which they rest. Descartes does not explain here what he means by foundations or principles. His claim that it is necessary "once in life" to demolish all things, however, recalls his use of this phrase in the *Regulae* to introduce the inquiry that must precede all other inquiries whatsoever. It is necessary, says Descartes, to investigate the powers and the proper objects of the mind prior to any inquiry into any other thing.[22] The purpose of the investigation is to establish the limits of the mind's cognitive powers and what it is that the mind can know of the natures of things. This inquiry shows that the human mind possesses three primary powers of knowing, namely, sensory-perception, imagination, and intellection. The method of doubt, in the First Meditation, is also structured by these three powers of knowing. The senses are doubted first, then the imagination by means of the doubt based on dreaming, and, finally, the intellect by means of the omnipotent deceiver doubt. In all of these instances it is necessary to uncover the well-considered and valid reasons for doubting the foundations or principles of the mind's opinions.

At the beginning of Descartes' examination, he identifies the foundation of all of his prior opinions with the senses. What the senses disclose to the mind is "most true," apparently, because the senses and only the senses make evident to the mind what is real and exists. He makes a distinction, however, between what is known "from the senses" and what is known "through the senses" (18, 15–16). Descartes explains, in the Burman manuscript, that this distinction expresses the difference between sight and hearing.[23] The existence of the stars can be known from sight but the existence of the biblical God can be known only through Revelation or through the reports of others. The distinction also seems to point to the ambiguous being of the sensible object in Descartes' account of sensory perception. The sensible object exists either in the sense organs or in the mind.[24] If the sense organs are instruments of the mind and the sensible object is a perception, then what is most true becomes evident to the mind only "through the senses."

---

22. Descartes says that "we ought once in our life carefully to inquire as to what sort of knowledge human reason is capable of attaining, before we set about acquiring knowledge of things in particular" (*Regulae*, Rule 8, AT X.396–97, CSMK I.30).

23. AT V.146, CSMK III.332.

24. *Optics*, Discourse V, AT VI.128, CSMK I.167.

Sensory deception is the first reason advanced to cast doubt on what is putatively known by means of the senses. The senses deceive the mind from time to time, and are therefore not trustworthy sources or principles of the mind's opinions. The senses present external objects to the mind in a manner that is not true of these objects. Large objects seen from a distance appear smaller than they are, and square towers seen from a distance appear round.[25]

Descartes rejects the testimony of the senses as a dictate of prudence. Since it is a matter of prudence "never to trust completely those who have deceived" one even once, and because the senses deceive the mind, it is prudent never to completely trust the testimony of the senses (18, 16–18). Prudence dictates that one only partially trust what the senses seem to teach about the world: it directs the mind to accept what the senses report about what exists outside of the mind, but to reject what they seem to teach about the natures of these things.

The next moment of the argument attempts to answer the objection raised against the senses by the initial reason to doubt. It concedes that the senses sometimes deceive the mind about "very small and distant things" but it denies that they are deceptive about the things of everyday human concern. The minute things may be too small to be visible and the distant things, even if they are quite large, may be too far away to be clearly seen. The answer takes advantage of recent discoveries in biology and astronomy made possible by the microscope and the telescope. Descartes, however, points to his own present situation of sitting by a fire, clothed in a winter robe, and holding a piece of paper as things known by means of the senses. In this context, the senses are reliable reporters of the existence and nature of these things. All of his senses agree that it is a fire that is burning before him. Knowledge of the things of everyday concernment and care has its basis in the senses. To cast doubt on this apparent knowledge Descartes does not stop to ask whether the fire exists as it seems to the senses but whether it exists at all. Doubt about whether the senses disclose the things of concern as they exist in truth is approached by way of doubt of the very existence of these things. Doubt of the existence of one's hands and body, however, seems to be impossible. Descartes asks, "How

---

25. VI.6, AT VII.76, CSMK II.53.

could it be denied that these hands or this whole body are mine?" (18, 24–26). The human body is not like any other body existing outside of the human mind. The mind is justified in regarding this body as its own.[26] The mind is not merely present in its body as a sailor is present in a ship, rather it is "very closely joined and, as it were, intermingled with it," such that the mind and the body "form a unit."[27] The unity of the mind-body composite nature of man is made evident to the mind by means of pain, hunger, thirst, and other similar sensations. Since the precise sense of mind or consciousness does not know whether it is corporeal or incorporeal it must lack the ideas of these sensations and the ideas of the mind's physical propensities toward "cheerfulness, sadness, anger, and similar emotions."[28]

Descartes seems nevertheless to have found a reason to doubt the existence of the human body. He says that if he were to compare himself with certain insane people whose brains are "damaged by the persistent vapors of melancholia" and found that he also was no less demented than they are, then his claim to have a body could be as groundless as the extravagant claims the insane make about themselves (18, 26 – 19, 5). The reason to doubt based on the supposition of insanity is problematic, however, because the doubt of the existence of the human body is based on the possibility that the doubter has a diseased brain. The doubt affirms the dependence of the existence of the human mind on the existence of the human brain. The mind proves to be dependent on the brain not only for its existence and well-being but also for its activity of thinking. Human physiology establishes that for every object present to the mind there exists a corre-

---

26 . VI.6, AT VII.76, CSMK II.52: "As for the body which by some special right I call 'mine,' my belief that this body, more than any other, belonged to me had some justification."

27. VI.13, AT VII.81, CSMK II.56.

28. VI.6, AT VII.74, CSMK II.52. Descartes explains in the Second Meditation that he can affirm of the mind only those things that are "known" to him. In this context, he can neither affirm nor deny that the mind is corporeal. He concedes that it is possible that the very things that he is "supposing" to be nothing, because they are unknown to him, are in reality "identical" with the mind of which he is aware. II.7, AT VII.27, CSMK II.18. If the mind of which he is aware felt sensations and experienced delight and distress, then it would already know that it was corporeal.

sponding motion in the brain.[29] This reason to doubt is therefore equivalent to the possibility that the brain motions corresponding to the mind's awareness of its hands and its whole body are activated not by the hands and the body as a whole but by a damaged part of the brain. Descartes' mind could be receiving from the brain all of the "signals" that persuade him that he is sitting by a fire, wearing a winter robe, and holding a piece of paper, when in fact his brain is being maintained and stimulated by unknown powers. The senses are therefore not immediately responsible for what the mind perceives of the world, for what they apprehend is known by the mind only by means of the brain. Certain operations of the brain translate the various motions that have their origin in the sense organs into the sensory perceptions that make up the elements of human experience.

The doubt based on insanity cannot however be a reason to doubt for Descartes, for he would seem no less demented than the mad if he were to take something from them as a model for himself (19, 5–7). The insane make claims either about their minds or about their nature as a whole that appear to be self-evidently false. These insane persons are evidently concerned with knowing the nature of the human mind and with achieving self-knowledge. They appear however to be mad because their claims about their minds and about their natures as a whole are not grounded in a prior investigation into the nature and cognitive faculties of the human mind.

Descartes appears to have contempt for his seemingly easy victory over the doubt based on madness. It is however not necessary to appeal to such an extravagant supposition to doubt the existence of the human body. Descartes finds a basis for this doubt in the everyday human experience of dreaming. If it is not possible to distinguish being awake from dreaming, then the doubter may be merely dreaming that he has hands and a whole body. This reason to doubt is however also problematic because the acknowledgment of the reality of dreams presupposes knowledge of the difference between dreaming and being awake. The reality of dreams is founded on Descartes' knowledge that he undergoes passively in dreams "all the same experiences while asleep as madmen do when awake—indeed sometimes even more improbable ones" (19, 8–11). Sometimes Descartes' thinking is even more deranged than the thinking of the insane and at these

---

29. VI.20, AT VII.86, CSMK II.59–60.

times he knows that he is dreaming and is not awake. Further, Descartes points to the passivity of dreams. When he is dreaming he is not the master of his thoughts. The model for the mastery of thought is the method of doubt. To be awake means to doubt an opinion or a conclusion of one's thinking. Being awake can therefore never be completely separated from being asleep because to dream is to opine and the mind's opinions are the subject matter of its thinking. The dream doubt therefore questions whether it is possible to know that an opinion has been sincerely doubted.

To establish that there is no known criterion to distinguish being awake from dreaming, it is necessary to make everyday experience and dreams sufficiently alike that their supposed differences are indiscernible. Descartes remembers being persuaded that he was seated next to a fire, wearing a winter robe, and holding a piece of paper when, in fact, he was "lying undressed in bed" (19, 11–13). What appears to be common to dreams and everyday experience is the passive acceptance of the mind's images of things and the absence of questions or doubts. Everyday experience is dream-like in that it persuasively deceives the mind about the natures of external things and that it is awake and not dreaming.

Descartes attempts to answer the dream doubt by testing its putative truth. The test introduces intention and deliberation into his acts of sensing. He attempts to make his perceptions more distinct by observing himself deliberately extending his hands and sensing. His perceptions are now more distinct because he has consciously willed himself to sense and to observe his sensing (19, 13–16). What is missing from the test, however, are any considerations that bear on his well-being or interests. Disinterested sensory perception cannot provide the required criterion and the test fails. Since the test can be performed in a dream, Descartes concludes that he plainly sees that "there are never any sure signs by means of which being awake can be distinguished from being asleep" (19, 19–21). It proves to be possible to know or plainly see even in a dream. The dream doubt cancels itself. Sensory perception proves incapable of establishing the difference between being awake and dreaming, however, only because Descartes abstracts from the mind's awareness of the sensations that cause delight and "distress of mind."[30]

---

30. VI.6, AT VII.76, CSMK II.52.

The dream doubt supposes not only that experience and dreams are experientially similar but also that the epistemic character of experience is indistinguishable from that of dreams. The faculty of the mind responsible for this understanding of the world is, however, not the senses but the imagination. The senses are not doubted because they are untrustworthy, rather they are doubted because what they contribute to human knowing presupposes the work of the human imagination. The dream doubt corrects the doubt based on insanity by replacing the brain with the imagination as the source of the mind's ideas of corporeal things. The second part of the dream doubt explores how the human imagination uses material supplied by the senses to form the mind's images of external things.

The second part of the dream doubt begins by granting the apparent conclusion of its first part by conceding that the doubter may be dreaming. The argument cannot however be literally about dreaming because Descartes now compares the human imagination to painters. He says that "it must surely be admitted that the visions which come in sleep are like paintings, which must have been fashioned in the likeness of things that are real" (19, 26–28). The things seen in dreams are not true things. The senses are dormant while the perceiver is asleep. What is seen in a dream are things similar to "paintings" that are formed in resemblance to true things. It appears that the imagination makes use of memory in its fabrication of the mind's dream images. What the imagination produces in the dream state is similar to what it produces in the waking state. Everyday experience is constituted by the mind's cognition of beings formed by and in the human imagination.

Descartes, however, says that the true things represented by the imagination by means of its images are not external things but certain other things that are more general than the external things. Descartes calls these more general things "kinds" or "natures" (19, 29–31). The argument therefore affirms the existence of external things because these things embody certain kinds or natures that make them both the beings that they are and capable of being known by the human mind. It denies, however, that the mind's images faithfully represent or resemble these things as they exist in truth.

Descartes uses the example of painters representing mythological creatures to clarify the present claim about the nature of the imagination's representations of things. The mythological creatures correspond to the things presumed to exist in the world. These things may be imaginary, but the painter is not at liberty to fashion them in whatever manner he wishes. He is compelled to make use of and to incorporate into his representations of these creatures the kinds or natures of different animals. What is real and exists, therefore, are the kinds or natures of things and not the things that may embody these natures.

The claim that the world may not exist because the mind's sole access to it is by means of images formed by and in the imagination without any assistance from anything existing outside of the mind is rejected because of the necessity to acknowledge the existence of certain things more general than external things. Originally, it appeared that the material supplied by the senses, namely, the sensible qualities of things, were understood to be imaginary while the more general kinds or natures of things were identified with the real. In the next moment of the argument, however, Descartes likens the imagination to certain painters that represent things that are "completely fictitious and unreal" (19, 31 – 20, 6). The kinds or natures of external things are now no longer identified with the real because the things that embody these kinds or natures are no longer being supposed to exist. But since the painters do not create the colors used to make their representations Descartes identifies the real with certain things that are even more general than the kinds or natures. The general kinds or natures, says Descartes, could be imaginary; nevertheless, it "must be admitted that certain other even simpler and more universal things are real. These are, as it were, the real colors from which we form all the images of things, whether true or false," that occur in human thought (20, 12–14).

The motion of the argument is from the particular and complex to the universal and simple. The complex particular things are being supposed to be unreal and imaginary while the simple universals are being identified with what is "real and exists." The world of everyday experience is constituted by means of the imagination's use of certain simple universals that are the material out of which it forms all the images of things that exist in human thought. The supposition of the existence of kinds or natures acknowledges the existence of irreducible difference but the supposition of the existence of simple universals affirms the existence of homogenized sameness. The apparent differences in things are now to be explained solely in terms of what is common to all things.

Descartes replaces the colors of the painters with the "real colors" used by the imagination to form the images of things. The real colors are however invisible and lack all other sensible qualities. They appear to be certain motions in the brain that are the material out of which the imagination forms the images of things perceived by the mind. There is reason therefore to suppose that what initiates the brain motions lacks any resemblance to the images formed by the imagination. What is real does not resemble the mind's spontaneous interpretation of the real. If this is so, what is the meaning of the claim that some of the mind's images of things are true? Is it the case that all of the mind's images that are not conscious constructions are true? Do particular things really exist outside of the mind that are nevertheless speciously represented by the human imagination?

The first simple universal mentioned by Descartes is "corporeal nature in general, and its extension" (20, 15–16). Corporeal nature is general because nothing exists that does not share in this nature. Descartes does not say what corporeal nature is; instead, he says that corporeal nature must possess, as one of its real properties, extension. It is impossible for corporeal nature not to occupy space or to be spread out in three dimensions. Descartes is therefore careful not to identify corporeal nature and extension. Extension is not the "essence" of corporeal nature.[31] The nature of corporeal nature is apparently unknown, but Descartes suggests that it can become partially known insofar as it is understood in terms of the intelligible concepts or simple universals of physics, beginning with extension.

Descartes claims that what is real is simple, but how is it known that extension is a real property of corporeal nature? The argument suggests that this is known only by means of experience. The intelligible understanding of things is inseparable from the imaginative understanding of

---

31. In the *Principles of Philosophy*, however, Descartes identifies extension with the nature or "essence" of body. *Principles* I.53, AT VIIIA.25, CSMK I.210; I.63, AT VIIIA.30–31, CSMK I.215; II.4, AT VIIIA.42, CSMK I.224. The nature or essence of something refers either to the cause responsible for something being the being it is or it refers to that which cannot be denied of something without contradiction.

things. Descartes insists that bodies have real properties that cannot be accounted for by means of the material simple universals or by any combination of them. Bodies, for example, possess, among other properties, the real properties of impenetrability and an inherent "striving" to remain in the "same state," whether this state be one of motion or of rest.[32] All of the other material simple universals or concepts do however follow from the reality of the extension and motion of bodies.[33]

Descartes distinguishes composite things and simple universals. He gives two examples of simples, namely, number and figure. Number and figure along with extension and magnitude were originally identified with the "real colors" of physics. The composite things are the things represented by the mind's images. If corporeal nature in general is that alone which exists, then all of the mind's images of things are "materially false" and the subject matter of physics, astronomy, and medicine is completely fictitious and unreal.[34] The distinction between the composite and the simple sciences corresponds therefore to the distinction between the empirical and the a priori sciences. The pure a priori sciences are certain and indubitable because their objects are existence-neutral. Descartes' claim about the doubtful character of physics, astronomy, and medicine pertains however only to the doubtful nature of the existence of body because he has just identified the subject matter of physics with the subject matter of geometry and "pure mathematics."[35]

The composite sciences are said to be dubitable not because the principles of these sciences are dubitable but because the existence of their respective objects are dubitable. Descartes does not however introduce a new reason to doubt the existence of the objects of the composite sciences.

---

32. Sixth Set of Replies, AT VII.442, CSMK II.298; *To More, 15 April 1649*, AT V.341–42, CSMK III.372; *Principles* II.37, AT VIIIA.62, CSMK I.240–41; *Principles* II.43, AT VIIIA.66–67, CSMK I.243–44.

33. *Principles* I.57, AT VIIIA.26–27, CSMK I.212; *Principles* II.14, AT VIIIA.47–48, CSMK I.229.

34. Material falsity occurs in ideas, says Descartes, when ideas "represent non-things as things" (III.19, AT VII.44, CSMK II.30).

35. V.16, AT VII.71, CSMK II.49. Descartes announces in the *Principles* that the "only principles" he accepts or requires in physics "are those of geometry and pure mathematics" (*Principles* II.64, AT VIIIA.78, CSMK I.247).

He seems to rely on the supposition that the imagination constitutes these objects out of material supplied by the simple universals as things really separate from the universal plenum. Now, however, Descartes extends the doubt to the principles of the composite sciences by means of his recollection of a "long-standing opinion" rooted in his mind of "an omnipotent God who made" him the "kind of creature" that he is (21, 1–3).

The omnipotent deceiver doubt has two parts. The existence of the world is doubted first, followed by doubt of the principles of reason and the axioms of the simple sciences. These two parts of the doubt are in tension with one another. The reason to doubt the existence of the world in the final moment of the dream doubt is founded on the claimed reality of the simple universals of physics. The world as it is known from the standpoint of physics does not resemble the world as it is cognized from the standpoint of experience. The doubt based on divine omnipotence supposes the absurdity that beings that do not exist do not resemble the mind's images of these beings. What is not doubted by means of the omnipotent deceiver doubt, however, is the existence of the mind of the doubter and time. God has annihilated the world "while at the same time ensuring that all these things appear" to the mind of the doubter "just as they do now" (21, 3–7). The doubter believes that the world exists, but he has an old opinion "firmly rooted" in his mind that persuades him that this may not be the case.

Descartes introduces the "incomprehensible" power of God as a reason to doubt the principles of reason. God may have made it the case that he is deceived whenever he adds two and three or counts the sides of a square. Descartes knows that it is possible for human beings to make mistakes because he remembers having judged that sometimes "others go astray in cases where they think they have the most perfect knowledge" (21, 7–9). Descartes believes he knows perfectly the sum of two and three. The people who err about what they think they know perfectly are not always in error, but Descartes may be always deceived about what he knows. God, "who can do all things," must therefore have the power to "bring it about that two and three added together are more or less than five."[36] God can create and make true what contains a "manifest contra-

---

36. III.4, AT VII.36, CSMK II.25.

diction." Omnipotence unlimited by the principle of contradiction is however identical to the principle of Descartes' own theology of creation. This theology teaches that God, in addition to being the Creator of everything that exists that is other than God, is also the Creator of the principles of truth and goodness. There is nothing, therefore, that does not depend on the divine will. "This applies not just to everything that subsists, but to all order, every law, and every reason for anything's being true or good."[37]

Since everything, in order to be, depends on the divine will, Descartes teaches that God is the Creator of the eternal truths.[38] The consequence of this theology is that the entirety of the a priori propositions of pure mathematics ceases to be necessarily true.[39] The truth of these propositions proves to be contingent on the indifferent will of God. The indifferent will of God is evident in His unconditioned freedom either to create or not to create the world.[40] Nothing outside of or prior to the divine will determines God to choose one alternative rather than the other. If this is so, however, then creation is an act of will in name alone, for there is nothing to choose.[41] The free acts of God appear, from the standpoint of the radical voluntarism of Descartes' theology of creation, to be nothing but the work of natural necessity because these acts are not acts of mind. Indeed, the claim that God, as the Creator of the world, can make "real and exist" what embodies a contradiction is a disguised way of denying that the cause of the whole of nature is mind. The omnipotent deceiver doubt is the doubt based on materialism in theological disguise.

The omnipotent deceiver doubt is in tension with Descartes' teaching concerning judgment and intellection. Descartes does not judge that, in his own case, he is ever in error. He recognizes that the human mind is

---

37. Sixth Set of Replies, AT VII.435, CSMK II.293–94.

38. *To Mersenne, 15 April 1630*, AT I.145–46, CSMK III.23; *To Mersenne, 27 May 1630*, AT I.151–52, CSMK III.25.

39. See Kennington, "Cartesian Rationalism and Eternal Truths," in *On Modern Origins*, 153–60; see 154.

40. According to the authors of the Sixth Set of Objections, "It is an article of faith that God was from eternity indifferent as to whether he should create one world, or innumerable worlds, or none at all" (AT VII.417, CSMK II.281).

41. Leibniz, *Theodicy*, par. 186.

compelled to affirm as true what it clearly perceives to be necessarily true.[42] The claim that God is the Creator of the eternal truths or the truths of pure mathematics is inconsistent with Descartes' teaching that the objects of pure mathematics have determinate natures that are "immutable and eternal"[43] and that these objects do not belong to a third ontological category between perceptible and intelligible being.[44] The objects of pure mathematics exist exclusively in the human mind and remain in their being existence-neutral.

Descartes attempts to answer the omnipotent deceiver doubt by means of another opinion about God. This opinion states that God is good. The divine goodness is apparently evident in His act of creation. God is good because God is the Creator of the world and all of God's creation is good.[45] Descartes appears to show that God's freedom of indifference is compatible with His independence and omnipotence but incompatible with His goodness. Descartes' theology of creation teaches that the divine will and power are "incomprehensible" or in no manner limited by principles of either truth or goodness.[46] The introduction of the divine goodness, however, restores to the argument from doubt the epistemic legitimacy of the principle of contradiction, for the supposed divine deception would contradict God's goodness.

Aquinas teaches, in contradistinction to Descartes' theology of creation, that omnipotence does not mean that God could will or create something contrary to the divine nature—not, however, because God lacks the power so to act but because such an act is not "something that can be done" even by God. Since "making it the case" that what contains a contradiction exists or is true is not something that can be done, the denial that God can do such a thing is not a challenge to or a reasonable doubt

---

42. Second Set of Replies, AT VII.145–46, CSMK II.104; *Regulae*, Rule 3, AT X.368, CSMK I.14.

43. V.5, AT VII.64, CSMK II.45.

44. *Regulae*, Rule 14, AT X.445–47, CSMK I.61–62; *Principles* I.59, AT VIIIA.27–28, CSMK I.212.

45. "And God saw every thing that he had made, and, behold, *it was* very good" (Gen. 1:31).

46. Descartes calls attention to the importance of the divine incomprehensibility in the Preface to the reader (AT VII.9, CSMK II.8), and in the Fourth Meditation (IV.6, AT VII.55, CSMK II.39).

of His omnipotence.[47] God's actions appear nevertheless to be independent of any limiting principle, for it is conceded by all theologians that God is free either to create or not to create the world. The theologians' affirmation of the divine freedom of indifference appears to be incompatible with the divine goodness.

Descartes, however, sees a deeper difficulty in the traditional theology of creation. The divine goodness does not seem to be compatible with the universal character of the deceptive nature of nature. The human mind, however, is deceived not because it possesses an imperfect intellect, as the omnipotent deceiver doubt may lead one to believe, but because human beings make false judgments about the "essential nature" of external things based on evidence supplied by the senses.[48] Descartes seems to imply that if God were good and the Creator both of the whole of nature and of the nature of the human mind, then nature would not have the character of being systematically deceptive. Inquiry into the nature of nature would still be required to discover the truth about nature but the experiential knowledge of things would point toward rather than away from the truth of things. As it apparently now stands, however, the surface or manifestation of things and the "essences" or natures of things are radically opposed to one another and this opposition is alien to the claimed goodness of God.

Descartes says that there "may be some who would prefer to deny the existence of so powerful a God rather than believe that everything else is uncertain" (21, 17–19). This powerful God is, of course, the Creator of the world. The Creator God of Descartes' theology of creation and of the omnipotent deceiver doubt has the power to make what is impossible actual. Since nothing is impossible for God, nothing is necessary. The materialists say that it is better to deny the existence of such a God than to believe that nothing is impossible or necessary. The Creator God of the Cartesian theology of creation is incompatible with the existence of nature.

The omnipotent deceiver doubt is extravagant in a manner not unlike the doubt based on madness and, as the madman doubt is followed by the dreaming doubt, so the omnipotent deceiver doubt is followed by the

---

47. *ST* I, Q 25, A 3.
48. VI.15, AT VII.83, CSMK II.57–58.

doubt based on materialism. Descartes says, concerning the materialists, "Let us not contradict them, but grant them that everything said about God is a fiction" (21, 19–20). The removal of the Creator God as a reason to doubt restores the principle of contradiction to the argument from doubt. It also, however, makes the issue of the cause of the human mind a new reason to doubt the existence of the world. Those who affirm the fictitious nature of God might suppose that the human mind has come to be "by fate, or chance, or a continuous chain of events" (21, 20–22). These persons implicitly deny that mind is a possible cause of mind. Mind is not first but is caused by and is therefore derivative of non-mind. The derivative character of mind does not however imply that the existence of mind is an illusion, for the mind never ceases to sense, imagine, and understand, or to be a "thinking thing." The derivative nature of mind does however imply the possibility that the mind is always deceived. Since "deception and error seem to be imperfections," the less powerful the materialists make the original cause of mind, "the more likely it is that" the human mind is "so imperfect as to be deceived all the time" (21, 22–26). The principle affirms a direct relation between the degree of imperfection of the mind and the degree of its vulnerability to constant deception. If the human mind were utterly imperfect, then it would be impossible for it to avoid being always deceived. The degree of imperfection of the human mind is a function of the degree of the power of its cause. It would be most improbable for the human mind to be constantly deceived if its author were supremely powerful. The materialists assert however that the cause of mind is either necessity or chance. If this is the case, then the cause of mind is not ordered toward the knowing of mind. If the mind comes to be through the aimless motions of blind matter, then there appears to be no basis in nature for the existence of a bond uniting the cognitive activity of the mind with the beings it seeks to know. In the dream doubt, this bond seemed to be supplied by the kinds or natures that could be abstracted from the mind's images of external things. This cognitive bond between the mind's images and the natures of external things is severed in the final moment of the dream doubt once the real is identified with the simple universals of physics. Since this identification entails the non-resemblance between the mind's images of things and the things themselves, the mind is always deceived. The mind is not deceived about the objects of pure mathematics, however, because these objects are at once intelligible to the mind and existence-neutral. The mind is, rather, systematically deceived about the natures of the things existing outside of the mind. What is known by the mind does not exist outside of the mind and what exists outside of the mind is not known by the mind.

The doubt based on materialism is the peak of Cartesian doubt. It makes evident the presuppositions that motivate the introduction of the material simple universals as a reason to doubt the existence of the world. The materialists claim that the mind is corporeal, and it comes to be from the motions of body. Is this not, however, a real basis to doubt the trustworthy character of intellection and reason? The autonomy of the mind or its independence from determination by the motions of body seems to survive the doubt based on materialism. Descartes says that this doubt is well considered and valid. Mind comes to be from the motions of body and yet it appears to enjoy a certain freedom from this causality. Perhaps the most obvious sign of this freedom of the mind is its capacity to doubt. Further, the power of reason to direct itself is confirmed in this context by its capacity to provide a remedy to the mind's vulnerability to deception. The mind is free to withhold its assent from opinions it formerly accepted as true. The standard that provides the proper degree of assent-withholding is supplied by the patently false. The freedom of the human mind is grounded in the finitude of the mind.

The theme of the First Meditation is the epistemic conflict that exists between experience and science as alternative modes of cognizing the world. The epistemic principle of experience is the imagination and that of science is the intellect. Experiential knowledge appears to be deceptive when measured by the intellect's understanding of the world. But since it is human experience that makes knowledge of the existence of the world available to the mind, deception and illusion continually infect the intellect's understanding of the world. For this reason, Descartes says that to have noticed that all of the mind's former opinions are dubitable is not sufficient to understand the nature of the world. In addition, care must be taken to remember the reasons to doubt the existence of the world, as these reasons are easily forgotten because of the power that the doubter's former opinions have over his thought (22, 3–6). In the context of the doubt of all things, the mind's freedom from alien determination is shown to be non-illusory, but in the context of everyday experience this same determination is shown to be sufficiently powerful to capture the doubter's belief.

Descartes' former opinions are simultaneously doubtful and probable. Powerful and well-considered reasons can be advanced against them and yet the mind can never break its habit of trusting in these opinions because it finds it more reasonable to accept than to deny them. The mind judges that it is more reasonable to believe than to deny that it has a body and yet the existence of body can be denied without contradiction. Doubt of the existence of the world and hence of the existence of the body of the doubter is a complex way of affirming the claim that the mind is epistemically unrelated to any being that exists outside of the mind. The hold that the mind's former opinions have over its beliefs, however, is a powerful challenge to this view.

Descartes originally declared the goal of the doubt to be the establishment of something indubitably certain. He now says that the doubt provides a counterweight to the "distorting influence" of the mind's assent to its habitual opinions so that its judgment is no longer detoured from the correct perception of things (22, 12–18). Things now exist and the supposed doubt of the existence of body is implied to be imaginary. This balance between the rational doubt and the acceptance of the mind's former opinions appears to be identical to the understanding of external things in terms of the simple universals of physics. This understanding consists, in part, of an account of the "forms of appearing" of these things.[49] The understanding of things in terms of the simple universals attempts to establish a necessary relation between the natures of things and how these things appear to the human mind.

Descartes concludes this section of the argument with the denial that his attempt at willful self-deception will court a moral error or danger. One might suppose that he had already courted this danger by not contradicting the materialists and granting that everything said about God is a "fiction." Now he is going to suppose that the cause of human knowing is not God but some evil genius or mind who employs all of his power and cunning to deceive the human mind (22, 23–26). The evil genius doubt is therefore invoked solely to advance the mind's correct perception of things.

---

49. II.12, AT VII.30, CSMK II.20.

The evil genius doubt is a recapitulation of the dream doubt. It also doubts the existence of all "external things." External things in this context, as in the dream doubt, are the things encountered in everyday experience. Color, for example, is interpreted as something external and the mathematical concept of shape is now the shapes of visible things. Absent from the list of things rendered dubitable by the evil genius are corporeal nature in general and the simple universals of physics. The deceptive power of the evil genius is a reason to doubt the existence of the body of the doubter, but this body is not the body machine of the physics, but the flesh and blood of a living human being.[50]

The evil genius doubt has two parts. In the first part what is outside of man is doubted and in the second part the human body is doubted. What is doubted in the second part appears to supply the principle animating the doubt of the first part. The evil genius appears to be a personification of the mind-body composite nature of man. Descartes suggests that what determines the human mind's spontaneous interpretation of the world is its desire for self-preservation. The human mind must have some means for making immediate judgments about what is advantageous and harmful for the human body and hence for making evident to the mind the bodies that ought to be pursued and those that ought to be avoided.[51] The best means available for this task appears to be the mind's sensory perceptions, images, and sensations.[52] The mind however misuses these things when it treats them as "reliable touchstones for immediate judgments about the essential nature of the bodies located" outside of the mind.[53]

If the evil genius is a personification of the composite nature of man, then the Creator God of the omnipotent deceiver doubt is a personification of corporeal nature in general. God is nature because the acts of God are indistinguishable from the causality of necessity. The two great persons of the First Meditation—God and the evil genius—comprehend between them the two senses of nature at work in this Meditation. Nature is both the subject matter of the science of the laws of nature and the com-

---

50. *Treatise on Man*, AT XI.201–2, CSMK I.108; *Discourse* V.9, AT VI.55–56, CSMK I.139.

51. VI.16, AT VII.83, CSMK II.57.

52. VI.22, AT VII.87–88, CSMK II.60–61.

53. VI.15, AT VII.83, CSMK II.57–58.

posite nature of man. This duality in nature is the indispensable condition for the possibility of mind.

The evil genius doubt seeks to make evident the presuppositions of the dreaming doubt. The attempt to doubt the existence of all external things goes against the grain of the nature of the mind. Descartes says that doubting is "an arduous undertaking, and a kind of laziness brings [him] back to normal life" (23, 9–11). He is compelled by his nature to fall out of meditation and to readopt the epistemic position of experience. The requirements necessary for thinking are not simply compatible with those of living. He implies that the evil genius has now completely succeeded in imposing upon and determining his thinking. He is compelled to suspend his search for something known with indubitable certainty.

Descartes likens his present condition to that of a prisoner who is enjoying an imaginary freedom in a dream. When he begins to suspect that he is sleeping he is afraid to be awakened and attempts to continue to enjoy the pleasant illusion. Descartes, in a manner not dissimilar to the prisoner, spontaneously falls back into his habitual opinions, and fears waking up because this "hard labor" would have to be spent not in some light but in the "inextricable darkness" of the problems already raised by the argument from doubt (23, 11–18). Descartes' comparison suggests that ordinary human knowing is a kind of prison within which the putative knower experiences the illusion of being free. In this context, the mind believes that it is acting independently of any determination by the composite nature of the human mind. What it takes to be its autonomous understanding is however an illusion generated by the mind's union with body. The doubt of all things is therefore an attempt by the mind to secure for itself its own freedom from the deceptive nature of human nature.

The mind that Descartes discovers necessarily exists is a thinking thing or consciousness. Consciousness is a power of awareness that cognizes thoughts or things present to the mind.[54] Consciousness, however, because it has no known bond to anything existing outside of itself, is ignorant of its union with the human body. Consciousness therefore senses, imagines, and understands, but it does not feel anything and hence cannot be conscious of any need, defect, or interest. There exists no basis in consciousness, there-

---

54. Second Set of Replies, AT VII.160, CSMK II.113.

fore, for it to doubt, make judgments, or reason. Indeed, such a mind could not be the mind of any being. The fundamental problem that the argument from doubt brings to light is how mind in the precise sense or mind conceived as consciousness can be unified with mind in the comprehensive sense, that is, with a mind that feels sensations and experiences delight and distress.

15

Montesquieu's Address to the Reader: The Prefatory Art of *The Spirit of Laws*

Stuart D. Warner

> There are some books the sentences of which resemble highways, or even motor roads. But there are also books the sentences of which resemble rather winding paths which lead along precipices concealed by thickets and sometimes even along well-hidden and spacious caves. These depths and caves are not noticed by the busy workmen hurrying to their fields, but they gradually become known and familiar to the leisured and attentive wayfarer.[1]
>
> Leo Strauss, "The Literary Character of the *Guide for the Perplexed*" (1941)

Montesquieu's Preface to *The Spirit of Laws*—surely written with most if not all of the manuscript already in hand—prepares his readers for the immensely long, difficult, and cavernous book that lies before them. The Preface, which consists of sixteen short paragraphs, appears to be flimsily constructed, the paragraphs precariously perched on top of each other.[2]

---

1. Cf. Leo Strauss, "Farabi's Plato," in *Louis Ginzberg: Jubilee Volume* (English Section) (New York: American Academy for Jewish Research, 1945/1946), 376–77.

2. Montesquieu's Preface has received surprisingly little attention. Cf., however, Thomas L. Pangle, *Montesquieu's Philosophy of Liberalism: A Commentary on "The Spirit of the Laws"* (Chicago: University of Chicago Press, 1973), 20–24 and 234–39; also, Charles Beyer,

In fact, it is artfully crafted, as the relationships among several of its paragraphs suggest. The opening paragraph alone reveals both its artfulness and some of the concerns that animate it:

> If among the infinite number of things that are in this book, there were some one that, contrary to my expectations, might give offense, there is at least none which has been placed there with evil intent. I have not by nature a disapproving mind. Plato thanked heaven that he was born in the time of Socrates; and I, I give thanks to heaven that it had me born in the government where I live, and that it has wanted me to obey those whom it had me love. (Pref. 1)[3]

The first part of this paragraph aims at disarming the reader. Given the endless array of things in the book, it is possible that one of them might, despite Montesquieu's finely wrought safeguards, offend the reader. If that occurs, Montesquieu assures us, such a thing has not been placed there with ill or evil intent. Of course, this suggests that there might very well be things that will offend the reader and that these things are intentionally written, but the intent is other than to cause ill. Moreover, there is some hint that things offensive will be lost in the almost overwhelming details of the book, something for which Montesquieu very much seems to hope. To heighten the effect of his implied concern that his book not have an unsalutary effect upon his readers, Montesquieu points out that he himself does not have a disapproving or censorious mind, encouraging his readers to follow the same path.[4] Nothing could be clearer but that Montesquieu is worried about political and religious persecution, and this worry casts a long shadow over the entire book. Being so worried, it would be astonishing if this were not reflected in the manner in which the book is composed.

Nature et valeur dans la philosophie de Montesquieu: Analyse méthodique de la notion de rapport dans "l'Esprit des Lois" (Paris: Klincksieck, 1982), 16–18.

3. All translations are by the author; quotations from *The Spirit of Laws* are cited parenthetically in the text.

4. Cf. Descartes, *Discourse on Method*, pts. 1–3.

Montesquieu adroitly allows us to notice that concern in the complicated comparison that he draws between Plato and himself. He silently borrows the remark about Plato from the end of Plutarch's *Life of Marius*, and it is virtually certain that he is using the French translation of Jacques Amyot rather than the Greek. In the Greek, Plutarch has Plato thanking his "daimon" and "fortune" for having him born in the time of Socrates; Amyot's translation has him thanking "the god" and "fortune."[5] In the first edition of *The Spirit of Laws*, Montesquieu has Plato thanking "the gods"; but this is corrected in the *errata* to the edition to "heaven,"[6] which is how it appears in all editions thereafter. Regardless, what is particularly striking about the remark is that the parallelism of the comparison between Plato and himself is entirely deceptive, but this very deception leads us to comprehend a more profound parallelism to which Montesquieu is actually pointing. In having Plato "thank" heaven, the verb that he uses is *remercier*, a term used to express thanks in everyday situations. When Montesquieu "thanks" heaven, he uses a composite verb, *rendre grâces*. This verb is used in circumstances in which respect or superiority is involved—for example, in church or with a lord. In the simple act of thanking, Montesquieu is indicating a pivotal difference between his own circumstances and those of Plato, namely, the power of the Catholic Church to affect a variety of matters. But this very difference leads us to the parallelism to which Montesquieu is recondtiely pointing. Plato was born in a time and place in which the philosopher was endangered—indeed, put to death—by a curious coalescence of politics and religion. Montesquieu also finds himself in a time and place in which the philosopher is endangered by a curious coalescence of religion and politics, albeit the religion is vastly different. Montesquieu is not pointing to a difference between Plato's circumstances and his own so much as he is pointing to a similarity of paramount importance. This claim is reinforced by recognizing the insincerity of his appeal to loving his government. Whatever the character of Montesquieu's love, it was not induced by the government itself; instead, heaven willed Montesquieu to obey those

---

5. Ch. 46 in the Loeb edition (Amyot's original has no chapters).

6. Cf. Montesquieu, *De l'esprit des loix*, ed. Jean Brethe de La Gressaye, 4 vols. (Paris: Société les Belles Lettres, 1950–61), 1:229.

whom it had him love.[7] This is a strange kind of love, indeed. Moreover, it is an ambiguous kind of love, for it is not clear exactly whom Montesquieu is supposed to love. The government appears as a reasonable possibility, but this seems to be only part of the answer—the other part being the Church. However, with respect to the government, Montesquieu indicates the inadequacy of this love many paragraphs later, when he remarks:

> If I could so arrange that everyone had new reasons for loving his duties, his prince, his fatherland, and his laws, that one might better feel one's happiness in each country, each government, and each post where one finds oneself, I would believe myself the happiest of mortals. (Pref. 11)

Thus, the old reasons for loving one's government—the reasons to which Montesquieu presumably refers in the opening paragraph—are insufficient, and thus not entirely the sort of thing for which one should give thanks.

We would be negligent in concluding this frame of thought if we did not note that the end of Montesquieu's opening paragraph contains a faint echo from the end of the opening of Tacitus' *Histories*: "It is the rare fortune of these days that someone may think what he wishes and say what he thinks" (*Hist.* 1.1). We suspect that Montesquieu is listening to Tacitus' voice, because his complaint is in part that he is not entirely free to say what he thinks, and Montesquieu, being an inveterate reader of Tacitus,[8] would surely have known this line. Moreover, as the quotation from Tacitus serves as the epigraph for each of the first two volumes of Hume's *Treatise of Human Nature* (1739), the relationship of this line to the public character of modern philosophy may very likely have been on his mind. Indeed, the freedom to philosophize was an even more pressing issue in the modern European state than it would have been for the ancients.[9]

---

7. Montesquieu's claim here in fact anticipates his discussion of the French feudal laws in the last two books of *The Spirit of Laws*.

8. In *The Spirit of Laws*, Montesquieu remarks that Tacitus was able in his writings to "abbreviate everything, because he saw everything" (30.2).

9. It suffices to mention the names of Bruno, Galileo, Hobbes, Descartes, Locke, Spinoza, Vico, Voltaire, and Rousseau.

Montesquieu begins his Preface by comparing himself to Plato, and thus the ancients. He ends his Preface by comparing himself to the moderns:

> If this work turns out a success, I shall owe much of it to the majesty of my subject; for all that, I do not believe that I have totally lacked genius. When I have seen that which so many great men in France, England, and Germany have written before me, I have been filled with admiration; but I have not lost courage: "And I too, I am a painter,"[10] have I said with Correggio. (Pref. 16)

These lines assert Montesquieu's own understanding that the magisterial character of his book comes from the nature of his subject and his own genius. Other moderns have written with great effect before him, but Montesquieu asserts a pride of place, believing that his work surpasses theirs in approach, comprehensiveness, and insight. While Montesquieu mentions France (perhaps Montaigne, Bodin, and Descartes), England (perhaps Hobbes, Harrington, Locke, and Newton), and Germany (perhaps Pufendorf and Leibniz)—Italy, on the other hand, is conspicuous by its absence, especially given what follows. And although it seems likely that Montesquieu had the aforementioned thinkers in mind—seen from the perspective of his mentioning two ancients in the opening paragraph—it appears telling that here in fact he remains silent about the names of any modern philosophers or political thinkers.

However, we should note that he does mention a modern by name, an Italian painter and not a philosopher, Correggio—and he is the only individual mentioned in the Preface apart from Plato and Socrates. In bringing forth Correggio's name, Montesquieu might have his painting *Ecce Homo* in mind. Better still, Correggio might be a placeholder for another Italian, someone about whom he is silent in the Preface—namely, Machiavelli. Montesquieu mentions Machiavelli twice in the body of *The Spirit of Laws*, once calling him "that great man" (6.5), and once alluding to him

---

10. [Montesquieu's note: *Ed io anche son pittore.*] Montesquieu's comment refers to an apocryphal remark attributed to the Italian painter Correggio upon seeing Raphael's *St. Cecilia*.

as a philosopher-legislator (29.19).[11] Also, in a chapter on "How commerce made its way into Europe through barbarism," Montesquieu asserts, "We have begun to cure ourselves of Machiavelism, and we will cure ourselves everyday" (21.20). Most importantly, there is a striking resemblance between the end of Montesquieu's Preface and the end of Machiavelli's "Dedicatory Letter" in *The Prince*. There, Machiavelli compares himself to a landscape artist, one who can understand both the nature of the prince—who can only understand the people—and the nature[12] of the people—who can only understand the prince. Thus, whereas both the prince and the people lack self-knowledge—both in the sense of their knowledge of themselves as human beings and their knowledge of themselves as individuals—Machiavelli is making a claim on both. The theme of self-knowledge constitutes the broadest horizon of Machiavelli's book *qua* treatise. In portraying himself as an artist, one who is very much like another artist who is contemplating the work of an Italian, Montesquieu slyly yet gracefully seems to turn the reader directly toward Machiavelli. *The Spirit of Laws* now comes into view as a book whose teaching is to be placed in relation to the teaching of Machiavelli.

Let us continue by noticing that from the moment of its publication, readers of *The Spirit of Laws* have questioned whether the book exhibits any order at all.[13] While it may appear to be haphazardly cobbled together, Montesquieu affirms in the second paragraph of the Preface the care with which it has been fashioned:

> I ask a favor that I fear will not be granted to me: it is not to judge by the reading of a moment a work of twenty years; to

---

11. He also mentions Machiavelli in a footnote (28.6), referring to a remark in his *Florentine Histories*.

12. Machiavelli appeals to nature four times in the epistle—twice directly and twice by pronoun. Cf. *The Prince*, ch.14, par.3; ch.25, par.1.

13. Cf., for example, H. Barckhausen, "Le Désordre de l'*Esprit des Lois*," in *Montesquieu: Ses idées et ses œuvres* (Paris: Hachette, 1907), 253–66; Leo Strauss, "Persecution and the Art of Writing," *Social Research* 8 (1941): 495n12; D'Alembert, *Éloge de Montesquieu* (1755), par.27; and David W. Carrithers, "Introduction: An Appreciation of *The Spirit of Laws*," in *Montesquieu's Science of Politics: Essays on "The Spirit of Laws*," ed. David W. Carrithers, Michael A. Mosher, and Paul A. Rahe (Lanham, MD: Rowman & Littlefield, 2001), 16–18.

approve or condemn the whole book, and not some sentences. If one wishes to seek the design of the author, one can discover it well only in the design of the work. (Pref. 2)

Montesquieu avers that his book does have a design, and that his intention for the work is inscribed in the book itself. However, his insistence suggests that the book will appear chaotic at first blush; only when one surveys the whole will the reader be able to discern that what appears chaotic is not, and hence that one should read the book with the idea that Montesquieu had a design in mind. The requirement to look for the design of the author in that of the book is redolent of the medieval and modern idea that the intention of God the creator can only be found in the order of the creation itself.[14] Montesquieu is, alas, silent about what his intention is, and it remains conspicuously hidden from view.

The second paragraph directs us to the penultimate paragraph of the Preface, for there too Montesquieu, self-reflectively poetic and dramatic, alerts the reader to the fact that the book has a design:

I have many times begun, and many times abandoned this work; I have a thousand times cast to the winds the leaves that I had written;[15] every day I felt my paternal hands drop;[16] I followed my object without forming a design; I knew neither the rules nor the exceptions; I found the truth only to lose it. But when I had discovered my principles, all that I sought came to me; and, in the course of twenty years, I have seen my work begin, grow, move forward, and end. (Pref. 15)

---

14. Cf. Basia Miller, "Montesquieu's *Esprit des lois*: Deferral for the Education of the Legislator" (unpublished PhD diss., University of Chicago, Department of Romance Languages and Literatures, 1989).

15. [Montesquieu's note: *Ludibria ventis.*] Vergil, *Aen.* 6.75: "playthings of the…winds." The words appear in the following remark: "Do not entrust verses to leaves, lest they fly in confusion, playthings of the swift winds."

16. [Montesquieu's note: *Bis patriae cecidere manus…*] Vergil, *Aen.* 6.33: "Twice the father's hands fell."

At the beginning of the Preface, Montesquieu's design seemed to be an almost effortless achievement, stated in an almost matter-of-fact way. Here, however, the difficulties of formulating and accomplishing that design come into focus, along with the weariness and frustration that must have accompanied his effort, a labor that is poeticized just as it is in the posthumously published *Invocation to the Muses*.[17] Intertwined with these difficulties is the image of Montesquieu as the father of his offspring, an evocation of the epigraph from Ovid at the beginning of *The Spirit of Laws—prolem sine matre creatam* (*Met.* 2.553). Of course, the offspring in Ovid is Erichthonius, who, as we know from other ancient sources, was fathered by Hephaestus, who, while chasing Athena, ejaculated upon her leg, as she was unwilling to give herself to him; and it was thus his semen, which Athena wiped to the ground, that provided the seed from which the child was born.

Montesquieu's two allusions to Vergil's *Aeneid* in the penultimate paragraph provide the first of the over 2,000 footnotes in the text itself. The last quotation and last footnote in the book also come from the *Aeneid*—"*Italiam... / Italiam*" (31.34; *Aen.* 3.523). Additionally, there is an epigraph from Vergil—"that which greatest Atlas taught"—which is properly understood as beginning the second half of *The Spirit of Laws*, as the book moves from the earth to places yonder, especially the high seas.[18] References to the *Aeneid* provide markers, then, indicating a long journey—both Aeneas' and Montesquieu's. The very idea of *The Spirit of Laws* as a voyage is fortified by a lexical register that Montesquieu invokes throughout the Preface: discovering (twice); seeking (four times); and finding (five times). It will turn out that the drama that is implied by the idea and image of a long, momentous voyage is fully played out in book twenty-one. However, lest we get too caught up in the drama of the moment, let us turn and consider Montesquieu's two allusions to Vergil.

---

17. The *Invocation*, originally written for *The Spirit of Laws*, appeared for the first time in one of Montesquieu's works in the year III (late 1794) (cf. *L'Esprit des Journaux, François et Étrangers*, tome XI [November, 1794], 337). However, it appeared four years earlier than that, albeit with one important variation, in [Michel-Jean-Louis Saladin] *Mémoire historique sur la vie et les ouvrages de M. J. Vernet* (1790), 27–29.

18. I argue for this in "By Land and By Sea: The Mythic Beginnings of Montesquieu's *Spirit of Laws*," in manuscript.

Montesquieu's first allusion is to book six of the *Aeneid*, where Aeneas ascends to the cave of the Sibyl to receive her prophecy. The practice of the Sibyl is to write her prophecy on leaves.[19] Aeneas, however, understands the difficulty inherent therein. The prophecy itself rests not only on the words entrusted to the leaves, but on the order of the leaves themselves: a different order will produce a different prophecy, one that will be at odds with the future to come. Knowing this, and feeling the wind around him, Aeneas asks the Sibyl to chant her prophecy.

Montesquieu commits the words that make up *The Spirit of Laws* to leaves of paper, and they were in fact always in danger of being moved; but the wind in this case winds up being Montesquieu himself. As the manuscript of the book reveals, he constantly shuffled chapters around. For example—and it by no means the most extreme—book thirteen, chapter fifteen, "The abuse of liberty," was at first chapter seven of that book, then eight, then eleven, then eight again, then fifteen, then sixteen, then, fourteen, then sixteen again, before its final resting place.[20] Thus, in marking this line about the Sybil in the *Aeneid*, Montesquieu is not only alluding to his continued dissatisfaction with what he wrote, presumably, both substantially and stylistically, but also and especially to the ordering that he imposed upon it. We are to infer from this that at some point the leaves were fixed, and that therefore the teaching of the book depends upon the order thereby created.[21] Furthermore, in comparing himself to the Sybil, Montesquieu seems to be portraying himself as a prophet, one who is pointing to a new world order still to come, a new world order that perhaps Montesquieu understands himself to be underwriting. A qualification to this, however, should be noted: Aeneas does not want the prophecy written down on the leaves, and the Sybil faithfully follows his request.

Montesquieu's second reference to the *Aeneid* turns on Vergil's description of the carvings that Daedalus marks into the stone of the sacred temple he is building for Apollo. Daedalus first depicts the story of the death of

---

19. Cf. Vergil, *Aen.* 3.444–53; and Dante, *Paradiso* 33.64–66.

20. Cf. Montesquieu, *Œuvres complètes de Montesquieu*, tome 3, *De l'esprit des loix* (Manuscripts), ed. Catherine Volpilhac-Auger (Oxford: Voltaire Foundation, 2008), 344.

21. Of course, the order and number of chapters of the 1748 edition undergo some changes in the 1757 posthumously published edition (for instance, ten additional chapters are added, raising the number from 595 to 605).

Androgeos, son of Minos, and the yearly punishment for this that the children of the Cecrops will have to pay. He further depicts the mating of Pasiphaë and the bull that gives birth to the Minotaur, and the labyrinth in which the Minotaur is kept, which, in the account of Apollodorus (*Bibl.* 3.15.8), Daedalus himself designed for Minos, and from which he alone knew how to escape. Despite Daedalus' inventiveness and mastery in various arts, however, twice, and only twice, he attempts to carve an image of his son Icarus, and twice his paternal hands fail.

In comparing himself to Daedalus, Montesquieu once again presents the image of himself as father to *The Spirit of Laws*, his offspring. What he seems to point to in this comparison is not only his labor, but, through Daedalus, the exquisite artistry his own creation involves. Yet we must not lose sight of the fact that Daedalus failed in his task, and in this respect he is quite like Hephaestus, who sought to copulate with Athena. Thus, both with reference to the epigraph from Ovid and here in the Preface, Montesquieu compares himself to two artisans, both of whom *failed* to do what they set out to do. By this device, Montesquieu is perhaps suggesting that his own progeny embodies the marks of a certain kind of failure, and that the book might thus lead the reader astray. But Montesquieu seems to imply that he is well aware of mistaken or misleading steps present in his book; indeed, perhaps these are central to the teaching of the book.[22] If these errors were intended, Montesquieu would presumably have provided some clues that would allow the reader to notice them and learn from them, clues that presumably would have to be found on the surface of the work.

Daedalus failed in his effort to carve his son into the stone of the temple. But he succeeded in carving the image of the labyrinth, and Montesquieu's emphasis on the order of *The Spirit of Laws* in the paragraph we have been examining steers us in the direction of that success. He insists in the second paragraph of the Preface, and calls our attention to the fact in the penultimate paragraph, that his book has a design. Given appearances to the contrary, one would need to discover a map or a thread

---

22. Cf. a letter from Leo Strauss to David Lowenthal, March 8, 1954, box 4, folder 12, Leo Strauss Archive, University of Chicago Special Collections, about the "'ascent' character" of "Montesquieu's argument," stating that "many things said in the early parts [of *The Spirit of Laws*] are revoked later."

that would allow one to make one's way through it successfully, without becoming hopelessly lost. In Apollodorus' account, Daedalus is the only one who understands how one can make one's way into and out of the labyrinth successfully—by the device of a thread. Toward the end of *The Spirit of Laws*, Montesquieu appeals to this very image: "If in the search for the feudal laws, I find myself in a dark labyrinth, full of paths and detours, I believe that I have hold of the end of the thread and that I am able to walk" (30.2). Although Montesquieu's remark is limited to only two books directly—thirty and thirty-one—it is likely that it is the image of the labyrinth that he intends to evoke in the reader's mind more generally through the comparison he makes between Daedalus and himself. Indeed, some readers of *The Spirit of Laws* seem to have understood the book in exactly this way. Voltaire, for example, in a dialogue he wrote in which Hobbes, Grotius, and Montesquieu are the principal subjects of discussion, has one of the three interlocutors rail at *The Spirit of Laws*: "I am annoyed that this book is a labyrinth, but without any thread."[23]

In the first paragraph, Montesquieu compares himself to the ancients; in the last paragraph, he compares himself to the moderns. The second paragraph introduces the theme of design; the penultimate paragraph too points to that theme. The third paragraph, as we will see, has an intimate connection to the antepenultimate one. The outer edge of the Preface thus reveals itself to be a ring composition.

In the third paragraph, Montesquieu claims that, "I have at first examined men, and I have believed that, in this infinite diversity of laws and morals, they were not solely guided by their fantasies" (Pref. 3). This is the second time in the Preface that Montesquieu has spoken of the infinite, the other time being the opening line. Montesquieu's appeal is hyperbolic; nonetheless, it achieves its purpose here in highlighting both the widespread differences in laws and morals among nations and peoples, and that Montesquieu thinks that there is some underlying logic to these differences.

The antepenultimate paragraph directs us to the metaphysical ground of those differences:

---

23. Voltaire, *L'A,B,C, Dialogue curieux traduit de l'Anglais de Monsieur Huet* (1762), "First Dialogue."

> It is in seeking to instruct men that one can practice that general virtue which comprises the love of all. Man, that flexible being, conforming himself in society to the thoughts and impressions of others, is equally capable of knowing his own nature when it is shown to him, and of losing even the sentiment of it when it is hidden from him. (Pref. 14)

The image of man as a flexible being is reminiscent of that found in La Fontaine's famous fable of "The Oak and the Reed."[24] This flexibility or malleability of human beings is ultimately responsible for the diversity of laws and morals that Montesquieu finds. Human beings are flexible in the sense that they "bend" themselves to the minds of others. Montesquieu obviously does not completely explain here in such a brief portion of his book how and why that happens, but he does provide some guidance. Our nature as human beings does not make itself evident to us—hence Montesquieu's comment about knowing our nature "when it is shown" to us—and it seems to be a hard-won achievement. Human beings are more readily disposed to conform themselves to a human world that is shaped and constituted by the thoughts and impressions of others, both past and present. Knowing our nature apparently orients us to act in certain ways that not knowing our nature fails to provide. What this means pivots on this essential question, the answer to which can only be found by a study of the whole of *The Spirit of Laws*: What is Montesquieu's understanding of nature?

The paragraph just prior to the antepenultimate one is a stepping stone to what is to come in that latter paragraph:

> I would believe myself the happiest of mortals if I could so arrange that men could cure themselves of their prejudices. I call here prejudices not that which makes one not know certain things, but that which makes one not know oneself. (Pref. 13)

---

24. This is so, in part, because of Montesquieu's use of the verb *se plier*. Cf. Stuart D. Warner, "Montesquieu's Prelude: An Interpretation of Book I of *The Spirit of Laws*," in *Enlightening Revolutions: Essays in Honor of Ralph Lerner*, ed. Svetozar Minkov (Lanham, MD: Lexington Books, 2006), 176.

Earlier in the Preface, Montesquieu had remarked that, "I have not drawn my principles from my prejudices, but from the nature of things" (Pref. 6). In returning to the theme of prejudice, Montesquieu addresses himself to the theme of self-knowledge; and the tone of the paragraph conveys the failure of most people in this regard. What impresses itself most upon the reader here is Montesquieu's linking his happiness to human beings being cured of their lack of self-knowledge. The self-knowledge to which Montesquieu adverts here can only be that knowledge that individuals have of themselves as human beings, that is, a knowledge or understanding of human nature. We presume that what Montesquieu intends as the agent of this cure is his book itself, and thus one of the aims of *The Spirit of Laws* is to articulate a conception of human nature.

The thirteenth paragraph of the Preface is in fact the final frame in a syntactical triptych. To understand it more deeply, we need to examine the other two frames (one of which we have already commented upon), both of which bear on Montesquieu's happiness and the project of the book itself.

> If I could so arrange that everyone had new reasons for loving his duties, his prince, his fatherland, and his laws, that one might better feel one's happiness in each country, each government, and each post where one finds oneself, I would believe myself the happiest of mortals. (Pref. 11)

> If I could so arrange that those who rule would increase their knowledge about that which they should prescribe, and those who obey would find a new pleasure in obeying, I would believe myself the happiest of mortals. (Pref. 12)

Whatever the philosophical project of *The Spirit of Laws* may be, there is also a political one. Indeed, the two appear as intimately related. The three paragraphs before us serve to orient us to this understanding.

What the three paragraphs have in common is clear enough: all three claim an interest in arranging certain things differently—in changing an already existing order to make it better in some manner; all three claim such new arrangements would lead Montesquieu to believe himself the happiest of mortals; all three are presented *hypothetically*. There are two important differences in these paragraphs, the first being a difference of matter.

Paragraph eleven looks at political life from the point of view of the citizen or subject. Put briefly, Montesquieu aims at providing new reasons for a person to love his country; and these new reasons would provide for a greater likelihood of one's being happy. Presumably, it is the intent of *The Spirit of Laws* to impart these reasons; however, Montesquieu does not explicitly tell us what these reasons are anywhere in the book.

Paragraph twelve looks at political life from the point of view of those who rule. The aim here is to augment their knowledge so that they prescribe better rather than worse laws. Interestingly, even here Montesquieu expresses interest in the happiness or pleasure of the citizens or subjects, and not that of the ruler. Once again, however, while presumably it is the intent of *The Spirit of Laws* to impart this knowledge, Montesquieu does not tell us what this knowledge is.

Paragraph thirteen does not look at political life at all. Rather one should say that its concern is philosophical: to present an understanding of being human whereby human beings can cure themselves of their lack of self-knowledge, an understanding that presumably *The Spirit of Laws* intends to provide. What this understanding is, Montesquieu here does not say. But his use of the word 'cure' is resonant of a remark to which we have referred earlier, namely, the importance of curing ourselves of Machiavelism.[25]

The second difference among these paragraphs is a matter of form. The thirteenth paragraph does *not* say, "If I could so arrange that men could cure themselves of their prejudices, I would believe myself the happiest of mortals." This Montesquieu easily could have written; he has gone out of his way to vary the syntax. By doing so, and avoiding the use of anaphora, Montesquieu calls special attention to this paragraph. By placing "I would believe myself the happiest of mortals" at the beginning, he wants to bring to mind that among the ideas in these three paragraphs, articulating an understanding of human nature whereby human beings might be able to cure themselves of their prejudices is of the foremost importance to him.

Indeed, that this is most important to him furnishes a clue for apprehending the logic of the three paragraphs: Citizens or subjects would have

---

25. Cf. *The Spirit of Laws*, 20.1.

new reasons to love their countries if rulers had increased knowledge about what laws to prescribe; rulers would have increased knowledge about what laws to prescribe only if they were able to cure themselves of their prejudices; and they could cure themselves of their prejudices only if they could endow themselves with a newfound understanding of what it is to be human, an understanding of nature that *The Spirit of Laws* perhaps affords to them. But does it afford that to them? Apart from all other considerations, this question must be raised because of the hypothetical formulation of the three paragraphs. Changes in things political require a change in philosophical outlook. Can a book such as *The Spirit of Laws* not only provide the needed understanding, but also lead people to cure themselves? If not, what does this imply about the political project of the book?

Some other contours of these questions can be seen by looking at the ninth and tenth paragraphs of the Preface, paragraphs that consider matters related to political change:

> I do not write in order to censure that which is established in any country whatsoever. Each nation will find here the reasons for its maxims; and one will naturally draw this consequence, that proposing changes belongs only to those who are born fortunate enough to penetrate by a stroke of genius the whole constitution of a State. (Pref. 9)[26]

> It is not a matter of indifference that people be enlightened. The prejudices of the magistrates began by being the prejudices of the nation. In a time of ignorance, one does not have any doubt, even when one is doing the greatest evils; in a time of enlightenment, one yet trembles doing the greatest goods. One feels the old abuses; one sees the correction; but yet one sees the abuses of the correction itself. One allows the evil if one fears what is worse; one allows the good if one is in doubt about what is better. One looks at the parts only in order to judge the whole; one examines all the causes in order to see all the results. (Pref. 10)

---

26. Cf. Descartes, *Discourse on Method*, pt. 2, par. 3.

One of the themes of these paragraphs is caution—in particular, Montesquieu's caution. He announces so that all can hear that whatever the political project of the book may be, he is not censuring the maxims of any country, for each country can find the reasons for its own maxims in his work. Of course, these reasons are reasons of explanation, not justification—but attaching the very term "reasons" to the maxims of a country confers a sense of legitimacy and respectability upon them. Furthermore, Montesquieu's declaration that he is not a censor is meant to encourage others not to be as well, especially of *The Spirit of Laws*. Unfortunately, Montesquieu's hopes were dashed when the work was placed on the Index of Prohibited Books in 1751.[27]

There is another sense of caution at play in these paragraphs, namely, political caution. At first, Montesquieu asserts that even the very act of proposing changes belongs only to a few—those who can completely grasp the constitution of a state. With an eye on book eleven, chapter six, of *The Spirit of Laws*, perhaps by "constitution" here Montesquieu means a political or legal constitution. Maybe, however, he means something more along the lines of what Plato or Aristotle or the ancients generally would have called a regime.[28] Regardless, the unalloyed claim here is that political change requires someone blessed by fortune with an acute understanding of the warp and weft of a state. This is a high standard, perhaps too high to be genuinely intended. Indeed, Montesquieu's remarks in paragraph eleven appear to point to just that. The divide between enlightened and unenlightened times is effectuated by an enlightened people. It is an enlightened people that makes for enlightened times: an enlightened people, Montesquieu implies, is the cure for magistrates corrupted by prejudice. But even under the dispensation of enlightened times and an enlightened people, one must be wary of effecting political change: whatever the blessing attached to some political change, there are always attendant curses. Indeed, what Montesquieu underscores in the passage at hand are the ever-present costs of political change and political life. However, as we have seen in examining the two paragraphs that follow, namely,

---

27. *Persian Letters* joined *The Spirit of Laws* on that list in 1761.

28. Cf. Leo Strauss, *What Is Political Philosophy? And Other Studies* (Glencoe, IL: Free Press, 1959), 34.

eleven and twelve, far from eschewing political change, Montesquieu anchors his happiness to it. Indeed, maybe we can now say that those two paragraphs, despite their hypothetical character, are meant to corrode the "conservatism" of the paragraphs that we have just examined. Regardless, it is unquestionably true that the tension between paragraphs nine and ten on the one hand, and eleven and twelve on the other, is emblematic of the tension between the daring and caution that thread their way through the entire Preface (and indeed the entire work).

The counterweight in the Preface to Montesquieu's five references to prejudice is enlightenment. This can hardly be unexpected, given Montesquieu's reputation as "an Enlightenment figure." Those who think of Montesquieu along these lines think of him as a modern. That he is a modern is in many significant senses undeniable, and thus the fifth paragraph, in which he relates himself in some measure to the ancient world, assumes a certain importance.

> When I have been called back to antiquity, I have sought to take on its spirit so as not to regard as similar those cases really different, and not to miss the differences of those that appear similar. (Pref. 5)

This paragraph seduces the reader into distorting Montesquieu's meaning. The reader expects that Montesquieu will take on the spirit of antiquity in order not to regard as similar cases really different, and not to regard as different cases really similar. But instead, Montesquieu tells us *twice* that he takes on this spirit in order to discern differences in cases where we might be tempted to see similarities when in fact none exists.[29] That Montesquieu seeks to take on the spirit of antiquity implies that his own spirit is that of modernity. But it further suggests that he can take on a spirit other than his own, and thereby understand the spirit of the ancients. Thus, he presents himself as someone who can see the modern

---

29. Cf. Warner, "Montesquieu's Prelude": "Montesquieu's two statements about the *differences* of things turn out to be statements that themselves are strikingly *similar* to each other: the two statements only *seem* markedly to differ, but they are in fact almost identical. While cleverly *telling* us twice to be aware of real differences amidst apparent similarities, what Montesquieu is *doing* is presenting us with a real similarity amidst apparent differences. Here we have the epitome of irony—a discrepancy between what

world through ancient lenses, and see the ancient world through modern lenses. Nothing human is occluded from his gaze because he is capable of alienating himself from the modern world, thus stripping away his own particularity. Like Herodotus, and unlike Gyges, Montesquieu is capable and willing to see that which is not his own (cf. Hdt. 1.9–13).[30]

What Montesquieu seems to suggest he is able to see is that the ancient and modern worlds are *really* different; and part of the effort of *The Spirit of Laws* is directed to uncovering and articulating some of these differences. Nevertheless, this last point does not explain why Montesquieu says twice what he could have said just once. This suggests that he is making a second point, a point concerning cases that *appear* similar but are *really* different, and I take it that these cases are entirely modern ones. Montesquieu is saying, among other things, that it is easy to confuse his book with the books of moderns that have come before his; apparent similarities thus will strike the reader immediately, but the careful reader will be able to take cognizance of the less than apparent differences. To this analysis, a particular question suggests itself: who or what called Montesquieu back to antiquity, and why?

In addition to being concerned with philosophy and politics, the testimony of an almost endless parade of historical examples throughout the course of the book[31] reveals a preoccupation with history itself. The idea that history is critical to the teaching of the book is first expressed in the fourth paragraph of the Preface.

> I have laid down the principles, and I have seen the particular cases conform to them as if by themselves—the histories of all nations being but the results of them, and each particular law bound to another law or dependent on another one more general. (Pref. 4)

Earlier, we looked all too quickly at the sixth paragraph of the Preface, where Montesquieu tells us that his principles came from nature, and not

---

Montesquieu says and what he does—and we should be ever so mindful of the possibility that irony is lurking in many other places in the work as well" (161).

30. Also in this context consider our earlier mention of Machiavelli's landscape artist.

31. With the important exception of the opening book of the work.

his prejudices. Now, in the light of the fourth paragraph, we are able to ascertain that nature itself—human and otherwise—furnishes the ground of the movement of history. In ascertaining this, we are in a position to see just how startling a claim Montesquieu is making. For in addition to *The Spirit of Laws* being political philosophy in the broadest sense of the term, it also presents itself as some kind of philosophy of history,[32] able to explain and trace the course of all nations.[33] Montesquieu obviously takes seriously the idea that human beings are ineluctably historical beings, and thus linked to time and place. An understanding of this can only be animated and furthered by an understanding of Montesquieu's principles.

However, not only does he not tell us explicitly anywhere in *The Spirit of Laws* what those principles are,[34] but also he does not even stop to tell us what he means by "principles." Here we can loosely assert that by principles he means the causes of the human phenomena that he seeks to explain, but it is more than likely true that by principles he means a high-order type of cause, and so at some point we would need to indicate at what level of abstraction these principles are to be found. As part of that analysis it would have to be shown that, for Montesquieu, history is not determined and unilinear. Furthermore, the central role of revolution in Montesquieu's vision of history would have to be unveiled.[35] What *can* be said at this point is that, beginning with book two, the dizzying array of historical examples that Montesquieu sets before the reader should be understood as the concrete manifestations that bear witness to his principles. What *must* be said here in the light of our discussion of paragraphs three, four, and five is that *The Spirit of Laws* should be seen as following the twin trajectories of nature and history, and in so doing, raising the fundamental question of what the relationship between these two is.

---

32. Cf. Catherine H. Zuckert, "At the Core of the Social Sciences: Montesquieu's *Spirit of the Laws*," in *Uniting the Liberal Arts: Core and Context*, ed. Bainard Cowan and Scott Lee (Lanham, MD: University Press of America, 2002), 102–12.

33. The important modern book to which Montesquieu's must be compared here is Vico's *New Science*.

34. Unless of course these principles are the principles Montesquieu discusses at the beginning of bk. 3, about which I am skeptical.

35. Cf., for example, *The Spirit of Laws*, bk. 21.

Throughout the Preface, things being hidden has been a pervasive theme.[36] In the most obvious cases, Montesquieu himself is hiding things, for example, the design of the book. Perhaps this is tied to his deep concern about matters of censorship. But viewed under the horizon of various remarks he makes about writing in his *Pensées*, it would appear that Montesquieu understands that the philosophical enterprise furnishes reasons in itself for keeping things hidden from the reader.[37] And there seems to be yet another source of this necessity, and that is the elusive, hidden character of nature itself. This issue must be raised because Montesquieu raises it. His desire to provide a circumstance in which individuals can cure their deepest prejudice is a desire to reveal something profound about human nature, a nature that can be virtually hidden from us. The fundamental question to ask in this regard is whether the cause of nature's being hidden lies in us or in nature itself. If it lies in us, then some kind of Enlightenment philosophical or political project holds some promise. However, if nature hides itself, then perhaps no enlightenment will be able substantially to ameliorate that feature of the human condition that renders us ignorant of ourselves. The alternatives in this regard are either political esotericism or metaphysical esotericism.[38] These alternatives are profoundly connected to the problem of nature and history adumbrated above.

In a certain fashion, what Montesquieu does not keep hidden in his Preface is himself, as he appeals to himself—I, me, my—no fewer than forty-two times. Curiously, the Preface is a most personal piece of writing.[39] In this regard, it begins with birth—Montesquieu's own—and ends

---

36. Cf. the second, fifth, seventh, thirteenth, and fourteenth paragraphs, for example.

37. For example: "When a work is systematic, it is necessary also to be sure that you have grasped the entire system well. Look at a great machine made in order to produce an effect. You see wheels that turn in opposite directions; you believe upon first glance that the machine was going to destroy itself; that all the wheels were going to hinder each other; that the machine was going to come to a standstill. It goes all the same: these parts, which appear at first to destroy each other, unite together for the proposed object" (*Pensées*, N° 2092).

38. On this distinction, cf. Seth Benardete, "Strauss on Plato," in *The Argument of the Action: Essays on Greek Poetry and Philosophy*, ed. with an introduction by Ronna Burger and Michael Davis (Chicago: University of Chicago Press, 2000), 409.

39. Montesquieu's name does not appear on the title page of any edition of *De l'esprit des lois* published in his lifetime. Nevertheless, *The Spirit of Laws* was immediately known

with birth—Montesquieu's child, *The Spirit of Laws*. When the nearly blind Montesquieu writes of his book coming to an end, one feels the unsettling pathos of a man's reflection that his life too is coming to an end. Of course, in the most important senses, his book and its influence were only just beginning.[40]

---

to be authored by him. Interestingly, Montesquieu's name does not even appear on the title pages of the 1757 edition, but D'Alembert's *Éloge de Montesquieu* is included in the first volume of that edition.

40. This essay is dedicated to Ronna Burger, a singular wayfarer. The author is deeply grateful to Svetozar Minkov for his ceaseless inspiration. He is indebted to various conversations with Stéphane Douard, Ralph Lerner, Thomas Merrill, and Andrea Radasanu, and to Josh Parens and the University of Dallas for an invitation to speak about *The Spirit of Laws* in the Spring of 2018. He is also thankful for the continued support of Roosevelt University, especially the support of his chair, Gina Buccola, and his dean, Bonnie Gunzenhauser.

16

Entering the Native Realm of Truth: The Advent of Self-Consciousness in Hegel's *Phenomenology of Spirit*

Robert Berman

I. Introduction

Hegel's 1807 *Phenomenology of Spirit*,[1] still the most-studied of the four books published during his lifetime, is celebrated for inviting the reader in with its wealth of concrete content, drawn from the full breadth and depth of human experience as well as from historical, literary, and philosophic traditions, mainly of the West. While excluding virtually nothing

---

One evening in July '77, exactly forty years ago, when the New York City blackout plunged our sixth-floor walk-up into pitch black, Ronna, ever resourceful, found candles and matches, and we passed some of the wee hours talking about Hegel's monumental philosophic *Bildungsroman*. This essay, reaching her now, is a late arrival, reflecting the starlight of its beginnings in the flickering flames of the wax lamps she lit on that eerie, adventuresome night four decades ago.

1. Throughout this essay, references to Hegel's *Phenomenology of Spirit* of 1807 use the italicized abbreviation "*Phenomenology*." Citations give the page numbers both from G.W.F. Hegel, *Phenomenology of Spirit*, trans. A.V. Miller (Oxford: Oxford University Press, 1977) and the German text, G.W.F. Hegel, *Die Phänomenologie des Geistes*, in *Werke in zwanzig Bänden*, ed. Eva Moldenhauer and Karl Markus Michel, vol. 3 (Frankfurt am Main: Suhrkamp, 1970). "M" abbreviates Miller's English translation, and "MM" the German Moldenhauer and Michel edition. Thus, citations will appear as follows: M; MM. In some cases I have modified Miller's English translation.

belonging to human existence—from simple sensory experience to religious faith and practice and all that lies between—access nevertheless remains notoriously difficult, owing to its single-minded preoccupation with fundamental questions of metaphysics concerning knowledge, truth, and being, formulated in the abstract vocabulary bequeathed by the philosophic tradition. These features of the work are clearly manifest in the fourth chapter, the central one of the three main sections of the book.[2]

Chapter IV plays the pivotal role in securing the unity of the *Phenomenology*'s single line of reasoning, which runs like a red thread through all of its eight chapters, by linking the shorter argument of the first three chapters with the vastly longer argument of the last four. As the locus of Hegel's phenomenological account of self-consciousness, the fourth chapter ushers in the shift from a broad investigation of knowledge to the more restricted focus on the question of self-knowledge, which becomes the abiding concern of the inquiry. At the same time, Chapter IV has attracted readers' attention with its memorable vignettes of the life-and-death struggle for recognition and the lord-servant relation. Though descriptively spare, those portrayals have had an outsized influence in the history of the reception of the book, thanks in large part to the interpretation of

---

2. The table of contents of the *Phenomenology* shows a three-level arrangement: There are eight chapters enumerated with Roman numerals; three divisions, each designated by a single capital letter—A. Consciousness, B. Self-Consciousness, and C. Reason; and four subsections of the Reason division, AA. Reason, BB. Spirit, CC. Religion, and DD. Absolute Knowing. Each of the eight chapters is assigned to a division, with the first three belonging to division A, the fourth alone to division B, and the remaining four chapters to division C. Uniquely in this tripartite scheme, the term "reason" does triple duty: It serves simultaneously as the title of the third division, the fifth chapter, the division's first, and of the first double-letter subsection.

Of the 435 pages of the Miller translation, the first two of the three divisions, which contain half the chapters, take up merely 79 pages, no more than a fifth of the total number of pages. This organization of the contents reflects the three-stage argument of the *Phenomenology* as a whole: It moves from the short argument of A to the long argument of C by way of the pivotal link provided by B.

That approximately 80 percent of the book is devoted to the analysis of the four-fold character of Reason is a further indication that Hegel intends his phenomenological approach to stand as an alternative to the Kantian critique of reason.

this material first sketched in unpublished writings of the young Marx and later developed by his followers, especially Kojève.[3]

The point of entry into the *Phenomenology* provided by the Marxist reception of Chapter IV might seem to justify an interpretation through the lens of anthropology and politics, which ignores or downplays the animating problem of knowledge at the heart of the work. If, however, the aim is to recover Hegel's original phenomenological intention, one has to go back behind the Marxist interpretation and highlight the linchpin function that Chapter IV performs in the larger argumentative whole: having exposed the irremediable incapacity of self-consciousness to measure up to the standard of self-knowledge it has inherited as the outcome of the preceding investigation, the chapter prepares for the rest of the inquiry by introducing the concept of spirit, which indicates the direction consciousness will need to follow if it is to have any chance of achieving its epistemic goal.[4] It is this greater purpose that dictates Hegel's choice and characterization of the well-known contents of Chapter IV—the preparatory discussion of life and desire, the pithy first formulation of the signature Hegelian concept of spirit (*Geist*), the celebrated descriptions of the life-and-death struggle for recognition, the dynamic reversals of the lord-servant relation, and the travails of the unhappy consciousness with which the chapter concludes.

---

3. This tradition of the reception of the *Phenomenology* began with Marx, whose notebooks from the 1840s—first made public in 1927 and now known as the *Economic and Philosophic Manuscripts of 1844* (also as the *Paris Manuscripts*)—document his reading of the *Phenomenology*, which concentrates its attention almost solely on the subsection of Chapter IV dealing with the lord-servant relation. This tradition culminates in Alexandre Kojève's influential lectures on Hegel in the decade following the publication of Marx's early writings. Excerpts from the 1947 French publication of Kojève's lectures, which contain his lecture notes together with some of their transcriptions, were translated into English and published shortly after Kojève's death in May 1968. See Alexandre Kojève, *Introduction to the Reading of Hegel*, trans. James H. Nichols, ed. Allan Bloom (New York: Basic Books, 1969).

4. This alternative approach is outlined in some detail in my "Self-Knowledge on Trial: A Vest-Pocket Guide to the Argument of Hegel's *Phenomenology of Spirit*," in *Writing the Poetic Soul of Philosophy: Essays in Honor of Michael Davis*, ed. Denise Schaeffer (South Bend, IN: St. Augustine's Press, forthcoming).

II. Before Entering: The Phenomenological Turn

If, as Hegel indicates, the *Phenomenology* is intended to serve as an introduction to a system of philosophic science[5]—why is that needed? The source of the need Hegel perceives can be traced to his heeding Kant's urgent call to decide once and for all the question of the very possibility of philosophy as metaphysics[6]—the ascent from opinion to comprehensive knowledge of the whole and of the highest being by means of unaided reason alone, dependent neither upon divine revelation nor empirical evidence. Kant reasons from the evident discrepancy between natural science and metaphysics: mathematical physics has made impressive advances in penetrating the secret lawful connections of nature, while metaphysics or first philosophy remains mired in intractable disagreements concerning both method and substance, which encourages the radical suspicion that philosophy is a quixotic quest. The goal that has traditionally animated lovers of wisdom, establishing metaphysics as a systematic science of being, looks to be in principle unattainable. It is this crisis of philosophy, the problem of metaphysics as identified by Kant, that motivates Hegel's phenomenological turn and forms the skeptical horizon of the project.[7]

To query the possibility of metaphysics without begging the question, the inquiry will have to be resolutely nonmetaphysical,[8] and this will

---

5. For Hegel's comment in the *Phenomenology* concerning its system-theoretical role, see its Preface, M: 20; MM: 38–39. For some discussion of this passage and related statements in the introductory portions of Hegel's *Science of Logic*, see, most recently, Richard Dien Winfield, *Hegel's "Science of Logic": A Critical Rethinking in Thirty Lectures* (Lanham, MD: Rowman & Littlefield, 2012), 36–43, which also includes citation and discussion of William Maker's earlier work on this issue in his *Philosophy without Foundations: Rethinking Hegel* (Albany: State University of New York Press, 1994).

6. Immanuel Kant, *Prolegomena to Any Future Metaphysics*, trans. and ed. Gary Hatfield, rev. ed. (Cambridge: Cambridge University Press, 2004), 5. For a recent discussion that reconstructs the philosophic connection between Kant's critical project and Hegel's *Phenomenology*, see Eckhart Förster, *The Twenty-Five Years of Philosophy: A Systematic Reconstruction*, trans. Brady Bowman (Cambridge, MA: Harvard University Press, 2012).

7. In the Introduction to the *Phenomenology* Hegel speaks of presenting the way of doubt (*Zweifel*), despair (*Verzweiflung*), and thoroughgoing skepticism (*vollbringende Skeptizismus*). M: 50; MM: 72.

8. The earliest reference to Hegel's "nonmetaphysical" intention for his systematic conception of philosophy as science is to be found, as far as I know, in Klaus Hartmann,

require an innovation in philosophy. Hegel rejects the transcendental philosophy devised by Kant precisely in order to carry out a critique of pure reason on the grounds that it violates the *petitio* prohibition by harboring residual metaphysical commitments. To avoid such a logical short-circuiting of the inquiry, Hegel makes his innovative turn by having recourse to the ancient tradition of Socratic elenchus. Adopting this stance, the philosopher, while refraining from offering knowledge claims or criteria of epistemic assessment of his own, examines whether his interlocutor is able to defend the truth of his own opinion by applying standards he himself is willing to accept. Hegel tailors this Socratic practice to fit the form of a thought-experiment that will make it possible to assess the prospects of metaphysics without having to practice it.[9] His strategy is to ask, and to observe a series of responses to this question: How would a philosopher dedicated to achieving metaphysical knowledge go about attaining his goal?[10]

"Hegel: A Non-Metaphysical View," in *Hegel: A Collection of Critical Essays*, ed. Alasdair MacIntyre (Notre Dame, IN: Notre Dame Press, 1972), 101–24.

9. On the maieutic image of elenchus and Socrates' account of his role as midwife, see Plato, *Tht.* 150b6–151b6.

    Hegel's own study of the tradition of ancient skepticism, which can be traced ultimately to its Socratic origins, made him acutely aware of the need to steer clear of the error of self-referential inconsistency that often afflicts skeptical doubts about metaphysics, of concluding from one's pretension to know the nature of human mind and knowledge that no human being can attain metaphysical knowledge. Hegel adopts his phenomenological stance to avoid this basic logical difficulty. See the Introduction to the *Phenomenology* (M: 46–49; MM: 68–72) for Hegel's considerations concerning epistemology that lead him to make his phenomenological turn. For Hegel's reception of ancient skepticism and its importance to his philosophic thought, see Michael N. Forster, *Hegel and Skepticism* (Cambridge, MA: Harvard University Press, 1989) and more recently, Dietmar H. Heidemann, *Der Begriff des Skeptizismus: Seine systematischen Formen, die pyrrhonische Skepsis und Hegels Herausforderung* (Berlin: Walter de Gruyter, 2007).

10. Hegel's phenomenological approach to Kant's urgent question is Socratic, then, in this one decisive respect: The Platonic Socrates can draw upon his dialogue partner's own operative standards to test the viability of the interlocutor's opinion without having to make any such epistemic commitments of his own. Whether it may be designated as elenchus or maieutics, this Socratic hoisting of the interlocutor on his own petard is an exercise in immanent criticism. Hegel's phenomenological investigation of the prospects of the metaphysical quest adopts this Socratic style of criticism, albeit not in the dramatic form of dialogue. For his nonmetaphysical inquiry, Hegel envisions

To maintain the bright line of demarcation between actor and spectator, Hegel envisions an investigation structured around a set of interrelated conditions. The aspirant to metaphysical knowledge will furnish his own criterion of epistemic success and assess his own efforts by applying his self-fashioned standard to himself. He can rightfully claim success if he measures up by his own lights and in the event of any failure, he will be able to continue as long as more than one path is open to him to attain the sought-for knowledge.[11] Finally, if he fails at every turn, and exhausts the limited number of paths available, he must concede the conclusion that metaphysics is unattainable. Hegel calls the epistemic agent engaged in this project "consciousness."[12] With that label, he designates an oppositional structure of cognition, based on what one might call a principle of realism: while cognition necessarily involves a relation to an object, the object is independent of and indifferent to that relation. The object is a thing in itself. It is essential that the aspiring philosopher of Hegel's thought-experiment be committed to realism, according to this understanding.[13]

---

an epistemic agent endeavoring to attain metaphysics, and affords him all the conceptual equipment he needs to embark on his project.

11. Thus, the candidate metaphysician has to undertake a first-person epistemic self-evaluation. Otherwise, the line of demarcation separating him from the phenomenological observer will be broken, undercutting the investigation. Hegel explains this crucial requirement governing his inquiry with admirable clarity and concision, using only a few paragraphs of his already brief, but indispensable eleven-page Introduction to the *Phenomenology*. See M: 52–54; MM: 75–78.

12. Hegel also uses the expression "natural consciousness" (M: 49; MM: 72), for example, but for convenience and brevity I am shortening it to "consciousness," since, as it seems to me, in the context of the *Phenomenology* Hegel uses the two expressions as notational variants.

13. With his comment on Kant's conception of the "Ding an sich" in the Bremen Lectures of 1949, Heidegger indicates that Kant operates with this idea of the object as it is in itself: "Das Ding an sich bedeutet für Kant: der Gegenstand an sich. Der Charakter des 'Ansich' besagt für Kant, daß der Gegenstand an sich Gegenstand ist ohne die Beziehung auf das menschliche Vorstellen, d.h., ohne das 'Gegen,' wodurch er für dieses Vorstellen allererst steht. 'Ding an sich' bedeutet, streng kritisch gedacht, einen Gegenstand, der keiner ist, weil er stehen soll ohne ein mögliches Gegen für das menschliche Vorstellen, das ihm entgegnet." Martin Heidegger, *Gesamtausgabe*, ed. Petra Jaeger, vol. 79, *Bremer und Freiburger Vorträge* (Frankfurt am Main: Klostermann, 1994), 16. Nowadays, this construal of the object as in itself—originally Kant's thing in itself of "transcendental realism"—is sometimes conveyed by expressions such as "mind-independence," "meta-

The principle of realism is built into the standard of success with which consciousness operates, that is, the traditional conception of knowledge as justified true belief. A belief is true when it accurately represents or corresponds to the object as it truly is, independent of its being known. And evidence of such correspondence, which must be accessible to consciousness, is what justifies the true belief. (Cf. Plato, *Tht.* 201b7–202c7.) Thus, metaphysical knowledge will require the aspiring philosopher of the thought-experiment to establish the truth of two self-ascriptive judgments. First, if he is to show that the class of metaphysical knowers is not a null set, he must have evidence about his own belief sufficient to warrant his claim that it accurately represents the object as it is in itself. Secondly, once he arrives at this self-knowledge about his belief, he has all the justification he needs to declare himself a charter member of that elite class.

In the course of the short argument that comprises the first three chapters of the *Phenomenology*, consciousness is shown arriving at the realization that it can never gain access to the truth of its object as it has preconceived it. It is led to the recognition, bespeaking Kant's Copernicanism, that the object it presumes to represent as it really is, entirely independent of the cognitive relation, is in fact the product of its own theoretical construction. For what it encounters is unavoidably "theory-laden," mediated by its own perceptual and conceptual cognition. Consciousness is thus compelled to conclude that knowledge, if attainable, must take the form of self-knowledge. The significance of this shift of focus to self-knowledge is revealed by the announcement at the beginning of the second paragraph of Chapter IV that "we have now entered the native realm [*einheimische Reich*] of truth."[14]

From this point forward, consciousness is committed to establishing that there is no objective truth other than itself, and correlatively, that its governing aim is to know nothing but itself. However, as consciousness, it cannot jettison the structural assumption that the objective reality it claims it knows is, given the principle of realism, other than itself, indifferent to

---

physical realism," or most simply, "realism." If we use "realism" to designate the view that the property of being in such an epistemic relation is a contingent relational property of what is to be known, then Hegelian phenomenology is concerned with investigating the prospects of the metaphysical quest characterized by its unquestioned commitment to realism.

14. M: 104; MM: 138.

its being known. The logical tension between these two underlying premises is key to interpreting the contents of Chapter IV, explaining why self-knowledge cannot be achieved in the shape of self-consciousness, why Chapter IV is transitional, and finally why Hegel's phenomenological thought-experiment will have to move beyond self-consciousness to examine the metaphysics of self-knowledge in the superior guise of reason. Because the narrowing turn to self-knowledge at the conclusion of the short argument has coincided with the advent of Hegel's treatment of self-consciousness, it seems that he identifies the two. Yet, this identity is belied by the need for the longer argument. Evidently, there is something about self-consciousness that is necessary but not sufficient for the self-knowledge required to satisfy the metaphysical aspirant's standard of success.

III. On the Way to Entry: The Short Argument

Hegel speaks of a "shape" of consciousness in describing each unique attempt in the series of its efforts to conform to its self-imposed standard of success.[15] Like all shapes of consciousness, sense-certainty, perception, and understanding, treated in Chapters I–III, respectively, are defined by distinct theories of truth, i.e., of the object as it is in itself. Notwithstanding their differences, these three shapes share an assumption that comes to light in Hegel's retrospective glance from the vantage point of self-consciousness, namely, the idea that the truth is to be found in what is other than consciousness.[16]

While failing to establish their respective knowledge claims, each sub-shape scrutinized in the short argument manages to contribute crucial premises necessary for the concluding shift to self-consciousness. The first, sense-certainty, construing truth as simple immediacy, holds that the object excludes all mediating factors, including all nonrelational as well as rela-

---

15. M: 21, 50, 51; MM: 38, 73, 74. Hegel uses the terms *"Gestalt"* and *"Gestaltung,"* which Miller often but not always renders with "shape" and "configuration," respectively. A shape of consciousness must be distinguished from the set of formal features that we can call the "form of consciousness," which defines Hegel's unique phenomenological conception of consciousness as it is spelled out in his Introduction (text cited in n. 12 above). This single underlying form of consciousness contrasts with the plurality of shapes of consciousness that will pass in review.

16. M:104; MM:137.

tional properties. Its commitment to immediacy implies its belief that knowledge of the object is direct, not dependent upon any special cognitive contribution of its own—thoughts, concepts, or representations of any sort. Precisely because sense-certainty endorses this most rudimentary of all possible conceptions of truth and knowledge—however indefensible it will turn out to be—it is the first shape of consciousness. Owing to the unsurpassable simplicity of its theory of truth, sense-certainty's contribution to the short argument is two-fold. Negatively, its epistemic failure eliminates from eligibility its preconceived theory of truth. On the positive side of the ledger, though, its failure proves the indispensability of universality and hence of mediation as a bare-minimum ingredient of any plausible theory of truth that consciousness might propose.[17]

Perceptual consciousness, whose object it construes as a thing of many properties, endorses universality as its theory of truth, although in continuity with sense-certainty it still presumes real knowledge to consist in a sensory encounter with a given multi-faceted object. For this reason per-

---

17. A note of clarification seems in order regarding Hegel's use of "universality" (*Allgemeinheit*) and its cognates throughout his treatment of the three sub-shapes of division A: Consciousness. Generically, universality is about the one/many relation, but the generic one/many relation turns out to have several distinct species: first, the set-theoretical conception involving the class characteristic/class member relation; secondly, the part/whole relation; thirdly, the substance/mode relation; and finally, the relation between opposites or contraries. In sense-certainty, the set-theoretical and whole-part species take center-stage, the former arising from the role that language plays in operating with both singular and general terms, the whole/part conception due to the temporal moments and spatial locations to which consciousness intends to refer in its attempts to establish singular reference to its spatio-temporal object in obedience to the strictures of immediacy, hence without the mediation-saturated benefit of language. The substance/mode or accident relation appears on the scene with the thing and its many properties, the object of perception. The relation between opposites makes its entrance initially with the distinction, introduced by perception, between being for itself and being for another. Understanding, the third and final shape of consciousness prior to self-consciousness, carries this distinction forward under the label of "unconditioned universality" and employs it to conceptualize its object, force. Thus, understanding distinguishes between force expressed and force repressed or withdrawn, in which each entails the other so that each already contains the reference to the other within itself, thus forming a unity of both. In conceptualizing the laws that govern force, understanding generalizes this relation of mutual entailment to arrive at the idea of inner difference, which is labeled "infinity."

ceptual consciousness only recognizes what Hegel calls "conditioned universality," for the universality of perception is still infected with the assumption taken over from sense-certainty.[18] Nevertheless, through its adherence to universality, perception supplies several premises needed for the derivation of self-consciousness. Perceptual consciousness infers from the principle of universality that its sensory encounters with the immediately given are vulnerable to misperception; hence it introduces the distinction between what merely seems to it and what really is. In this context Hegel inserts for the first time the idea of reflection: If consciousness is to perceive truly, it must arrive at its veridical perception by discounting the way the thing merely seems to be, which it assumes to reflect its own cognitive contribution. It must, therefore, subtract from the object as it really is whatever extraneous additions it discovers that its cognition imposes. Perceptual consciousness recognizes the distinction between two modes of cognition, sensory perception and conceptualization, and it explicitly acknowledges the role the latter plays in mediating its sensory encounter with the property-laden thing. Finally, to account for the individuation of the thing, perception distinguishes between essential and accidental properties. However, if a thing's essential constitution is what differentiates it from other likewise individuated things, then it must also be acknowledged that what things are in themselves depends essentially on their reciprocal relations to one another. The formal concepts of being for itself and being for an other are intertwined in a correlated unity, which Hegel designates as "unconditioned universality" to indicate that in this one-many relation there is no logical space left in the theory of truth for any residual immediacy.[19]

---

18. M: 76; MM: 105. Operating with the idea of conditioned universality, perception oscillates back and forth between the substance/mode relation, according to which the many properties inhere in the thing as their underlying unity, and the whole/part relation, according to which the thing is a whole constituted by properties that are thought to be independent parts, as bricks are to a wall.

19. In the same paragraph, only a few lines after he speaks of conditioned universality, Hegel first introduces the contrasting expression "unconditioned universality" (M: 77; MM: 105). This comes in preparation for the transition to the third subshape, understanding, whose guiding theory of truth will go by this name. See M: 79; MM: 107.

The short argument culminates with the examination of understanding, the shape that conceives its object as the force underlying and lawfully governing perceived things, holding that force, as the truth, instantiates unconditioned universality. Understanding thus sets up a dichotomy between the world of appearances, the entirety of things given to perception, and the inner, supersensible world of force knowable, if at all, solely by conceptual means alone. Real knowing, accordingly, consists in conceptual cognition, not sensory perception, just as the objective truth to be known is a theoretical rather than an observable entity. On the premise that the totality of perceptible objects has no independent being of its own, but is rather the product of the inner, supersensible force,[20] the goal of understanding is causal explanation: appearances are the law-governed effects of non-apparent force functioning as their causal ground.

Because understanding construes truth as unconditioned universality, no factor operating in the supersensible world can be left indifferent to and unmediated by relations to other such factors, which equally entail reciprocal interaction.[21] Yet, as consciousness, understanding is at the same time subject to the structural assumption that objective truth, here the supersensible world of force, has the ontological status of being in itself, indifferent to, hence not essentially, but only contingently mediated

---

The Platonic Socrates, it appears, first articulated the idea of unconditioned universality, which Hegel will reformulate later in Chapter III as the principle of inner difference, i.e., infinity (see n. 24 below). Cf. Plato, *Tht.* 156a3-157c2.

20. This is not simply a notational variant of the seems/is distinction recognized by perception; for that distinction is marked by the contrast between what pertains only to perception's own reflection and what is intrinsic to the object in itself, the truth that perception claims it can actually come to perceive.

By implication, understanding insinuates into its conceptual repertoire the ground/grounded distinction, and maps onto it the epistemic distinction it deploys between *explanans/explanandum*.

21. It is not sufficient for understanding to declare, as perception already was forced to acknowledge, that its guiding principle is at work in the sensory world of appearances populated by things and their properties exhibiting "the play of forces" (M: 87; MM: 116). The supersensible world must also exhibit the character of unconditioned universality. This explains why it finally reveals itself to understanding as an "inverted world" (M: 95-96; MM: 127-28).

by relation to another. In effect, therefore, understanding inconsistently holds that what is in itself does not have the character of in-itselfness.[22]

Hegel reformulates unconditioned universality as the principle of inner difference (which, for several reasons, he labels "infinity"), to set it off from the indifferent difference that defines in-itselfness. He repeatedly characterizes inner difference as "the difference that is no difference" to indicate that it is in a unity with its other, hence a one that is already a two and a two that is always already a one. This marks the most significant contribution understanding makes to the short argument. The principle of inner difference puts the lie to the assumption shared by all three shapes examined in the short argument, namely that objective truth must be sought in what is other than consciousness. Face to face with infinity, understanding is forced to reject this assumption about the locus of truth. Implicit in this repudiation is the affirmative claim that the epistemic relation to the objective truth must also conform to the strictures of inner difference.[23] Consequently, the quest for knowledge must now be reconceived

---

22. The difficulty for understanding is that if it applies the principle of inner difference, as it must, to the inner, supersensible causal ground of appearances, then the inner must itself display thoroughgoing mediation, but in doing so it loses its character as unmediated ground. To avoid this implication, understanding tries to confine the application of the principle of inner difference to explanation, i.e., to its own reflection, leaving the inner free of inner difference. This is but a momentary stop-gap, however, since if inner difference is confined to explanation, the inner, supersensible world has no determinate character of its own, with two devastating implications. If it is thus indeterminate, not only can it not play the role of causally-determining, law-governed ground of appearance; even worse, there will be no determinate truth to be known. Thus, understanding must grant that inner difference does in fact apply to the real, inner supersensible world if it is to avoid abandoning its claim to know. But conceding this means that its object forfeits its presumptive status as what is true or in itself.

23. M: 99; MM: 131. Hegel explicitly introduces the expression "infinity" in order to capture in a word that which provides, thanks to understanding's dilemma, a principle of unity in opposition: unity in opposition implies a one that is already a two and a two that is always already a one. It implies difference that, because it is an opposite or contrary, is what it is in virtue of not being what it is not. Its relation to its other is essential, and so an inner difference cannot be indifferent to that contrastive relation. A difference that can be indifferent is what we can call an indifferent difference. Consequently, Hegel's formula that with infinity we have "a difference that is no difference," can be restated so that it means simply that the difference of infinity is inner difference, not indifferent difference.

as tantamount to the search for self-knowledge. This completes the short argument and underwrites the transition to the new shape of self-consciousness. Since infinity threatens the very idea of consciousness, whose structure of opposition includes indifferent difference as an essential feature, the thought-experiment will have to proceed by tolerating their mutual exclusivity, at least provisionally, until the epistemic agent discovers how to square the circle or acknowledges that an assault on the peak of metaphysics, undertaken under the auspices of consciousness, is doomed to defeat.

IV. Inside the Native Realm of Truth

As the outcome of what has preceded in the short argument, the successor shape of self-consciousness is path-dependent: the relation to its predecessor shapes is much the same as the relation that the conclusion of a deductive argument has to its premises. To do justice to this path-dependence, Hegel has self-consciousness, en route to establishing self-knowledge, enact the falsification of the previous shapes' shared assumption about objective truth while being guided by its own alternative conception. For this reason the object of self-consciousness must be doubled. Consciousness relates both to what is other than itself and to itself, the one home of truth. Thus, like the previous shapes, all of which are object-related, self-consciousness, too, relates to an objective domain. Because the principle of inner difference is operative, however, self-consciousness encounters not merely—and not merely theoretically—physicochemical objects, otherwise inert, propertied things whose law-governed motions are externally generated by the play of forces, but also individual instances of what Hegel calls "life."[24] Instantiat-

---

This structural principle of infinity is understanding's most important contribution, because it undermines the assumption understanding shares with its two preceding brethren shapes—that its object harbors no determinacy fundamentally at odds with its putative status as truth or unmediated in itself. It carries an even more explosive implication: it denies the basic assumption anchored in the oppositional structure of consciousness, namely that the truth that consciousness claims to know is indifferently different to that cognitive relation.

24. As an object immediately given to itself, self-consciousness belongs to the sphere of life as a living thing, thus subject to all the vicissitudes of the dynamic life process. But the world of life is not a life-world, if by the latter one has in mind a *geistige Welt*, i.e., a network of socio-economic, political, and cultural interrelations among self-

ing inner difference, living things are entities whose organs are the functioning parts of self-organizing wholes, self-moving organisms that relate both to objects in the inorganic realm as well as to other organisms. Living things come to be and pass away as modes of an all-encompassing, hence cosmic environmental system that itself exhibits the dynamics of the inner difference by comprehending both the physicochemical and the biological aspects of objectivity.

Since consciousness in its new shape claims self-knowledge, it takes itself to be an object and, therefore, to belong to the totalizing sphere of life as one of its denizens. Yet, this new shape is founded on the falsity of the assumption that the entire sphere of objectivity accessible to perception and understanding is where truth is to be found. With this alethic demotion, the object of self-knowledge cannot be sought in the natural sphere of life. Self-knowledge requires another kind of object that transcends the otherness comprising the domain of life.

Correlative to the doubling of the object of self-consciousness is the distinction Hegel introduces between desire and its satisfaction. Objects encountered through perception and understanding in the sphere of life are desired by self-consciousness; they are not objects of sheer contemplation. These objects of desire, however, are precisely those which self-consciousness takes to be other than itself and for that very reason not the locus of truth. Only an object that self-consciousness knows to be itself can satisfy its desire. Thus, the task before it is to demonstrate success in actually meeting up with such an object. But that places self-consciousness before the following difficulty. As desire, it must acknowledge the object as other, while its attitude toward the desired object must be utterly negative, since it is not the truth. Yet, as self-consciousness, it claims to have no other object before it but itself and to know itself, rather than something other, to be the objective truth. It must, therefore, eliminate the object of immediate desire in order to prove that such an object is neither itself nor true. It can try to effect this elimination in one of two ways. It can opt to annihilate the desired object altogether and thus show that there is no candidate vying against

---

conscious individuals and groups of such individuals, mediated by artifacts and constituted by practices whose rules (*nomoi* or laws) define the social roles and thus the individuals whose identities are determined by those roles.

itself for the status of objective truth.[25] Yet, this strategy of elimination is self-defeating. For the desire relation is a necessary condition of self-consciousness, and to annihilate the desired object would amount to destroying that relation; success would undermine self-consciousness itself.[26]

The other option available to self-consciousness is elimination without annihilation. To accomplish this, consciousness must desire an object that as desired is other, yet gain the satisfaction of self-knowledge in the object in virtue of knowing the object as itself. How, if at all, can self-consciousness consistently satisfy both of these seemingly mutually exclusive demands?

It can do so, Hegel argues, but only on one condition: the desired object must be another self-consciousness. For in that unique case alone, the object of its desire is, as its object, other, but as self-consciousness, another instance of the same kind as itself. Self-consciousness can conform to this double requirement of desire and self-knowledge if it is numerically different from its desired object, an other self-consciousness, but not eidetically different, that is, not different from it in kind.[27] The double requirement echoes the formulations Hegel offers to articulate the concept of spirit (*Geist*)—introduced into the argument here for the first time—as reciprocal recognition, as infinity realizing itself in self-consciousness and, most concretely, as "the I that is We" and "the We that is I."[28] If it is to actualize self-knowledge, self-consciousness must assume the character of a class member who knows

---

25. By destroying all other competitors for truth, it recapitulates the dynamic of the predecessor shapes of consciousness, whose failure to establish their claims to know the truth has led directly to self-consciousness.

26. M: 109; MM: 143: "Desire and the self-certainty obtained in its satisfaction are conditioned by its object; for self-certainty is through sublating (*Aufheben*) of this other: that the sublating might be, this other must be."

27. For the thesis that this idea of a numerically differentiated instance of same kind reconstructs Hegel's account of individuality in his *Science of Logic*, see my "Ways of Being Singular: The Logic of Individuality," in *Hegel's Theory of the Subject*, ed. David Gray Carlson (London: Palgrave Macmillan, 2005), 85–98.

28. M: 110; MM: 145. The thesis (mentioned in n. 28) about Hegel's logical concept of individuality entails that strictly speaking the spiritual I must be an individual.

Hegel explicitly invokes the principle of infinity right after introducing the concept of spirit when he writes that the concept of the unity of self-consciousness with itself in its duplication is the concept "of infinity realizing itself in self-consciousness." See M: 111; MM: 145.

his class characteristic as instantiated in his fellow members, just as they, for their part, recognize themselves in him and in one another. Yet, if self-consciousness were, by dint of actualizing spirit's reciprocal recognition, to achieve self-knowledge, would that not mean in effect the identification of the shape of self-consciousness with that of spirit? And if so, would this convergence not warrant the further inference that Chapter IV brings the argument of the *Phenomenology* to a conclusion? Of course, this is actually not what ensues. What, then, is defective or insufficient about self-consciousness as a shape that prevents it from closing out the phenomenological investigation in favor of metaphysics?

Recall that self-consciousness as a shape emerged as a result of the falsification of the thesis, guiding all its predecessor shapes, that truth is to be found in what is other than consciousness. The premise for the entire discussion of self-consciousness is the opposing thesis, that the truth lies solely with consciousness. Built into the very conception of the shape of self-consciousness is the assumption that these loci of truth oppose one another, forming an exclusive disjunction. Self-consciousness must, as a consequence, grant that there are living things other than consciousness, yet deny them the status of truth. Correlatively, it achieves the satisfaction of its desire only if the object of desire has this entirely negative significance for self-consciousness.

Earlier, it looked as if self-consciousness had two options available to solve the problem posed by the doubling of its object, the one of desire, and the other itself as the true object of knowledge. And it was clear that only the second offered the prospect of a solution by leaving open, at least in principle, the possibility of a successful pursuit of self-knowledge. Adopting the second option, however, requires locating truth in what is in one sense other than consciousness, namely in another self-consciousness. Yet under the assumption of exclusive disjunction, locating truth in another self-consciousness is not possible without reverting to the preconception about truth—namely, that truth resides precisely in what is other to consciousness—that in part defined the prior shapes. But self-consciousness has defined itself essentially by its rejection of that former conception. Knowing oneself in another self-consciousness in conformity with the dual requirements of desire and self-knowledge entails locating truth both in what is other than self-consciousness and within itself. The concept of spirit accommodates this dual requirement. Therefore, if self-consciousness is to take advantage of the promise held out by the second option, it has to abandon the assumption of exclusive disjunction about the locus of truth. But this is a bridge too far; for that assumption is essential to the very shape of self-consciousness. Because the shape of self-consciousness is congenitally wedded to the assumption of exclusive disjunction, consciousness in this shape cannot realize spirit and thus cannot possibly attain self-knowledge.

Hegel vividly depicts this necessary failure of the shape of self-consciousness in the sequence of five content-rich, influential vignettes in Chapter IV. In each of these sketches, consciousness is portrayed as confronting the dilemma that stems from its inescapable acceptance of the assumption of exclusive disjunction—that truth lies either in what is other than consciousness or in consciousness, but necessarily not in both. Since this assumption is intrinsic to its character as self-consciousness, consciousness cannot do without it: it cannot locate truth both in the other as well as in itself without undermining itself as self-consciousness altogether. Self-consciousness cannot, therefore, avail itself of the option that would allow it to relate to the other as another self-consciousness in which it knows itself. It is condemned, as a consequence, to pursue the first, self-defeating option available to it, and it tries, accordingly, in a sequence of five increasingly fraught variations, to annihilate the other as a competing candidate for the truth, ultimately turning on itself when it turns itself into that very other.[29]

In the struggle for life and death, to begin with, each living self-consciousness exhibits its contempt for life in himself and in his adversary by both risking his own life and aiming to kill the other. Each is victorious only if there is mutually assured destruction, but this reciprocal annihilation is a pyrrhic victory, in which neither self-consciousness can succeed in prevailing, thereby proving that he alone is what truly is.[30] In the following scenario, the lord again enacts disdain towards his living other, the servant, but cannot, for that very reason, know himself in that other self-

---

29. M: 123; MM: 160. Skepticism is the subshape of self-consciousness that first turns fully against itself, but the unhappy consciousness takes this self-abnegation to its extreme.

30. M: 113–15; MM: 148–50.

consciousness, even while acknowledging his needy dependence on him, preventing the lord from establishing himself as the sole independent reality. The servant, on the other hand, cannot know himself in his lord, whose way of life is so totally other; and while the servant, doing the work of his lord, both sublimates his own desire and refashions the objective domain of nature, stamping it with labor's form, he fails to find in the artifacts he makes another self-consciousness. However, his fear of death, bespeaking his attachment to life in the face of the lord's power to destroy it, opens the way to the all-inclusive thought of one's own existence as whole.[31]

Both stoicism and skepticism, presented immediately after the lord-servant relation, exhibit in their respective relations to the objectively given the comprehensive attitude toward themselves that first came to light when the servant trembled before the terrifying prospect of his own death. The stoic shape of self-consciousness once more shows contempt for desire and its objects. In liberating himself from life and desire by his complete indifference, he identifies himself and thus the truth with his thought. As the servant transformed the naturally given through labor, the stoic imposes conceptual form on all that he encounters through thinking. However, in subjecting everything given to the form of thought, the stoic only makes evident that such a purified self-relation leaves the specific content unaffected by thought. The skeptic avoids such indeterminacy. His thoughts are filled with specific content, but at the price of continually moving from one determinate thought or desire to another, affirming at one moment what he denies in the next. The skeptic is driven to this negative attitude toward particular thoughts, since, as particular, all are as opposed to the universal form of thought as such as they are different from one another. Nor can he settle on the determinate thought of himself as one who, by skeptically thinking through this entire movement of particular thoughts, arrives thereby at self-knowledge of his own ignorance. Instead, he not only adopts a negative attitude toward his determinate thoughts, limited as they are by the particularity of life and desire, but his global skepticism leaves him vulnerable to the charge of self-referential inconsistency unless, which is no better, he disavows even his own thought about himself.[32]

---

31. M: 115–19; MM: 150–55.

32. M: 119–26; MM: 155–62.

The curtain-closing scene opens with the unhappy consciousness explicitly avowing the self-contradictory character of self-consciousness, caught as it is between what to it are two mutually exclusive selves. The one, its given self, determined by the particular reality of life and desire, it disavows, endeavoring to transcend this otherness within itself. It aspires to know as its true self a self it projects as completely free from the taint of life and desire. Self-consciousness in this unhappy shape is resigned to its imprisoning dissatisfaction. It has internalized the struggle for life and death, and cannot deny that it is a living, desiring, laboring, and thinking creature; but this means it is an enemy to itself and the truth is to be found in itself only as a self that gains victory over the opponent it harbors within. In its most extreme form, it attempts to overcome its innate unhappiness through a full-blown asceticism, promising joyful liberation through complete self-renunciation. This thoroughgoing self-denial demands, among other things, that the unhappy consciousness subordinate entirely its thought and will to the guiding counsel of another self-consciousness, who mediates between the ascetic in his unhappiness and the standpoint he envisions as the unity of desire and self-knowledge that he wants and prays to achieve through self-abnegation. Looking to his advisor with neither envy nor resentment, which would only reanimate the enemy lurking within, but with the eye of hope, the unhappy consciousness sees a living creature like himself, whose voice he regards nonetheless as absolutely authoritative; for he takes the counselor himself to incarnate the internal reconciliation granted to a self that is sufficiently universal to be shared by all other selves, the very type of self for which he yearns to know himself to be. In hearing the advisor's pronouncements and commands, the unhappy consciousness experiences himself as being, as it were, in the presence of God's vicar on earth, who embodies the very joy of inner harmony for which the miserable ascetic longs, while acknowledging that it remains forever beyond his grasp.[33]

V. Conclusion: Toward the Long Argument

The unhappy ascetic finds that what he longs for but cannot attain is fulfilled in the way of life he envisions is enjoyed by his counselor. That vantage point, considered from the phenomenological perspective, supplies

---

33. M: 126–38; MM: 163–77.

the premise for the long argument that follows, probing beyond the confines of self-consciousness, the prospects of reason, the final major shape under investigation. The promise of reason rests on the rejection of the assumption that the sought-for truth resides either in consciousness or in what is other than consciousness, but can never simultaneously be united in both—the exclusive disjunction that self-consciousness has not been able to overcome. Reason claims that it can avoid the dilemma of this either/or by exploiting the both/and of spirit; for, in uniting I and we, it demonstrates that truth is one, that self and object are, in the decisive respect, one and the same.

But it remains to be seen whether, and if so, how the spiritualization of reason can be reconciled with the structural opposition of consciousness. This furnishes the touchstone for Hegel to complete the phenomenological thought-experiment; for only with that reconciliation can rational consciousness in the shape of spirit succeed in its claim to have actualized self-knowledge.[34]

---

34. For a detailed analysis of Chapter V, the first phase of the long argument that charts the course that reason follows leading to its adoption of the shape of spirit, see my "Reason, Idealism, and the Category: Kantian Language in Hegel's *Phenomenology of Spirit*," in *The Linguistic Dimension of Kant's Thought*, ed. Frank Schalow and Richard Velkley (Evanston, IL: Northwestern University Press, 2014), 205–36.

17

Absolute Longing
in Kant, Hegel, and Kierkegaard

Paul T. Wilford

> Sicut cervus desiderat ad fontes aquarum,
> ita desiderat anima mea ad te, Deus.
>
> —Psalm 42

Although "every human being by nature desires to know," only a subset are animated by the desire to know the whole. As Seth Benardete observes, the desire to know is not the same as the love of wisdom: to aim at the perfected state of knowing is a universal characteristic applicable to every member of the species, but to love wisdom is something else entirely.[1] In fact, a vast gulf separates the two, and Aristotle is certainly *not* claiming "that all of us desire to learn"—an activity incumbent upon the recognition that although the desire to know does not distinguish between kinds of knowledge, the love of wisdom does (*Met.* 980a22).[2] Metaphysics, or the investigation into being *qua* being, only begins once we have distinguished knowing from loving wisdom, particulars from universals, experience from knowledge of causes, and, moreover, discovered a peculiar human type that

---

1. Seth Benardete, "On Wisdom and Philosophy: The First Two Chapters of Aristotle's *Metaphysics A*," in *The Argument of the Action*, ed. Ronna Burger and Michael Davis (Chicago: University of Chicago Press, 2000), 397.

2. Benardete, 396–98.

is relentlessly concerned with querying the given, who when confronted with "the that" is always prompted to ask for "the why."[3]

What motivates such questioning, however, is not perfectly clear: it appears to be undertaken solely for its own sake by one who wonders, finds himself at an impasse, judges himself ignorant (or deficient), and flees his ignorance. Thus, although such knowledge is free, since "it alone is for its own sake" and not for any practical utility, our pursuit of it appears to be compelled by necessity in the guise of the pain of ignorance (*Met.* 982b10–983a11). In other words, if "wonder is a certain kind of conscious neediness (*aporia*)," philosophy appears as the remedy for our neediness, and thus, even in philosophy, we remain subject to necessity.[4] Alternatively, perhaps this inquiry into first things is motivated by the same desire as those inquiries more immediately proximate to the human, namely a concern with understanding "what makes the beautiful and just things good."[5] Thus, if wisdom is knowledge of first principles and the pursuit of such knowledge is motivated by wonder, but wonder can lead to self-forgetting, then "self-knowledge ... completes wisdom."[6] Knowledge of the goodness of philosophy is the eccentric core of first philosophy.

I. Finite Reason and Infinite Longing on Kant's Critical Path

For Kant, philosophy exemplifies the impulse inherent to rational beings to get to the bottom of things. Human reason is driven by some inner compulsion to ask "Why?" But every answer prompts a further question, and the mind moves ever onward and upward in search of an ever more encompassing perspective, seeking ultimately to grasp the whole. Reason strives to ascend from the local, particular, finite, and parochial, in search

---

3. Benardete, 396.

4. Benardete, 400.

5. Ronna Burger, *Aristotle's Dialogue with Socrates: On Aristotle's "Nicomachean Ethics"* (Chicago: University of Chicago Press, 2008), 21. For Burger's elaboration on the relation between "the that" and "the why," see, inter alia, 3–4, 20–21, 33, 70, 102. Cf. Arist., *NE* 1095b4–8. Consider the conclusion to Benardete's comparison of philosophy with mathematics: "Wisdom is the proper union of the playful and the serious; and that union is perhaps the same as maintaining the difference and the sameness of the beautiful and the good." Benardete, "On Wisdom and Philosophy," 402–3.

6. Benardete, 404.

of the universal, the infinite, and the eternal. The end of all this striving is the absolute or what Kant calls the unconditioned. Yet what is this most fundamental ground? Is it an object of contemplation, or an indubitable foundation for the erection of a system? Will it provide a place of rest—some form of satisfaction for the ostensibly insatiable desire to know? And what is this kind of knowing?

The traditional name for this activity is first philosophy or metaphysics —the highest form of the ascent to first principles that Aristotle thought marked all philosophy as opposed to science.[7] But what if this is an impossible task, and we desire a knowledge that transcends the human-all-too-human and therefore remains unattainable? What if the whither and wherefore are forever beyond our grasp? If such is our lot, is this not an absurd condition? Like Sisyphus condemned to eternal labor, philosophy would be engaged in an endless endeavor, compelled to strive for something divine but never able to attain it. For Kant the human condition is marked by incongruity, disjunction, and opposition. The rational animal is such an odd composite that he would be fit for a comedy if not a farce. He is not by nature at home in the world, and his attempts to improve his condition are often self-defeating.[8] The human person suffers

---

7. Thus to transform metaphysics into a science is to reject Aristotle's claim that an answer to the question "what is being" (*ti to on*) was sought long ago, is sought now, and forever will be sought. Arist., *Met.* 1028b2–4.

8. The root of the problem is that man inhabits two realms, to which two forms of reason—theoretical (or speculative) and practical—apply. Man's awareness of an "ought" implies that "the is" will always appear deficient. For the description of man's existence as a dramatic spectacle, see Kant, "On the common saying: That may be correct in theory, but it is of no use in practice," trans. Mary J. Gregor, in *Practical Philosophy*, ed. Mary J. Gregor and Allen W. Wood (Cambridge: Cambridge University Press, 1996), 8:308. Man's doubleness is described as arising from the fact that he belongs to two species—one natural and one moral—in "Conjectural beginning of human history," trans. Allen W. Wood, in *Anthropology, History, and Education*, ed. Günter Zöller and Robert B. Louden (Cambridge: Cambridge University Press, 2007), 8:116. This doubleness is the principal challenge confronting any rational account of the historical activity of mankind. "Idea for a universal history with a cosmopolitan aim," trans. Allen W. Wood, in Zöller and Louden, *Anthropology, History, and Education*, 8:17–18. All Kant citations refer to *Kants gesammelte Schriften*, Deutsche Akademie der Wissenschaften (Berlin: Walter de Gruyter, 1900–) by volume and page number, save the *Critique of Pure Reason*, which references pages of the first and second editions.

the diremption of being locally individuated, situated in space and time, and yet capable of infinite reflection. Although he aspires to a God's eye view of the world and longs to overcome the limitations of his narrow horizon, the deficiencies and inadequacies of all discursive reasoning expose his neediness. Even in that domain where he appears most exalted, he requires the givenness of experience, rendering all his knowledge subject to limitations of the first-person perspective.[9] For Kant, our doubleness as finite rational beings is the enduring mystery at the heart of the world, the deepest problem of self-knowledge, and the stumbling block for all morality.[10] It is the source of the painful limitation of the mind as it aspires to rise above its local habitation. In the opening words of Kant's *Critique of Pure Reason*,

> Human reason has the peculiar fate in one species of its cognitions that it is burdened with questions which it cannot dismiss, since they are given to it as problems by the nature of reason itself, but which it also cannot answer, since they transcend every capacity of human reason. (*CPR*, Avii)

Our lot is to be burdened with insoluble questions; our nature is defined by a capacity that cannot achieve satisfaction. In the dawning awareness that "reason's business must always remain incomplete because the questions never cease," "reason sees itself necessitated to take refuge in principles that overstep all possible use in experience, and yet seem so unsuspicious that even ordinary common sense agrees with them" (*CPR*, Avii–viii). But our reach exceeds our grasp; we fall into "obscurity and contradiction," and soon we have fallen back to earth and find ourselves

---

9. As Kant's discussion of "the unity of apperception" indicates, this limitation is implied in our capacity to append to all our judgments the words "I think." Kant, *Critique of Pure Reason*, trans. and ed. Paul Guyer and Allen W. Wood (Cambridge: Cambridge University Press, 1998), B130–35 (hereafter cited as *CPR*).

10. See Kant's two related descriptions of man: "a limited rational being" and "a finite thinking being," *CPR*, B72. Cf. Yirmiyahu Yovel, *Kant's Philosophical Revolution: A Short Guide to the "Critique of Pure Reason"* (Princeton: Princeton University Press, 2018), 1–20, 88–89, 101–4. Cf. Karl Jaspers, "The Finiteness of Man and the Limits of Reason," in *Kant*, trans. Ralph Manheim, ed. Hannah Arendt (New York: Harcourt Brace, 1962), 97–101.

engaged in endless polemics on the battlefield of metaphysics (*CPR*, Aviii). We may soon tire of this frenzied activity, but we cannot long remain indifferent to the questions of the ultimate ground of beings, of the first principles of the cosmos, or of the nature of the human soul. Man simply cannot rest content in apathetic resignation.

Misology beckons; for while human beings are characterized by what Kant calls *metaphysica naturalis*—longing for knowledge of God, freedom, and immortality—our pursuits run aground on unavoidable antinomies of reason that are the source of endless controversy (*CPR*, Bxiv–xv, Bxxx).[11] Not only is the human being a peculiar, incongruent composite of mind and body, but human reason proves to be "divided against itself," and, even when independent of sensibility, speculative reason nevertheless falls into a "wholly natural antithetic."[12] But we might discipline reason to rein in its ambitions, to circumscribe its aims, and to settle for what Socrates called "human wisdom"—that form of self-knowledge Kant thought available through an investigation into the limits and powers of reason. If we bring reason itself and its desire to know before the tribunal of reason, we might know the sources of our errors, recognize that the longing for the unconditioned is built into the structure of the finite rational being, and thereby secure a limited knowledge adequate to answering the most urgent and important of all questions—how should I live, or what is the right way of life? (*CPR*, Axi; *CPR*, B22–26).

By reflecting on "the origin of this disunity of reason with itself," I can attain knowledge of a whole—namely that of human reason (*CPR*, A464/B492). I come to know the whole that is accessible to me from the perspective I inhabit as a finite rational agent. For Kant, such *must* be the theoretical activity of metaphysics because our "natural predisposition" to metaphysics is inextirpable. As long as "human reason . . . has thought,

---

11. Cf. Kant, "Groundwork of The metaphysics of morals," in Gregor and Wood, *Practical Philosophy*, 4:395–6 (hereafter cited as "Groundwork").

12. Alfredo Ferrarin, *The Powers of Pure Reason: Kant and the Idea of Cosmic Philosophy* (Chicago: University of Chicago Press, 2015), 14; *CPR* A407/B433. Kant continues: this "leads reason into the temptation either to surrender itself to a skeptical hopelessness or else to assume an attitude of dogmatic stubbornness. . . . Either alternative is the death of a healthy philosophy, though the former might also be called the euthanasia of pure reason."

or rather reflected (*nachgedacht*)," there has always been metaphysics (*CPR*, A842/B870). As a consequence,

> we will always return to metaphysics as to a beloved from whom we have been estranged, since reason, because essential ends are at issue here, must work without respite either for sound insight or for the destruction of good insights that are already to hand. Thus the metaphysics of nature as well as morals, but above all the preparatory (propaedeutic) critique of reason that dares to fly with its own wings, alone constitutes that which we can call philosophy in a genuine sense. (*CPR*, A850/B878)

Having completed the critique of reason, reason no longer risks the fate of Icarus, for it has come to know precisely what it is capable of achieving. Thus, Kant announces the magnitude of his accomplishment: if metaphysics is as old as thought itself, but we have learned how to fly only with the publication of the *Critique of Pure Reason*, Kant has transformed the world we inhabit.[13] Every generation hereafter is the beneficiary of Kant's Herculean labors, for we now know the proper employment of reason. This achievement, however, strikes us as less grand if we remember that it consists in demonstrating "through the critique of our reason [that] we finally know that we cannot in fact know anything at all in its pure and speculative use" (*CPR*, A769/B797). The finite rational being overcomes the endless controversies that have dogged all previous philosophy and thrown man into confusion, only to learn that this enables him to plod along the critical path, content in the knowledge that he is justified in confirming the most quotidian of truths. Kant's critical enterprise would appear to feed hungry souls with the thinnest of gruel.

However, Kant's great philosophical revolution contains a second moment. Far from being fruitless, Kant's critical labors disclose a whole new world; for by disciplining theoretical reason, Kant opens a domain for the activity of practical reason, the justification of morality, the revelation of freedom, and the formation of grand theological-political projects

---

13. See "History of Pure Reason" (*CPR*, A852/B880–A855/B883). Cf. Aristotle's conclusion to his survey of previous philosophy in *Met.* 993a11–17.

(*CPR*, A807/B835–A819/B847).[14] Thus, by denying knowledge "in order to make room for faith," Kant provides a new way of relating to that absolute we originally sought in philosophic speculation (*CPR*, Bxxx).[15] In the "good will" we find an indubitable principle, something truly unconditioned; for the "good will" is good without qualification, without limitation ("Groundwork," 4:393–99).

With this new beginning, we also discover a new end. We find in the moral realm the whither and wherefore of our lives. Practical reason provides the *telos* and undergirds the "moral theology" that plays an "immanent use, namely for fulfilling our vocation here in the world by fitting [it] into a system of all ends" (*CPR*, A819/B847).[16] Thus, we escape from the uncertainty and doubt that plague the human condition and confidently follow the critical path—avoiding the Scylla of skepticism and the Charybdis of dogmatism—in pursuit of a moral whole, a world transformed in accordance with the highest good, secure in our knowledge that if we do our duty we are justified in our hope that the kingdom of ends may be realized, that justice may reign on earth, that virtue and happiness may one day converge, and that the painful diremption that characterizes the human soul may ultimately be overcome. In projecting such an idea of reason we envision a form of wholeness that preserves our freedom, establishes our dignity, and secures the rights of man. Though exalted, such an end is not the product of a fevered imagination, but an a priori construct of reason. By taking guidance solely from reason itself, mankind secures its self-sufficiency and guards against the dangers of enthusiasm.[17]

---

14. Cf. Kant, "Critique of practical reason," trans. Mary J. Gregor, in Gregor and Wood, *Practical Philosophy*, 5:3–6; 5:107–13.

15. Richard L. Velkley, *Freedom and the End of Reason: On the Moral Foundation of Kant's Critical Philosophy* (Chicago: University of Chicago Press, 1989).

16. The core of moral theology is the priority of practical reason: "So far as practical reason has the right to lead us, we will not hold actions to be obligatory because they are God's commands, but will rather regard them as divine commands because we are internally obligated to them. We will . . . believe ourselves to be in conformity with the divine will only insofar as we hold as holy the moral law that reason teaches us from the nature of actions themselves." On the basis of Kant's new revelation of freedom, one serves the divine will by promoting what practical reason judges to be best for the world.

17. Kant, "What does it mean to orient oneself in thinking?," trans. Allen W. Wood, in *Religion and Rational Theology*, ed. Allen W. Wood and George di Giovanni (Cambridge:

In giving itself such a project and securing the possibility of progress towards this *telos*, philosophy works to preserve mankind's autonomy, to stave off the threat of misology and to avoid the twin evils of melancholy and misanthropy.[18] The absolute longing that threatened to lead the noblest souls into despair finds its true outlet in furthering "the whole vocation of mankind, the philosophy of which is called moral philosophy" (*CPR*, A840/B868). The philosopher's eros has become moral; our longing for wholeness finds expression in advancing mankind's moral purpose.

II. The Travails of the Unhappy Consciousness on Hegel's Highway of Despair

Hegel's inquiry in the *Phenomenology of Spirit* is animated by the very same *Erkenntnisproblem* that spurred Kant to undertake the "experiment" of the Copernican Turn.[19] But Hegel rejects the Kantian solution to the epistemic problem; whereas Kant aims to transform metaphysics into a science by delineating the boundaries of pure reason, Hegel seeks to uncover a mode of cognition that overcomes the disjunction at the heart

---

Cambridge University Press, 1996), 8:133–46. Reason's autonomy depends on a salutary self-limitation: the self-sufficiency of reason to legislate practically is secured through self-mastery. By reining in our "natural predisposition" to attempt to answer "the questions that pure reason raises," we moderate that impulse that makes human reason so susceptible to superstition and religious enthusiasm (*CPR*, B22).

18. Cf. Kant, "On the common saying," 8:307–12.

19. Following Rockmore, I employ the term *das Erkenntnisproblem* as a catchall formula, including a range of interrelated epistemic and metaphysical questions. Tom Rockmore, *German Idealism as Constructivism* (Chicago: University of Chicago Press, 2016). Cf. Kant to Marcus Herz, 1772, in *Philosophical Correspondence, 1759–99*, trans. and ed. Arnulf Zweig (Chicago: University of Chicago Press, 1967), 70–76. Nevertheless, Kant's formulation of the problem as the question, "How is metaphysics possible as a science?" is especially significant, for it encapsulates how Kant's resolution of metaphysical quarrels would amount to the end of philosophy (as it is traditionally understood)—future practitioners would be scientists, i.e., operating upon an already established foundation or justified set of first principles that require no further investigation. Yet, as argued in Part I, this is the necessary trade-off: the alternative is skepticism leading to nihilism (*CPR*, Aix–xii, Bxxxiii–xxxv, A855/B883). Paul W. Franks aptly captures this aspect of German Idealism in *All or Nothing: Systematicity, Transcendental Arguments, and Skepticism in German Idealism* (Cambridge, MA: Harvard University Press, 2005).

of the Kantian world between phenomena and noumena (appearances and things-in-themselves).[20] Hegel's speculative sublation of Kant proceeds on multiple levels: from a dismissal of the possibility of attaining partial or limited truth while the absolute remains obscure to the rejection of Kant's anxiety about reason's tendency (and therewith philosophy's) to fall, like Thales, into the well of dialectical illusion.[21] Instead, Hegel believes that human reason can ascend from understanding (*Verstand*) to reason (*Vernunft*), and grasp the speculative truth expressed in all genuinely philosophical propositions (*PhS*, §61). To this end, the *Phenomenology* undertakes a comprehensive analysis of the understanding's possible forms of cognition. The progression of these "shapes of consciousness" exhibits a logic that leads ultimately to a radically new theoretical position that transcends the structural dichotomies that foreclosed the possibility of knowledge of first things in Kant's critical philosophy. However, this does not entail the discovery of a single foundational moment or an Archimedean point of indubitable certainty upon which a comprehensive system can be constructed. Rather, the insight available at the culmination of the *Phenomenology* is that insofar as "the true is the whole," then the enterprise of philosophy is foundationless—the system must be a self-supporting whole in which the beginning is the end and the end, the beginning (*PhS*, §§20–26).[22]

While Hegel's critique of Kant is at times perfectly explicit, especially in his charge of the empty formalism of the categorical imperative and his exposition of the practical postulates, Hegel's running disagreement with Kant in fact constitutes a red thread throughout the book,[23] as the Kantian formulation of the subject-object duality is merely the sharpest and clearest expression of the basic epistemic orientation and metaphysical problem

---

20. Hegel, *The Science of Logic*, trans. and ed. George di Giovanni (Cambridge: Cambridge University Press, 2010), 26–30.

21. Hegel, *The Phenomenology of Spirit*, trans. and ed. Terry Pinkard (Cambridge: Cambridge University Press, 2018), §§73–75 (hereafter cited as *PhS*). On reason's propensity to dialectical illusion, which Kant calls "alluring and natural," see *CPR*, A704/B732.

22. Cf. William Maker, *Philosophy without Foundations: Rethinking Hegel* (Albany: State University of New York Press, 1994).

23. Philip J. Kain, *Hegel and the Other: A Study of the "Phenomenology of Spirit"* (Albany: State University of New York Press, 2005).

that animates the book as a whole. The *Phenomenology*, in its exposition of the understanding, attempts to run through every possible iteration of the subject-object relation; every possible way in which the world could be conceived as "given to the mind" is examined and found wanting.[24] The book as a whole is therefore a grand *reductio ad absurdum* argument demonstrating the inadequacy of any dualist metaphysics—as though the subtitle of the book were: *Cartesianism delenda est!*[25]

Hegel describes this record of failure as "a highway of despair," the purpose of which is a self-consummating skepticism—a skepticism so complete that it exhausts the possible maneuvers available to what Hegel calls "natural consciousness" (*PhS*, §78). Moreover, consciousness brings each failure upon itself. The *Phenomenology* depicts each failed attempt at apprehension of the world as a product of the distinct inflection of "the opposition of consciousness" that defines each "shape of consciousness." Consequently, each failure is a condemnation of a shape of consciousness or a possible orientation of the mind to the world. The engine of this development, as Hegel underscores in the *Introduction*, is built into the structure of consciousness. Consciousness is characterized by the unrelenting (*unaufhaltsam*) pursuit of true knowledge, namely, that form of knowing which "no longer needs to go beyond itself, that is, where knowledge comes around to itself, and where the concept corresponds to the object and the object to the concept" (*PhS*, §80). Only at this point does consciousness achieve satisfaction (*Befriedigung*), but in this moment, consciousness transcends itself, and finally comes to know itself as spirit.[26]

---

24. Compare Hegel's immanent critique of all forms of the opposition of consciousness with Wilfrid Sellars' account of "the myth of the given." Ultimately, Hegel rejects any correspondence theory of truth or any way in which the mind "pictures" or "represents" the world to itself. See Robert Berman's essay in ch. 16 of this volume for an elaboration of Hegel's phenomenological method.

25. For an illuminating commentary focused on the Cartesian epistemic dynamic between certainty and truth, see Tom Rockmore, *Cognition: An Introduction to Hegel's "Phenomenology of Spirit"* (Berkeley: University of California Press, 1997). Cf. Antón Barba-Kay, "We Are, Nonetheless, Cartesians: A Prodigal Johnnie Reports Back," *St. John's Review* 59, nos. 1–2 (2017–18): 1–21.

26. Cf. Kant's claim that the critical path will provide the complete satisfaction (*völlige Befriedigung*) of human reason "in that which has always (*jederzeit*), but until now vainly, occupied its lust for knowledge (*ihre Wißbegierde*)" (*CPR*, A856/B884).

Prior to this self-transcending moment, however, consciousness is continually "driven out of itself" by its own activity; for in "all the stations on the way" to true knowledge, consciousness is "for itself its *concept*" and the concept belongs *to* consciousness. Consequently, consciousness continually outstrips itself, i.e., its specific determination as *this particular* shape of consciousness. Thus, "consciousness suffers violence at its own hands and brings to ruin its own restricted satisfaction" (*PhS*, §80).[27] Consciousness thus performs a self-consummating negation of itself, whereby it undermines every pretension to knowledge, and, in repeatedly performing "this dialectical movement on itself," generates the exhaustive series of shapes of consciousness which emerge out of one another through a series of determinate negations (*PhS*, §86). The movement as a whole can be viewed from two perspectives as either:

> the path of natural consciousness which presses forward towards true knowledge, or the path of the soul as it wanders through the series of the ways it takes shape, as if those shapes were stations laid out for it by its own nature so that it both might purify itself into spirit and, through a complete experience of itself, achieve a cognitive acquaintance of what it is in itself. (*PhS*, §77)

Thus, the different "shapes of consciousness" in which spirit appears are but so many guises spirit adopts as it struggles to fully realize itself, express its essential nature, and thereby be at home in the world. Hegel's text is a record of the various forms in which spirit attempts to express its content, to be "for itself" what it is "in-itself," and thereby to truly know itself.

---

27. Cf. Kierkegaard's description of the skepticism driving "self-reflection" in Hegel's philosophy. *Concluding Unscientific Postscript to Philosophical Fragments*, trans. and ed. Howard V. Hong and Edna H. Hong, 2 vols. (Princeton: Princeton University Press, 1992), 1:335 (hereafter, *CUP*). The problem as presented concerns thought's relation to being, but as Kierkegaard's elaboration in a footnote indicates, the question is decisive for Christianity: if Hegel's method is sound and one can pass from doubt to certainty or "that by doubting everything one in this very doubt wins truth without a break and an absolutely new departure, then not one single Christian category can be maintained, then Christianity is abolished" (*CUP*, 1:336).

The central turning point in spirit's journey to know itself is the transition from *Consciousness* to *Self-Consciousness*. Here, the knowing subject is said to step out from "the colorful semblance of the sensuous world and the empty night of the supersensible other-worldly beyond into the spiritual daylight of the present" (*PhS*, §177). Although the full emergence of spirit into daylight requires the subsequent development of *Reason*'s claim "to be all reality," the trajectory of self-consciousness is clear: the self-conscious being will ultimately find its satisfaction only in transcending the obscurities attendant upon all forms of representation (*Vorstellung*), and achieving a form of knowing that Hegel calls conceptual comprehension (*begreifendes Wissen*), which is the key to speculative philosophy insofar as it grasps the identity-in-difference structure that is the essence of spirit. When self-consciousness understands itself as spirit, knowledge is finally possible, and with this knowledge the individual finds her rest and satisfaction—self-knowledge and being-at-home in the world prove to be coextensive.[28]

However, prior to this final dialectical *Aufhebung*—which occurs through the transfiguration of the content of religious representation (*Vorstellung*) into the philosophic, conceptual form of absolute knowing—self-consciousness is marked by a restless, unremitting desire. According to Hegel, "self-consciousness is desire above all (*Begierde überhaupt*)" (*PhS*, §167).[29] Therefore, the deepest substratum of the self-conscious being is anawareness that the world is something other than itself; it strives to negate this otherness, to deny the independent validity of the world, and thereby to affirm its self-certainty (*Gewißheit seiner selbst*) (*PhS*, §§166–67).[30] Whereas *Consciousness* in its three iterations—Sense-certainty, Per-

---

28. The rest is not a static self-sameness but the maintenance of self-identity through continual activity. Consider the Bacchanalian revelry image (*PhS*, §47). Cf. Hegel's decision to conclude the *Encyclopedia of Philosophical Sciences* with Aristotle's description of thought thinking itself in *Met.* 1072b18–30. Hegel's *"Philosophy of Mind,"* trans. W. Wallace and A.V. Miller, rev. M.J. Inwood (Oxford: Clarendon Press, 2007), §577.

29. On the relation of *Begierde* to eros and/or *oregesthai*, see Peter Kalkavage, *The Logic of Desire* (Philadelphia: Paul Dry, 2007), 102–5.

30. Cf. Robert Pippin, *Hegel on Self-Consciousness: Desire and Death in the "Phenomenology of Spirit"* (Princeton: Princeton University Press, 2010). Pippin lucidly and persuasively presents Hegel's account of the self-conscious subject as a response to recognizably Kantian problems, but he does not address the figure of the unhappy consciousness,

ception, and Force and Understanding—sought knowledge on the basis of the principle that what is true for consciousness is something *other than* itself, in the turn to *Self-Consciousness* the knowing subject takes the opposite tack and attempts to work out the proposition that truth lies exclusively *in the knower*.

In this epistemic dynamic (i.e., concept-object relation), we hit upon Hegel's reworking of Kant's *Copernican Revolution* (*CPR*, Bxvii–xviii). Kant, having been rudely awoken from dogmatic slumber by Hume, posed the question whether the objects of the world conform to the structure of our mind, rather than our mind conforming to the objects of the world.[31] Hegel's appropriation of the turn to subjectivity, however, runs the risk that it will encounter precisely those difficulties that dogged the Kantian subject, who longs both for knowledge of the unconditioned and for the convergence of the realms of nature and freedom in the highest good.[32] Hegel is well aware of this possibility, and he explores the experience of such a subject under the rubric of the "unhappy consciousness" (*unglückliches Bewußtsein*)—a figure that reappears throughout the *Phenomenology* at moments of tension, when the individual self-conscious agent finds herself bereft and isolated in a world drained of meaning.[33] Nevertheless, Hegel describes the unhappy consciousness as "the perfection of self-consciousness" (*PhS*, §673). Something about the comportment of the unhappy consciousness exemplifies the essence of the self-conscious being. Thus, spirit's self-knowledge requires grappling with the unhappy consciousness, and seeing its pitiable condition as potentially our own.[34]

---

which serves as a stalking-horse for the bad infinity Hegel believes inherent in Kantian critical philosophy. Hegel, *Science of Logic*, 207–12.

31. Kant, "Prolegomena to any future metaphysics that will be able to come forward as science," trans. Gary Hatfield, in *Theoretical Philosophy after 1781*, ed. Henry Allison and Peter Heath (Cambridge: Cambridge University Press, 2002), 4:257–60.

32. *CPR*, A707/B735–A708/B736, A840/B868, A808/B836–A815/B843.

33. *PhS*, §482; §527, §658, §§752–58, §785. Compare also *PhS*, §527 with §768.

34. Of twentieth-century commentators who explore the metaphysical implications of this line of thought, Jean Wahl is especially insightful. Jean Wahl, *Le Malheur de la conscience dans la philosophie de Hegel* (Paris: Reider, 1929).

Following Hegel's famous poetic presentation of the life and death struggle for recognition between two self-conscious agents, each of whom enters the struggle seeking to prove their self-sufficiency (*Selbständigkeit*), there emerges a hierarchical social ordering of master and servant, of recognized and recognizing. This is the first intersubjective relation in the *Phenomenology*, and the inequality between the two subjects is a reflection of their behavior in the primordial struggle for recognition. Whereas the master is willing to risk everything, even his life, to prove his dominion over any possible determination of or limitation to his will, the servant, unwilling to risk life and limb, submits to the master (*PhS*, §§187–90). Unable to prove himself independent of natural existence (i.e., "life"),[35] the servant suffers a corresponding spiritual (because intersubjective) subordination, reflecting his essential lack of self-sufficiency; their hierarchical arrangement reflects the normative claim that one who fears death is not truly free, and therefore deserves to be socio–politically subordinate.[36] Whereas the master achieves external confirmation of his essence as self-sufficient, the locus of all authority, the center around which the world turns, the servant experiences the profound alienation of dependency— the essence of his selfhood is outside himself. The master knows himself as absolute and unconditioned; his will is law; his whim governs the world. There is no higher authority for the master, and he finds his exalted position reflected back to him in the obsequious actions of the servant, who labors to transform the given natural world in accordance with the master's desires.

---

35. Cf. Hegel's description of "life" as the object of "self-consciousness" (*PhS* §162, §§168–74).

36. Although not stated so simply, this principle undergirds both the confrontation and the consequent intersubjective relation between the two self-conscious agents. That is, the struggle is *not* primarily about defeating a rival, but about proving to oneself and to the other—through staking one's life (*das Daransetzen des Lebens*)—that freedom (*Freiheit*) is the essence of self-consciousness: "the essence for self-consciousness is...not *being*, not the *immediate* way self-consciousness emerges, not its being absorbed within the expanse of life—but rather, it is that there is nothing on hand in it itself (*an ihm nichts vorhanden*) which could not be a vanishing moment for it, that is, that self-consciousness is merely pure *being-for-itself*" (*PhS*, §187). Only thereby can self-consciousness raise its certainty of *existing for itself* to truth.

The master appears to have achieved a stable form of satisfaction. But this proves not to be the case for two decisive reasons: first, the master receives recognition from an inferior and such recognition is woefully inadequate. Second, the master has nothing further to do; there is no activity for the master to undertake—he becomes a passive consumer of the products of the servant's labor. Satisfying his pleasures, which can never be particularly sophisticated because they must occur without mediation, the master has returned to the original state of the isolated solitary self-conscious subject, whose primary activity was simple consumption of the given. In other words, the irony of the master is that, in his dominion over the servant, he is little better than a dumb brute.

The servant, however, compelled by the external necessity of his physical subordination, becomes psychically more sophisticated, as he discovers heretofore undisclosed depths to the human soul. The development of interiority begins with the harrowing experience of absolute fear (*absolute Furcht*). In the life and death struggle,

> this consciousness was not driven with anxiety about just this or that matter, nor did it have anxiety about just this or that moment; rather, it had anxiety about its entire essence. It felt the fear of death, the absolute master. In that feeling, it had inwardly fallen into dissolution, trembled in its depths, and all that was fixed within it had been shaken loose. However, this pure universal movement, this way in which all stable existence becomes absolutely fluid, is the simple essence of self-consciousness; it is absolute negativity, pure being-for-itself, which thereby exists in this consciousness. (*PhS*, §194)

This radical face-to-face confrontation with the all-consuming negativity of death proves to be the condition for the servant's discovery that he "possesses a mind of his own" (*PhS*, §196).[37] Or, as Hegel provocatively suggests, quoting Proverbs: "the fear of the Lord is the beginning of Wisdom (*die Furcht des Herrn der Anfang der Weisheit ist*)" (*PhS*, §195).[38] In fear and trem-

---

37. Cf. Heidegger, *Being and Time*, trans. and ed. John Macquarrie and Edward Robinson (San Francisco: Harper & Row, 1962), 306–8.

38. Cf. Prov.1:7; 9:10.

bling before that absolute Lord (*absoluter Herr*), i.e., the fear of death, self-consciousness discovers its capacity for independent thought (*PhS*, §194).[39]

Thus, in laboring on behalf of the master, the servant discovers a realm of interiority independent of any external authority. The development of this wholly new dimension of the self-conscious being is the theme of the second half of chapter 4, entitled *The Freedom of Self-Consciousness*. The logic governing the exploration of this new realm of freedom is the principle that "consciousness is a being that thinks, and that consciousness holds something to be essentially important, or true and good only in so far as it *thinks* it to be such" (*PhS*, §198). The development of the servant's interiority occurs in three logical moments, expressed in three figures: the stoic, the skeptic, and finally the unhappy consciousness, each of whom struggles to unite its particularity (or individuality) with the universality of thought. The question of the self-conscious being has become: how does an individual existing being (*Dasein*) constrained by contingent externality exercise the capacity for free, unbounded thought? How does the self-conscious subject unite the finitude of man disclosed in mortality with the divinity of infinite reflection?

As depicted in the travails of the unhappy consciousness, the first crude attempts are pitiable and tragic. Self-consciously suffering its own incoherent sublation of the stoic and the skeptic, the unhappy consciousness attempts to combine the stoic's assertion of independence *from* (through indifference *to*) the world with the skeptic's discovery that the negativity, which secured the stoic's withdrawal from the world, could be turned back on one's own selfhood. The unhappy consciousness becomes "*for itself* the doubled consciousness of itself as self-liberating, unchangeable, selfsame self-consciousness, and of itself as absolutely self-confusing, self-inverting—and it is the consciousness of its being this contradiction" (*PhS*, §206). Cognizant of its diremption, the unhappy consciousness struggles to attain unity with itself by negating its own particularity, and by bringing its capacity for pure thought into a relation with an absolute being, the source of all essentiality. It wants to abide in the presence of this being, but it fails to achieve such communion, and is instead wracked

---

39. Cf. the description of the fear of death as the absolute lord in *Absolute Freedom and Terror* (*PhS*, §593).

by an "infinite yearning" (*unendliche Sehnsucht*) for unity with this absolute Other, which it locates in a transcendent, other-worldly beyond (*PhS*, §217; cf. *PhS*, §238). While Hegel describes the unhappy consciousness as wretched and pitiable, this shape of consciousness marks a decisive advance beyond stoicism and skepticism, because it holds together pure thinking and particular individuality. And, although it cannot reconcile this doubleness, it squarely faces up to the fact that this is *the* essential problem for a self-conscious subject.

If we recall that self-consciousness is desire above all, and that desire is the longing for unity with oneself, mediated by a relation to what is other than oneself, we can see the unhappy consciousness as expressing a profound metaphysical longing. The unhappy consciousness does not think it can be whole unless it can be united with the absolute, but it believes its own individuated particularity to be the barrier between itself and its desired object.

The unhappy consciousness is defined by a desire that in principle cannot be satisfied given the limitations of its own nature. The contingent facticity of its own existence thwarts its aspirations. The unhappy consciousness cannot help but fall into despair and even self-loathing, as it believes its own finitude precludes its satisfaction. It has come to abandon the naïve belief in its own self-sufficiency that drove the master into the life-and-death struggle. But, having internalized the doubleness that previously existed between two self-conscious beings, it conceives of itself as a paradoxical synthesis of opposed elements that must relate to one another, but the unhappy consciousness cannot conceive how such a relation is possible (*PhS*, §§206–10). Rather than constituting a whole, it is a combination of incongruous elements; rather than expressing a unity, it suffers a seemingly external, and therefore contingent, necessity. The unhappy consciousness embodies what Hegel calls "bad infinity" (*die schlechte Unendlichkeit*).[40]

In light of the *Phenomenology* as a whole, the unhappy consciousness exemplifies the experience of natural consciousness suffering violence at its own hands. Its attempts at self-purification—even the extreme morti-

---

40. Cf. Donald Phillip Verene, "The True and the Bad Infinity," in *Logos and Eros: Essays Honoring Stanley Rosen*, ed. Nalin Ranasinghe (South Bend, IN: St. Augustine's Press, 2006), 260–71.

fication of the flesh—are but concrete, physical manifestations of the impulse that animates all shapes of consciousness, for it too is aiming at an adequate correspondence between concept and object.[41] But all its efforts come to naught. Its profound longing remains shut up within its own solitude, merely implicit, or "in-itself," lacking the externalization that would enable its identity to be for others, and therefore "for-itself." The unhappy consciousness is the perfection of self-consciousness because it is the awareness that the self-conscious subject, when burdened by the opposition of consciousness, is structurally unable to achieve its *telos*. It reveals the problem inherent in self-consciousness.

Moreover, if we recall that Hegel's dismissal of Kant's critical philosophy culminates in a criticism of the possibility of distinguishing "between an absolute truth and some other kind of truth" (*PhS*, §75), then we see that the unhappy consciousness reveals the lamentable state of the self-conscious cognitive agent if there is no remedy for our peculiar fate described by Kant. As later appearances of the unhappy consciousness illustrate, the redirection of man's metaphysical longing to the practical aim of transforming the whole into a moral world simply repeats the problem of projecting into an other-worldly beyond the wholeness we seek here and now.[42] In Kant, the goal of realizing the highest good remains an ideal we can, at best, asymptotically approach, but never actually attain. The disjunction endures between ought and is, freedom and nature. Our pursuit of a perfectly good will (a "holy will") is an infinite task. While we long to be angels, we remain tethered to the earth by the discursivity of reason. Wholeness remains elusive as we are fated to tread indefinitely on Kant's critical path that "leads only to a progression from bad to better extending to infinity."[43]

---

41. Consider, for example, the destructive fury of absolute freedom, which negates particularity in pursuit of achieving an adequate relation between its concept and the object it intends to know (*PhS*, §§590–93).

42. Thus for Hegel, the pursuit of such purity in fact leads to the hard heart of the beautiful soul, a figure Hegel describes as suffering a fate worse than the unhappy consciousness, for "this time it is conscious of being the concept of reason, something which the unhappy consciousness was merely *in itself*" (*PhS*, §658).

43. "Groundwork," 4:439; Kant, "Religion within the boundaries of mere reason," trans. George di Giovanni, in Wood and di Giovanni, *Religion and Rational Theology*, 6:3–8,

III. Kierkegaard, the Single Individual, and the Self-Forgetting of Philosophy

Although Kierkegaard is engaged in a running dialogue with Hegel throughout his literary career, his criticism is often wrapped in layers of irony. Like the Delphic oracle, Kierkegaard "neither reveals, nor conceals, but gives a sign." An especially prominent sign appears in *Either/Or* in a section entitled "The Unhappiest One" and subtitled "An Inspired Address to the *Sumparanekromenoi*: Peroration at the Meeting on Fridays."[44] While Kierkegaard's argument for the paradoxical nature of human existence and thus Hegel's misunderstanding of the dilemma of self-consciousness is anything but straightforward, with an explicit reference to the unhappy consciousness, he provides a jumping-off point for exploring his fundamental critique of Hegel. By unraveling Kierkegaard's enigmatic presentation of the metaphysical problem confronting the unhappy consciousness, we uncover the deepest stratum of Kierkegaard's objection to Hegel.[45]

Through this peculiar address to the *Sumparanekromenoi*—a group "who do not believe in the game of gladness or the happiness of fools, ... who believe in nothing but unhappiness"—Kierkegaard explores the sources of human unhappiness.[46] The address, which resembles a sermon delivered

---

6:46–48, 6:51. Cf. the third stage in Nietzsche's "How the 'True World' Finally Became a Fiction: History of an Error," in *Twilight of the Idols*, trans. Richard Polt, ed. Tracy Strong (Indianapolis: Hackett, 1997), 23.

44. Kierkegaard's authorship, especially in *Either/Or*, can appear haphazard. Nevertheless, Kierkegaard claimed "that there is a plan in *Either/Or* from the first word to the last." Kierkegaard, *Papers and Journals: A Selection*, trans. and ed. Alastair Hannay (London: Penguin, 1996), 163 (hereafter cited as *PJ*). Reflecting subsequently on the work that announced his arrival on the literary scene, Kierkegaard asserts that although his contemporaries cannot grasp the design of his work, "each essay in *Either/Or* is only a part in a whole, and then the whole of *Either/Or* a part in the whole; that's enough to drive you mad, think my petty-bourgeois contemporaries" (*PJ*, 227). If Kierkegaard can be said to imitate Socrates in his ironic posture and his role as gadfly, he also imitates Plato in practicing his own form of logographic necessity.

45. As Kierkegaard makes explicit in *CUP*, *Either/Or* is an "indirect polemic against speculative thought, which is indifferent to existence. That there is no conclusion and no final decision is an indirect expression for truth as inwardness and in this way perhaps a polemic against truth as knowledge" (*CUP*, 1:252).

46. Kierkegaard, *Either/Or*, trans. and ed. Howard V. Hong and Edna H. Hong (Princeton: Princeton University Press, 1987), 220.

to a congregation, takes the form of an imagined competition as to who would most deserve the title of "the unhappiest one." In his search for insight into the criterion for evaluation the orator remarks:

> In all of Hegel's systematic works there is one section that discusses the unhappy consciousness.... The unhappy one is the person who in one way or another has his ideal, the substance of his life, the plenitude of his consciousness, his essential nature, outside himself. The unhappy one is the person who is always absent from himself, never present to himself. (*Either/Or*, 222)

According to the sermon, one approaches such passages with trepidation—with "an inner awareness" and "palpitation of the heart." Like an unexpected *memento mori* introduced suddenly into a moment of high drama in literature, the very phrase "the unhappy consciousness" makes one "tremble like a sinner" (*Either/Or*, 222).

Yet how is the unhappy consciousness not himself? According to Hegel, he has his essence "in either past or future time." With this insight, the orator concludes that "the whole territory is thereby adequately circumscribed," and *for* this insight we ought to thank Hegel, since given "this firm limitation," unhappiness has been conceptually circumscribed and delineated. Our investigation into unhappiness has taken a substantial step: unhappiness is transformed into a universal genus and further specified into two subspecies. With Hegel as our guide, we appear to have arrived at the cause of unhappiness and therewith at a standard for judgment. Yet, the author continues, "since we are not only philosophers who view this kingdom at a distance, we shall as natives consider more closely the various stages contained therein" (*Either/Or*, 222). And thus we take the first step towards dismantling Hegel's resolution to the paradox of existence. We are not merely spectators but denizens of this vale of tears.

As the remainder of this section of *Either/Or* demonstrates, any verdict on the relative unhappiness of the contestants will prove inadequate. For although in possession of Hegel's conceptual map and seemingly in earnest about the competition, the orator's presentation raises a series of further difficulties, the first of which is the perspective from which to judge our fellow inhabitants of this kingdom. We are exhorted to make ourselves worthy to sit as judges and fellow contestants so that we do not lose the overall view, are not confused by the particulars, for the eloquence of grief is infinite and infinitely inventive. We shall divide the unhappy into specific groups, and only one from each will be heard. We shall not deny that no particular individual is the unhappiest one; it is rather a class, but we shall not therefore have scruples about awarding the representative of this class the title of the unhappiest one. (*Either/Or*, 222)

But from what perspective could one judge the suffering of another consciousness? The high altitude of the conceptual analysis leaves the distinct individual behind.[47]

As the imagined contest unfolds, it becomes increasingly absurd; for the evaluation of the contestants requires comparison, but disinterested contemplation proves to be a stumbling block to genuine comprehension. The philosopher views from a distance what can only be understood through the passionate identification with the suffering of another. The contest exposes thereby the pretensions of judging the existing individual from the outside, according to some measure, as though suffering were uniform and quantifiable. But who can know the infinite passion that attends the grief of remorse or the longing of hope? By definition, the displacement of the unhappy consciousness's essence can receive no adequate external objectification; indeed, part of the sorrow is its incommunicability. Built into the structure of the unhappy consciousness is precisely what precludes comparison and vitiates the competition. The very attempt to categorize and to compare, to examine representative exemplars of different types of unhappiness, is absurd in principle; for the root of all unhappiness is particularity *qua* particularity.

The irony is compounded by the invocation of Hegel; for particular individuality is precisely the problem that Hegel identifies in the unhappy consciousness. The unhappy consciousness cannot divest himself of his changeable, contingent facticity and he understands his being a particular

---

47. Implied but never stated explicitly is that the kind of judgment the *Sumparanekromenoi* desire to render is reserved for God alone; that is, it is a judgment about the worth of individual souls with constant reference to mortality.

"that" to preclude his becoming "what" he truly is. Hegel resolves this dilemma only by transforming the ineliminable particularity of the unhappy consciousness into a conceptual problem, thereby making an existential problem susceptible to logical resolution.[48] The unhappy consciousness is sublated through the magical power of the logic of determinate negation into the rational consciousness that "expresses itself to itself," and is thereby "the certainty of being all reality" (*PhS* §§231–32). Through the negativity of consciousness, consciousness raises itself, like Baron Munchausen, out of disconsolate despair to supreme self-confidence.[49]

If we recall that along the *via dolorosa* that is spirit's journey to self-purification in the *Phenomenology* the unhappy consciousness makes his last appearance in the final act of the drama, at the denouement of Hegel's dialectic, then the almost magical character of the process becomes evident. In the final development of *Die offenbare Religion*:

> The death of this representational thought contains at the same time the death of the *abstraction of the divine essence* which is not yet posited as a self. That death is the painful feeling of the unhappy consciousness that *God himself has died*. This harsh expression is the expression of the inmost simple-knowing-of-oneself, the return of consciousness into the depth of the night of the I = I which no longer distinguishes and knows anything external to it. This feeling thus is in fact the loss of *substance* and of the substance taking a stance against consciousness. (*PhS*, §785)

In Hegel's account, this is religious representation's depiction of the conceptual development of spirit as it sheds its particularity and is transfigured into the spiritual life animating the community: "Death is transfigured from what it immediately means, i.e., from the *non-being* of *this individual*, into the *universality* of spirit which lives in its own religious community, dies

---

48. See Kierkegaard's discussion of negation in logic and ethics in *The Concept of Anxiety*, trans. and ed. Alastair Hannay (London: Liveright, 2014), 17–18 (hereafter cited as *CA*).

49. For the Baron Munchausen image, see Charles Taylor, *Hegel and Modern Society* (Cambridge: Cambridge University Press, 2015), 38.

there daily, and is daily there resurrected" (*PhS*, §784). What occurred in the past and required recollection in order to be present is now constitutive of lived actuality. The beyond we longed for as recompense for our diremption in the present is made immanent to the activity of the community. The eternal is now animating every moment of the present. Like Shakespeare's late romance plays, a seemingly miraculous and abrupt turn suddenly transforms the tragedy of spirit into the joy of the revelation of good news: consciousness can be at home in the world. It need not be displaced by its overreaching impulse; inhabiting the present, it no longer experiences its own self-negation as death, but as a moment of divine life.[50]

However, in undertaking what Fackenheim calls a trans-mythologizing, Hegel has drained the historical moment of the crucifixion of its existential heft together with the individual's knowledge of her own anticipated death.[51] Where is the doubt, the anxiety, the lamentation? Death is no longer that harrowing encounter with nothingness described in the life-and-death struggle, but merely the negation of particularity in the ascent of spirit to universal self-consciousness.[52] Moreover, although the unhappy consciousness is depicted as having a genuine experience of the loss of what it would mean for the world to become a wilderness and to be thrown back into the isolation of the solipsistic I = I (where consciousness cannot escape the confines of its own subjectivity), the reader remains a disinterested spectator, confident that Hegel has already transformed "the

---

50. Cf. *PhS*, §19, §32, §80. For the description of spirit as essentially an "overreaching" power, see Emil L. Fackenheim, *The Religious Dimension of Hegel's Thought* (Bloomington: Indiana University Press, 1968), 96–112. According to Fackenheim, overreaching (*übergreifen*) "is perhaps Hegel's most important term, and the presence of overreaching power in spirit may be called without exaggeration the decisive condition of the possibility of the complete philosophic thought" (98).

51. Emil L. Fackenheim, "Demythologizing and Remythologizing," in *The Jewish Return into History* (New York: Schocken, 1978), 118–20.

52. Compare Hegel's previous discussion of burial in *Sittlichkeit*, *PhS*, §§451–52. Self-consciousness transfigures mortality through ritual and elevates the human above mere natural existence. Cf. Benardete's thesis that burial is one of the "pillars of definitional law" that "says what man is or what he is not through his regular performance of some rite"; "burial denies that man is either a beast or carrion." Quoted in Ronna Burger, "Definitional Law in the Bible," in *The Eccentric Core: The Thought of Seth Benardete*, ed. Ronna Burger and Patrick Goodin (South Bend, IN: St. Augustine's Press, 2018), 13. In Hegel's terms, such rituals affirm that man is essentially spirit.

historical Good Friday" into the "speculative good Friday."[53] For Hegel, the tension between the eternal and the temporal has been mediated in the self-differentiating movement of the concept.

From Kierkegaard's perspective, however, the death of the mediator in the mediation of the concept is not the resurrection of spirit in the community, but the loss of the reality that is Christ.[54] The integration of the unhappy consciousness into the atemporal logical movement of the whole is achieved only by losing touch with the eternal outside of time—an Archimedean point that would make being-with-oneself in the present actually possible. The satisfaction of the unhappy consciousness through conceptual mediation comes at the price of the eternal. Having lost the eternal, Hegel also loses the existing present. The singular existing individual is swallowed up in the abstractions of systematic philosophy. Speculative theology claims to unite religion and philosophy in one inquiry, but this requires bridging the chasm between existence and thought (*CUP*, 1:118).[55] Yet this can be achieved only by denying what makes the human unique among creation—our personhood. The subjectivity of selfhood is not a logical problem, but an ethical one to be wrestled with by each individual in every generation.[56]

From Kierkegaard's perspective, outside the unhappy consciousness, there is no true passion in Hegel's system, and together with the grief for a *deus abscondus*, true freedom has been lost in the dialectical *Aufhebung* of the concept.[57] The passionate inwardness of the unhappy consciousness—the "infinite grief" of the unhappy consciousness when uttering that hardest of sayings: "*Gott ist gestorben*"—has lost its infinite significance. Unmoored from the existing individual, inwardness has become abstract—a mood has been rendered into a concept (cf. *CA*, 19–21, 50–53). And, con-

---

53. Hegel, *Faith and Knowledge*, trans. and ed. Walter Cerf and H. S. Harris (Albany: State University of New York Press, 1977), 190–91. Contrast *CUP*, 1:98.

54. Cf. "Philosophy's concept is mediation—Christianity's the paradox" (*PJ*, 138).

55. Cf. "Existence is always particular; the abstract does not *exist*" (*CUP*, 1:330).

56. Kierkegaard, *Fear and Trembling*, trans. Sylvia Walsh, ed. C. Stephen Evans and Sylvia Walsh (Cambridge: Cambridge University Press, 2006), 107–9 (hereafter cited as *FT*).

57. Cf. the connection between anxiety (*Angst*), sin, and freedom in *CA*. Note especially Kierkegaard's definition of anxiety: "Anxiety is freedom's actuality as the possibility of possibility" (*CA*, 51).

versely, without infinite longing, without grief at the past and hope for the future, the individual has been flattened.[58] The delicate balance of possibility and actuality that makes choice a reality is obviated in the necessary dialectical march of the concept.

As the address to the *Sumparanekromenoi* states (with subtle reference to Hegel), "Happy is the one who can write such a paragraph [about the unhappy consciousness], and even happier is he who writes the next" (*Either/Or*, 222). But as the framing of the contest of "the unhappiest one" suggests, such a person must have forgotten death—a moment one must face alone and that cancels all one's conceptual comprehension. For it is mortality that individualizes; our finitude is the obverse of our individuality. Rather than understanding ourselves as particular instances of universal categories, we ought to grapple with the facticity of an existence experienced in light of the eternal. Thus, in a final irony, Kierkegaard suggests that Hegel is truly the unhappiest one, having relinquished the temporality of life for the atemporal stasis of abstract thought—the process of becoming for the conceptual comprehension of the whole. By trying to live neither in the past nor the future, one does not affirm the present but merely drains life of its dynamism. One might successfully let go of one's grief and abandon one's hopes, but in doing so one gives up on the concrete actuality of the present. True being-at-home with oneself requires an eternal moment, but this transcendence of time in order to be timely depends on faith—"the substance of things hoped for, the evidence of things unseen" (Heb. 11:1). In other words, faith in the paradox of the divine mediator is the only adequate response to the "paradox of existence."[59]

The paradox of existence, according to Kierkegaard, is the paradox of the being that can say "I" and stand apart from the crowd in possession of an identity that eludes all conceptual comprehension. For Kierkegaard, true self-knowledge does not answer the question: "What am I?" but rather "Who am I?" Hegel argues persuasively that "the nature of sci-

---

58. See the discussion of the "young lover" in *Either/Or*, 223–25.

59. "Faith is therefore no esthetic emotion but something much higher, precisely because it presupposes resignation; it is not a spontaneous inclination of the heart but the paradox of existence" (*FT*, 40). Abraham grasps "the whole of temporality by virtue of the absurd, and this is the courage of faith"; for "temporality, finitude is what it is all about" (*FT*, 41, 42).

ence" demands "that the individual all the more forget himself," and in the dawning age of true science (*die wahre Wissenschaft*), when "the universality of spirit has grown so much stronger," it is fitting that

> what is purely singular (*die Einzelheit*) has become ever more a matter of indifference (*soviel gleichgültiger*).... [Thus] although the individual must become what he can and must do what he can, there is nonetheless even less which must be demanded of him, just as he in turn must both anticipate less for himself and may demand less for himself. (*PhS*, §72)

But what the individual human being most needs is a truth to live and die by—"a truth which is true *for me*" (*PJ*, 32–37). The problem of the particular individual is the repeated refrain of Kierkegaard's writings, but this existential lament has a philosophic question at its core: "What is this 'I' that thinks?" The effort to understand the subject runs aground on the reflexive realization that in pursuit of understanding one abstracts from the contingent and particular, but that the agent doing the abstraction is recalcitrant to himself becoming abstract. As Kierkegaard states: "I can abstract from everything but myself" (*PJ*, 51).[60] In all abstraction, there is this stubborn remainder, namely, this 'I' that does the abstracting. This is the hard kernel of fact that cannot be categorized as an instance of the transcendental ego *à la* Kant or sublated in the universal truth of spirit in Hegel's systematic philosophy.[61]

Thus, Kierkegaard calls attention to the possibility that the unhappy consciousness is a chink in Hegel's conceptual armor, as though the figure embodies the bad conscience of the system; for the unhappy consciousness is the cognizance of the dilemma of particularity. Although Hegel knows he must address this figure, his attempts belie the truth—his efforts are woefully inadequate. For the voice crying out in the wilderness, Hegel holds out the most meager consolation: not a loving relationship with the

---

60. Cf. Hegel, *Elements of the Philosophy of Right*, trans. H. B. Nisbet, ed. Allen W. Wood (Cambridge: Cambridge University Press, 1991), 68–69.

61. Cf. *CUP*, 1:314: "For the existing person, existing is for him his highest interest, and his interestedness in existing is his actuality. What actuality is cannot be rendered in the language of abstraction."

word made flesh but recognition of the "rose in the cross of the present" and the insight that "the rational is actual and the actual rational." According to Hegel, the most that those peculiar souls "who have received the inner call *to comprehend*" can hope for is *"reconciliation* with actuality."[62] As in Spinoza, freedom is the knowledge of necessity and philosophic longing must be satisfied with the intellectual comprehension of necessity. For a soul animated by the intense longing that the unhappy consciousness embodies, this seems an almost farcical form of satisfaction. How, then, does Hegel achieve the remarkable feat of convincing his audience that he is in earnest?[63]

From Kierkegaard's perspective the philosopher achieves this conjuring trick by turning faith into a trifle.[64] Philosophy can justify itself and reconcile itself to its limited satisfaction (in Hegel) or to the infinite task of transforming the world (in Kant) only by denying the reality of faith or the possibility of grace.[65] That is, the philosopher can justify himself only by denying the possibility of the wholeness a soul might experience when it "rests transparently in God" (*SUD*, 46). Philosophy denies that the singular individual as a singular individual can exist in fellowship with God by relinquishing the objective certainty of conceptual comprehension

---

62. Hegel, *Elements of the Philosophy of Right*, 20–22.

63. Cf. Kierkegaard, *The Sickness unto Death: A Christian Psychological Exposition for Upbuilding and Awakening*, trans. and ed. Howard V. Hong and Edna H. Hong (Princeton: Princeton University Press, 1980), 5–6 (hereafter cited as *SUD*). Cf. *CA*, 19: "An error of thought has dialectics outside; the absence of mood or its falsification has the comical outside, as its enemy." The system's other—which it could not include within itself—is laughter. Against ridicule, the system has no defense. Laughter, born of the incongruity in man's nature, makes a mockery of all systematic mediation.

64. *FT*, 108, 27–28, 40–41, 60–61.

65. For Kierkegaard, like Hegel confronting skepticism, the argument is an all or nothing proposition: either faith is the paradox of Abraham's transcendence of universal categories, ethical duty, and intersubjective communication in an immediate relation to a loving personal God, or Abraham is a murderer and a madman. Either Kierkegaard is right and Abraham is the father of faith, or Kant is right and Abraham violated the moral law, sacrificed his autonomy, denied the dignity of his son, and practiced the most debased form of "religion of rogation." Kant, "Religion within the boundaries of mere reason," 6:51; 6:87, 6:187. Cf. Kant, "The conflict of the faculties," trans. Mary J. Gregor and Robert Anchor, in Wood and di Giovanni, *Religion and Rational Theology*, 7:63–66.

for the subjective certainty of faith.[66] Philosophy must deny that the soul's wings were fashioned for transcendence, for an ascent from the unconditional duty of the categorical imperative to the unconditional love of God and one's neighbor. Whereas Kant warns against flying too high lest we come crashing down like Icarus and succumb to misology and misanthropy, Kierkegaard thinks anything short of existing in an absolute relation to the absolute is the utmost despair.[67]

What Kant denied as enthusiasm and Hegel warned against as madness, Kierkegaard sees as the soul's only salvation. Beyond the boundaries of reason, there lies a highest good accessible in faith and commensurate to the depth of our longing.[68] Beyond the horizon of the universal, the single individual discovers a loving God who has no need of conceptual abstractions, but knows the particular as particular.[69] In the words of 1 Corinthians 13, the soul longs to see God face-to-face, to know and to be known, to love and to be loved. And so, the problem with philosophy, as Ronna Burger once wryly observed, is that wisdom doesn't love you back.

---

66. See *FT*, 106. Cf. James 2:23–24. On subjective versus objective truth see *CUP*, 1:199, 201, 203–4. Cf. "The absolute significance of the category of the particular ... is precisely the principle of Christianity" (*PJ*, 254).

67. *FT*, 61–62, 71, 81–82; *SUD*, 46.

68. Kierkegaard, *Three Discourses on Imagined Occasions*, trans. and ed. Howard V. Hong and Edna H. Hong (Princeton: Princeton University Press, 1990), 18.

69. *SUD*, 121: "God does not avail himself of an abridgement; he comprehends actuality itself, all its particulars; for him the single individual does not lie beneath the concept." Cf. Arist., *Met.* 982a4–12.

Selected Works by Ronna Burger

Monographs and Books

On Plato's "Euthyphro." Munich: Carl Friedrich von Siemens
    Foundation, 2015.

Aristotle's Dialogue with Socrates: On the "Nicomachean Ethics."
    Chicago: University of Chicago Press, 2008.

The "Phaedo": A Platonic Labyrinth. New Haven, CT:
    Yale University Press, 1984. Reprinted with a new preface.
    South Bend, IN: St. Augustine's Press, 1999.

Plato's "Phaedrus": A Defense of a Philosophic Art of Writing.
    Tuscaloosa: University of Alabama Press, 1980.

Edited Books

The Eccentric Core: The Thought of Seth Benardete. Edited by Ronna
    Burger and Patrick Goodin. South Bend, IN: St. Augustine's
    Press, 2018.

*The Archaeology of the Soul: Platonic Readings of Ancient Poetry and
    Philosophy.* Essays by Seth Benardete. Edited with an
    introduction by Ronna Burger and Michael Davis.
    South Bend, IN: St. Augustine's Press, 2012.

Encounters and Reflections: Conversations with Seth Benardete. With
    Robert Berman, Ronna Burger, and Michael Davis. Edited
    with a preface by Ronna Burger. Chicago: University of
    Chicago Press, 2003.

The Argument of the Action: Essays on Greek Poetry and Philosophy.
By Seth Benardete. Edited with an introduction by Ronna Burger
and Michael Davis. Chicago: University of Chicago Press, 2000.

Articles

"Chance, Divine Providence, or Human Prudence?: On the Book
of Esther." In *Writing the Poetic Soul of Philosophy*, edited by
Denise Schaeffer. South Bend, IN: St. Augustine's Press,
forthcoming.

"Eros and Mind: Aristotle on Philosophic Friendship and the Cosmos
of Life." *Epoché: A Journal in the History of Philosophy* 23, no. 2
(Spring 2019): 365–80.

"Definitional Law in the Bible." In *The Eccentric Core*, 3–17.
South Bend, IN: St. Augustine's Press, 2018.

"The Thumotic and the Erotic Soul." In *The Eccentric Core*, 81–100.
South Bend, IN: St. Augustine's Press, 2018.

"Woman and Nature: The Female Drama of the Book of Genesis."
In *Athens, Arden, Jerusalem: Essays in Honor of Mera
Flaumenhaft*, edited by Paul T. Wilford and Kate Havard,
227–42. Lanham, MD: Lexington Books, 2017.

"Socrates' Odyssean Return: On Plato's *Charmides*." In *Socratic
Philosophy and Its Others*, edited by Denise Schaeffer and
Christopher A. Dustin, 217–35. Lanham, MD: Rowman &
Littlefield, 2013.

"Maimonides on Knowledge of Good and Evil: *The Guide of the
Perplexed* I 2." In *Political Philosophy Cross-Examined:
Perennial Challenges to the Philosophic Life*, edited by
Thomas L. Pangle and J. Harvey Lomax, 79–100.
New York: Palgrave-Macmillan, 2013.

"The Nonlover in Aristotle's *Ethics*." In *Logos and Eros: Essays
Honoring Stanley Rosen*, edited by Nalin Ranasinghe, 105–17.
South Bend, IN: St. Augustine's Press, 2006.

"The Thumotic Soul." *Epoché: A Journal in the History of Philosophy* 7, no. 2 (Spring 2003): 151–67.

"Hunting Together or Philosophizing Together: Friendship and Eros in Aristotle's *Nicomachean Ethics.*" In *Love and Friendship: Rethinking Politics and Affection in Modern Times,* edited by Eduardo A. Velásquez, 37–60. Lanham, MD: Lexington Books, 2003.

"Aristotle on *Mimēsis*: The Visual Image and the Plot of Tragedy." In *Key Writers on Art: From Antiquity to the Nineteenth Century,* edited by Chris Murray, 7–11. New York: Routledge, 2003.

"Male and Female Created He Them: Some Platonic Reflections on Genesis 1–3." In *The Nature of Woman and the Art of Politics,* edited by Eduardo A. Velásquez, 1–18. Lanham, MD: Rowman & Littlefield, 2000.

"Imitation and Representation: *Mimēsis* in Aristotle's *Poetics.*" In *Encyclopedia of Aesthetics,* edited by Michael Kelly, 1:165–67. 2nd ed. 1998; repr., Oxford: Oxford University Press, 2014.

"Plato's Non-Socratic Narrations of Socratic Conversation." In *Plato's Dialogues: The Dialogical Approach,* edited by Richard Hart and Victorino Tejera, 121–42. Studies in the History of Philosophy 46. Lewiston, NY: Edwin Mellen Press, 1997.

"Ethical Reflection and Righteous Indignation: *Nemesis* in the *Nicomachean Ethics.*" In *Essays in Ancient Greek Philosophy: Aristotle's "Ethics,"* edited by John P. Anton and Anthony Preus, 4:127–39. Albany: State University of New York Press, 1991.

"Is Each Individual the Same as Its Essence?: *Metaphysics* Z.6–11." *Review of Metaphysics* 41, no. 1 (Sept. 1987): 53–76.

"Socratic *Eironeia.*" *Interpretation: A Journal of Political Philosophy* 12, no. 2 (May 1985): 143–49.

"Socratic Irony and the Platonic Art of Writing: The Self-Condemnation of the Written Word in Plato's *Phaedrus,*" *Southwestern Journal of Philosophy* 9, no. 3 (Nov. 1978): 113–26.

Lectures and Discussions Online

"Plato's Aristophanic Speech on Eros and the Biblical Story of Adam and Eve." Harvard Program on Constitutional Government, June 2018. https://www.youtube.com/watch?v=T2cc3akVKhg.

"Women and Nature in the Book of Genesis." Montesquieu Forum, Roosevelt University, Chicago, November 2016. https://www.youtube.com/watch?v=LVSN5dtisxQ.

"Ronna Burger on Seth Benardete." Foundation for Constitutional Government, Contemporary Thinkers, August 2015. https://contemporarythinkers.org/seth-benardete/.

"Ronna Burger on Plato's *Republic*." Foundation for Constitutional Government, Great Thinkers, August 2015. https://thegreatthinkers.org/plato/multimedia/.

"Ronna Burger on Aristotle." Foundation for Constitutional Government, Great Thinkers, August 2015. https://thegreatthinkers.org/aristotle/.

"Ronna Burger on the Hebrew Bible." Foundation for Constitutional Government, Great Thinkers, August 2015. https://www.youtube.com/watch?v=e4OJY9dEfJM.

"Divine Plan and Human Agency: The Biblical Story of Joseph." St. John's College, Santa Fe, August 2014. https://www.youtube.com/watch?v=rQpdzv4gWGs.

"In the Court of an Oriental Despot: The Book of Esther." Tulane University Judeo-Christian Studies, New Orleans, March 2014. https://www.youtube.com/watch?v=MMHbyjoACS4.

"The Best Human Life: On Aristotle's *Ethics* I.5." Emory University, Atlanta, February 2013. https://www.youtube.com/watch?v=fa1dZpO0fFM.

"Maimonides on the Knowledge of Good and Evil." Montesquieu Forum, Roosevelt University, Chicago, November 2011. https://www.youtube.com/watch?v=5GWaM__oRlA.

"Laughter, Anger, and the Philosopher-King in Plato's *Republic*." Montesquieu Forum, Roosevelt University, Chicago, April 2011. https://www.youtube.com/watch?v=U2fTVGVddwQ.

"In the Wilderness of Sinai: Moses as Lawgiver and Founder." Montesquieu Forum, Roosevelt University, Chicago, October 2008. https://www.youtube.com/watch?v=qQ6978844mM.

Contributors

Seth Appelbaum
Tutor, St John's College, Santa Fe

Steven Berg
Professor of Philosophy, Bellarmine University

Robert Berman
Professor of Philosophy, Xavier University of Louisiana

Michael Davis
Professor of Philosophy, Sarah Lawrence College

Derek Duplessie
Postdoctoral Fellow, Department of Government,
Harvard University

Jacob Howland
McFarlin Professor of Philosophy, University of Tulsa

Mary P. Nichols
Professor Emerita of Political Science, Baylor University

Matthew Oberrieder
Associate Professor of Humanities, Rogers State University

Clifford Orwin
Professor of Political Science, Classics, and Jewish Studies,
University of Toronto, and Senior Fellow of the Berlin/Bochum
Thucydides Center

Evanthia Speliotis
Professor of Philosophy, Bellarmine University

Nathan Tarcov
Karl J. Weintraub Professor, Committee on Social Thought,
Department of Political Science and in the College,
University of Chicago

Jason Tipton
Tutor, St. John's College, Annapolis

Peter Vedder
Independent Scholar

Richard Velkley
Celia Scott Weatherhead Professor of Philosophy,
Tulane University

Stuart D. Warner
Professor of Philosophy and Founding Director
of the Montesquieu Forum, Roosevelt University

Roslyn Weiss
Clara H. Stewardson Professor of Philosophy, Lehigh University

Paul T. Wilford
Assistant Professor of Political Science, Boston College